P9-CQN-604

DISCARDED

Human Visual Cognition

A STUDY IN EXPERIMENTAL
COGNITIVE PSYCHOLOGY

by

PHILIP H. K. SEYMOUR

ST. MARTIN'S PRESS
NEW YORK

 For information, write:
St. Martin's Press, Inc., 175 Fifth Avenue, New York, NY 10010
Printed in Great Britain
First published in the United States of America in 1979

ISBN 0–312–39966–9

Library of Congress Cataloging in Publication Data

Seymour, Philip Herschel Kean, 1938–
Human visual cognition.

Bibliography: p.
Includes indexes.
1. Cognition. 2. Visual perception.
3. Symbolism (Psychology) 4. Lexicology.
5. Memory. I. Title. [DNLM: 1. Visual
perception. WW105 S521h]
BF311.S46 1979 153.7 78–27246
ISBN 0–312–39966–9

ACKNOWLEDGEMENT

I am grateful to the University of Dundee and my colleagues in the Department of Psychology for their support during the preparation of this book; also to my family for their forbearance; to Margaret Grubb, Anna Shewan and Aileen Sandilands for their patient typing of the manuscript; to Patrick Seymour for expert preparation of the diagrams; and to Maureen Jack for helpful comments on the text.

PREFACE

This book about *Human Visual Cognition* is a product of my research and teaching at the University of Dundee, Scotland, during the last ten years or so. My interests were originally in educational psychology and the then popular topic of 'programmed instruction'. From this I developed an interest in the psychology of reading skill, which extended naturally to the studies of the processing of visual symbols which were conducted during the 1960s. Since that time *cognitive psychology* has grown and flourished. I have tried to the best of my ability to keep pace with those aspects of this development which have most interested me, and this book represents my own attempt to make sense of the outcomes of the numerous cognitive research projects which have been conducted in past few years.

In order to place some limit on the range of research which I am seeking to systematize I have defined the limits of my subject matter somewhat strictly. I have excluded research relating to episodic memory, about which much has been written in recent years, and also research in artificial intelligence relating to complex language and picture processing abilities, much of which belongs more obviously to the conceptually-oriented disciplines of linguistics, philosophy and computational science than to the empirically-oriented discipline of experimental cognitive psychology. One is then left with a large body of experimental reports which aim to provide a detailed analysis of the cognitive processes which occur when competent individuals perform simple but fundamental tasks. I have tried to make sense of that section of this literature which is concerned with the recognition and interpretation of visual symbols and visual objects.

My hope is that this effort to perceive coherence in an ongoing research enterprise will be of some benefit to those students of psychology who have found experimental studies of cognition fragmentary or uncertain in their goals or direction, and that it will also provide a structured summary of recent research for workers in allied fields of application, such as education and neurology.

Dundee
Christmas, 1977

P. H. K. Seymour

CONTENTS

PART TWO
THE LEXICAL MEMORY

Introduction

CHAPTER I
Visual Cognition

I.1 INTRODUCTION

In his influential book on *Cognitive Psychology* Neisser (1967) proposed a major topical division between visual and auditory cognitive processes. He used the term *visual cognition* to refer to those processes which occur in the human brain when visual events are recognized, categorized and interpreted. Much of his treatment of this topic was concentrated on an analysis of the processing of symbolic and lexical information, though he also included a chapter on imagery and visual memory for pictures.

Since Neisser's book appeared cognitive psychology and psycholinguistics have been established as central topics in human experimental psychology. Numerous experimental studies have been conducted, and the painstaking reports of their methodologies, results and theoretical interpretations are scattered through a range of technical journals and published collections of articles. The pace of this activity has been so rapid that some observers have experienced bewilderment and discomfort, and have questioned whether experimental cognitive psychology is indeed a theoretically coherent enterprise which is building a properly integrated and cumulative body of knowledge about human cognition (Newell, 1973; Allport, 1975).

These considerations suggested that it might be worthwhile to look again at the topic of visual cognition with the aim of clarifying its conceptual structure, and evaluating the contribution of a decade or more of intensive experimental investigation. A problem for the contemporary student of cognitive psychology is to perceive the major topical divisions of the subject, and to diagnose the rules which allow the reference of individual experimental reports to be determined. For academics, this is a practical problem of devising a topically structured filing system for storage and retrieval of offprints of published papers. Anyone who has attempted to keep pace with the flood of experimental cognitive articles appearing weekly on the library shelves must have confronted this problem, and the labelling of his offprint filing system will give some clues to the manner in which he has attempted to solve it.

In the absence of a sensible topic structure experimental cognitive research must indeed appear as a fragmented and directionless collection of small-scale local enterprises (Newell, 1973). It will also appear as a difficult and often unrewarding field of study to a majority of students of psychology who may be looking for a readily intelligible structure and a clarification of the nature of human cognition which is applicable to human problems in educational and clinical contexts. For this reason one of the major aims behind the writing of this book has been to formulate a usable topic structure for one branch of cognitive psychology.

I.2 SYMBOLIC, LEXICAL AND PICTORIAL DOMAINS

The title *Visual Cognition* helps to signal some important limitations on the scope of this book. As a *cognitive* text it will discuss the logical structure of mental processes, but not their instantiation in functioning physiological systems. No consideration will be given to the photoreceptive and neural mechanisms mediating the activity of the eye–brain system, or to neuropsychological conclusions concerning the functions of the different anatomical regions of the brain. Since the text emphasizes *visual* processes, the topics of speech perception and interpretation, and of memory for auditory verbal events, will not be treated in any detail. Finally, the term *visual cognition* is taken to refer to a limited class of cognitive activities which relate relatively directly to visual events occurring in an observer's immediate environment. On these grounds no attempt will be made to cover research relating to the more complex and abstract forms of thinking, problem solving and comprehension.

The topic of visual cognition is not to be equated with the study of visual memory. By *visual memory* is meant a capability for storage and subsequent reinstatement of a knowledge of visual properties of past events. This is often referred to as *episodic memory* (Tulving, 1972). Visual cognition, on the other hand, is taken to refer to the mental processing which occurs when visual events are recognized or interpreted. These capabilities for recognition and interpretation rest upon permanently established processing facilities and accessible stores of information concerning essential semantic properties of words and objects. In a text about visual cognition the primary objective must be to clarify the nature of these permanent information processing facilities, and of the store of fundamental knowledge which is consulted whenever visual input is interpreted.

Having sought to isolate Visual Cognition from some immediate conceptual neighbours, we can turn to a consideration of those subtopics which appear to be good candidates for detailed consideration in this text. As a start we will assume that *Visual Cognition* is a superordinate label for two major areas of human competence. The first of these concerns a person's competence to deal intelligently with the configurations of *objects* which he encounters moment by moment as he moves about within his world. The other relates to his competence in interpretation of visual *symbols*. This latter competence encompasses literacy and numeracy, and refers most directly to the ability to read and to use symbols in mathematical and scientific problem solving. Such a distinction finds some empirical support in factor analytic studies of the components of the human intellect. For example, Vernon (1951) distinguished between verbal/educational and spatial/mechanical forms of intelligence. Guilford (1967) has also argued that abilities for solving *figural* and *symbolic* types of test item are to some degree independent.

Developmentally, the achievement of competence in the handling of objects precedes the achievement of literacy and numeracy, which are, in their turn, dependent on the development of an auditory symbolism for referring to objects in spoken language. On the other hand, written language comes to play an increasingly dominant role in the cognition of literate and educated members of contemporary western society. For this reason, literacy—the cognition of visual language—appears as a socially more salient issue than a generally taken-for-granted competence for living in a world of objects. This bias is also evident in the experimental psychological literature on the visual cognitive processes of adult subjects. A large majority of these studies has investigated the processing of visual symbols. The essential methodology for this type of research has also been developed in the context of studies of symbolic information processing. From the viewpoint of the experimental psychologist, therefore, and perhaps also of the student of cognitive psychology, the topic of the visual cognition of written symbols appears to enjoy a certain priority. This ordering has been followed in this book, which will deal first with the cognition of visual symbols, and only later with the cognition of visual objects.

When one examines the many experiments on the processing of visual symbols a major division is evident between studies in which the materials used are alphanumeric symbols (the letters of the alphabet and the numerals), and those in which the materials are words or sentences. The first group is concerned with a person's knowledge of the letters and the numerals, where these are viewed as arbitrary sets of two-dimensional visual forms having assigned names, conventional sequence, and various internal classifications. In the discussion that follows this limited though important area of human competence will be referred to as the *Symbolic Memory.* The second group of experiments aims to investigate a person's knowledge of the written vocabulary of his language, and his competence in interpretation of sentences and larger segments of text. This area of competence is extensive, and of great social and educational significance, since it is the basis of a person's literacy—that is, his ability to read with understanding, and to acquire new knowledge by reading. This form of competence will be referred to as the *Lexical Memory.*

The major topic divisions of this book derive from these distinctions. Some preliminary comments on methods and assumptions of Cognitive Psychology are contained in this and the following chapter. Thereafter, the book is divided into three large sections, each containing a number of chapters. *Part One* will discuss research relating to that area of human competence which is subsumed under the label of *Symbolic Memory.* This will deal primarily with studies of recognition, categorization, naming, short-term retention and comparison of arrays of alphanumeric symbols, and will serve incidentally to illustrate some general theoretical considerations together with an experimental methodology for investigation of mental activities. *Part Two* considers research relating to a person's vocabulary knowledge, and his capabilities for interpretation of sentences and text. This area of competence has been called the *Lexical Memory.* The chapters in this section deal in the main with the experimental analysis of the fundamental components of reading skill, including the recognition of visual words, their phonological and semantic interpretation, and the evaluation of the truth and falsity of sentences. Finally, *Part Three* examines research concerned with capabilities for recognition and interpretation of objects or scenes, this area of competence being referred to as the *Pictorial Memory.* This final section also considers some aspects of the referential relationship between objects and the words used to describe them.

This division between Symbolic, Lexical and Pictorial areas of visual competence has allowed a relatively straightforward tripartite categorization of the experimental literature. Experimental reports have been considered to relate to the *Symbolic Memory* if they have employed unstructured arrays of alphanumeric symbols as materials, to the *Lexical Memory* if they have employed words, sentences, or larger segments of text, and to the *Pictorial Memory* if they have employed pictures of objects or scenes.

I.3 DISPOSITIONS AND FUNCTIONS

The expressions *Symbolic Memory*, *Lexical Memory* and *Pictorial Memory* may properly be viewed as labels for areas of human competence. As such, they refer to collections of behaviours (or behavioural dispositions) which exemplify each domain (see Ryle, 1949), and which could, in principle at least, be listed in the course of a conceptual analysis of the domain. Such a list would identify the essential observable performances in terms of which visual cognitive competence is defined. The list would not in itself constitute a psychological analysis of competence. However, we can shift the discussion to a psychological level by arguing that the competence labels may also be treated as names for neurological systems whose activity underlies the successful performances through which competence is exemplified.

This may be illustrated for the case of the *Symbolic Memory*. Possession of a *Symbolic Memory* is demonstrated by a variety of commonplace achievements, such as naming and writing letters and numbers, reciting the alphabet, counting, calculating, and so forth. We may reasonably suppose that these activities have their origin in a neurological system. If, by misfortune, this system was to be selectively destroyed the behaviours exemplifying knowledge of the alphabet and numerals would no longer be observable, and we would speak of the impairment or destruction of the *Symbolic Memory*. Thus, the term *Symbolic Memory* may be transferred from its proper dispositional usage to become the name for a neurological system.

Certain of the properties of the underlying neurological system can be derived from the analysis of competence. This specifies certain elementary tasks which a person possessing a *Symbolic Memory* is capable of performing. These tasks, in their turn, identify the capabilities of the neurological system for transformation of an input to an observable output. For example, one aspect of the competence defining the *Symbolic Memory* is a capability for the vocal naming of visually presented symbols. Hence, a characteristic of the underlying neurological system is an ability to accept input of a visual symbol and to generate the name of that symbol as speech output.

By considering a full list of the defining capabilities of the *Symbolic*

Memory one could specify a complete set of types of input-output transformations which the neurological substrate of the Memory is able to achieve. We could from this list derive statements about the different *functions* which are carried on within the system. These include functions for recognition, name retrieval and production, comparison, and the like. Thus, we know from observation of behaviour that comparison of symbols can be achieved by competent individuals, and infer from this that *comparison* is a function performed within the neurological substrate of the Symbolic Memory. Although *comparison* is properly viewed as a name for a set of behavioural dispositions, it too may legitimately be transferred to become a label for a segment of neurological activity during which internal comparison of symbols occurs. We will refer to these neurological activities as *mental functions*.

The concept of a *mental function* provides a second basis for categorization of experimental tasks. An examination of the input-output transformations performed within the Symbolic Memory (see Chapter III) suggested the existence of five significant and essential mental functions. These will be referred to as:

ENCODING —an operation for transformation of an external stimulus into an internal neural code

REPRESENTATION—the maintenance of a code in short-term memory

RETRIEVAL —the accessing in permanent memory of a code defining an alternative representation of a symbol

COMPARISON —an operation for the determination of the equivalence of symbols or symbol sets

EXPRESSION —an operation for the transformation of an internal code to an observable output in speech or action

Justification for these categories will be provided in some detail in the chapters contained in Part One, which deal respectively with visual ENCODING of symbols (Chapter IV), REPRESENTATION of symbols in visual short-term memory (Chapter V), RETRIEVAL functions (Chapter VI), and COMPARISON operations (Chapter VII).

The classification of *mental functions* can be seen to correspond approximately to the operations category in Guilford's (1967) model of the 'structure of the intellect'. Guilford identified operations of (1) Cognition (perception or interpretation of input), (2) Memory (the storage of input), (3) Production (the retrieval of information from storage), and (4) Evaluation (comparison or assessment against a standard). He sought to develop psychometric tests which selectively created difficulties for each of the operations in turn, and used these in the assessment of individual differences in efficiency of mental functioning in different domains. As will become evident, an analogous approach is adopted in experimental psychology, where the study of the mental functions has depended on the development of techniques which allow the experimenter selectively to vary the processing load imposed on a particular function. This methodology will be outlined in greater detail in Chapter II.

I.4 CONCLUSIONS

This introductory chapter has sketched the general approach which will be followed in this book. We shall be discussing experimental approaches to the analysis of mental functions which occur during the processing of visual symbols, words and objects. The methods and assumptions of experimental cognitive psychology will initially be explicated by reference to research on aspects of the *Symbolic Memory* (Part One). The extension of these methods to the analysis of the larger *Lexical* and *Pictorial Memories* will provide the subject matter for Parts Two and Three.

CHAPTER II

Mental Functions

THE ADDITIVE FACTOR METHODOLOGY

II.1 INTRODUCTION

In the preceding chapter it was argued that we may derive from a dispositional analysis of a domain of competence the notion of an underlying neurological system which is characterized by certain functions and facilities. We may identify these as *mental functions* and view them as the primary objects of research in experimental cognitive psychology.

Mental functions are, in the first instance, the products of a conceptual analysis of competence. However, the transition to a psychological analysis can be achieved if one is willing to accept that each function corresponds to neural activity of some kind, and to make the assumptions that: (1) neural activities occupy measurable intervals of time, and (2) such activities may be more or less successful in their outcomes. These assumptions lead naturally to empirically-based research in which measurements of speed of reaction and accuracy of performance are taken to support inferences about the detailed structure of individual mental functions. Of course, one may also argue that any such investigation of detail must be undertaken in conjunction with a logical analysis of the function in question.

In what follows, the discussion of mental functions will proceed at various times at any one of four distinct levels, these being: (1) A conceptual analysis of competence, leading to identification of permanent memory systems and their component functions and facilities; (2) An analysis of the logical structure of a function, such as COMPARISON or RETRIEVAL; (3) A description of the failures of performance which occur under specified circumstances, including neurological damage; (4) Measurements of speed of reaction (RT) in simple tasks, combined with analytic techniques which allow time variations to be localized within a particular mental function.

The first two levels are conceptual in nature, and may be based on the intuitions of an investigator concerning human competence, and on logical criteria. The third remains a study of competence, but has an empirical basis in systematic sampling of performance under controlled conditions. It is characteristic of research in developmental and educational psychology, and in neuropsychology. It is only at the fourth level, that is the measurements of the time taken up by the mental functions, sometimes referred to as *mental chronometry*, that a study of the events underlying competent performance becomes possible. This approach is fundamental to experimental cognitive psychology, and will be evident in the great majority of the research studies to be discussed in this book.

II.2 THE ASSUMPTION OF SELECTIVE INFLUENCE

The major problem posed for attempts at psychological analysis of individual mental functions is that performance on experimental tasks necessarily involves the activity of more than one function. Even a simple reaction task, such as calling out 'Oh' each time a light is switched on, must depend on the functions of ENCODING (for internal representation of the occurrence of the signal) and EXPRESSION (for production of the vocal response). Hence, a measurement of the average RT for this task will include the times taken up by both functions, and either function might be a source of performance errors. This problem is exaggerated when more complex tasks are considered.

The possibility of a psychological analysis of individual mental functions is therefore crucially dependent on the development of techniques which allow variations in RT or accuracy of performance to be related to the activity of a particular function. These techniques derive from a chain of argument which states: (1) For each mental function there exist sets of external conditions which, if varied, will exert a *selective influence* on the efficiency of the function, or the duration of its activities; (2) These internal variations will, in their turn, produce externally observable effects on the accuracy of performance, or on the overall RT.

We can refer to elements from the set of relevant external conditions as *experimental factors*, each of which may be varied at two or more levels. For example, in the simple reaction experiment, the brightness of the signal light might be treated as a factor varying at several levels, each corresponding to a different degree of brightness. Associated with each factor there is an assumption of *selective influence* which resolves to a set of assertions identifying the function influenced by the factor and defining the nature of the influence. This might be referred to as the *expected internal effect* of the factor. Speculation concerning these internal effects is clearly closely related to the conceptual analysis of component functions and their logical structures. Hence, it might be more appropriate to maintain that the conceptual analysis of each function may be taken to a point at which a set of assertions about potentially influential external conditions is derived. Finally, it is assumed that internal variations in the efficiency or temporal extension of a function will have observable influence on *external indicators*, such as error frequency or RT, and this may be referred to as the *expected external effect*.

These arguments suggest that the psychological study of the mental functions might be regarded as conditional on the validity of two rather general assumptions. The first of these states that external conditions may have a consistent influence on mental activity. In support of this one might cite the very extensive body of experimental literature in which subtle variations in experimental conditions are shown to yield reliable effects on RT and error frequency. The second is the more questionable, though crucial, assumption that certain conditions produce internal effects which are selectively localized within a particular, identifiable function. The remainder of this chapter will be devoted on an evaluation of this assumption of selective influence.

II.3 THE ADDITIVE FACTOR METHODOLOGY

In a number of influential papers Sternberg has provided a clear explanation of a methodology which has been designed to validate the assumption of selective influence (Sternberg, 1969a, 1969b, 1971). The method is based on the statistical procedures of analysis of variance (Winer, 1962), and particularly on the notions of additivity and interaction of effects of experimental factors, and is frequently referred to as the *additive factor method*.

The argument underlying the method is as follows. Suppose that there are two mental functions, F_1 and F_2, and that these are respectively influenced by the experimental factors, E_1 and E_2. If variation in the level of factor E_1 selectively alters the time taken up by function F_1, whereas variation in the level of factor E_2 selectively alters the time taken up by function F_2, and if these internal influences give rise to observable external effects on the overall RT for a task implicating functions F_1 and F_2, then it follows that the factors E_1 and E_2 will produce independent and additive effects on the RT.

This will be true so long as functions F_1 and F_2 occur in strict succession to one another, and provided that factor E_1 influences only function F_1 and factor E_2 influences only function F_2.

Sternberg generally refers to the mental functions as *processing stages*. This captures well the view that the mental functions depend on complex neurological activity extending over an appreciable interval of time. The extra assumption is that performance on a task will involve a series of processing stages, with each stage waiting for completion of the preceding stage before it starts its work. Such an assumption finds support in the conceptual analysis, since the mental functions identified in the analysis of a task often imply a number of temporal dependencies. For example, in a comparison task ENCODING necessarily precedes COMPARISON, and EXPRESSION necessarily follows COMPARISON.

A particular processing stage may be influenced by more than one experimental factor. Suppose that factors E_{1a} and E_{1b} both influence the processing stage which we define as the neurological realization of the mental function, F_1. Under such circumstances the impact of factor E_{1b} might well differ depending on the level of factor E_{1a} with which it was combined. If so, the effects due to concurrent variation of the levels of the two factors need not be additive, and it is perhaps more likely that an interaction would be observed, with the size of the effect for each factor being related to the level of the other. On the basis of these expectations Sternberg has argued that factors which yield interacting effects when combined orthogonally in an experiment probably exert a selective influence on the same stage of processing.

The task of naming numerals has been studied by Sternberg (1971) in an experiment which illustrates the application of the additive factor method. In a numeral naming task the *S* must respond to each of a series of visually displayed numerals by calling out its name as rapidly as possible. The RT from onset of the numeral to initiation of the *S*'s vocal response is recorded. Accurate performance on the task appears to require the mental functions of ENCODING (for internal representation of the test symbol), RETRIEVAL (for retrieval of a representation of its name from permanent storage), and EXPRESSION (for overt production of the name in speech). There is also a logical ordering of the functions, since ENCODING precedes RETRIEVAL, and RETRIEVAL precedes EXPRESSION. Hence, the preliminary analysis of the task suggests that three sequentially occurring processing stages might be involved.

In order to apply the additive factor method to this situation it is necessary to carry the conceptual analysis of the three functions to a point at which potentially influential external conditions may be identified. In the case of ENCODING, for example, conditions which vary the legibility of the test numerals are likely to be effective. There are a number of ways in which legibility could be varied, all involving changes in physical characteristics such as brightness, size, figure-ground contrast, or exposure duration. These define a set of experimental factors which appear, *prima facie*, to be related to the ENCODING function. Sternberg has used the term *stimulus quality* to refer to the members of this set, and chose to examine in particular the effects of figure-ground contrast, test numerals being presented against a clear background or against a checkerboard background. There were, therefore, two levels for the factor of stimulus quality, which may be referred to as Level 1 (intact) and Level 2 (degraded). We assume that there is a processing stage which performs the function of ENCODING, and that the duration of this stage will be increased when the test symbol is degraded.

The EXPRESSION function is defined as a capability for translation of an internal representation of a name to an observable speech output. Conditions which alter the directness of the relationship between the numeral name and the overt response should exert a selective influence on the processing stage underlying EXPRESSION. Such variations can be achieved by altering the *instructions* given to the experimental *S*. For example, he may be told to give the name of the displayed numeral under one instruction, but to give a transformation of that name under another. Possible transformations would be to give the number of letters in the name, to give the first or the last letter, to say the name backwards, or to give a word which rhymed with the numeral name. Sternberg instructed his *S*s to give the name of the numeral following the one on the display. These instructional variants define a further set of experimental factors, to be referred to as variations in *response compatibility*, which might be expected to affect the duration of the EXPRESSION processing stage. This factor also had two levels in Sternberg's experiment, which may be described as Level 1 (compatible) and Level 2 (incompatible).

If we are correct in assuming that ENCODING and EXPRESSION correspond to real stages of processing, and if these stages are selectively influenced by the factors of stimulus quality and response compatibility, orthogonal combination of the levels of the two factors should lead to additivity of effects on the RT. The results of an experiment carried out to test this expectation are shown in Figure II.3.1. The figure shows the naming RT plotted in relation to the two levels of stimulus quality (intact versus degraded) and the two levels of response compatibility (direct naming versus naming with addition of one). These data present a clear example of additivity of effects. The RT was delayed by about 40 msecs when the test symbol was degraded, and this effect was of the same magnitude for compatible and incompatible responses. Similarly, the RTs for naming with addition were greater than the RTs for direct naming, and this effect was not altered by variation in stimulus quality. This result is consistent with the view that ENCODING and EXPRESSION are independent and successive mental events which are selectively influenced by the stimulus quality and response compatibility factors.

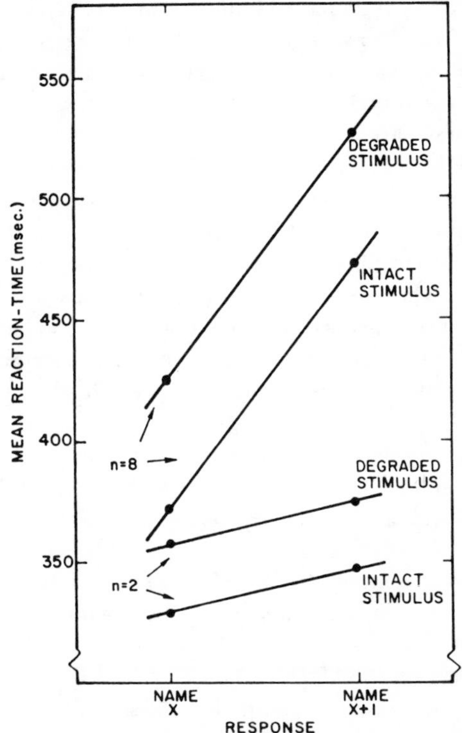

Figure II.3.1 Reaction time data from an experiment on naming of numerals. The factors of stimulus quality and response compatibility produce additive effects, but the factor of ensemble size (n = 2, n = 8) interacts with both compatability and quality. (From Sternberg (1969a)). Reproduced by permission.

Sternberg also incorporated into his experiment a third factor, the *size of the ensemble* of numerals presented for naming, which was varied at 2 and 8 alternatives. The relationship between this factor and response compatibility is also shown in Figure II.3.1. In this case, the data provide a clear instance of an interaction, since the effect of number of alternatives was greater for incompatible than for compatible naming, and the effect of compatibility was greater for 8 alternatives than for 2 alternatives. Sternberg also reported that the effect of stimulus quality increased slightly under the 8 alternative condition.

In the conceptual analysis of naming it was proposed that the task depended on the functions of ENCODING, RETRIEVAL and EXPRESSION. The RETRIEVAL function is required for identification of a visually represented numeral (pattern recognition) and for addressing of the location in permanent storage containing a representation of the name of that numeral. It is perhaps reasonable to suppose that the processing stage corresponding to this function may be reduced in duration when the size of the set of stimulus numerals becomes small. If so, size of ensemble might be a factor having a selective influence on a RETRIEVAL stage. It is also reasonable to argue that more complex retrieval processes are required for naming with addition than for direct naming. This is because naming with addition utilizes knowledge of the ordinal positions of numerals in the number sequence, whereas direct naming need not do so. Finally, since RETRIEVAL incorporates a pattern recognition component, it is possible that reductions in stimulus quality will affect this as well as ENCODING.

These comments lead to the formulation of a processing stage model of numeral naming of the kind shown in Figure II.3.2. The model consists of the three conceptually defined mental functions arranged in their logical order of occurrence. Each function is assumed to correspond to a temporally extended stage of processing which is subject to influence by externally controlled factors. Stimulus quality is thought to have its main influence on ENCODING, but a secondary effect on RETRIEVAL is suggested by the occurrence of an interaction between stimulus quality and size of ensemble. Response compatibility affects EXPRESSION, but also increases the complexity of RETRIEVAL, resulting in an interaction of effects of ensemble size and response compatibility. Additivity of effects occurs only for stimulus quality and response compatibility, as is expected if these factors exert selective influence on ENCODING and EXPRES-

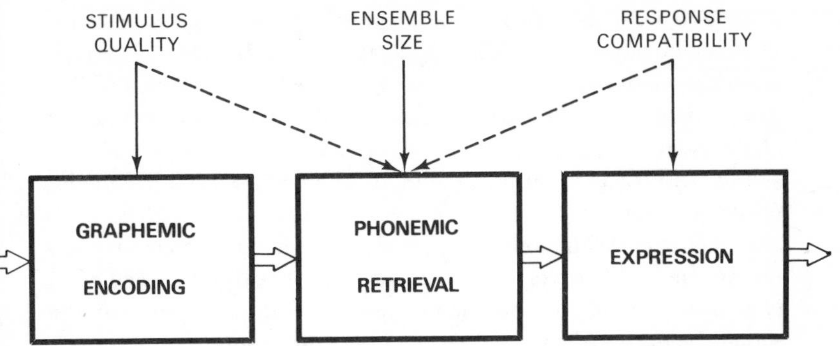

Figure II.3.2 A 'processing stage' model of numeral naming, in which it is assumed that an ENCODING stage is influenced by stimulus quality, that variations in ensemble size affect name RETRIEVAL, and that response compatibility has effects on both EXPRESSION and RETRIEVAL. A subsidiary effect of stimulus quality on RETRIEVAL is also indicated.

SION stages which are separated from one another by the intervening RETRIEVAL stage.

II.4 THE SYMBOL CLASSIFICATION TASK

A much more extensive effort to identify the factors influencing the processing stages corresponding to the different mental functions has been carried on in the context of a *symbol classification task* introduced by Sternberg (1966, 1967). In this task, the *S* is given a short list of symbols to hold in memory, and is then presented with a probe symbol which he must classify as a member or non-member of the memorized set. His decision can be indicated by pressing one of two response keys, or by vocally reporting 'Yes' or 'No'. A new memory set may be presented on each trial of the experiment (varied set procedure), or the memory set may be held constant over a block of trials (fixed set procedure). The RT is recorded from onset of the probe symbol to production of the indicator response.

The task has proved a valuable tool for research because it mobilizes many of the resources of the Symbolic Memory. The memory set must be maintained for a short time in the temporary storage registers, requiring the functions of ENCODING (for internal representation of each of the symbols in the set), and REPRESENTATION and RETRIEVAL (for cyclic refreshing and recoding of the symbol descriptions). When the probe is presented, it must be identified, compared with the items in the memory set, and a decision about membership or non-membership of the set must be taken and translated into an overt response. This requires operations of ENCODING (for representation of the test symbol), COMPARISON (for matching of the symbol against the items in the memory set), RETRIEVAL (for selection of a response code), and EXPRESSION (for production of the response).

If the mental functions correspond to distinct and successive segments of neurophysiological activity, the time between the occurrence of the probe stimulus and the emergence of the indicator response should be occupied by a sequence of four processing stages, referred to as ENCODING, COMPARISON, RETRIEVAL and EXPRESSION. To validate this assumption we need to identify one or more experimental factors which appear likely to exert a selective influence on each of these stages. In the case of ENCODING, *stimulus quality* has already been identified as a relevant factor. Sternberg has proposed that COMPARISON may be selectively influenced by variation in the number of symbols in the memory set. The levels of this factor of *memory set size* will be referred to by the letter M, and generally take values of 1–6 symbols. There is, built into the symbol classification experiment, a factor of *decision outcome*, since on each trial the probe may be classified as a member or a non-member of the memory set. This factor could affect comparison, but might also influence RETRIEVAL and EXPRESSION of the indicator response. In addition, Sternberg suggested that the RETRIEVAL and EXPRESSION stages might be affected by variation in the *relative frequencies of positive and negative responses*. If, for example, positive responses are required on 75 per cent of trials, and negative responses on only 25 per cent of trials, the RETRIEVAL and EXPRESSION stages may come to occupy less processing time for positive than for negative decision outcomes.

There are, therefore, three factors—stimulus quality, memory set size and response frequency—which appear likely to exert a selective influence on distinct processing stages. The fourth factor, the decision outcome, is uncertain in its locus of influence. A test of the validity of the assumption of selective influence can be made by conducting experiments in which the levels of each of the possible pairs of factors are orthogonally combined. According to the reasoning behind the additive factor method, additivity of effects on RT should be observed for pairs of factors which influence distinct processing stages, and interactions should be observed for pairs of factors which influence the same stage.

Figure II.4.1 shows RT data obtained by Sternberg from experiments in which five of the six possible combinations of pairs of four factors were studied, these being stimulus quality in relation to memory set size and decision outcome, memory set size in relation to decision outcome and relative frequency of response, and decision outcome in relation to relative frequency of response. In each case the effects on the RT of concurrent variation of the two factors appear to be additive. Degradation of the probe symbol raises the general level of the RT, but this effect is independent of the size of the set of symbols in memory or the decision outcome. The RT increases as size of the memory set is increased (M = 1, 2 or 4), but this effect is independent of decision outcome and relative frequency of response. Finally, the RT decreases as the relative frequency of a response is increased (response probability = ·25, ·50 or ·75), but this effect is additive with the effect for decision outcome.

These results are consistent with the conclusion that the processing stage performing the function of COMPARISON of a representation of the probe against a representation of the memory set is independent of stages of ENCODING of the probe and RETRIEVAL and EXPRESSION of a response. Since the factor of decision outcome does not interact with either memory set size or relative frequency of response Sternberg has argued for the existence of an additional stage, called *binary decision*, occurring after COMPARISON but before response RETRIEVAL and EXPRESSION. The formulation preferred here, and developed in Chapter VII, is that the COMPARISON function depends on two subsidiary functions, one being concerned with executive control over a process of matching components of a probe description against components of a memory set description, and the other with a judgement as to whether accumulating match/mismatch evidence is sufficient for a positive or negative decision about memory set membership.

Further experimental research which supports the view that processing stages underlying the major mental functions may be isolated by application of the additive factor method has been carried out by Briggs and his associates. In addition to the factors of stimulus quality, memory set size and decision outcome, Briggs introduced variations in: (1) Instructional emphasis on speed or accuracy; (2) the number of probe symbols presented; and (3) the number of alternative response categories. Speed instructions were found to reduce the general level

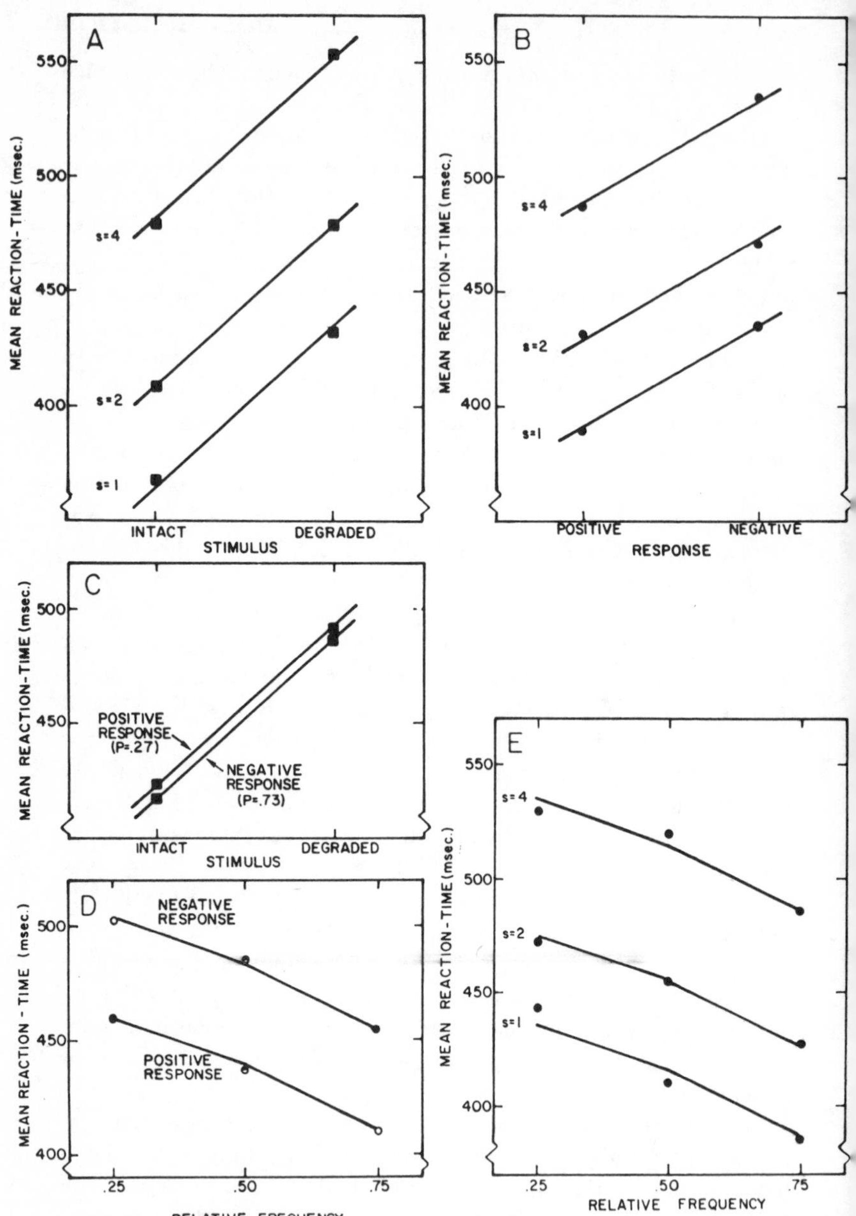

Figure II.4.1 Reaction time data from experiments on symbol classification illustrating additivity of effects for factors of stimulus quality, memory set size, decision outcome and relative frequency of response. (From Sternberg, 1969a.) Reproduced by permission.

of the RT, but to be independent of effects due to variation of memory set size (Lyons & Briggs, 1971). This implies that the instructions do not affect the COMPARISON stage, and Briggs has presented arguments suggesting ENCODING as the probable locus. Variation in *display size* was achieved by presenting 1, 2 or 4 probe items, one of which matched a memory set item on positive trials. This factor can be referred to as *display load*, symbolized by the letter D, having the levels D = 1, 2 or 4. When D and M (memory set size or *memory load*) are varied independently, an interaction is typically obtained, the effect of D increasing as the number of items in the memory set, M, increases. On the other hand, effects of D are generally independent of effects due to variation in stimulus quality (Johnsen & Briggs, 1973). This implies that an increase in display load affects the duration of the COMPARISON stage, but not of the ENCODING stage.

Briggs & Swanson (1970) have described experiments in which the factor of *response load* (symbolized by the letter R) was varied in addition to M and D. Probe symbols were presented in upper or lower case and in different type faces. The number of response keys which might be used to indicate a positive or negative decision was varied between groups of *S*s, choice of key being contingent on the type face and case of the probe symbols. Response load was varied at R = 2, 3 or 4 in one experiment, and at R = 2, 4 or 8 in a second experiment. The RT increased as response load increased, but this effect was independent of the effects of M or D, and did not alter the form of the M × D interaction. This is consistent with the conclusion that response load is a factor which selectively influences the stage of RETRIEVAL and EXPRESSION of a response, this stage being independent of ENCODING or COMPARISON.

On the basis of these findings we can propose a 'processing stage' model of the mental activities occurring during symbol classification. This has been represented diagrammatically in Figure II.4.2. The model proposes an ordered sequence of stages which successively perform the functions of ENCODING, COMPARISON, and RETRIEVAL and EXPRESSION of a response. Each stage is correlated with external factors which influence its duration, these being stimulus quality for ENCODING, memory load (M) and display load (D) for the first (feature matching) stage of COMPARISON, positive or negative decision outcome for the second (judgemental) stage of COMPARISON, and response load (R) and relative frequency of response for the RETRIEVAL and EXPRESSION stages in response production.

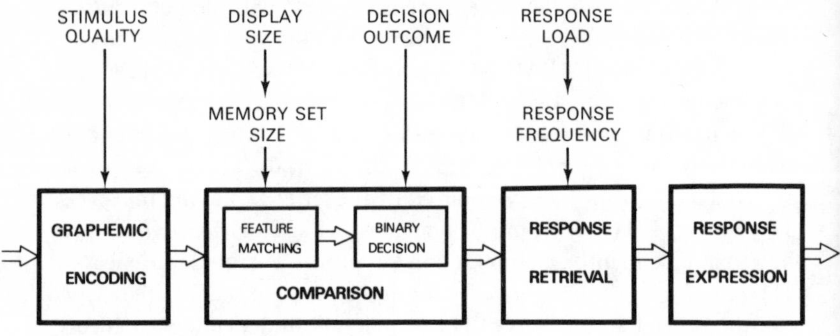

Figure II.4.2 A 'processing stage' model of symbol classification identifying factors exerting a selective influence on ENCODING, COMPARISON and response RETRIEVAL.

II.5 SLOPE AND INTERCEPT PARAMETERS

An important contribution of the research discussed in the preceding section has been the demonstration that COMPARISON is a distinct processing stage which may be selectively loaded by varying memory set size and display size. Variation of the levels of these factors alters the amount of processing activity which must occur before a decision about the status of the probe as a member or non-member of the memory set can be taken.

If average RTs obtained in a symbol classification experiment are plotted in relation to M, the size of the memory set, an almost universal finding is that RT increases as a function of M. The relationship often approximates linearity, although, for a substantial number of experiments, a better fit is obtained if RT is plotted in relation to a logarithmic transformation of M (Briggs, 1974). Either way, it is possible to define the RT as a linear function of memory set size, such that:

$$RT = A + B(M) \text{ msecs}$$

In this equation, M is a variable taking the different values of memory set size (or logarithmic transformations of those values), and A and B are constants. B is the time added to the overall RT for each additional symbol in the memory, and thus defines the *slope* of the function relating RT to M. Sternberg has proposed that this value may be treated as an index of the *rate of functioning* of the COMPARISON stage. The zero intercept parameter, A, can then be regarded as a measure of the accumulated durations of all processes other than

COMPARISON. It follows that A can be defined as an index to ENCODING and response RETRIEVAL and EXPRESSION, although these input and output stage durations are not separable in this analysis. In typical experiments, Sternberg (1966) reported that $\overline{RT} = 397 + 38(M)$ msecs for the varied set procedure, and $\overline{RT} = 369 + 38(M)$ msecs for the fixed set procedure.

The interpretation of the slope parameter, B, as an index of rate of COMPARISON is, of course, dependent on the conceptual analysis of the mental functions, and the adequacy of the empirical validation of the assumption of selective influence. However, if it is accepted that the underlying assumptions are adequately proven, the intercept and slope parameters can be used as convenient indications of the probable locus of experimental effects. If a new factor is introduced into the symbol classification experiment, an investigator can ask whether its effect is on the slope or the intercept of the function relating RT to M. Factors which alter the slope of the function are considered to influence the COMPARISON stage, whereas factors which influence the intercept are said to influence one of the other stages.

Numerous examples of such an interpretation of the slope and intercept parameters may be found in the experimental literature. As mentioned earlier, Sternberg (1967) introduced the factor of stimulus quality into the standard symbol classification experiment. He reported that degradation of the probe symbol produced its main effect on the intercept of the RT function, though there was also a small effect on the slope in the first session. A subsequent replication of the experiment showed an intercept effect but no slope effect (Bracey, 1969). Sternberg concluded that stimulus degradation increased the duration of the ENCODING stage (indexed by the change in the value of the parameter, A), and possibly exerted a small influence on COMPARISON in the earlier stages of practice (indexed by variations in the values of B).

Chase & Calfee (1969) varied the modality of presentation (visual or auditory) of both the memory set and the probe in an otherwise standard symbol classification experiment. The modality of the probe affected the value of the intercept, A, being 385 msecs for auditory probes and 498 msecs for visual probes. This probably reflects a difference in the durations of auditory and visual ENCODING processes. The slope parameter, B, was greater when the memory set and probe were presented in different modalities than when they were presented in the same modality, the values being 66 msecs per symbol in memory as against 50 msecs per symbol in memory. An implication is that both the memory set and the probe are represented in the modality of input, and that this incongruity must be resolved by recoding during the COMPARISON stage. Cruse & Clifton (1973) taught *S*s letter-digit equivalences, A-1, B-2, C-3, etc. Memory sets consisted of letters or digits, and probes were drawn from either category, *S*s being instructed to respond positively if the probe was a member of the memory set, or the equivalent of a member. The equation relating RT to M took the values: $\overline{RT} = 464 + 37(M)$ msecs when the probe and memory set were from the same category, and $\overline{RT} = 429 + 94(M)$ msecs when they were drawn from different categories. This again suggests that an incongruity between probe and memory set descriptions was resolved during the COMPARISON stage.

Briggs has proposed that effects of factors other than M can be clarified by plotting the value of A or B in relation to the various levels of the factor. For example, in the experiments by Briggs & Swanson (1970), variation in response load altered the value of the intercept parameter, A. It was found that A increased approximately linearly with a rise in the value of R, the number of alternative responses, so that one could state: $A = 242 + 84(R)$ msecs. This may imply that the RETRIEVAL phase of response selection is influenced by response load, being delayed by 84 msecs for each additional response which must be considered. The intercept value of 242 msecs could then represent ENCODING and perhaps the final stages of response EXPRESSION. In experiments in which both display load and memory load are varied, the value of B is found to increase as D becomes larger. Briggs suggested that this could be expressed by the equation: $B = 20 + 50(D)$ msecs, and proposed that COMPARISON might involve an operation of retrieval of a memory set item, requiring 20 msecs, and an operation of matching that representation against a display item, requiring 50 msecs. This interpretation appears to go somewhat beyond the legitimate conclusions which may be drawn from the data. The main point is that the slope parameter, B, is dependent on display load as well as memory load, increases in either D or M being sufficient to increase the duration of the COMPARISON stage.

II.6 CONCLUSIONS

This chapter has undertaken a preliminary exploration of the relationship between *mental functions* and 'processing stages'. Sternberg's additive factor method provides a conceptual and experimental framework within which the sensitivity of the mental functions to experimentally manipulable factors can be investigated. The research by Sternberg and others on the tasks of symbol naming and symbol classification was taken as an example of the application of the method. It seemed that it was possible to identify factors which exerted a selective influence on the durations of processing stages concerned with ENCODING, COMPARISON and response RETRIEVAL. In general, factors exerting a selective influence on distinct stages of processing yielded additive effects when combined in an experiment whereas factors influencing the same stage produced interactive effects.

PART ONE

The Symbolic Memory

CHAPTER III
The Symbolic Memory
STRUCTURE AND RESOURCES

III.1 INTRODUCTION

It is convenient to begin a discussion of research and theorizing in the topic of human Visual Cognition by considering a relatively specialized system which is involved in storage, representation and manipulation of the alphanumeric symbols. This system, which is referred to here as the *Symbolic Memory*, has been the object of extensive experimental study, chiefly because the letters and digits provide convenient sets of stimulus materials which are known to be familiar to a great majority of adult *S*s.

As explained in the two preceding chapters, the expression *Symbolic Memory* is in the first instance a label for a set of human capabilities or *behavioural dispositions* which exemplify knowledge of the alphanumeric symbols. A person who knows the letters and digits can, *inter alia*: (1) Name visually presented symbols, irrespective of variations of form, size and colour; (2) indicate whether pairs of simultaneously presented symbols are 'same' or 'different' according to a specified criterion; (3) select a verbally designated symbol from an array; (4) hold one or more symbols in memory and indicate whether or not they correspond to a subsequently presented set of probe symbols; (5) draw the shapes of verbally designated symbols; (6) categorize the symbols according to various criteria, such as letters versus digits, upper case versus lower, odd numbers versus even, vowels versus consonants; (7) list by speech or writing in correct order the letters of the alphabet or the numerals; (8) make decisions about the relative locations of letters and digits within their respective sets; (9) apply elementary arithmetical operations to number pairs.

This list of behavioural dispositions may readily be translated into a list of *experimental tasks*. These are tests which might be given to a child or a brain-damaged patient if one wished to assess competence in the use of the alphanumeric symbols. Since, by definition, the tasks depend on knowledge of the symbols for their accurate completion, they define an appropriate set of experimental situations for study of the Symbolic Memory system in mature and intact *S*s.

III.2 FUNCTIONS OF THE SYMBOLIC MEMORY

It was suggested in the introductory chapters that the dispositional analysis of a memory system might imply a set of essential functions which the neurological substrate of the system must be capable of carrying out. A candidate list of such functions will be presented for the Symbolic Memory in this section.

The formulation of this list can start from the assumption that the neurological system serves the individual through its capabilities for *interpretation* of external events, and for *initiation* of environmentally relevant action. If we accept that the internal language of the neurological system is at once distinct from the external world while being at the same time required to represent characteristics of that world, it follows that mental functions are needed to translate external events into an internal code, and to transform internal codes into externally observable actions. These functions will be referred to by the labels of ENCODING and EXPRESSION.

The ENCODING function is taken to be a process by which external energy variations are translated to an internal code or description. In this book we shall restrict our attention to *visual* ENCODING, although analogous encoding operations are required for each sensory modality. The visual ENCODING function will be discussed in some detail in Chapter IV, where it will be suggested that ENCODING is in fact a two-stage operation, involving first the coding of information entering the field of clear vision, and secondly the selective processing of limited portions of that information. An assumption has also been made that encoding is modality-specific. Thus, in speaking of visual ENCODING we are referring to a process by which an internal description of *visual* properties of an external event may be formed. It is true that subsequent processes may transform this visual description to some quite different code, such as the representation of a name or a class, but these later coding transformations will not be taken to be part of the ENCODING process.

The EXPRESSION function will not be discussed at any length in this text. In much of the experimental work to be considered experimenters have required *S*s to make responses which are perfunctory in nature and serve primarily to indicate the outcomes of prior decision processes. Theoretical interest has focused on the inferences about these processes which may be derived from the study of response latency and accuracy, but not on the response *per se*. Nonetheless, the present analysis assumes an EXPRESSION function for translation of internal codes to observable output. Like ENCODING, this function is seen as being peripheral in nature, and also modality specific. Thus, separate EXPRESSION functions are envisaged for translation to output in speech, writing, drawing, or motor reaction.

Aside from the peripheral ENCODING and EXPRESSION functions, the listing of capabilities which provide the dispositional definition of the Symbolic Memory suggests a requirement for three important internal functions. Firstly, successful performance on tasks which demand that symbol sets be held in memory for a short interval of time implies a capability of the neurological substrate of the Symbolic Memory for maintenance of internal symbol descriptions. This is the topic which has traditionally been discussed under the heading of *short-term memory*. In the present text it will be referred to as the REPRESENTATIONAL function. Its purpose is seen as one of maintaining symbol descriptions (representations) in temporary storage. Some discussion of this function is undertaken in Chapter V, with special reference to the REPRESENTATION of visual codes. Secondly, it is apparent that a number of the capabilities mentioned in the previous section presuppose the possibility of transformations from one form of descriptive code to another. The naming of symbols involves a visual-phonological transformation, whereas a search for a verbally designated symbol probably involves a phonological-visual transformation. These instances of recoding imply a capacity of the system for RETRIEVAL from permanent storage of alternative codes which are associatively equivalent to a currently maintained code. This RETRIEVAL function will be discussed in Chapter VI. It will be argued there that RETRIEVAL, like ENCODING, is analysable into two subsidiary functions, involving pattern recognition and the addressing of locations in permanent store.

Finally, a number of the tasks seen as defining the Symbolic Memory clearly involve some procedure by which symbol descriptions may be matched and evaluated for equivalence. This function, which will be referred to as COMPARISON, has in practice provided a central point of discussion in cognitive psychology, and many of the experimental studies to be discussed are based on comparison tasks of one kind or another. The COMPARISON function will be considered in detail in Chapter VII. The main argument there will be that the function is conceptually divisible into two subsidiary aspects, one involving the matching of components of symbol descriptions, and the other the formulation of a judgement of equivalence.

The candidate list of essential functions of the Symbolic Memory therefore contains five members, to be called: ENCODING, REPRESENTATION, RETRIEVAL, COMPARISON and EXPRESSION. These concepts, and the preliminaries of their logical analyses, are assumed to be derivable from a purely formal consideration of the Symbolic Memory. The psychological validation of these assumptions will be undertaken in Chapters IV–VII.

III.3 STRUCTURAL MODEL OF THE SYMBOLIC MEMORY

Each of the functions identified in the previous section is a name for a collection of related procedures—akin to routines of a computer programme which have been labelled in a manner that indicates the kind of work they do—which may be utilized in manipulation of symbol descriptions. These descriptions are the objects of the functions, in the sense that ENCODING is the *formation* of a descriptive code, REPRESENTATION is the *maintenance* of such a code, RETRIEVAL is the *accessing* of a code in permanent memory, and COMPARISON is the *evaluation* of codes with regard to their equivalence. The *descriptive codes* therefore form a second essential element in the analysis of the Symbolic Memory, since they constitute the data on which the mental functions must operate.

We can derive certain conclusions about the descriptive codes from the dispositional analysis of the Symbolic Memory. In this we assume that the descriptive codes are internal representations of those characteristics of the alphanumeric symbols about which competent individuals are evidently knowledgeable. Successful performance on the defining tasks mentioned at the beginning of this chapter requires a knowledge of the visual forms of the symbols, their assigned names, and the sequential structures and classes into which they may be organized. We assume that this knowledge is internally realized in the form of neural representations or codes, separate codes being required for description of visual properties, phonological properties, classifications and sequential organization of the members of the symbol sets. In the discussion that follows these will be referred to as the *graphemic code* (for representation of visual information), the *phonemic code* (for representation of speech sounds), and the *categorial* and *structural codes* (for representation of class membership and location in a sequential structure).

The validation of these assumptions concerning descriptive codes depends on the development of techniques of demonstrating that the data manipulated by the mental functions do indeed take the form of coded descriptions of graphemic, phonemic, categorial or structural properties of the symbol sets. Some comments on methods of investigating this question will be included in Chapters V and VI.

The notions of mental functions and descriptive codes may be combined to complete the conceptual analysis of the Symbolic Memory. If these functions are to be applied to the descriptive codes in the service of successful performance on the defining tasks, the Symbolic Memory must incorporate certain essential facilities or resources. These appear to fall under three main heads. Firstly, we have to assume that the codes representing the graphemic, phonemic, categorial and structural aspects of the symbol sets are held in a permanent form of storage. We will therefore assume that one resource of the Symbolic Memory is a *permanent storage space*. It is permissible to divide this space along conceptual lines, so as to differentiate between graphemic, phonemic, categorial and structural *data stores*. Secondly, we must assume that descriptive codes which have been retrieved from permanent store or created by application of encoding functions to sensory input may be temporarily represented in a manner which allows them to become the focus of operation of the mental functions. This implies the availability of *temporary storage space* in which currently active descriptive codes may be held and manipulated. This space may again be divided conceptually to distinguish between the different types of representational code. In what follows the term *register* will be used to refer to these temporary stores, and we will speak of the *graphemic register* (for temporary representation of visual properties), the *phonemic register* (for temporary representation of speech sounds), and the *categorial* and *structural registers* (for temporary representation of class membership and sequential location).

A third important requirement is a facility allowing for transformation from one code to another. These transformations are achieved by application of the RETRIEVAL function. For RETRIEVAL to occur, a code held in one temporary storage register must be used to access a location in permanent storage so that the description held at that location can be placed in a second temporary register. We will assume that the various possible transformations are mediated by associative systems which will be referred to as *interface structures*. An interface must contain a set of *pattern recognizers*, specialized for

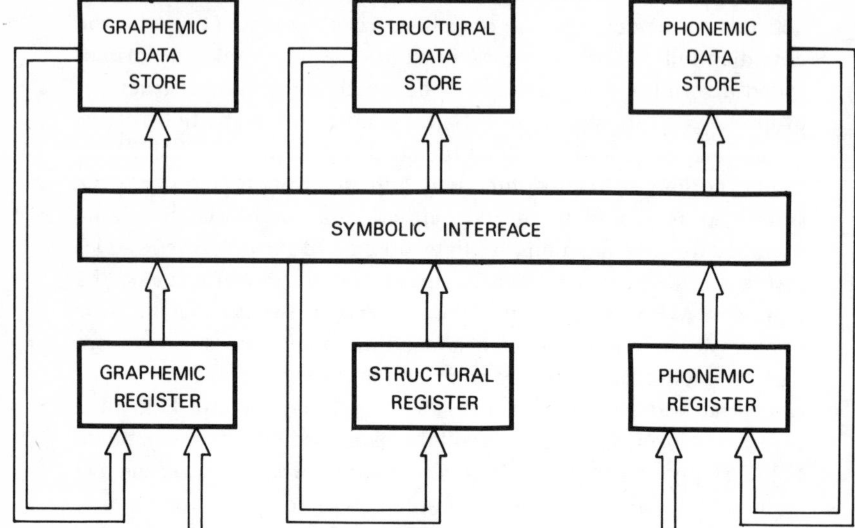

Figure III.3.1 Schematic representation of the major components of the Symbolic Memory, including the temporary storage registers, the permanent data stores, and the symbolic interface structure.

identification of codes held in a particular temporary storage register, and an *address register* which contains pointers to locations in one of the permanent data stores. The interface includes links between particular recognizers and particular addresses which allow for RETRIEVAL of alternative codings of a symbol.

The resources of the Symbolic Memory may be represented in a diagrammatic form, as shown in Figure III.3.1. It is to be emphasized that the diagram does not purport to be a map of anatomically separate neurophysiological systems in the brain. It is merely a convenient pictorial summary of conceptually distinguishable storage and addressing facilities which are considered to be a necessary part of the Symbolic Memory system. The following are the principal features of the diagrammatic model. Firstly, sensory information entering the system via the visual or auditory modalities is transformed, by application of the ENCODING functions, from external physical energy into a set of internal descriptions or codes. Visual input leads to formation of a visual description which is initially placed in the graphemic register. Auditory input of speech sounds is transformed to a phonemic code which is initially placed in the phonemic register. Secondly, the memory system contains permanent data stores for graphemic, phonemic, categorial and structural properties of the symbol sets. These stores are accessible through the interface structure. This has been represented as a single entity in the diagram, but may be conceptually differentiated with regard to the code providing input to the interface and the target data store. Retrieval of the name of a visual symbol would involve input from the graphemic register to the interface, accessing of a location of the phonemic data store, and placement of the contents of that location in the phonemic register. Thus, each permanent store has an associated temporary register, and descriptions retrieved from permanent store are always placed in the register belonging to the store from which they are taken. Maintenance of a code by the REPRESENTATIONAL function could be achieved by allowing a descriptive code to access its replica in its own data store. For example, a graphemic code could be maintained by cyclic input of graphemic information to the interface and accessing of descriptions in the graphemic data store.

The diagram represents the facilities required for operation of the mental functions, but does not represent the functions themselves. Each function has a sphere of activity within the diagram, ENCODING being concerned with sensory input, EXPRESSION with generation of output, and REPRESENTATION and RETRIEVAL with maintenance or transformation of descriptive codes by use of the temporary and permanent stores and the interface structure. The calling and chaining of these functions, and the detailed modulation of their activities, is the province of an *executive level* which is superordinate to the diagram. This is also true in the case of COMPARISON, which is an executive procedure capable of focusing on a specific coding register, sampling its content, and arriving at a 'same' or 'different' decision.

III.4 CONCLUSIONS

This chapter has outlined a schematic model of the *Symbolic Memory*. The model is intended to emphasize that knowledge of the letters and the numbers is internally represented in the form of codes which are descriptive of properties of symbols. It has been supposed that this coding system is conceptually divisible with respect to the types of codes which may be formed (graphemic, phonemic, categorial and structural), and with respect to the components or facilities which are logically required (permanent storage, temporary storage, and associative interface).

The *Symbolic Memory* emerges from this account as a system for representation of properties of symbols (the mental codes) which contains the data that are operated upon by various routines or procedures (the mental functions). In the chapters which follow we shall discuss experimental studies which serve to validate our assumptions concerning the mental codes, and to clarify the nature of the mental functions.

CHAPTER IV

Visual Encoding Functions

FORMATION OF THE GRAPHEMIC CODE

IV.1 INTRODUCTION

The first of the mental functions identified in the previous chapter was called ENCODING. This term is taken to refer to a preliminary processing stage by which visual (or auditory) sensory input may be transformed to an internal description or code. It was considered that visual ENCODING is a processing stage which is selectively influenced by factors of *stimulus quality*, and this view was validated by the various demonstrations that stimulus quality combined additively with factors thought to influence other stages of processing (Sternberg, 1967, 1969b).

This chapter will undertake a more detailed analysis of the logical structure of the ENCODING function, and will also consider the results of some relevant experimental studies. The basic experimental situation which we seek to analyse is one in which an array of symbols is briefly presented, and the *S* is required to indicate whether or not a target symbol is present, or to identify the symbols occupying particular locations in the array. Investigators have in general relied on RT measurements and error frequencies in report and forced-choice detection tasks as indicators of the duration and efficiency of the ENCODING stage. They have sought to determine the capacity of the stage, both with regard to spatial aspects (the number of symbols that may be encoded simultaneously, or array locations which may be preferentially processed), and temporal aspects (the time required for the proper functioning of the stage). This has been approached by introducing variations in the factors of *display load*, D, and *stimulus quality*, generally through use of tachistoscopic presentation combined with masking.

The visual ENCODING function is part of a set of executive procedures which control an individual's orientation to the external world by voluntary movements of the head and body, and, more especially, adjustments in the aim of the two eyes. The main characteristics of the eye-movements which occur during inspection of printed symbols have been known for many years (Tinker, 1958). The eyes make rapid shifts, known as *saccades*, interspersed by longer fixation pauses which average 200–250 msecs in duration. It is considered that uptake of visual information occurs during the pauses. ENCODING is therefore part of a larger programme of search activity. To emphasize this point we will use the label INSPECTION as a name for the higher order executive. It is assumed that INSPECTION controls the trajectories of the eyes and calls on ENCODING as a complex routine which is applied during each fixation pause.

IV.2 VISUAL SEARCH

If one wishes to examine the rate of functioning of the INSPECTION programme it is convenient to use a *visual search task* of the kind popularized by Neisser (1967). He presented *S*s with columns of 50 lines of symbols and instructed them to scan down the column and close a switch as soon as a row containing a target symbol was encountered. The position in the list of the critical item varied unpredictably. RT was measured from presentation of the column of symbols to closure of the switch by the *S*. Neisser reported an approximately linear relationship between RT and target position, P. We can therefore state that $RT = A + B(P)$ msecs, where A and B are intercept and slope constants, and P is the position of the target item. As in Sternberg's analysis of memory search, B may be taken as an index of the rate of functioning of the INSPECTION process.

If other experimental factors are introduced, and can be shown to alter the value of the slope parameter, B, it will follow that they also influence the rate of INSPECTION. Neisser (1963) examined a number of such factors, including: (1) search for presence of a target versus search for its absence; (2) variation in the number of letters per row; (3) similarity of non-target context letters to the target; (4) practice on the visual search task. All of these factors altered the slope of the RT function relating search time to target position.

We might conclude from such results that INSPECTION—which incorporates the ENCODING function which is the main object of interest in this chapter—is sensitive to the factors of display load and target-background confusability, and also to factors influencing the amount of processing required to classify items as non-targets. On the latter point, Neisser argued that search for absence of a target is slower than search for its presence because the search for absence requires positive identification of a critical letter whereas a search for presence requires only a failure to detect certain defining features before INSPECTION can take the decision that a target has not been found and shift the eyes so as to continue the search. Thus, INSPECTION appears to be a serial self-terminating search process. The operations of moving the eyes and encoding information from the symbol display are applied reiteratively until the target is found, and search time is directly dependent on the number of symbols that must be scanned and rejected as non-targets.

IV.3 DISPLAY SEARCH TASKS

Neisser's visual search task is not a satisfactory tool for analysis of the ENCODING function because it fails to separate ENCODING from INSPECTION. Thus, although we know that visual search rate is affected by visual and conceptual confusability (Neisser, 1963; Brand, 1971), we cannot say whether this is an influence on the duration of the ENCODING stage or on the programming of the saccadic eye-movements by INSPECTION. A better procedure is to present small arrays of symbols for an interval approximating the duration of a fixation pause and to record RT from display onset to occurrence of a response indicating whether or not a target is present.

This can be referred to as a *display search task*. It is the converse of Sternberg's symbol classification task. The latter involves a single display item which must be matched against a variable number of items in memory. In display search there is usually only one item in memory, but the number of items on the display is varied. The procedure may be used, therefore, to determine the effects of display load, D, on the RT. It has, however, an inherent limitation in that it must always be difficult to determine whether an obtained effect of D is occurring during ENCODING or during a subsequent COMPARISON stage. Indeed, the experiments of Briggs & Swanson (1970) indicated that D affected the slope of the RT function in symbol classification but not the intercept (see Section II.4 above). This was taken to imply an effect of D on COMPARISON, but no effect on ENCODING.

For this reason effects of D obtained in display search experiments might most properly be assigned to a COMPARISON stage in which display items are matched against a memorized target representation. The display search task is useful for the study of ENCODING only if circumstances allow the *S* to dispense with a COMPARISON stage and to base his decision directly on tests applied during ENCODING.

Such cases can be detected if the effects of D on ENCODING are of a markedly different magnitude from those exerted on COMPARISON. In practice, investigators have generally been interested in the possibility that D has little or no influence on ENCODING, since this would constitute evidence for parallel processing of a number of spatially distinct symbols during the ENCODING stage.

Some relevant experiments have been reported by Egeth, Jonides & Wall (1972). Their *S*s made a positive response only when a digit was included on a display of letters. The display load, D, was varied at 1–6 items, and a circular array was used. It was found that the effect of D on the RT was slight and statistically insignificant, the data being fitted by the equation: $\overline{\mathrm{RT}} = 369 + 4(\mathrm{D})$ msecs. This result also occurred for positive responses when *S*s reacted to both presence and absence of the target. Further experiments, described by Egeth, Atkinson, Gilmore & Marcus (1973), compared linear and circular displays and digits and letters as background items. Circular displays composed of digits yielded non-significant effects of D, but linear arrays containing letters produced effects of the order of 10 msecs per display item. Egeth has also shown that responses to absence of a target are more likely to produce effects of D than are responses to presence of a target. In the experiments of Egeth, Jonides & Wall (1972), negative RT was related to D by the equation: $\overline{\mathrm{RT}} = 458 + 26(\mathrm{D})$ msecs.

An alternative way of running the display search task is to instruct the *S* to respond positively if all items on the display are the same, and negatively if there is an odd-man-out. This situation also yields data in which RT is not affected by D. For example, Beller (1970) presented *S*s with arrays of 2, 4 or 8 letters, and required them to respond positively if all the letters were physically identical or had the same name (e.g. AAAA or AAaA). The positive RT for physically identical arrays was about 466 msecs, and was unrelated to D. This was also true of same name displays, although the general level of the RT was somewhat higher at 537 msecs. Egeth, Jonides & Wall (1972) obtained comparable results with circular displays of 2–6 symbols. Connor (1972) also found no effect of D = 3, 6 or 12 letters. Giving *S*s a small set of digits to hold in temporary memory immediately prior to presentation of the display had no effect on this outcome.

These experimental findings appear sufficient to establish that the ENCODING stage may, under certain circumstances, appear insensitive to variations in D, the display load. There is no effect of D when the task is merely to test for homogeneity of the display. Tests for presence of a target item, or a member of a target class (any digit), may also show only slight effects of D, especially when circular arrays are used. An effect of D is likely to occur, however, when the *S* must search for a target letter within a linear array of letters. For example, Atkinson, Holmgren & Juola (1969) presented arrays of 1–5 consonants delimited by dollar signs at either end. A single target consonant was specified on each trial. The RT was significantly related to D on both positive trials, where $\overline{RT} = 444 + 24(D)$ msecs, and negative trials, where $\overline{RT} = 474 + 26(D)$ msecs. No consistent effects for serial position of the target in the array were obtained.

Jonides & Gleitman (1972) have presented evidence to suggest that conceptual similarity of target and background items is an important factor underlying display size effects. They reported no effect of D when *S*s searched for a target letter among digits, or a target digit among letters, where D = 2, 4 or 6 items. When the target and background were drawn from the same class a significant linear effect of D was obtained, having a slope of 26 msecs per item. It proved possible to replicate this finding when the target symbol, O, was defined as a digit or letter. There was no effect for D when *S*s searched for the letter O among digits, or for the digit O among letters, but the effect was reinstated when the target description and the display items were from the same class. A slope of 24 msecs per item was found when *S*s searched for the letter O among letters, or the digit O among digits.

Effects of D on display search can also be assessed in a *forced-choice detection task*. Two targets (or sets of targets) are defined, and the *S* must indicate which target was present on a briefly flashed display. Estes (1972) examined this situation, using arrays of 4, 6 or 8 items, and mutually exclusive target sets of 1, 2 or 4 items. The number of signal items on the display was also varied. When the non-target elements were simply matrices of dots on an oscilloscope display, variation in D affected neither RT nor accuracy of detection, and there was no effect due to duplication of target letter. However, when the non-targets were other letters, RT was related to D by a linear slope of 11 msecs per item, accuracy declined with increases in D, and both dependent variables were affected by the number of redundant target items.

These experiments may be taken as confirming that, under some circumstances, RT in display search tasks may be shown to be independent of D, the display load. The result is most secure in the case of the odd-man-out task of Beller (1970), but may occur in display search and forced choice tasks provided that the target and non-target items are not visually (or conceptually) confusable. Use of confusable items, especially linear arrays of letters, tends to give rise to effects of D on the RT, although these are typically somewhat smaller in magnitude than the effects of M obtained in symbol classification tasks by Sternberg and others.

IV.4 SELECTIVITY IN 'ENCODING'

The experiments showing an absence of effects of D on display search RT may be taken as support for the conclusion that the ENCODING stage has available to it a number of processing channels which operate in an independent and parallel manner to convey information about symbols occupying distinct spatial locations in an array. Referring back to the diagrammatic model of the Symbolic Memory shown in Figure III.3.1, one might suppose that these channels transmit information about symbol characteristics directly from the retinal receptors to the graphemic register. There are, however, certain logical and empirical objections to this supposition which will be considered in this section.

The main problem is that it seems essential to assume the involvement of a *selective process* at some point during ENCODING. We know that the sensitive foveal region of the retina occupies a visual angle of about 2°. In normal reading, the eyes track along a line of print, processing horizontally arrayed groups of symbols. Although symbols on lines above and below the immediate focus of attention also fall within foveal vision they are hardly seen and generally do not interfere with the reading process (Neisser, 1969). If the book is rotated through 90° and the lines are read vertically, symbols to the right and left of the current focus will not be seen. Thus, not all information that is potentially available for detailed analysis by the ENCODING stage is in practice privileged by such analysis. A degree of spatial selectivity is involved.

Experimental demonstrations of this selective property of ENCODING come chiefly from studies of accuracy of report of tachistoscopically presented arrays of symbols. When *S*s are instructed to report as many symbols as they can (known as the *whole report* method) they typically fail to remember more than 4–5 items although they often claim to have been aware of more than this at the time of the tachistoscopic flash. This limitation is referred to as the 'span of apprehension' or 'span of immediate memory' (Miller, 1956) and is characteristic of whole report tachistoscopic experiments.

Sperling (1960) introduced a *partial report* method of studying the amount of information initially encoded from complex arrays. *S*s were presented with 3×3 and 3×4 matrices of symbols followed immediately by a tone signal indicating which of the three rows should be reported. Sperling found that a high level of accuracy could be maintained on whichever row was cued, and concluded that a representation of the entire display was available for selective processing at the time when the cue signal occurred. The representation must be located within the visual system, since the physical display was no longer present when the *S* received and interpreted the signal. Subsequent studies suggest that post-stimulus selection may be based on visual properties, such as spatial location, size, or colour, but not on more conceptual properties, such as orientation or the distinction between letters and digits (Sperling, 1960; von Wright, 1968).

Sperling also examined the effects of delaying onset of the partial report cue. If the proportion of items correctly reported from the cued row of the display is taken as an estimate of the proportion of all display items available following interpretation of the cue, his data suggested a decline from about 80 or 90 per cent for an immediate cue to about 40 per cent at a 1 sec delay. A similar decay function was obtained by Keele & Chase (1967) for visual cueing of single locations on a 10-item circular display. Partial reports were no more accurate than whole reports at delays of 250 msecs or more. At shorter delays performance was affected by luminance of the display, and errors were shown to depend on visual rather than acoustic confusability.

These experiments have been taken to imply that a representation of a visual display may be retained in the processing system for a short time after the display has been switched off. Following Neisser (1967) we will refer to this representation as the *icon*. Sperling's results indicate that the icon is a briefly persisting memory of visual characteristics of a tachistoscopic presentation, and that spatially selective encoding operations may be applied to this representation.

IV.5 TWO-STAGE MODEL OF 'ENCODING'

We take Sperling's findings to establish that ENCODING is a spatially selective process, even though characteristics of non-selected symbols are represented in the system. From this we can conclude that two temporary storage registers may be necessary for the proper functioning of the ENCODING stage. The first of these might be called the *iconic register*. It is required for brief retention of a neural representation of the visual field projected onto the retinal mosaic at the outset of each fixation pause. The second is the *graphemic register* mentioned in Chapter III. It is supposed that those contents of the iconic register which are selected for further processing are transferred to the graphemic register, and that it is this information that forms the durable product of the ENCODING stage.

The assumption that two storage registers are required for visual ENCODING leads naturally to a two-stage model of the process. A first sub-stage is needed for transformation of retinal stimulation to a representation in the iconic register. We might refer to this as the *icon formation sub-stage.* A second sub-stage is required for selection of information in the iconic register and its transfer to the graphemic register. This could be called the *selective encoding sub-stage.*

These comments point towards a description of the ENCODING function which is stated in terms of the temporary storage facilities on which its operations depend. If we assume distinct temporary stores, and transfer of data from one store to the other, we must also provide communication *channels* to carry information from the retinal level to the iconic register, and from the iconic register to the graphemic register. It has already been argued, on the basis of experiments showing an absence of effects of D on the RT in display search tasks (Section IV.3), that the ENCODING function may have access to a number of these channels, and that the channels may transfer data independently of one another and in a temporally parallel fashion.

The temporary storage and data transfer resources of the ENCODING stage can be represented diagrammatically, as shown in Figure IV.5.1. It is suggested in the figure that a large number of channels is available for parallel transfer of information from the retinal level to the iconic register, but only a relatively small number for transfer from the iconic register to the graphemic register. It has appeared convenient to assume that each channel has a terminal register which may contain information about relative spatial location and about symbol properties. These termini form the cells of the temporary storage registers, and will, when active, contain a spatially labelled representation of characteristics of a symbol array (the graphemic codes, $G_{1...n}$, and the spatial codes, $S_{1...n}$).

As mentioned earlier in this chapter, the operation of the ENCODING stage is subordinate to a higher order executive function called INSPECTION. The stage will operate whenever INSPECTION initiates a saccadic movement of the eyes and stabilizes convergence

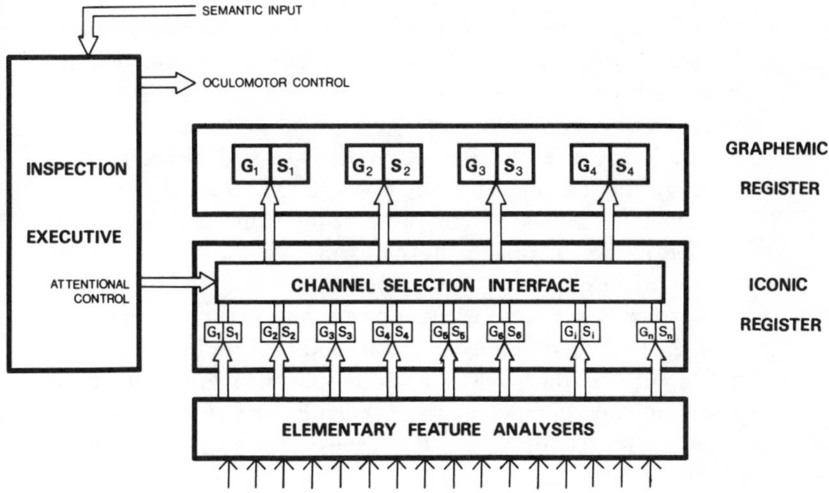

Figure IV.5.1 Diagrammatic representation of the temporary storage and data transfer facilities required by the graphemic ENCODING function. Processing is controlled by the INSPECTION executive which receives instructions in the form of semantic codes and which determines eye-movements and attentional selectivity at the level of the channel selection interface. Incoming visual stimuli are processed by elementary graphemic feature analysers, and a representation is formed in the iconic register which specifies the spatial location of each symbol (indicated by the labels S_1, S_2, ...S_i .... S_n) and its graphemic properties (indicated by the labels G_1, G_2, ... G_i .... G_n). A limited number of these graphemic/spatial representations may be transferred to the graphemic register following instructions from the INSPECTION executive.

and fixation at the end of the trajectory. It seems reasonable to suppose that the first sub-stage of icon formation is then automatically carried out. The second sub-stage of selective encoding will, on the other hand, be dependent on instructions from the executive as to which locations in the iconic register should be processed. In Figure IV.5.1 this intervention has been represented as an interface structure through which cells in the iconic register may be linked to the channels connecting with the graphemic register. It is supposed that the executive continuously revises these links so as to maintain an appropriate attentional field in reading, or to respond to the instructions given in a partial report experiment.

IV.6 EFFECTS OF PRESENTATION RATE

In order to validate the two-stage model it is necessary to find experimental procedures which successfully differentiate the two representational levels which have been proposed. This is most easily approached through tachistoscopic experiments in which accuracy of forced choice detection or partial report is treated as the primary indicator of the functioning of the ENCODING stage. In one type of experiment symbols are displayed sequentially and the *rate of presentation* is varied, usually by manipulating the delay between successive brief exposures of the symbols. The *S* may be instructed to make a forced choice as to whether or not a target symbol has been presented. If such a decision can be taken at the termini of the input channels, either in the iconic or in the graphemic register, and if the channels do indeed function independently and in parallel, it is anticipated that performance should show relatively little effect of presentation rate.

A study by Eriksen & Spencer (1969) provides some relevant data. A ten-channel tachistoscope was used to present letters at locations on a circular array. The letter A was designated as a target, and the letters T and U as non-targets. Each letter was displayed for approximately 2 msecs in sequences of 1–9 items, and the interval between letters varied from 5–30 msecs. The *S*s were instructed to indicate whether or not the sequence had contained an A. When a target did occur, it might be inserted near the start, middle or end of the sequence. The data were analysed within the framework of the theory of signal detectability (Egan & Clark, 1966). The measure of the observer's sensitivy, d', did not vary with either rate of presentation or target location in the sequence. This is consistent with the view that ten symbol processing channels were available, each capable of testing for the occurrence of the target, A, the functioning of each being independent of the states of other active channels.

In a related experiment, Eriksen & Collins (1969) displayed sequences of digits at a single location on a screen. The digits were presented in order, but the starting point varied, and one digit was always omitted. A target digit was specified prior to each trial, and *S*s were instructed to indicate whether or not that digit had been presented. The digits were displayed for 10 msecs each, and the interval between them varied over the range 50–125 msecs. It was found that an interval of 75 msecs or more was sufficient for almost perfect detection of presence or absence of the target digit, but that there was some deterioration of performance at the 50 msec interval. There were no effects due to the position of the target in the sequence.

The important contrast between this and the Eriksen & Spencer study is that the digits were displayed at a single location. If input channels are assigned on a spatial basis, it follows that only one channel was available for processing of the sequence of digits. Under these circumstances, it is expected that presentation rate will become an important factor as soon as the interval between symbols is reduced below the time required for normal operation of the channel. The results of the Eriksen & Collins study therefore suggest that about 85 msecs may be required for processing and testing of an individual symbol.

In a somewhat more complex experiment, Sperling, Budiansky, Spivak & Johnson (1971) combined variation in display size and presentation rate, *S*s being instructed to detect the occurrence of a digit embedded in one of a rapidly presented series of letter arrays. The factors in the experiment were display size (D = 2–25 items per display), interval between arrays (20–230 msecs), and number of arrays preceding the one containing a target. Sperling analysed the accuracy of reports of the location containing the target to derive estimates of the number of locations successfully processed. For a 9-item array performance was optimal for two practised *S*s when the inter-display interval was 40-60 msecs. Accuracy data suggested that 3–6 locations might be processed at this presentation rate.

The interpretation favoured here is that these studies reveal characteristics of a decision process operating at the level of the iconic register. Possibly target descriptions can be duplicated at the termini of all input channels, so that what was referred to by Estes (1972) as a *primary detection response* can be generated as output from whichever channel happens to contain a target. This account can also apply for display search experiments in which effects of D are found to be small or absent. Detection of an odd-man-out, as in Beller's (1970) study, might also depend on processing at this level, perhaps through application of a routine for comparing the content of each channel terminus with the content of every other. If this interpretation is correct, the experimental data may be taken as consistent with the view that the input channels function in parallel during icon formation, and that the time required for transfer of data along these channels is somewhat less than 100 msecs.

This interpretation can be supported by showing that quite different effects of presentation rate occur when symbols must be identified, rather than being evaluated for correspondence with a predesignated target. The study by Eriksen & Collins (1969) may again be consulted. They presented sequences of digits, each shown for 10 msecs, with intervals of 100–200 msecs between each digit. On every trial one digit was omitted from the sequence. *S*s were given the name of a digit, and were instructed to indicate whether or not it had occurred in the sequence. It seems likely that each digit had to be processed at least to the level of the graphemic register (from which a structural coding of the number sequence is accessible) for this decision to be taken. Eriksen & Collins reported that it was only at the 200 msec delay that *S*s were able to perform this task accurately. Rather similar results were obtained by Kolers (1970) in a study in which letters making up words were displayed successively at a single location. An interval of about 250 msecs between letters was required for correct identification.

These effects of presentation rate are markedly different from those obtained in the experiments on detection. It is proposed that they reflect the duration of the whole ENCODING stage, that is both the icon formation and selective encoding sub-stages. One can note that the estimate obtained is close to the duration of a fixation pause in reading (Tinker, 1958). It is also in agreement with results of whole report experiments using masking techniques. For example, Smith & Carey (1966) presented a 6 × 6 matrix of letters for 20 msecs followed by a second matrix at an inter-stimulus delay of 80, 180 or 380 msecs. The *S* was required to make a whole report of the letters in a particular row of the matrix, and the dependent measure was the number of masked exposures required for achievement of accurate report of all six letters. Relative to performance with an unmasked 20 msec exposure, masking disrupted report accuracy at the 80 msec and 180 msec delays, but not at the 380 msec delay.

IV.7 EFFECTS OF MASKING

A second kind of experiment which is useful in validating the proposed distinction between icon formation and selective encoding is one in which visual masking is combined with Sperling's partial report procedure. In masking experiments an array of symbols is briefly presented, followed, after a variable delay, by presentation of a visual noise field. The critical manipulation is the temporal interval between the display and the masking field, sometimes referred to as the *stimulus onset asynchrony*. Under the partial report procedure, an auditory or visual indicator is presented which tells the *S* which location to report. The delay of the indicator relative to the display may also be varied.

It is known, from studies such as those of Sperling (1960, 1963, 1967) or Smith & Carey (1966) that accuracy of report is impaired when a tachistoscopic display is followed by a masking field. In a two-stage model of ENCODING, of the kind diagrammed in Figure IV.5.1, these *backward masking effects* might arise in either of two possible ways. Firstly, a masking field presented in close temporal proximity to the symbol array could disrupt the icon formation sub-stage by degrading the information transmitted along the input channels. Secondly, a masking field occurring later in processing could disrupt the activity of the selective encoding sub-stage by deleting content from the iconic register during selective transfer to the graphemic register.

On the basis of the studies of effects of presentation rate on target detection described in the preceding section we could anticipate that the icon formation sub-stage of ENCODING should be vulnerable to masking during the period of 80–100 msecs following onset of the target array. Eriksen (1966) has argued that test and masking fields presented at these short stimulus onset asynchronies may combine to reduce contrast and legibility. In support of this view he has shown that two closely successive inputs may be integrated to form a composite pattern description. Arrays of dots, each appearing random when viewed in isolation, were displayed for 6 msecs each separated by intervals of 0, 25, 50, 75 and 100 msecs. When superimposed the dots outlined a three-letter nonsense syllable. This syllable could be identified by *S*s at intervals of 50 msecs or less, implying integration of successive inputs during the icon formation sub-stage of ENCODING (Eriksen & Collins, 1967, 1968).

A study of masking effects occurring within this temporal region has been reported by Spencer (1969). He presented circular arrays of 12 letters together with a visual pointer indicating which letter the *S* was to report. When the array was followed by a blank masking field a stimulus onset asynchrony of 50–75 msecs was sufficient for achievement of a level of accuracy equivalent to that observed in a no mask control condition. A patterned masking field was somewhat more disruptive, a delay of about 150 msecs being required before performance approximated the control condition. It may be noted that in this experiment a selective encoding process was not required, since the partial report indicator was presented simultaneously with the symbol array. It is therefore reasonable to suppose that the accurary variations recorded by Spencer reflected the impact of masking on the icon formation sub-stage of ENCODING.

In order to study an effect of masking on the selective encoding sub-stage it is necessary to conduct a somewhat more complicated experiment. If the partial report indicator is delayed relative to the display, as in the original study by Sperling (1960), we assume that icon formation occurs prior to onset of the indicator, and that a selective encoding operation is initiated when the indicator has been processed and interpreted. If masking can disrupt this selective process it should be possible to show disruption of performance when a mask occurs after offset of the indicator. The study by Spencer (1969) included a condition of this kind. The 12-letter circular array was followed after a delay of 100 msecs by an indicator pointing to a particular position, and the *S* was instructed to identify the letter which had occupied that position. Presentation of a blank masking field after offset of the indicator had no influence on performance. However, presentation of a patterned mask had a substantial deleterious effect over a period of 300 msecs or so after presentation of the delayed indicator. Since this disruption occurred over a much greater temporal interval than the masking effects observed when the indicator was presented simultaneously with the display there seems to be a strong suggestion that the interference relates to the later selective processes in ENCODING.

It is possible masking disrupts selective encoding by replacing the contents of the iconic register. In Spencer's study the effect was obtained for a patterned mask, but not for a blank field. Thus, although the blank field can apparently interfere with icon formation it seems that it does not lead to creation of a new icon. This occurs only when patterned information possessing some graphemic characteristics enters the ENCODING stage. For the stage to function efficiently it is important that it should be protected from new input over an interval of 200–250 msecs from the start of processing. This delay is sufficient for icon formation and selective encoding, that is for entry of symbol descriptions into the graphemic register. The graphemic register defines a deeper level of temporary storage which is not thought to be vulnerable to masking effects (Coltheart, 1972), and its contents may be used to access alternative codings of symbols.

IV.8 DIRECTIONAL ASPECTS OF 'ENCODING'

A further factor on which the icon formation and selective encoding sub-stages may be differentiated is in accuracy variations due to the *serial positions* occupied by symbols in linear arrays. If symbol processing occurs in independent parallel channels during icon formation we might anticipate that each serial position should be processed with equal efficiency. However, studies using a visual partial report indicator have generally shown that report performance is related to array position by a W-shaped function in which accuracy is highest at the ends and centre of the array (Averbach & Coriell, 1961; Haber & Standing, 1969).

It seems likely that this W-shaped function is characteristic of the icon formation sub-stage of processing. If so, the parallel channel model must be modified to allow for preferential processing of central and end locations. Merikle & Coltheart (1972) have argued that channels are assigned to symbol locations in a temporal succession, the end positions being processed earliest, followed by the central positions, and finally the intermediate positions. In support of this they demonstrated that forward masking of a briefly exposed 7-letter array selectively impaired accuracy of reports of the end locations, whereas backward masking had a selective effect on the central locations. An interaction of masking and serial position effects of this kind is to be expected if both factors influence the same icon formation stage of processing. Merikle (1976) has further reported that these effects combined additively with other factors, notably the modality of presentation and the delay of the partial report indicator, which may be assumed to influence the selective encoding sub-stage.

Serial position effects attributable to the selective encoding sub-stage generally show evidence of a superiority of symbols on the left of the array over those on the right. In whole report experiments, where correctly reported symbols have presumably been selectively transferred from the iconic register to the graphemic register, it is often found that report is most accurate for the upper rows of complex displays, and for the lefthand items (Sperling, 1960; Averbach & Coriell, 1961; Heron, 1957). Merikle, Coltheart & Lowe (1971) reported data for 8-letter linear arrays which show a clear left-to-right decline in accuracy combined with a vestigial advantage for the central locations. Comparable data have been reported by Bryden (1966) and Merikle, Lowe and Coltheart (1971).

Mewhort, Merikle & Bryden (1969) selectively masked the left or righthand halves of 8-letter arrays, the array being presented for 40 msecs and delay of the mask being set at 0, 20, 40, 60 or 80 msecs. When the righthand side was masked, accuracy of report of the rightmost four letters improved as a function of mask delay, but this factor had no effect on reports of the lefthand letters. By contrast, when the left side was masked, delay of the mask improved performance on both sides of the array. Thus, masking on the left disrupted selective encoding of letters on the right (unmasked) side of the display, although there was no corresponding effect due to masking of letters on the right. The implication is that selective encoding is a serial process operating in a left-to-right direction across the contents of the icon.

Shaw (1969) has described an experiment which suggests that left-to-right processing may occur in detection tasks as well as in whole report tasks. He presented arrays of letters extending to the right of a fixation mark. The *S* was required to indicate which of two possible letters occurred in the leftmost position, and which of two other target letters had occurred somewhere else on the display. Under conditions where *S*s discriminated the lefthand letter almost perfectly the detectability of the target letter declined as it was shifted to the right across the array. This again suggests a serial left-to-right process operating on the rapidly fading contents of the iconic register. However, Shaw also reported that a space to the right of the target letter brought about a substantial improvement in accuracy of discrimination. This is not consistent with the notion of a progressive left-to-right scan across the entire array. It could relate to the superior identifiability of end items commented on earlier. Possibly the leftmost block of letters on an array containing a space was treated as a unit, with priority being assigned to the end locations at the icon formation sub-stage. If descriptions of these locations were superior to those formed for other locations, this might account for the advantage found by Shaw for items preceding a space.

These directional effects may be interpreted within the two-stage model of ENCODING by assuming that the INSPECTION executive normally programmes transfer from the iconic to the graphemic register according to spatial criteria. This requires that the contents of the iconic register should be spatially labelled, and that the executive should take account of location in linking iconic cells to the channels mediating transfer to the graphemic register. Probably, this selective encoding routine has emerged as a by-product of the development of reading skill, and tends to follow the left-right and top-down directionality which is a conventional part of Western literacy. It is not clear whether the selective transfer involves parallel use of a small number of channels, as implied by Figure IV.5.1, or whether the channels operate in a more strictly serial fashion. Either way, it is arguable that left-right differences in report accuracy arise because information is lost from the iconic register before more than 4-5 symbols can be transferred to the more durable levels of temporary storage.

IV.9 POST-ICONIC VISUAL STORAGE

An important assumption underlying the two-stage model of ENCODING is the proposal that graphemic information may be represented at two distinct levels. The existence of the first *iconic* level is reasonably well attested in the experiments of Sperling and many others. A second, post-iconic graphemic register has perhaps been less widely accepted because many investigators have assumed that information may be transferred directly from the icon into a speech-based short-term memory system. In fact it seems essential that there should be a durable mode of graphemic storage which will outlast the icon and which is not vulnerable to overwriting by new visual input (Coltheart, 1972, 1976). The difficulty in demonstrating this point experimentally is simply that visual symbols may be transformed to phonemic and other internal codes which cannot readily be distinguished from the graphemic code. Some tachistoscopic experiments which confront this issue will be discussed here, and the whole topic will be treated more extensively in Chapter V.

An experiment by Mitchell (1972) may be cited as a preliminary to this discussion. He displayed a single digit or letter-like form to *S*s for 30 or 40 msecs followed by a masking field. After a delay of 0·5, 3 or 6 secs, a second form was presented, and the *S*s were instructed to indicate whether or not it was same as the first. For digits accuracy of discrimination remained constant across the three delay intervals. This was also true of letter-like forms for which *S*s reported using made-up names. Forms which had not been named produced a decline in accuracy across the intervals although, even with a delay of 6 secs, performance remained well above chance level with about 70 per cent of discriminations correct. If one accepts that the unnamed forms could not have been retained as phonemic or articulatory codes the experiment provides evidence for a graphemic representation persisting over a period of seconds.

Henderson (1972a) has shown that *S*s retain information about spatial locations of symbols on a 3 × 3 matrix display, and has argued that maintenance of data of this kind in a linguistic code would overtax the capacity of the phonemic-articulatory system. A more reasonable proposal is that position information is held in a visual code. A good procedure for establishing this point is to occupy the phonemic-articulatory system with a subsidiary memory task and to test for an effect of this extra load on accuracy of report of a tachistoscopic display. Henderson (1972b) found that *S*s could retain a sequence of more than five auditorily presented digits at the cost of loss of only one half of an item in accuracy of report of tachistoscopically displayed letters. Given Sperling's (1960) finding that *S*s can report only 4–5 items from a visual display, this evidence for a combined span of 9–10 items is strongly suggestive of dual representational systems, one graphemic and one phonemic, as indicated in Figure III.3.1.

Scarborough (1972) employed a methodology similar to that of Henderson (1972b). *S*s were given an auditory sequence of digits to remember followed directly by a 250 msec exposure of a visual array of 6 letters. An auditory cue at display offset indicated to the *S* whether he should report the digit sequence or the letters on the display. Neither type of report was affected by the memory load imposed in the alternative modality. With delay of the cue accuracy of visual report remained constant in the absence of an auditory load, but showed a slight decline when an auditory load was imposed. Processing of the visual displays had virtually no effect on retention of the auditory digit sequences. These findings are consistent with those of Henderson, and may be taken as experimental validation of the conceptual distinction between the graphemic and phonemic temporary storage registers, and, *a fortiori*, of the existence of a post-iconic mode of visual representation.

Henderson (1972b) also examined the effect on tachistoscopic report of imposition of a spatial load. *S*s were required to remember the positions of 6 cells blacked in on a 5 × 5 matrix while reporting identities and locations of letters displayed tachistoscopically on a 3 × 3 matrix. They were able to retain an average of 4·8 of the 6 locations without loss of efficiency in the tachistoscopic task. This implies that the graphemic register is not used for temporary storage of a non-symbolic spatial array. Analogous results were reported by Sanders & Schroots (1969) for storage of a sequence of spatial locations following visual presentation of a list of 6 consonants. When a consonant list was followed by a digit list increases in the number of digits impaired performance, but less severely than when consonants were followed by further consonants.

These experiments appear collectively to validate the assumption that visually presented symbols may be represented in a post-iconic graphemic register over a period of at least some seconds. We further suppose that the register is specialized for representation of visual properties of graphemes, and is relatively independent of temporary storage facilities for speech sounds (the phonemic register) or non-symbolic visual information (the pictorial register).

IV.10 CONCLUSIONS

This chapter has provided an analysis of the first of the major mental functions, the ENCODING stage of processing. It has not been possible to review in detail the very extensive experimental literature on this topic, or to explore many of the subtleties of interpretation of the data. Nonetheless, it is hoped that the discussion may have been sufficient to clarify some of the more general characteristics of ENCODING, and to indicate the kinds of experiments which are valuable in the study of this stage of processing.

The process which has been described is an operation of *graphemic* ENCODING. That is, it has been assumed that we are dealing with a process which has been developed for the purpose of forming internal descriptions of printed symbols, and that other, no doubt comparable, ENCODING processes are involved in the analysis of non-symbolic pictorial events. Thus, the whole ENCODING function which has been discussed in this chapter is a developmental achievement dating from the period of early schooling when children normally acquire the fundamental aspects of reading skill. As Gibson (1965, 1970) has stressed, an important part of this achievement is the development of a knowledge of those features of the letters of the alphabet which are useful in differentiating one letter from another. We assume that the symbol descriptions formed at the levels of the iconic and graphemic registers are stated in terms of these basic differentiating features. Indeed, the function of a graphemic ENCODING process is precisely to translate retinal stimulation into an internal description of grapheme features.

A second important function of the ENCODING stage is to preserve information about the relative positions of symbols in arrays. It has been assumed that the iconic and graphemic registers incorporate a structure for labelling of spatial locations in addition to their capabilities for representations of graphemic features. The partial report experiments establish that location information is readily utilized during selective encoding. A capacity to represent position information of this kind is probably fundamental for acquisition of basic word recognition skills.

The ENCODING stage has been analysed into two sub-stages,

called icon formation and selective encoding. It was assumed that the first sub-stage operates automatically each time the eyes fixate a graphemic array. The second is subject to the INSPECTION executive, which controls the trajectories of the eyes and also marks out those channel termini in the iconic register which have priority. This selective transfer process also appears closely linked to the development of reading skill. The INSPECTION executive is modified to favour left-to-right processing for both eye-movements and selective encoding when a child learns to read.

CHAPTER V

Representational Functions

MAINTENANCE AND MANIPULATION OF THE GRAPHEMIC CODE

V.1 INTRODUCTION

The preceding chapter discussed the ENCODING function by which retinal stimulation may be transformed into an internal description of an array of symbols. This description, which may be referred to as the *graphemic code*, is placed in the graphemic register of Figures III.3.1 and IV.5.1 as an end-product of ENCODING, and is viewed as a representation of visual features of graphemes and of their relative locations in an array. It seems likely that the graphemic code is of critical importance during the acquisition of basic reading skills since the establishment of associative links between spellings and sounds or between words and meanings requires a facility for accurate and durable representation of visual symbol arrays.

This chapter will review further experiments which have been designed to validate the assumption that the graphemic code is a description of *visual* properties of symbols which can be manipulated by mental operations of various kinds. Three types of operation appear particularly relevant. There is firstly an operation of *graphemic comparison* which is involved when symbols are judged to be 'same' or 'different' with respect to their visual properties. Secondly, it is evident to introspection that we are able to imagine symbols in different orientations, in the sense that we know what a k would look like if it was rotated clockwise through 270°, or what letter would be formed if a p was rotated through 180°. These phenomena suggest that graphemic codes may be manipulable by quasi-spatial operations which could be viewed as a form of *mental rotation*. Finally, it has already been pointed out that the graphemic code enters into a variety of RETRIEVAL operations. The code provides input to the interface structure of Figure III.3.1 when grapheme features are transformed to alternative codes or are maintained in the graphemic register by cyclic application of the REPRESENTATIONAL function. It also occurs as the output of RETRIEVAL when alternative codes are used to address locations in the graphemic data store.

The *graphemic comparison* process will be given only preliminary discussion in this chapter. A point to emphasize is that experimental instructions can cause the COMPARISON function to focus on the contents of the graphemic register, and that such comparisons are sensitive to the visual similarity of graphemes. A fuller treatment of the comparison of arrays of symbols will be postponed until Chapter VII. From an experimental viewpoint, the topic of *mental rotation* resolves to a demonstration that the rotation process occupies time, and that it can be used to prepare a graphemic description of a symbol in a specified orientation. It is also worth commenting that the proposal that the graphemic code is formulated in terms of elementary features of graphemes tends to favour the view that mental rotation is a process of revision of spatial co-ordinate values within a descriptive structure.

The REPRESENTATION and RETRIEVAL of the graphemic code are assumed to depend on a system of the kind shown in Figure V.1.1. The REPRESENTATIONAL function requires that grapheme features should occur as input to a set of graphemic pattern recognizers in the interface structure, and that these recognizers should be linked to the addresses of their own canonical forms in the graphemic data store. Activation of the links results in transfer of a grapheme description from the data store to the graphemic register. Cyclic application of this procedure has the effect of maintaining a description in the register. In RETRIEVAL the input to the interface comes from another temporary storage register—the phonemic register in Figure V.1.1—and the pattern recognizers relating to that register are linked to the graphemic address register. This application allows the spoken name of a symbol to retrieve a description of its visual properties. The converse operation of RETRIEVAL of a phonemic code for a visually represented symbol will be discussed in Chapter VI.

V.2 GRAPHEMIC COMPARISONS

Posner & Mitchell (1967) reported a series of experiments which demonstrated nicely the manner in which the focus of COMPARISON may be shifted from one coding register to another by changing the definition of equivalence applied by the *S* in judging symbols as 'same' or 'different'. If the criterion for a 'same' decision is stated in terms of *physical identity* the comparison must focus on the graphemic

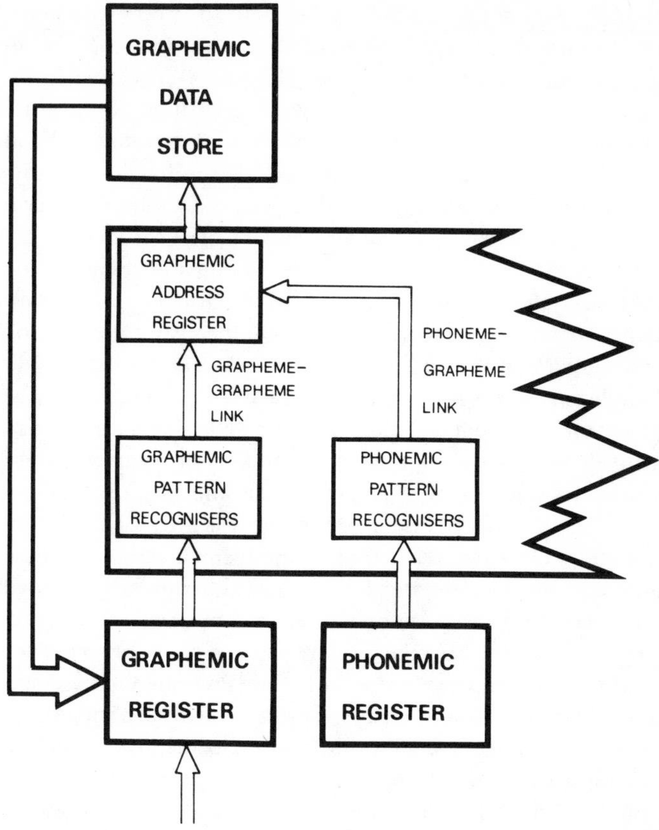

Figure V.1.1 Schematic illustration of the graphemic REPRESENTATION and RETRIEVAL functions. The figure shows the graphemic and phonemic temporary storage registers, the permanent graphemic data store, and a part of the symbolic interface structure, including graphemic and phonemic pattern recognizers, internal links, and a graphemic address register.

register. Definition in terms of *nominal identity* will cause a shift of focus to the phonemic register, where forms such as A and a, which are assigned quite different graphemic descriptions, receive equivalent phonemic descriptions.

It is well-established that judgements of physical identity are sensitive to variations in the visual similarity of graphemes. Posner & Mitchell (1967) reported that 'different' RT was greater for visually similar letter pairs, such as Cc, Ff, Kk, than for dissimilar pairs such as Aa, Ee or Bb. There are also variations in the similarity of nominally different graphemes within both the upper and lower case alphabets which influence 'different' RT and which may be used to assess the *visual confusability* of pairs of letters (Gibson, 1970). These graphemic comparisons are relatively insensitive to variations in phonemic similarity. Posner & Mitchell found that nominally identical pairs, such as Aa, were classified as 'different' no less rapidly than pairs, such as Ae, which did not share the same phonemic description.

It seems very likely that judgements of physical identity are not true comparisons of segregated entities so much as responses to more global or configurational properties of the display. The situation in which two symbols are presented simultaneously for comparison is a limiting case of the oddity detection task used by Beller (1970) in which display size is fixed at D = 2. It will be recalled that in Beller's experiment *S*s responded positively to arrays of same letters and negatively to arrays containing one or more discrepant letters. Positive RT was not affected by variations in D, and negative RT became faster as the number of discrepant letters was increased. The absence of an effect of D suggested that the judgement might be based on sampling of signals generated by a feature matching routine operating simultaneously on the contents of all pairs of cells currently active in the iconic (or graphemic) register. It could be that this procedure generates one output which is unambiguously characteristic of a homogeneous display, another which is characteristic of a heterogeneous display, and a third output which contains a mixture of homogeneity and heterogeneity signals.

If it is assumed that the homogeneity and heterogeneity signals are outcomes of elementary feature matching operations this account can be extended without difficulty to the case in which two symbols are presented for comparison. A pair of 'same' symbols, such as AA, generates an unambiguous homogeneity signal, whereas a pair of 'different' symbols, such as AB, generates an unambiguous heterogeneity signal. It is only in the case of confusable pairs, such as Cc, KX, MW, that an ambiguous signal, characteristic of both homogeneity and heterogeneity, is generated. These instances lengthen the 'different' RT, either because sampling of homogeneity evidence delays accumulation of a critical amount of heterogeneity evidence, or because detection of ambiguity results in a switch to a more analytic processing mode.

Fox (1975) proposed that display homogeneity might be defined in terms of higher order characteristics, such as symmetry. The letter pair, TT, is symmetrical about a vertical axis, whereas the pair EE is symmetrical about a horizontal axis. Since these forms of symmetry are characteristic of 'same' displays the detection of symmetry may in itself provide sufficient evidence for production of a positive response. Fox reported experiments which suggested that these factors had a greater influence on the judgemental RT than physical variations which increased the difficulty of segregating the two members of each pair, such as overlapping of their outlines. This is consistent with the proposal that judgements of physical identity depend on detection of global symmetry or homogeneity rather than on the formation and matching of two discrete graphemic descriptions.

An implication of this view is that non-essential features which tend to reduce the symmetry of the display will delay 'same' decisions, whereas features tending to increase symmetry will delay 'different' decisions. It has been shown that 'same' RTs are indeed delayed when the members of the letter pair differ in orientation (Buggie, 1970), in brightness (Corcoran & Besner, 1975), or in colour (Well & Green, 1972; Kroll, 1977). In a number of experiments Krueger (1970, 1973a) has examined the effects of addition of irrelevant lines to the display. Flanking of the letters by vertical lines delayed 'same' and 'different' RT and selectively increased 'different' RT when the height of the bracketing lines approximated that of the letters. In another study one, both or neither of the letters presented were underlined. The symmetrical arrangement of underlining both or neither of the letters facilitated 'same' decisions, whereas the asymmetrical arrangement of underlining only one of them facilitated 'different' decisions (Krueger, 1973b).

These findings are all consistent with the conclusion that RT in graphemic comparison tasks reflects the influence of configurational properties of the test display on a judgemental process. Since the evidence on which these judgements are based is generated during graphemic ENCODING we might reasonably anticipate that graphemic comparisons should be insensitive to variations in the *familiarity* of symbols. This expectation was supported by Posner & Mitchell (1967) who found that *S*s matched letter-like forms of the kind devised by Gibson, Gibson, Pick & Osser (1962) no less rapidly than the familiar shapes of digits and letters of the alphabet. However, Ambler & Proctor (1976) have more recently demonstrated that English-speaking *S*s match unfamiliar Japanese letters slightly less rapidly than English letters, and that the reverse is true for Japanese *S*s. This implies that the critical factor may be the familiarity of the differentiating features of the graphemes rather than of the letter shapes themselves.

Ambler & Proctor suggested that this aspect of familiarity influenced a COMPARISON stage of processing rather than ENCODING, since they found in a symbol classification experiment that the slope of the function relating RT to M was greater for Japanese than for English letters but that there was no effect on the intercept.

If matching is based on sampling of configurational properties of the display a systematic change in the orientation of the symbols should not affect the RT. Inversion of the 'same' display, AA, to give ∀∀ does not alter the symmetry or homogeneity of the display, even though it does involve the presentation of familiar symbols in an unfamiliar orientation. However, Egeth & Blecker (1971) reported that inverted letter pairs were classified as 'same' less rapidly than normally oriented pairs, although inversion had no effect on the 'different' RT. This finding was replicated by Ambler & Proctor (1976) but was shown by them to be dependent on the mixing of normal and inverted displays in the trial sequence. When these conditions were blocked the effect of rotation on the RT disappeared.

The familiarity effect obtained by Egeth & Blecker parallels the results from experiments on 'word superiority effects' in graphemic comparison tasks which will be discussed in Chapter IX. A possible explanation is that access to the symbolic interface occurs coincidentally during visual matching, and that successful access evokes an internal affirmative code which modifies the 'same' decision process.

V.3 MENTAL ROTATION

It was suggested in the introduction to this chapter that the graphemic coding of a symbol might be manipulable by a quasi-spatial operation called *mental rotation.* Ingenious procedures for demonstrating this point experimentally were introduced by Cooper & Shepard (1973). They employed a graphemic comparison task in which visual input of a symbol was matched against a graphemic description retrieved from permanent storage. The *S* was presented with normal or mirror-image versions of familiar symbols, and required to react positively to the normal versions and negatively to the mirror-image versions. In terms of the diagram in Figure V.1.1 this task requires that the test symbol should be ENCODED as a graphemic description, that this code should be used to RETRIEVE a standard description from the graphemic data store, and that the two descriptions should then be matched by a COMPARISON operation.

Cooper & Shepard examined the effect on RT in this task of variation in the orientation of the test symbol. Normal and mirror-image symbols were presented upright or rotated through 60°, 120°, 180°, 240° or 300° clockwise from the vertical. When symbols are transformed in this way they remain relatively easy to identify although it is difficult to tell which are rotated normal forms and which are rotated mirror-image forms without carrying out a mental activity phenomenally akin to shifting the symbol back to an upright orientation. Cooper & Shepard reported that the normal/mirror-image discrimination RT increased as a function of the clockwise or anti-clockwise rotation of the test symbol from the vertical. The data have been summarized in Figure V.3.1, and appear as the uppermost curve, labelled as Condition N. It can be seen that the RT increased as the test symbol was tilted through successive 60° angles in either direction from the vertical, but that the relationship was not strictly linear, chiefly on account of the delay in classification of inverted symbols.

A reasonable interpretation of these data is that the relationship between RT and test symbol orientation indexes an operation of mental rotation which is applied to the graphemic representation of the symbol. The operation may be viewed as a processing stage which is called on to eliminate a structural incongruity existing between the description formed during ENCODING and the description retrieved from the permanent data store. In order for COMPARISON to match these descriptions it is necessary that both should be formulated by reference to a common co-ordinate system. Cooper & Shepard's results suggest that this ROTATION stage operates by *progressive* revision of co-ordinate values.

If ROTATION is a processing stage interposed between the initial ENCODING and RETRIEVAL stages and a subsequent COMPARISON stage the effects of test symbol orientation should combine additively with effects due to factors influencing the other stages. This prediction was not rigorously tested by Cooper & Shepard, since their experiments did not incorporate a stimulus quality factor likely to influence ENCODING or a memory set size factor likely to influence COMPARISON. However, they reported that the orientation effect combined perfectly additively with a difference between positive and negative responses, and also with effects due to presentation of advance information about the identity of the coming test symbol or the orientation in which it would appear. Results for these latter conditions have been included in Figure V.3.1 as the curves labelled I (Identity information) and O (Orientation information). Both types of advance information reduced the RT by about 100 msecs, but this effect was not influenced by test symbol orientation.

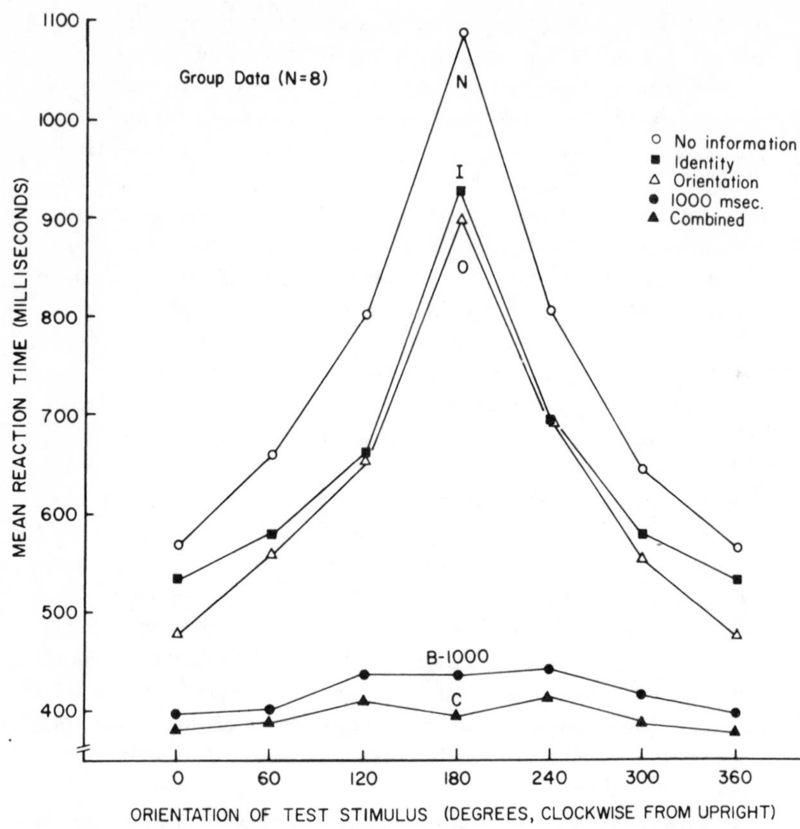

Figure V.3.1 Reaction time data for discrimination between normal and mirror-image symbols rotated from the upright by 60° steps. The curve labelled N gives results for a control condition in which no advance information was given before display of the symbol. In the other conditions, warning was given of the identity of the coming stimulus (Condition I), its orientation (Condition O), or both of these aspects (Conditions B–1,000 and C). (From Cooper & Shepard (1973)). Reproduced by permission.

Provision of advance information about the identity of the test symbol could have the effect of eliminating the need for RETRIEVAL of the canonical description of the test symbol from the graphemic data store. Advance information about orientation, on the other hand, specifies the true vertical axis of the test symbol and its upper and lower extremities. These data are necessary to the ROTATION function, since they can be used to define the starting point, direction and stopping point of the trajectory required to yield a normally-oriented symbol description. This suggests that we might think of ROTATION as a two-stage procedure, having *axis determination* as a first sub-stage, and *co-ordinate revision* as a second sub-stage. The angle of the test symbol influences the duration of the second sub-stage only.

V.4 'REPRESENTATION' OF THE GRAPHEMIC CODE

Posner and his colleagues developed a useful methodology for the study of the persistence or decay of graphemic codes over a period of time (Posner, Boies, Eichelman & Taylor, 1969). Evidence from tachistoscopic studies suggesting that the graphemic code may be maintained for some seconds without support of phonemic recoding was discussed at the end of the last chapter. Posner's findings from RT measurements in 'same'–'different' judgemental tasks provide an additional source of converging evidence.

In the simultaneous matching experiments of Posner & Mitchell (1967) it was found that decisions about nominal identity of letters were faster by about 80–90 msecs for a physically identical pair, such as AA, than for the nominally identical pair, Aa. Nominal judgements were also facilitated by the visual similarity of such pairs as Cc and Kk. Thus, although it is likely that nominally 'same' and 'different' pairs are classified by consideration of retrieved phonemic codes (Dainoff & Haber, 1970), it appears that physically identical pairs are matched by a graphemic comparison process even under nominal identity instructions. If so, the difference in 'same' RT between nominally identical (NI) and physically identical (PI) letter pairs which is obtained under nominal instructions may be taken as an index of the involvement of graphemic codes in the matching process. In what follows we will refer to this index as the NI–PI difference.

If the matching experiment is modified so that the two letters to be compared are presented in succession with a variable inter-stimulus interval (ISI) interposed between them, persistence of an NI–PI difference can be taken to indicate survival of the graphemic coding of the first letter, whereas diminution of the difference is indicative of the decay of the graphemic code.

Parametric studies of the relationship between the NI–PI difference and the ISI were conducted by Posner, Boies, Eichelman & Taylor (1969). It was found that the NI–PI difference decreased as the ISI lengthened, such that, by ISI = 2 secs, the advantage of PI pairs had entirely disappeared. A result of this kind is suggestive of decay of the graphemic code and its replacement by a phonemic code (Dainoff,

1970). However, Posner has argued that these results are characteristic of a 'mixed list' experimental design in which the case of the second symbol varies unpredictably, and only 25 per cent of trials involve physically identical stimuli. The *S* possibly maintains a graphemic description of the first symbol for long enough to retrieve its phonemic representation, and then focuses on the phonemic code as the most likely basis for the comparison.

Evidence of parallel maintenance of both graphemic and phonemic codes was given by Cohen (1969). Two three-letter arrays were presented for matching with an intervening ISI of 5 secs. On 'different' trials the second array differed from the first at one letter position. The replacements were considered to be non-confusable (c or t replacing q), visually confusable (b or p replacing q), acoustically confusable (p replacing c or t) or visually and acoustically confusable (b replacing d or p). Cohen reported that 'different' RT was equivalent for the non-confusable, visually confusable, and acoustically confusable displays, but was delayed by nearly 100 msecs for visually and acoustically confusable displays. She argued that graphemic and phonemic codes for the first array were maintained during the ISI, and that the comparison was focused on both representations. If the decision was based on whichever comparison finished earlier, confusability effects might be apparent only when both registers were affected.

Cohen's study agrees with others (see Section IV.9) in indicating that the graphemic code may be maintained over a period of seconds. Posner has argued that maintenance of the code is an option which the *S* will take up under appropriate circumstances. In a 'pure list' experimental design, in which the case of the second letter of the test sequence was held constant, he found that RT for PI comparisons did not alter with ISI, and remained consistently faster than the RT for NI comparisons. Thus, the NI–PI difference was maintained despite increases in ISI when the experimental conditions encouraged the *S*s to base their decisions on a graphemic code (Posner, Boies, Eichelman & Taylor, 1969).

Extensions of this methodology have been undertaken by Parks, Kroll, Salzberg & Parkinson (1972). Using a procedure analogous to that of Scarborough (1972), they imposed a secondary task of repeating aloud a sequence of auditorily presented digits during an 8 sec ISI. This task might be expected to pre-empt the resources of the phonemic register, thus forcing the *S* to base his comparison between letters on a maintained graphemic code. In line with this expectation, they found that the NI–PI difference was preserved over the ISI. In a further experiment, Kellicutt, Parks, Kroll & Salzberg (1973) presented pairs of letters in normal or mirror-image orientation, with an 8 sec ISI between pairs. As in the previous study, the interval was filled by shadowing of auditory digits, and it was shown that the NI–PI difference survived the ISI. However, *S*s matched mirror-image letters less rapidly than normal letters, except after extensive practice. This implies that the graphemic representation of the first letter pair was not a direct copy of the original input, but a canonical description retrieved from the graphemic data store.

Experiments reported by Kroll, Kellicutt, Berrian & Kreisler (1974) examined the possibility that colour information might be preserved as part of the graphemic code. Letter pairs, printed in red or green, were presented for matching at 1 and 8 sec ISIs with imposition of an auditory shadowing task. Preservation of the NI–PI difference was observed at both ISIs, but there was no effect of colour congruity. In a second experiment the salience of the print colour was enhanced by instructing *S*s to report the colour of the first letter pair following the 'same' or 'different' response. A clear effect of colour congruity was obtained combined with maintenance of the NI–PI difference. This indicates the availability of an option to maintain chromatic information in addition to the graphemic coding of symbols.

V.5 'RETRIEVAL' OF THE GRAPHEMIC CODE

The experimental evidence discussed thus far appears in agreement with the proposal that visual ENCODING of a symbol leads to formation of a graphemic code which may be operated upon by COMPARISON and ROTATION functions, and which may be maintained in the graphemic register by application of the REPRESENTATIONAL function. Also implicit in Figures III.3.1 and V.1.1 is the assumption that the graphemic coding of a symbol may be retrieved from permanent storage when a phonemic description of the symbol name is placed in the phonemic register.

This possibility was also investigated by Posner, Boies, Eichelman & Taylor (1969). Their method involved measurements of RTs for nominal identity matching of a visual test letter against a previously presented visual letter or spoken letter name. We will refer to these as visual-visual (VV) and auditory-visual (AV) comparisons. In a first study the ISI was fixed at 750 msecs and *S*s were tested under the 'pure list' and 'mixed list' conditions. The VV presentation replicated the previous findings, showing an NI–PI difference of 25 msecs for mixed lists and 60 msecs for pure lists. On AV trials the case of the visual letter was held constant (pure list arrangement) or allowed to vary (mixed list arrangement). Following practice, *S*s classified pure list auditory-visual presentations about as rapidly as pure list visual-visual presentations. Under mixed list arrangements the AV comparisons also showed RTs which were approximately similar to VV comparisons of physically identical letters. These results are consistent with the possibility that the auditory letter names were recoded in a graphemic format during the ISI of 750 msecs.

The time required for phonemic-graphemic recoding of this kind can be estimated from a study of changes in the magnitude of the difference between auditory-visual and visual-visual RTs which occur as the ISI is lengthened. Figure V.5.1 shows data from an experiment by Posner, Boies, Eichelman & Taylor (1969) in which the ISI was varied at 0, 500 and 1,000 msecs. It can be seen that by the longest ISI the RTs for auditory-visual comparisons were equivalent to RTs for physically identical visual-visual letter pairs obtained under pure list conditions. Under the mixed list arrangement the RTs for the visual-visual physically identical and nominally identical pairs converge, reflecting the progressive loss of the graphemic code. The auditory-visual trials show an opposed trend, with the RT tending to decrease as a function of the ISI, and to cross the curve for visual-visual physical identity comparisons at an ISI of 750 msecs. This pattern of RT data was taken by Posner as an indication that an interval of this order was required for graphemic recoding of a letter name.

A judgement of the nominal identity of upper and lower case letters could depend on RETRIEVAL of phonemic codings of the letters (Dainoff, 1970) or on RETRIEVAL of a graphemic description of the alternative case of the first letter presented. Posner (1973) cited studies by Boies (1969, 1971) which suggest that a graphemic-graphemic transformation of this kind may sometimes occur. In one experiment Boies presented pairs of visual letters in immediate succession. The duration of the first letter was varied at 500, 1,000 or 1,500 msecs. An NI–PI difference of 83 msecs observed at the shortest display time was eliminated at the longest display time. This reflected a tendency for the NI 'same' RT to decline while the PI 'same' RT increased by about 30 msecs as the presentation interval was lengthened. It is unlikely that loss of the graphemic code was responsible for this effect since the first letter was physically present throughout the interval. Boies suggested that the graphemic register might come to contain descriptions of both cases of the displayed letter. This could be viewed

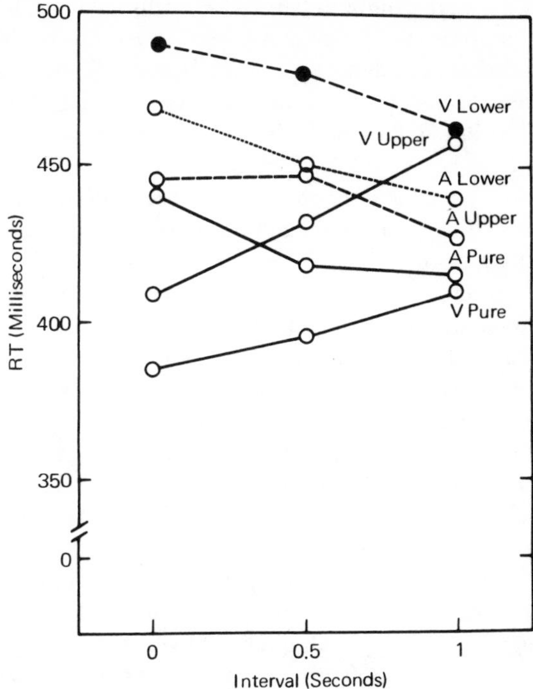

Figure V.5.1 Reaction times for matching visual test letters against a visual or auditory memory letter at varying inter-stimulus intervals. The curves labelled 'A Pure' and 'V Pure' give the results for auditory–visual and visual–visual comparisons under 'pure list' conditions. The remaining curves are for 'mixed list' conditions, and are labelled with respect to the modality of the memory letter (A or V), and the case of the second letter (upper or lower). (From Posner, Boies, Eichelman & Taylor, 1969). Reproduced by permission. Copyright 1969 by the American Psychological Association.

as an increase in memory set size from M = 1 to M = 2, which might be expected, on the basis of Sternberg's (1966) data, to raise the level of the RT by 30–40 msecs. When the *S* was certain that the test letter would always be opposite in case to the first the effect did not occur, suggesting that the description of the alternative case effectively replaced the original in the graphemic register.

V.6 SELECTIVE PREPARATION

The RETRIEVAL of a graphemic description from permanent store and its placement in the graphemic register may be viewed as a form of selective preparation for an anticipated input. Beller (1971) demonstrated that priming of this kind facilitated the RT. His *S*s matched simultaneously displayed letters under PI and NI instructions. On alternate trials a visual or auditory letter matching one or both of the expected display items was presented. Under PI instructions, this priming facilitated 'same' RT, but had no effect on 'different' RT. Under NI instructions, priming facilitated both PI and NI comparisons, and the effect on NI comparisons was greater for auditory than for visual presentation of the priming letter.

Especially clear demonstrations of selective preparation for visual input were given by Cooper & Shepard (1973). It will be recalled that speed of discrimination between normal and mirror-image symbols is affected by orientation of the test symbol (see Section V.3 above). If the *S* is given advance information about both the identity and the orientation of the coming symbol it should be open to him to retrieve the canonical description and rotate it to the appropriate angle before presentation of the test. The co-ordinates of the prepared description and the one formed during ENCODING should then be congruent, thus eliminating the need for a mental ROTATION stage. It follows that the effects of orientation of the test symbol on the RT should no longer be observed. Reference back to Figure V.3.1 will confirm that this was the result obtained by Cooper & Shepard. The two lowest curves of the figure are for conditions in which *S*s were presented with advance information in the form of a tilted symbol or a normal symbol followed by an arrow to indicate orientation. Both conditions yielded fast RTs which were effectively independent of orientation of the test symbol.

When the advance warning consists of a normal symbol followed by an arrow an operation of mental rotation becomes part of the process of preparing for the expected stimulus. Since ROTATION is a time-consuming activity the elimination of orientation effects under this condition should be observed only if the ISI between the arrow and test symbol is long enough for completion of the rotation process. Cooper & Shepard reported that the stimulus orientation effect was reinstated as the interval was shortened below a value of 1,000 msecs.

These findings suggest that *S*s can prepare graphemic descriptions of rotated symbols. An implication is that presentation of a test symbol in an orientation other than the one expected will produce a coding incongruity. A further rotation operation may then be required to make the normal/mirror-image judgement possible. As a test of this, Cooper & Shepard conducted an experiment in which symbol names were presented auditorily, followed by a series of commands, each requiring mental rotation of the symbol clockwise through 60°. At an unpredictable point a test symbol was displayed for normal/mirror-image discrimination. On 50 per cent of the trials the orientation of the test symbol did not match the orientation the *S* should have reached in the preparatory rotation, and the degree of discrepancy varied from 60°–180°.

The experiment demonstrated the anticipated dependence of RT on the degree of angular difference between the orientation the *S* expected and the orientation of the test symbol. However, there was a substantial interaction between the factors of orientation of the probe and the magnitude of the discrepancy. To encounter an inverted test symbol when expecting an upright one appeared far more disruptive than to encounter an upright test symbol while expecting an inverted one.

V.7 CONCLUSIONS

The research discussed in this chapter suggests that symbols may be retained in temporary storage in a distinctively visual and spatially manipulable format which we have called the *graphemic code*. A measure of experimental ingenuity has been devoted to the validation of the existence of this code, perhaps because the notion of a *visual* representation is suggestive of concepts of imagery which have appeared distasteful to some psychologists. In fact, the evidence considered in this chapter is in no way dependent on subjective criteria or reports, and the experiments provide a useful methodology for the objective validation of the general assumption of modality-related codes.

CHAPTER VI

Retrieval Functions

NOMINAL AND STRUCTURAL CODES

VI.1 INTRODUCTION

In the two preceding chapters we discussed the processes by which a graphemic description may be formed during visual ENCODING, retrieved from permanent storage, and maintained in the graphemic register by the REPRESENTATIONAL function. The graphemic code also provides input to the RETRIEVAL stage when visual symbols are recoded as phonemic descriptions of their names or are interpreted with respect to their class membership or location in the alphabetical or numerical series. These RETRIEVAL operations will constitute the main focus for this chapter.

It was proposed in Chapter III that the RETRIEVAL function depends on an *input register* to hold the code which is to be transformed, an *output register* to receive the product of retrieval, a *permanent data store* from which the retrieved code is copied, and an *interface structure* which mediates recognition of the input code and addressing of the output code. A consequence of this analysis is that RETRIEVAL can be viewed as a processing stage which is logically divisible into two sub-stages. The first of these is required for *pattern recognition* of elements of the code held in the input register. The second is required for *addressing* of a location in permanent storage, and for the transfer of information to the output register.

This two-stage account of RETRIEVAL can be represented diagrammatically in the manner shown in Figure VI.1.1. The diagram shows the graphemic and phonemic data stores and temporary registers, together with part of the interface structure of the Symbolic Memory. The two-stage assumption is incorporated into the interface in the form of separate banks of pattern recognizes for the graphemic and phonemic registers, and distinct address registers for the graphemic and phonemic data stores. This principle is also applicable to the other representational codes of the Symbolic Memory—the categorial

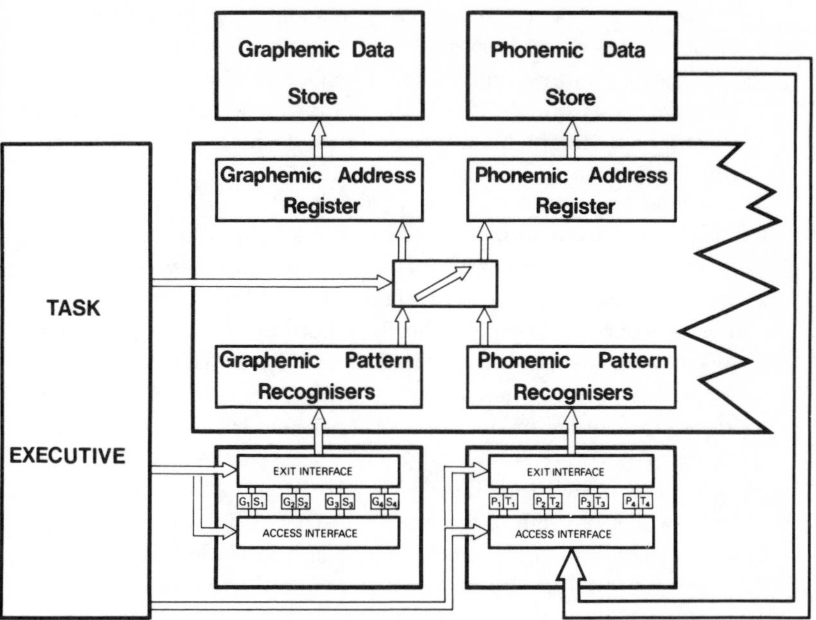

Figure VI.1.1 Schematic representation of RETRIEVAL functions in the Symbolic Memory. The TASK executive controls exit from and access to the cells of the graphemic and phonemic registers and also makes and unmakes links between pattern recognizers and address registers within the symbolic interface. In the diagram the system is set to transform the graphemic codes, $G_{1\text{-}4}$, to the phonemic codes, $P_{1\text{-}4}$, and to translate the spatial codes, $S_{1\text{-}4}$, into the temporal codes, $T_{1\text{-}4}$.

and structural codes—which are not represented in the diagram.

If the interface is to be useful in mediating a variety of types of coding transformation, and if these are to be scheduled in a manner which meets the requirements of a particular task, it is desirable that they should be controlled by an external executive, also represented in Figure VI.1.1, which has been called TASK. A first requirement is that TASK should determine the coding transformation which is to occur at a given point in processing by forming a *link* between a set of pattern recognizers and an address register. In the diagram this capability appears as an influence of the executive on a central component of the interface in which connections between pattern recognizers and address registers can be made and unmade. This component must also handle inputs from categorial and structural codes, and addressing of locations in the categorial and structural data stores. Although it is in principle possible that every combination of pattern recognizer and address register could be formed, this need not be so in practice. For example, the categorial distinction between vowels and consonants might be accessible to phonemic codings of letters but not to graphemic codings (Posner, 1970).

A second important function of the interface is to preserve or transform structural properties of the codes held in the temporary storage registers. A frequently encountered situation is one in which a visually presented array of symbols is recoded as a list of symbol names. Readers of English typically report the identities of letter arrays in a left-to-right order, implying that RETRIEVAL involves a systematic transformation of a spatial order in the graphemic register to a temporal order in the phonemic register. It seems likely that recoding of structure is also subject to executive control. The suggestion incorporated into Figure VI.1.1 is that TASK controls the order in which the cells of the input register pass information to the pattern recognizers in the interface, and also the order of placing of the codes retrieved from permanent store into the cells of the output register.

The functioning of the system can be briefly illustrated by an account of the phonemic recoding of an array of visual symbols. We assume that the array is represented as a spatially structured graphemic code in the graphemic register. The TASK executive must then make the link between the graphemic pattern recognizers and the phonemic address register. The graphemic code occupying the left-most cell of the graphemic register is then transferred to the interface, and the phonemic code retrieved is entered into the first cell of the phonemic register. The executive then revises its control over the input and output registers and repeats the cycle until all grapheme descriptions have been recoded. An analogous type of transformation is involved when a structural coding of part of the alphabet or number series is used to generate a phonemic sequence of digit or letter names or visual imagery of the symbols.

VI.2 PHONEMIC RECODING OF SYMBOLS

It will be convenient to concentrate in the first instance on the relatively simple situation in which a single visual symbol is recoded as a phonemic description of its name. This graphemic-phonemic transformation can be studied in the context of symbol naming tasks and symbol matching tasks using nominal identity instructions. In both cases we assume that an initial operation of graphemic ENCODING is followed by a phonemic RETRIEVAL stage which precedes an EXPRESSION stage in the naming task, or a COMPARISON stage in the matching task.

If we are to view phonemic RETRIEVAL as a processing stage it is desirable that we should be able to associate with it experimental factors which selectively influence its duration. The relevant factors have usually been thought to consist of a set of procedural manipulations which alter the *S*'s uncertainty about the identities of the symbols which will occur on each trial of the experiment. These include variations in the size of the ensemble of stimuli and their probabilities of occurrence. Since both manipulations affect the frequency of repetition of stimuli in the experimental series it is possible that their effects are mediated by this variable.

A number of experiments can be cited which demonstrate that factors of this kind can influence symbol naming RT. Fitts & Switzer (1962) reported that letter naming RT was affected by the frequency of occurrence in text of the letters of the alphabet. In the study by Sternberg (1971) digits were named faster in an ensemble of two digits than in an ensemble of eight digits, although other experimenters have failed to demonstrate an effect of ensemble size or probability (Alluisi, Muller & Fitts, 1957; Brainard, Irby, Fitts & Alluisi, 1962; Morin & Forrin, 1962; Theios, 1972), and indeed symbol naming has often been treated as an exception to the well-established relation between such variables and choice RT (Welford, 1968). However, Fitts & Switzer (1962) showed that reductions in ensemble size could yield consistent reductions in naming RT when the symbols included in the ensemble formed a familiar sub-set, such as ABC or 123.

Effects of stimulus repetition on symbol naming RT were examined by Eichelman (1970a). The stimuli were upper and lower case letters organized in a trial sequence so that half of the trials involved repetition of the naming response given on the preceding trial. These repetition trials were equally divided between physical identity repetitions, in which the letter appeared in the same case on both trials, and nominal identity repetitions, which involved a case alternation. The response-signal interval between completion of a naming response and onset of the next stimulus was varied at 200 and 700 msecs. At the shorter interval Eichelman obtained a 75 msec facilitation effect for physical identity repetitions but no effect for nominal identity repetitions. However, at the longer interval significant facilitation for nominal repetitions was observed.

Marcel & Forrin (1974) presented mixed sequences of letters and digits for naming at response-signal intervals of 300, 1,600 and 2,900 msecs. They examined the effects of repetition of an individual symbol (item repetition) and of successive presentation of different symbols from the same category (class repetition). Both types of repetition facilitated the RT at the shorter response-signal interval, although item repetitions produced a larger effect than class repetitions. A more detailed analysis was carried out on class repetition effects within the set of numerals. It appeared from this that the facilitation reflected a gradient of proximity within the number sequence, being greatest for successively displayed numerals which were adjacent or close to one another on the number scale.

These experimental findings suggest that the duration of the phonemic RETRIEVAL stage may be modifiable by variations in the frequency of repetition of symbols presented for naming. As matters stand, they do not establish which sub-stage of RETRIEVAL is affected. We might think of the pattern recognizers as evidence accumulators with thresholds (akin to the *logogens* in Morton's (1969a) theory of word recognition). These accumulators could incorporate a permanent bias in the form of threshold variations determined by general frequency of usage, and might retain some residual activation for a short period following recognition of a symbol, thus giving rise to repetition effects. However, it is equally reasonable to suppose that such biases and temporary adjustments are located in the links between the pattern recognizers and the address registers, or in the operation of accessing information in permanent storage.

An approach to the resolution of this issue is suggested by the experiment on symbol naming described by Sternberg (1971). It may be recalled from the discussion in Chapter II that this study was conducted within the framework of the additive factor methodology, and that it examined the effects of combining the factors of stimulus quality and ensemble size. Stimulus quality has been viewed as a factor influencing ENCODING whereas ensemble size has been seen as a factor influencing RETRIEVAL. Nonetheless, Sternberg reported that the two factors interacted, the stimulus quality effect being larger for the eight digit ensemble than for the two digit ensemble. It was suggested in Chapter II that such an interaction might occur because stimulus degradation both increased the duration of ENCODING and reduced the rate at which graphemic features were passed to the RETRIEVAL stage. It seems evident that an interaction of this kind would be expected to arise at the pattern recognition sub-stage of

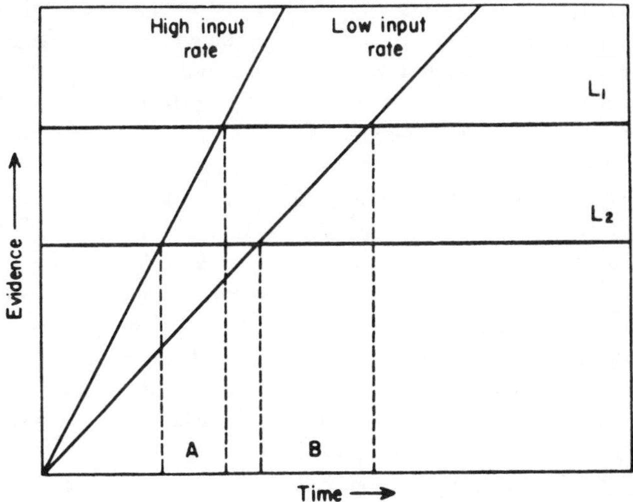

Figure VI.2.1 Illustration of manner in which a factor influencing the rate of input of information into a pattern recognition system may interact with a factor affecting the evidence requirements of the recognizers. The evidence requirements are defined by the threshold levels, L_1 and L_2. At a high input rate the time to achieve recognition is A units greater for the L_2 setting than for the L_1 setting. If the input rate is reduced by degradation of the stimulus, this difference increases to B units of time. (From Seymour (1977)). Reproduced by permission. Copyright by Academic Press Inc. (London) Ltd.

RETRIEVAL. The underlying mechanism has been illustrated diagrammatically in Figure VI.2.1. We assume that a particular pattern recognizer has its threshold set at level L_1 or L_2, depending on the size of the ensemble. When an intact stimulus is presented evidence accumulates in the recognizer as a function of elapsed sampling time according to the function labelled 'high input rate'. It is apparent that the duration of the pattern recognition sub-stage of RETRIEVAL will depend on the threshold setting of the unit (L_1 or L_2). If the effect of degradation of the stimulus is to damage the quality of the graphemic coding of the symbol, and if a consequence of this is a reduction in the *rate* at which evidence is accumulated in the recognizer, stimulus degradation will enlarge the ensemble size effect. The reason for this is that the reduction in rate of accumulation enlarges the impact on sampling time of the threshold difference.

It seems possible, therefore, that stimulus quality variations will combine interactively with manipulations which exert a selective influence on the pattern recognition sub-stage of RETRIEVAL. It follows that the occurrence of such interactions could be treated as evidence for the localization of an effect in this sub-stage. Factors influencing the later sub-stage of RETRIEVAL should not be vulnerable to stimulus quality effects, and should therefore combine additively with stimulus quality variations. An example of such additivity is contained in a study by Pachella & Miller (1976). The experiment was a letter matching task of the kind used by Posner & Mitchell (1967) and incorporated variations in factors of stimulus quality and stimulus probability. When nominal identity instructions were in force stimulus probability did not affect physical identity 'same' judgements but did influence nominal identity 'same' judgements and 'different' judgements. This is consistent with the assumption that stimulus probability influenced the duration of a phonemic RETRIEVAL stage. Reductions in stimulus quality raised the level of the RT, but this effect combined additively with the probability effects. According to the argument presented here this additivity might be taken to imply that probability affected the later sub-stage of RETRIEVAL.

VI.3 RECODING OF STRUCTURE

The more complex function of the RETRIEVAL system is to preserve the spatial or temporal structure of an array while transferring symbols from one register to another. This capability will be discussed by reference to two types of experimental task. The first of these is the tachistoscopic report experiment considered in Chapter IV. If the *S* is shown a visual array of symbols and is required to make a *whole report* of their identities, a transformation from spatial order in the array to temporal order in the report is necessarily involved. The second task is one of listing the letters of the alphabet. In this case the array structure which is preserved during RETRIEVAL is held in permanent store—the structural data store of Figure III.3.1—and is transferred, segment by segment, into a structural register prior to addressing of phonemic descriptions of the letter names. The account of the transfer process outlined in the introduction to this chapter, and illustrated in Figure VI.1.1, is applicable to both of these situations.

In the tachistoscopic whole report experiment the *S* responds to a briefly displayed array of letters or digits with a vocal or written report of the items he has seen. These reports typically follow a left-to-right order (Bryden, 1966, 1967). We would suggest that this occurs because the graphemic ENCODING process and the phonemic RETRIEVAL process are biased in favour of a left-to-right directionality following the acquisition of reading skill. Thus, a normal occurrence may be for selective encoding to transfer grapheme features from the iconic register to the graphemic register in a left-to-right spatial order, giving rise to the left field superiority which is apparent in many whole report studies (Heron, 1957; Bryden, 1966; Merikle, Lowe & Coltheart, 1971), and for RETRIEVAL to follow the same order when recoding items from the graphemic register to the phonemic register.

According to this account there are two sources of executive intervention which give rise to a left-to-right directionality in tachistoscopic reports. The INSPECTION executive which controls the selective encoding process typically programmes a left-to-right transfer of information into the graphemic register, although this may be modifiable by instruction or by presentation of mirror-image letters (Harcum & Filion, 1963; Harcum & Smith, 1963; Asso & Wyke, 1967). If the *S* is given an instruction to reverse his normal order of report—that is to report the letters in a right-to-left order—before presentation of the tachistoscopic flash, it may be open to the INSPECTION executive to alter the direction of selective encoding, thus reversing the usual left field superiority (Freeburne & Goldman, 1969; Scheerer, 1972). An instruction which occurs after the display cannot modify the ENCODING process, and should therefore leave the left field superiority unaltered, although it may well conflict with the order of transfer preferred by the TASK executive during RETRIEVAL. Experiments demonstrating a persistence of a left field superiority when report order is controlled by a post-stimulus cue are consistent with these proposals (Scheerer, 1972, 1973). Bryden's (1960, 1967) findings that instructions to reverse the normal report order create greater difficulties with alphabetic than with non-alphabetic arrays suggest that left-to-right directionality is a specialized capability of the Symbolic Memory system developed for processing of written language.

This element of stereotyped directionality is also evident in the structural coding of the alphabet. Most adult *S*s will recite the letters of the alphabet rapidly in a forward direction, requiring only 3.5–4 secs for production of the 26 letter names in overt or covert speech (Landauer, 1962; Weber & Castleman, 1970). Attempts at reverse listing give rise to delays, confusions and claims that forward rehearsal is often necessary before a letter sequence can be reversed. Qualitatively similar comments were made by Bryden's *S*s after they had attempted to report tachistoscopic arrays in a right-to-left direction.

Weber and his colleagues have investigated the process of generation of the alphabetic sequence and have attempted to determine the nature of the underlying structural code. It appears likely that the code contains phonemic descriptions of the letter names organized within a temporal structure. When *S*s are asked to *visualize* the letters of the alphabet—that is to form graphemic descriptions of the letters—they function much less rapidly than in the phonemic sub-vocalization task, requiring an average of 13 secs for one pass through the alphabet (Weber & Castleman, 1970).

Two experimental procedures were employed by Weber with the aim of providing a more objective demonstration that the structural coding of the alphabet accesses phonemic codes directly and graphemic codes only indirectly. In a study reported by Weber, Kelley & Little (1972) *S*s were instructed to visualize the letters of the alphabet in lower case and classify each as possessing or not possessing an ascender or descender. In one condition *S*s spoke each letter name and reported the graphemic categorization immediately afterwards. In the other condition only the categorization responses were required. Weber found that the rates for these two conditions did not differ, and concluded that this was because evocation of a phonemic code was a necessary preliminary to the retrieval of a graphemic description of each letter.

A second approach derived from research reported by Brooks (1968). Brooks instructed *S*s to categorize the words of a memorized sentence as nouns or non-nouns. The *S*s found this task more difficult when they responded vocally than when they marked visual yes/no symbols on a page. It appeared that the production of the vocal 'Yes' and 'No' responses interfered with maintenance of a speech-based representation of the sentence. If generation of a sequence of graphemic descriptions of letters of the alphabet also depends on the speech system it should be more difficult to categorize letters by vocal reports than by some other non-verbal method. This was confirmed by Weber in a study which demonstrated that *S*s were faster to indicate graphemic classifications of letters by making slash and dot marks on a page than by making 'Yes' and 'No' reports.

These experiments on alphabetic retrieval illustrate the point that certain links between pattern recognizers and address registers may not be established in the interface of the Symbolic Memory. A structural coding of a segment of the alphabet can be linked to the phonemic address register but not to the graphemic address register. Hence, visualizing the letters of the alphabet requires that the structural code should access phonemic codes, and that these should then access the relevant graphemic codes. Similar specialization is evident in the categorization of letters as vowels or consonants. Posner & Mitchell (1967) and Posner (1970) noted that a decision that two letters were both vowels or both consonants was facilitated when the letters were also nominally identical although this was not true of decisions indicating whether or not two symbols were both letters or both digits. The implication is that the categorial distinction between a letter and a digit is directly accessible to the graphemic representation of a symbol, whereas the vowel-consonant distinction requires prior phonemic recoding.

VI.4 THE STRUCTURAL CODE

One of the points which has been emphasized from time to time in the preceding discussion is that the temporary storage registers of the Symbolic Memory contain feature descriptions of individual symbols and *structural descriptions* of symbol arrays. This capability for structural representation, and for the recoding of structure during retrieval operations, appears fundamental in the analysis of skills of processing written language, since our knowledge of the spellings of words and numbers depends on structural codes which can support two-way spatial-temporal transformations. The principle may be extended to the syntactic conventions of language and mathematics, where temporal and spatial orderings of elements are of logical significance.

Specification of the nature of the structural code poses difficult theoretical and experimental questions. So far we have concentrated on modality-related structural codes, assuming that the contents of the graphemic register may be labelled with respect to spatial position whereas the contents of the phonemic register are labelled with respect to temporal position. It is possible that this distinction is also applicable to permanent memory representations of structure, such as those underlying knowledge of the alphabet or number series. If so, the notion of a structural register and data store which is incorporated into Figure III.3.1 could be viewed as superfluous. We might say that the alphabetic sequence is retained in the phonemic data store, and that segments of it may be loaded directly into the phonemic register. This could also apply for spellings of words, which might be retained in the phonemic or graphemic data stores (Weber, Kelley & Little, 1972).

A problem with this modality-specific account of structural coding in permanent memory is that it appears not to place a sufficient emphasis on the semantics of the number series or alphabet. The numbers are not reducible to a chant: 'One, two, three, four, five . . .', but must also represent more abstract variations in magnitude, quantity and position. This is also true of the alphabet since dictionary users possess a generalized knowledge of positions of letters in the series which can be accessed directly without rehearsal of the whole sequence. The position favoured here has been that this form of coding can usefully be distinguished from the spatial and temporal codes used to organize the contents of the graphemic and phonemic registers. The latter might take the form of simple statements of adjacency which link items in a sequence, whereas the proposed structural code specifies semantic attributes of symbols, such as (large), (small), (early), (late) or (central).

Tasks which are useful in the experimental investigation of the structural codes are those which explicitly query the *S*'s knowledge of magnitudes of numerals or positions of letters in the alphabet. For example, Hovancik (1975) presented *S*s with single letter probes and instructed them to respond with the name of the letter lying one or two steps beyond it in the alphabetic sequence. He reported that the RT for two-step retrieval was greater by 350 msecs than RT for one-step retrieval, and that this effect combined additively with an effect due to the position of the probe in the alphabet. The RT tended to increase across the letter positions A .... L, but was constant across the positions M .... X. We might take this position effect as an index of a process of localization of the probe, that is of an operation of retrieval of a structural coding of its position in the alphabet, followed by retrieval of the relevant segment of the alphabet and its placement in the phonemic register. The effect of number of steps might then reflect an operation on the content of the phonemic register. Had Hovancik (1975) instructed *S*s to name the letters occurring *before* the probe he would no doubt have found that backward RETRIEVAL was slower than forward RETRIEVAL —a result obtained by the present author in experiments on other sequentially structured categories, such as months of the year or days of the week (Seymour & Sanford, 1975; Seymour, 1976a).

When applied to the numerals this retrieval task becomes an investigation of elementary addition and subtraction operations. Given a problem such as: $7+2=?$, the *S* might localise the 7 with respect to the structural coding of the numerals, place the phonemic coding of 7–8–9–10 into the phonemic register, and then move 2 steps through this sequence to obtain the answer. It is quite likely that children do solve addition problems in this way when they first acquire the basic arithmetical skills. Groen & Parkman (1972) reported that the reaction times of American first-graders to simple addition problems were described by the function: $\overline{RT} = 2{,}530 + 340(X)$ msecs, where X was the value of the smaller of the two digits presented. This finding is consistent with a counting model of addition, and the rate appears slow enough for us to accept that implicit speech activities might be involved. A similar counting rate was noted in Hovancik's (1975) study of the alphabet, and also in the author's studies of months of the year and days of the week (Seymour, 1976a).

It is, on the face of it, improbable that adults solve problems in elementary arithmetic by resorting to counting operations. In experiments studying evaluation of the correctness of addition and multiplication sums the function relating RT to the smaller number typically has a slope of only 20 msecs per counting step (Parkman & Groen, 1971; Parkman, 1972), and problems involving a single digit only, such as $5+5$ or 5×5, produce fast and atypical RTs. Although some experimenters have maintained that these data index computational operations the studies have not really been adequate to support such an interpretation. It is more likely that the elementary number facts are directly represented in the permanent storage component of the Symbolic Memory, and that the answers to simple problems can be accessed by appropriate retrieval operations. We might suppose, for the sake of argument, that specialized sets of links between pattern recognizers for visual or auditory digits and phonemic representations of number names are formed during the learning of basic arithmetic, and that the TASK executive can switch in the links which are relevant for a particular operation of addition, subtraction, multiplication or division. If so, variations in RTs to solve simple arithmetical problems index the speed of the RETRIEVAL function rather than the occurrence of high speed computational activities.

Certain other types of experiment have appeared better adapted to the analysis of the structural code. DeRosa & Morin (1970) used a variant of Sternberg's symbol classification experiment in which consecutive digit sequences, such as 3–4–5–6, were the memory sets. They reported that both positive and negative RTs were delayed for probe numerals whose position in the number series placed them close to the boundaries of the memory set, that is at the transitions 2–3 and 6–7 in this example. The negative RT was found to be a decreasing function of the remoteness of the probe from the positive set (see also Morin, DeRosa & Stultz, (1967), and Marcel, (1970a)). Similar effects can be obtained with months of the year when *S*s classify month names into dichotomous classes, such as first half versus second, central versus peripheral, or warm versus cold (Seymour, 1976a). It would be useful to know if this pattern also obtains for the alphabet, but a study by Waugh & Anders (1973) which used consecutive letter sequence as memory sets unfortunately avoided cases where negative probes fell at the set boundaries.

These findings suggest that *subset boundary effects* may be characteristic of the structural coding of such sequences as numerals and months of the year. This implies that the sequence is represented as an array on which boundary locations may be marked. Discrimination problems arise when probes which lie close to the boundaries are encoded. This boundary effect shades into a *distance effect*. As the distance on the array from the boundary to the probe is increased the RT is reduced. We may note that this is the converse of the graded repetition effect obtained in a symbol naming task by Marcel & Forrin (1974), who reported that reductions in the distance between successively presented numerals facilitated naming RT. A distance effect is also observed when *S*s judge whether pairs of symbols are correctly or incorrectly ordered. Lovelace & Snodgrass (1971) found that RT for order judgements about pairs of letters increased with depth into the alphabet and with reductions in the size of the gap between the letters.

An experimental task which has proved particularly useful in highlighting the influence of structural properties of the number series and alphabet on the RT is the *relative judgement task*. *S*s are presented with pairs of numerals (or letters), one to the left and one to the right, and press a left or right key to indicate which is the larger (or smaller) of the two. Moyer & Landauer (1967) reported that the discrimination RT was subject to a distance effect, tending to increase as the difference in magnitude between the two numerals became smaller. However, Parkman (1971) pointed out that an experimental design in which all possible digit pairs are presented systematically confounds magnitude difference with the values of the larger and smaller members of the pairs. He demonstrated that RT for both 'choose larger' and 'choose smaller' instructions was related to the size of the smaller digit by a linear function with a slope of 12–18 msecs per unit, although his data also showed evidence of a distance effect of the kind described by Moyer & Landauer (1967).

In a similar experiment Parkman (1971) obtained relative judgement RTs for the alphabetical sequences A–J and K–T. These RTs were greater by 200 msecs or so than those observed in the digit task. As in the experiments of Hovancik (1975) and Lovelace & Snodgrass (1971)the RT was greater for the K–T than for the A–J series. There was evidence of an effect of distance between the letters. However, the impact of the position of the earlier letter was weak in the A–J series, and absent in the K–T series, where RT was inversely related to the position of the later letter.

Banks, Fujii & Kayra-Stuart (1976) have recently formulated a comprehensive model of relative judgement which accommodates the distance effects and the effect of size of the smaller digit. They propose that digits, once graphemically encoded, access codes which specify approximate magnitude as abstractions of the form (small) or (large), depending on whether the digit lies above or below a cut-off point in the numerical series. This cut-off point is assumed to vary, but generally falls below the mean value of the series, so that the digits 1–3 might be classified as (small) and the digits 4–9 as (large). The experimental instruction to 'choose the larger' or 'choose the smaller' is represented in the same abstract format, and is matched during a COMPARISON stage against the digit codes. Provided that the digit codings lie either side of the cut-off, one being coded as (small) and the other as (large), the matching against the instructional code is straightforward, and leads to a rapid response. A delay of RT occurs if the digits have been assigned the same coding, since it will then be necessary for a finer discrimination of relative magnitude to occur. Banks argued that the probability of a duplicated coding should increase as the absolute values of the digits become larger and the magnitude difference between them becomes smaller. With these assumptions the model will generate effects of magnitude difference and value of the smaller digit, and will also produce an interaction between instructions and digit magnitude known as the *semantic congruity effect.* This reflects a tendency for the instruction 'choose smaller' to be slower than 'choose larger' when the digits to be classified are large though not when they are small. An experimental demonstration of these effects was provided by Banks, Fujii & Kayra-Stuart (1976).

Banks has, therefore, localized effects of structural properties of the number series in a COMPARISON stage of processing. This is in line with the earlier conclusions regarding the graphemic and phonemic codes, where it appeared that factors of code congruity influenced RT through selective effects on COMPARISON. His discussion also emphasizes that the structural code for the numerals is an integral part of the semantics of the number system.

VI.5 CONCLUSIONS

This chapter has discussed the RETRIEVAL function which mediates transformations between coded representations within the Symbolic Memory system. This function enhances the temporary storage capacity of the system by providing graphemic–phonemic recoding facilities as support for the representational function discussed in the last chapter. It also allows the graphemic and phonemic codings of symbols to access representations of class membership and of the structural properties of the alphabet and number system.

It has been assumed that REPRESENTATIONAL and RETRIEVAL functions depend on a central component of the Symbolic Memory which has been called the interface structure. This contains banks of pattern recognizers corresponding to the different types of representational code (graphemic, phonemic, categorial and structural), and registers of addresses of locations in permanent storage. An executive programme, referred to as TASK, controls the moment-to-moment functioning of the Symbolic Memory by making and unmaking links between particular sets of pattern recognizers and particular address registers.

These recognition and addressing functions occur with a high degree of speed and efficiency in literate adults. Indeed, it is a characteristic of the elements of symbol systems that they should be recognized and recoded by direct and semi-automatic procedures (LaBerge & Samuels, 1974). This is exemplified in the more rapid naming of symbols than of objects (Fraisse, 1967, 1969), and in the relative independence of symbol naming RT of variations in stimulus ensemble size and stimulus probability (Brainard, Irby, Fitts & Alluisi, 1962; Morin & Forrin, 1962; Forrin, Kumler & Morin, 1966).

The Symbolic Memory emerges, therefore, as a highly efficient system for representation and manipulation of symbolic entities, which is acquired as part of the learning of the basic skills of literacy and numeracy in the early years of schooling. In the terms used here, this learning involves the development of a capability for feature description of graphemes (the ENCODING function of Chapter IV), the laying down of symbol descriptions and structural codes in the permanent data stores, and the construction of pattern recognizers, address registers and mediating links within the interface structure. The system can suffer selective neurological damage in later life. In certain cases of acquired dyslexia the naming of individual letters has been shown to be severely impaired (Patterson & Marcel, 1977), and Morton (1977b) has recently discussed a case in which recitation of the alphabet was impaired although the ability to use knowledge of its structure for referencing purposes was relatively well preserved.

A further aspect of the Symbolic Memory which has its origins in the early development of literacy is the capability for transformation of array structure during recoding. Representations of spatial position in the graphemic register are transformable to representations of temporal position in the phonemic register, and *vice versa*. Although these directional aspects of recoding are controlled by the TASK executive they become partially automatic and cannot easily be reversed.

It has been proposed that the Symbolic Memory contains a semantic component in the form of structural representations of alphabetic sequence and numerical magnitude. Structural coding of the numerals is fundamental to arithmetic skills, although, as was noted, competence in arithmetic may also depend on the establishment, in the symbolic interface, of connections allowing direct RETRIEVAL of answers to standard addition, subtraction, multiplication and division problems. A further possibility, discussed by Seymour & Porpodas (1978), is that the structural code is involved in the permanent storage of information about spellings of words.

CHAPTER VII

Comparison Functions

SAMPLING AND DECISION MODEL

VII.1 INTRODUCTION

Throughout the preceding chapters we have made frequent reference to 'same'–'different' judgemental tasks, and to the impact of various experimental factors on a COMPARISON stage of processing. Indeed, the sensitivity of this stage to variations in the similarity, congruity and structure of the representational codings of symbols has been basic to much of the methodology used in the study of the Symbolic Memory. Aside from this, COMPARISON is a mental function of great generality which enters in a significant way into many types of intelligent performance (Miller, Galanter & Pribram, 1960). A more detailed analysis of the COMPARISON stage will be undertaken in this chapter.

COMPARISON may be viewed as a specialized type of RETRIEVAL operation by which symbol codes are transformed to a semantic representation of sameness or difference. For this transformation to occur we require initially that descriptions of symbols or symbol arrays should be entered into a *comparison register*. This register could be equated with the temporary storage registers previously discussed. However, since the COMPARISON function is treated as conceptually distinct from the RETRIEVAL and REPRESENTATIONAL functions, the cause of consistency will be better served if a distinction at the level of the registers is also assumed. It is convenient to represent the comparison register as two rows of cells. Each cell may contain a featural description of a symbol, and higher level structures are available for labelling of spatial locations (or other organizational properties) of a symbol array.

On the basis of experimental evidence introduced in previous chapters we will assume that the elementary operation in COMPARISON is one of *feature matching*. We might imagine that the comparison register incorporates a facility for matching components of feature descriptions occupying homologous locations in any pair of cells. For reasons to be developed later it is necessary that specification of these feature tests should be subject to an external executive which we shall call MATCH. This property of the register can be represented as an internal interface structure which contains optional links between corresponding cell locations We assume that MATCH can enable and disable these links on a moment-to-moment basis and thus control the logic and timing of the comparison process. A diagrammatic representation of this account of the comparison register is included in Figure VII.1.1.

When symbol descriptions have been entered into the cells of the register, and a MATCH routine is in operation, the comparison register will produce as output a sequence of signals, each indicating a binary match or mismatch outcome of an elementary feature matching operation. We will for the present assume that these signals are generated at a high rate, and that they flow along a single channel to a *judgemental component* of the comparison system. The judgemental component can be viewed as an interface structure which contains two pattern recognizers and facilities for addressing locations in a semantic data store. As in previous discussions, the pattern recognizers can be represented as evidence accumulators having a threshold level at which access to the semantic store is achieved. We assume that one recognizer, to be called the *'same' accumulator*, responds to match signals, whereas the other, to be called the *'different' accumulator*, responds to mismatch signals. When either accumulator passes a threshold, a link to the address register becomes active. This allows for retrieval of a semantic coding of affirmation or denial, that is an abstract representation of (same) or (different). This code is placed in a semantic register, and may be used for retrieval of response codes. These ideas are also represented diagrammatically in Figure VII.1.1.

In anticipation of later discussion, it is assumed that the MATCH executive may influence the judgemental component of COMPARISON by adjusting the thresholds of the 'same' and 'different' accumulators. There are a variety of types of adjustment which might occur. For example, the two thresholds could be raised or lowered in tandem, one could be raised or lowered unilaterally, or they could be adjusted in a reciprocal fashion, one being lowered as the other was raised.

It will be evident from the preceding account that COMPARISON is seen as a complex process having two distinct aspects.

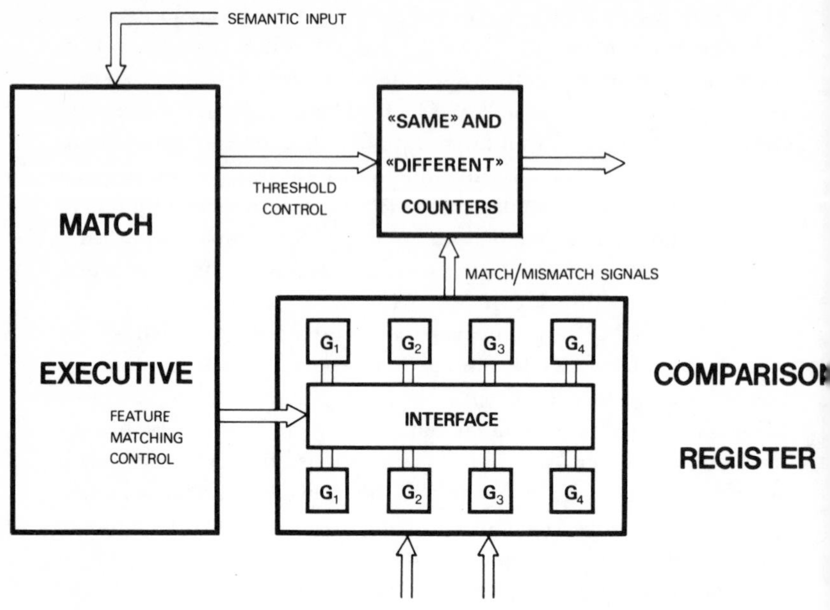

Figure VII.1.1 Schematic representation of the structure of the COMPARISON function. The arrays to be matched are initially transferred to the comparison register and placed in the cells labelled G_{1-4}. (The use of four cells in the diagram is not intended to imply a capacity limitation). The executive MATCH programmes a sequence of feature comparisons by making and unmaking links in the interface of the register, and a stream of match and mismatch signals is generated. These signals are counted by 'same' and 'different' accumulators, and a semantic coding of sameness or difference is retrieved when one or other accumulator passes its threshold. The MATCH executive receives instructions in the form of semantic codes, and acts upon these by adjustments to the accumulator thresholds and by alterations in the feature matching routine.

One of these is the transformation of symbol descriptions to match and mismatch signals which is achieved within the comparison register. The other is the evaluation of this evidence which occurs within the judgemental component. Both parts of the system are subject to control by the external MATCH executive, which sequences the feature matching operations and determines the relative settings of the 'same' and 'different' thresholds.

VII.2 FACTORS INFLUENCING 'COMPARISON'

Within a system of this kind the time required for operation of the

COMPARISON stage, that is the time elapsing between entry of symbol codes into the comparison register and entry of a (same) or (different) code into the semantic register, will be dependent on: (1) the *rate* at which evidence supporting the correct decision flows to the judgemental component; and (2) the *threshold setting* of the evidence accumulator corresponding to the correct decision. It follows that experimental factors exerting a selective influence on COMPARISON should have an impact on one or both of these aspects.

A number of relevant factors may be identified by reference to research which has already been discussed. These include code congruity and similarity, the size of the memory set, M, and the size of the display set, D. When two arrays are presented for comparison, either simultaneously or successively, the number of symbols common to the two arrays, or the number of positions containing the same symbol, may also be important. We will use the letter C to label such variations in the communality of the arrays. These factors, which define the sizes and the degree and nature of the correspondence between arrays presented for comparison, may influence the feature matching aspect of COMPARISON, and thus affect the rate of flow of match/mismatch evidence. By contrast, differences between positive and negative decisions which are found in many studies appear to relate more obviously to the judgemental aspect of the process, and might be thought to reflect differences in threshold settings. A clear-cut distinction of this kind was proposed by Sternberg (1969a, 1975), who argued that a judgemental stage, influenced by decision outcome, occurred after completion of a COMPARISON stage, influenced by M.

In the following discussion we will argue that this separation is an over-simplification. Given the analysis proposed here, it must obviously be incorrect to represent the feature matching and judgemental aspects of COMPARISON as *successive* processing stages. Generation of match/mismatch signals and their accumulation by the 'same' and 'different' counters are better viewed as concurrent activities which terminate when one of the counters exceeds a threshold value. Indeed, it will be argued that D and M affect the duration of COMPARISON through alterations in both the rate of evidence accumulation and threshold settings.

A further factor of importance relates to the instructions given to the *S* regarding the *definition of equivalence* which he is to observe in classifying arrays as 'same' or 'different'. This is in part tied up with code congruity, since instructions indicate to the *S* whether 'same' is to be defined in terms of physical, nominal or semantic levels of equivalence. However, instructions also determine the manner in which the *S* classifies partially equivalent arrays. To illustrate, we might consider a comparison task in which pairs of four-letter arrays are presented, as, for example:

ABCD	ABCD	A BCD
ABCD	ABXY	WXYZ

The extreme examples are either *same* at all positions, or *different* at all positions, and are unambiguously classifiable as 'same' or 'different'. The middle example contains matching letters in two positions, and mismatching letters in two positions. If the *S* has been instructed that *same* arrays must have the same letters in each position he will classify this example as 'different'. If, on the other hand, he has been instructed that the arrays are *same* if they contain any same letters in corresponding positions, he will classify the example as 'same'.

This instructional variable is important in the analysis of the COMPARISON stage. Since identical configurations may be classified as 'same' under one instruction and 'different' under another, it appears essential to assume the involvement of an executive MATCH component with a capability for modification of the evidence accumulation and judgemental processes which will yield decision outcomes that are appropriate to the task definition. Just how this might be achieved will be a main topic for consideration in this chapter.

VII.3 CONJUNCTIVE AND DISJUNCTIVE DEFINITIONS OF EQUIVALENCE

The instructional factor introduced above relates to the stringency of the definition of equivalence which the *S* must apply. The most stringent definition of equivalence is the one which will tolerate no discrepancy between the arrays and which insists that the arrays should be *identical* with regard to the symbols they contain and the positions occupied by those symbols. This stringent definition, which nonetheless appears quite a natural one, may be referred to as a *conjunctive definition* of equivalence. It states that the two arrays may be classified as 'same' if they are: (*Same* at P_1) *and* (*Same* at P_2) *and* (*Same* at P_3), and so on up to (*Same* at P_n), where P represents 1 . . . . n display positions.

When the stringency of the definition of equivalence is relaxed, so that a degree of non-correspondence between the arrays becomes tolerable, the effect is to create a number of alternative conditions which are all acceptable as a basis for a 'same' decision. This could be achieved by stating that the arrays can be regarded as equivalent if they contain the same letters, regardless of position, or one or more same letters in corresponding positions, or one or more same letters without regard to position. These may be referred to as *disjunctive definitions*. For example, the requirement that there should be one or more same symbols in corresponding positions might be represented by the disjunction: (*Same* at P_1) *or* (*Same* at P_2) *or* (*Same* at P_3) up to (*Same* at P_n), and including conjunctions of two or more same positions.

Experimental studies have suggested that *S*s generally find conjunctive definitions of equivalence easier to work with than disjunctive definitions. A study by Nickerson & Pew (1973) provides some relevant data. Their *S*s were presented with two successively displayed pairs of letters, so that M = D = 2. The correspondence, C, between the arrays varied in the manner shown in Table VII.3.1, and can be seen to include: (1) two matching symbols with or without correspondence of position; (2) one matching symbol, again with or without correspondence of position; and (3) no matching symbols. One group of *S*s classified displays of this kind under a conjunctive definition of equivalence, a positive response being required only when symbols occurred in corresponding positions. It can be noted that 'same' RT was in general faster than 'different' RT, and that 'different' RT varied with the degree of correspondence of the arrays, being fastest when different letters were presented, and slower when same letters occurred in non-corresponding positions, or the left display position contained same letters. As will be shown later, this pattern of RT data is quite characteristic of performance under conjunctive instructions. The most frequent errors were false 'same' responses to *different* displays containing matching letters.

Nickerson & Pew (1973) also obtained RT data for classification of these displays under two types of disjunctive instruction. One group of *S*s was instructed to respond positively if the arrays contained the same letters, regardless of position. Results for this condition are included in Table VII.3.1. 'Same' responses now occurred to identical arrays, and to arrays containing the same letters in reversed positions. It may be noted that reversal of position delayed the 'same' RT by over 90 msecs. 'Different' RTs were slower for displays which shared one symbol than for those which did not. Further, if we compare

Table VII.3.1 Reaction times (msecs) for comparison of successively presented letter pairs of varying correspondence for conjunctive and disjunctive decision rules. (Adapted from Nickerson & Pew (1973)).

Type of display correspondence	Example	Decision rule for responding 'same'					
		Conjunctive rule (Same letters in same positions)		Disjunctive rule (Same letters, position not critical)		Disjunctive rule (One or two same letters, position not critical)	
		'Same'	'Different'	'Same'	'Different'	'Same'	'Different'
Same letters, same positions	AB AB	353		407		438	
Same letters, reverse positions	AB BA		432	499		478	
Leftmost letters same	AB AC		430		500	503	
Rightmost letters same	AB CB		398		515	528	
Right-left correspondence	AB CA		399		485	584	
Left-right correspondence	AB BC		390		507	593	
No correspondence	AB CD		373		444		619

'same' RTs for identical displays obtained under this instruction with those obtained under the conjunctive instruction it can be seen that the disjunctive instruction has led to a delay of 50 msec or so. For 'different' responses to displays containing no common elements the disjunctive instruction induced a delay of about 70 msecs.

A third group of *S*s was instructed to respond positively if the arrays contained any common element, regardless of position. Under this instruction, *S*s may respond positively to all displays except those containing no common symbols. The results given in Table VII.3.1 indicate that under this instruction 'same' RT increased as the similarity of the arrays was reduced. RTs averaged 438 msecs for identical displays, 478 msecs for displays containing the same letters in reversed position, 515 msecs for a single same letter in the same position, and 588 msecs for a single same letter with reversal of position. This trend is the direct converse of that obtained for 'different' responses to these displays under the conjunctive instruction. Finally, it can be noted that 'different' RT averages 619 msecs, which is greater than the slowest 'same' RT and 246 msecs greater than RT to classify arrays having no elements in common under the conjunctive instruction.

A number of points can be made on the basis of Nickerson & Pew's data. Firstly, the shift from conjunctive to disjunctive definitions of *same* is associated with a general increase in RT, which is possibly related to the number of alternative display configurations which satisfy the criterion for a positive response. Secondly, increases in display correspondence result in facilitation of 'same' decisions, and in retardation of 'different' decisions. Error frequencies follow the same trend, being high for *different* displays which contain common elements and for *same* displays having few common elements.

The data also illustrate a theoretically puzzling asymmetry in the relationship between positive and negative RT and the conjunctive and disjunctive instructions. For *S*s in the third group, where *same* was defined as correspondence of one or two letters without regard to position, the 'different' RT was greater than the slowest 'same' RT. This is consistent with the view that *S*s test for all possible types of display correspondence and reach a 'different' decision only when sufficient time has passed for completion of these tests. A reasonable expectation is that the converse pattern of results should be found for the first group of *S*s who employed a conjunctive definition of *same*. For this condition there is a variety of types of non-correspondence of the arrays which are sufficient for a 'different' decision, and it seems logically necessary that the 'same' decision should be delayed until all of these have been considered. The RT data obviously run against this expectation, since the 'same' RT was 20 msecs faster than the fastest of the 'different' RTs. This phenomenon of fast 'same' responses will provide a main point for discussion in the following section.

VII.4 JUDGEMENTS OF IDENTITY

Three types of experimental task have been found useful in the study of judgements of identity, that is tasks in which a conjunctive definition of equivalence is adopted by the *S*. The first of these is the oddity detection task of Beller (1970) which was briefly discussed in Chapter IV. The other two involve comparisons of symbol arrays of equal length. Where the arrays are presented successively, as in the study by Nickerson & Pew (1973), the first array is a memory set of size M, and the second is a display of size D. A constraint is that M = D, and the *S* is instructed to respond positively if M and D contain the same symbols in the same positions. The arrays may be presented simultaneously, either side by side or one above the other, in which case we can speak of a first and second array of sizes D_1 and D_2, where $D_1 = D_2$, and the *S* responds 'same' if the arrays contain the same symbols in the same positions.

In the oddity detection experiment reported by Beller (1970) the 'same' RT averaged 466 msecs and was independent of D (2, 4 or 8 symbols). It will be recalled that *S*s were instructed to respond positively if all letters in a single array were identical, and negatively if one or more discrepancies were encountered. The 'different' RT averaged 479 msecs for arrays of D = 4 or 8 containing all different letters, and was slightly slower at 528 msecs when D = 2. A reduction in the number of different letters increased the 'different' RT, so that, for D = 8, the RT was 510 msecs when there were four same letters and four different letters, 566 msecs when there were two sets of four same letters, and 650 msecs when there were seven same letters and only one discrepant letter. This latter condition produced a large rise in error rate.

The experiment illustrates the paradox of the fast 'same' responses. *S*s required 650 msecs to indicate the presence of a single different letter in an 8-item array. We anticipate that they should require at least this amount of time to determine absence of discrepancy in an array of identical letters before responding 'same'. Yet the 'same' RT for an 8-item array was only 454 msecs.

Experiments on comparison of simultaneously presented arrays generally show effects of D, the display size. A representative study, using letter arrays of length $D_1 = D_2 = 1$, 2, 4, or 6, was reported by Eichelman (1970b). The arrays were presented one above the other, and *S*s were instructed to press a 'same' key if all array positions contained identical letters, and a 'different' key otherwise. RT for 'same' responses increased as a function of D, having a slope of $B = 60$ msecs per item. Beller (1970) conducted a similar experiment in which $D_1 = D_2 = 1$, 2 or 4, and sameness was defined in terms of nominal equivalence. 'Same' RT for arrays containing physically identical letters yielded a slope of $B = 63$ msecs per item. Nominally equivalent arrays produced a steeper slope of $B = 143$ msecs per item.

'Different' RT in array matching tasks is related to D and to C, the number of same symbols occupying corresponding positions. Both Beller (1970) and Eichelman (1970b) reported that the RT increased as a function of D, and also as a function of C. The latter effect is to be taken as meaning that 'different' RT increases as the number of same letters on the display increases. For example, in Beller's experiment, displays of $D_1 = D_2 = 4$ produce 'different' RTs of 745 msecs when $C = 0$, as against 937 msecs when $C = 3$. The data also reproduce the relative advantage of 'same' RT which has already been commented on. The 'same' RT for four-item arrays was 747 msecs. This is close to the value for 'different' RT for arrays containing no same letters, and markedly faster than RT for arrays containing only a single discrepant letter. Silverman & Goldberg (1975) obtained very similar results in a study involving matching of four-item digit arrays.

Some additional points have been made by Henderson & Henderson (1975). In their study four-letter arrays were presented for comparison, with the number of corresponding letters, $C = 3$ or 1. The factor of number of correspondences was held constant within blocks of trials. When $C = 3$, 'different' RT increased as the position of the single discrepant letter shifted from left to right across the display. By contrast, when $C = 1$, the 'different' RT declined slightly as the position of the single same letter was shifted from left to right. By blocking the levels of C, Henderson & Henderson were able to demonstrate an effect on both 'same' and 'different' RTs. Both responses were faster when $C = 1$ than when $C = 3$, that is when *different* arrays differed at three of four possible positions. The relation between 'same' and 'different' RT was also influenced by

C, 'same' RT being faster than 'different' RT when C = 3, but marginally slower when C = 1.

Detailed analyses of a successive presentation version of the array matching task have been undertaken by Bamber (1969) and Taylor (1976a). In Bamber's experiment array size was varied at M = D = 1, 2, 3 or 4. For *different* arrays the number of corresponding letters was varied between C = 0 and C = D – 1. Thus, the arrays could differ at all positions, or at fewer positions, including the case where only one discrepant location was present to signal the 'different' response. Bamber reported that 'same' RT increased as a function of D at a rate of B = 20 msecs per symbol. This result was also obtained by Taylor (1976a), who obtained a slope of approximately 25 msecs per symbol. In a subsequent study, with a nominal definition of equivalence, the obtained slope value was 69 msecs per symbol (Bamber, 1972). These estimates are lower than those obtained by Beller (1970) for simultaneous comparisons, although the two types of experiment agree in showing that 'same' RT increases linearly with D, and that the slope is steeper for NI than for PI comparisons.

In Bamber's experiment RTs to respond 'different' were affected by D and C. As in previous studies, the RT increased as D became larger, and decreased as C, the number of same letters, became smaller. When there was only one discrepant item, so that C = D – 1, 'different' RT was related to D by a slope of B = 32 msecs per symbol. In the nominal identity experiment this value increased to B = 81 msecs per symbol. When there were no same letters, so that C = 0, the RT was effectively unrelated to D in the physical identity experiment, and showed a much reduced effect in the nominal identity experiment. A frequent source of error was again the occurrence of false 'same' responses to different displays containing only one discrepant letter. These findings were replicated in their essentials by Taylor (1976a). Both experiments also illustrate the phenomenon of fast 'same' responses. The 'same' RT was faster by about 50 msecs than the 'different' RT for displays containing a single discrepancy.

Attempts at interpretation of this pattern of results initially focused on a *serial self-terminating model* of COMPARISON (Bamber, 1969; Eichelman, 1970b). Unlike the feature-matching model outlined at the beginning of this chapter, this theory makes the assumption that the elementary operation of COMPARISON is a judgement of the equivalence of two symbols. The model states that the *S* compares symbols occupying corresponding locations in a seriatim fashion, and that he terminates COMPARISON and initiates a 'different' response as soon as a mismatch is encountered. An account of this kind is reasonably descriptive of the basic findings for 'different' RT. If we assume a random order of processing of locations, increases in D will raise RT by increasing the number of comparisons which must be made, and decreases in C will reduce RT by raising the probability that a mismatching location will be encountered early in processing.

In practice, this serial self-terminating model is difficult to distinguish from models which assume parallel processing of items combined with a limitation on available processing capacity (Corcoran, 1971; Townsend, 1971; Taylor, 1976b). Taylor (1976a) has argued that a self-terminating limited capacity parallel model of this kind produces a slightly better account of the 'different' RT data obtained by himself and Bamber than does the serial model. The feature matching model discussed earlier is also of this general type. In such a system processing is serial at the level of feature comparisons but may appear parallel at the level of item comparisons. If outcomes of feature tests are passed to the judgemental accumulators by a single channel, and if mismatch signals are counted by the 'different' accumulator as evidence of non-correspondence of the displays, increases in the value of C will be expected to raise the 'different' RT. This is because match signals generated by feature tests on same letters will come to occupy the channel, thus slowing the rate at which mismatch signals arrive at the 'different' accumulator. If $C = 0$ this occupation of the channel will not occur, and the RT may appear effectively unrelated to D, as reported by Bamber. If multiple channels were available, RT would tend to decrease as D increased unless a capacity limitation of the kind considered by Corcoran was operative.

As it stands, Bamber's serial self-terminating model does not satisfactorily explain left-to-right trends found in the 'different' RT data (Henderson & Henderson, 1975), or the prevalence of false 'same' responses to *different* arrays having large values of C. Its more serious defect is its failure to predict the function for 'same' RTs. Bamber (1969) used his 'different' RT data in conjunction with formulae deriving from the assumptions of the serial model to obtain an estimate of the time required for each judgement that two symbols matched which preceded the discovery of a mismatching pair and termination of the COMPARISON stage. The obtained value of about 60 msecs was more than twice as large as the observed rate at which 'same' RT increased with D. This establishes that the serial model cannot be descriptive of both 'same' and 'different' judgements. If it were we would expect 'same' RT to be related to D by a slope of 60 msecs per item, and to fall at a level greater than that obtained for 'different' RTs when C = D – 1.

Both Bamber and Taylor have sought to get around this problem by invoking the possibility that 'same' judgements may be different in kind from 'different' judgements. Bamber suggested that 'same' judgements might be based on a fast operation of *gestalt* matching which he referred to as the *identity reporter*. He thought that this might be a response to configurational properties of the display which allowed a 'same' reaction to be initiated without recourse to the slower and more analytic serial comparison process. Taylor (1976a) considered that premature termination of processing and guessing might contribute to the fast 'same' RT at the cost of some false 'same' responses. However, adjustments for guessing were not adequate to account for the effect, and he also concluded that some special characteristic of 'same' decisions allowed the COMPARISON stage to be by-passed on 60–75 per cent of trials.

Although the two-process theory about judgements of identity put forward by Bamber has some attractive features it has not fared well in subsequent tests. If the identity reporter responds to *gestalt* properties of the display we might expect it to be disabled when *S*s make nominal comparisons of letters. Yet Bamber (1972) was not able to fit the serial self-terminating model to both 'same' and 'different' RTs in his nominal identity experiment. In a further study, Bamber & Paine (1973) presented a four-item memory set followed by a test array which could contain some blank locations. *S*s were instructed to respond positively if the filled locations corresponded to memory set items. Bamber considered that the blank locations would destroy configurational properties of the display and thus disable the identity reporter. However, he was again unable to fit 'same' RTs to the serial self-terminating model.

On these grounds we may feel inclined to doubt the explanatory value of Bamber's indentity reporter. The notion is perhaps most obviously applicable to an account of the response to duplication of symbols which occurs in Beller's (1970) oddity detection task. It was suggested that the evidence required for a decision that all display items are identical might become available during ENCODING if a feature-matching routine tested for display homogeneity at the termini of all active input channels. A characteristic of this type of decision was an observed independence of the 'same' RT from D. If the same type of decision process was involved in array comparison we might anticipate a similar independence of D. However, the experiments by Beller (1970), Eichelman (1970b), Bamber (1969) and Taylor (1976a) all show an approximately linear relationship between 'same' RT and D. Since D has been taken to be a factor influencing COMPARISON this implies that array matching requires entry of symbol descriptions into the comparison register and application of the feature-matching and judgemental procedures of the COMPARISON stage.

When viewed within the framework of a sampling and decision model of the kind described at the beginning of the chapter, array comparison involves the application of a specialized routine for matching features of symbols occupying corresponding spatial locations. Provided that this routine is well-disciplined, identical displays will generate a sequence of match signals at a rate which is independent of D. A failure of discipline, resulting in matching of features of symbols in non-corresponding locations, will reduce the rate of accumulation of match signals on account of periodic occupation of the channel by spurious mismatch signals. Thus, if the threshold of the 'same' accumulator was maintained at a constant level we would expect 'same' RT to appear independent of D, unless increases in D were associated with increased laxity in control over the feature sampling process.

As it stands such a formulation is not adequate because it leaves the system prone to errors in classification of *different* arrays. As has already been remarked, the rate of accumulation of mismatch evidence is expected to be independent of D when all locations contain different symbols, but will become slower as C, the number of same symbols, increases. Hence, if the 'different' threshold is maintained at a constant level, RT is expected to increase as a function of C, as is indeed observed. This delay of the 'different' decision is attributable to the occupation of the channel by match signals which are counted as evidence by the 'same' accumulator. If the threshold on this accumulator was held at a constant level the critical value would often be exceeded when *different* displays having large values of C were presented, giving rise to many false 'same' decisions.

A natural way of minimizing such errors is to arrange for the MATCH executive to shift the threshold of the 'same' accumulator upward as display size increases to a level sufficient for processing of a *different* display for which $C = D - 1$. We have noted that 'same' RT does indeed increase as a function of D, and at a rate similar to 'different' RT for single discrepancy displays. However, although this is consistent with the theory, we are left with the paradoxical observation that the absolute level of 'same' RT is lower than that of 'different' RT, implying that 'same' decisions are taken before sufficient time has been allowed to avoid errors on *different* displays containing same letters.

Two ways of adapting the model to handle the problem of the fast 'same' responses suggest themselves. Firstly, we could suppose that the 'same' threshold is adjusted to a level which is sufficient to allow for detection of an incongruity on the display but not for complete achievement of a 'different' decision. This would require that the MATCH executive should monitor the accumulation of mismatch evidence and raise the 'same' threshold to a safe level if a minimal indication of incongruity was present. The time required for this would be expected to increase as a function of D and C. Relatively accurate performance could be maintained with a low setting of the 'same' threshold combined with an adjustment for display size which was generally sufficient for detection of incongruity.

Another possibility is that the feature-matching routine may focus selectively on particular cells of the comparison register. Given detection of an incongruity, the MATCH executive might limit the acquisition of match/mismatch evidence to a sub-set of display locations. The left–right differences described by Henderson & Henderson (1975) and in various of the papers by Bamber suggest that this kind of selectivity of processing may occur. If MATCH monitored variations in the rate of accumulation of mismatch evidence as the focus of the comparison was shifted, the approximate location of the incongruity could be determined, and sampling could then be concentrated on that region. As focus improved the proportion of match signals deriving from comparisons of features of same letters would be expected to fall. This would reduce the rate of accumulation of evidence in the 'same' accumulator, and hence the risk of early termination of processing by a false 'same' decision. If we assume that localization of the source of an incongruity can be achieved early in the feature matching process, but that the necessary sampling interval is dependent on the sizes of D and C, accurate performance could be maintained by setting the 'same' threshold at a value sufficient for achievement of focus for single discrepancy displays at each level of D.

The proposal, therefore, is that the phenomenon of fast 'same' responses and the logical requirement that 'same' decisions should be delayed relative to slow 'different' decisions may be reconciled by assuming that the 'same' decision is delayed relative to completion of an early though critical phase of COMPARISON. Given the active involvement of MATCH in the process it is perhaps not surprising that occasional miscalculations are made, and erroneous 'same' responses are allowed to occur. The theory is, of course, speculative, though not outrageously so. The assumption that the level of the 'same' threshold may be adjusted is supported by Henderson & Henderson's (1975) demonstration that 'same' RT and the relative levels of 'same' and 'different' RTs are influenced by variations in the value of C. Our further assumption that MATCH may control the fine detail of the feature matching process seems a reasonable conclusion given Nickerson & Pew's (1973) demonstration of a need for strategic flexibility in the COMPARISON process.

VII.5 DISPLAY SEARCH AND MEMORY SEARCH

Most of the other comparison tasks which have been investigated have been based on disjunctive definitions of equivalence. Two special cases will be considered in this section, both of which have already received quite extensive discussion. These are the display search task, in which the *S* reacts to presence or absence of a target symbol on an array of varying size, and the memory search task in which a single probe symbol is classified as a member or non-member of a memorized set. In display search memory set size is held constant at M = 1, and display size varies at D = 1 . . . . n. For memory search, D = 1 and memory set size varies at M = 1 . . . . n.

In both tasks M and D are classified as 'same' whenever the isolated member of one set corresponds to a member of a larger set. Equivalence is defined by the disjunction: (*Same* at P_1) *or* (*Same* at P_2) *or* (*Same* at P_3), and so on up to (*Same* at P_n). There is therefore a range of alternative conditions each of which may satisfy the requirements of a 'same' decision. This situation is a direct converse of that obtaining when equivalence is defined conjunctively. In identity comparisons of the kind discussed in the preceding section there is a range of alternative configurations which may lead to a 'different' decision, but only one possibility which will support a 'same' decision.

It follows that our expectations regarding the relative levels of 'same' and 'different' RTs will reverse when experiments using disjunctive definitions of equivalence are considered. We would now anticipate that the 'different' decision should be delayed until sufficient time has elapsed to allow each of the possible *same* outcomes to be evaluated. Thus, 'different' RT should be greater than 'same'

RT, and should increase so as to maintain this separation under circumstances which delay the 'same' RT. A relatively cursory glance over the experimental literature will confirm that 'different' RT is usually found to be slower than 'same' RT in display and memory search tasks, and that this effect is often preserved when variations in M or D alter the level of the 'same' RT.

With regard to display search, it will be recalled that some experiments have demonstrated an independence of the 'same' RT and D. The conditions giving rise to this appeared to be related to target/non-target confusability and possibly the shape of the display (Egeth, Jonides & Wall, 1972; Jonides & Gleitman, 1972; Egeth, Atkinson, Gilmore & Marcus, 1973; Estes, 1972). This implies that under certain favourable circumstances 'same' decisions in display search can be based on tests of display homogeneity of the kind involved in the oddity detection experiments. Taylor (1976c) has recently demonstrated that effects of D on display search RT are very small when non-target elements are repetitions of a single symbol. If homogeneity detection could also operate at a level of higher order features, such as those distinguishing letters from digits, the account might be extended to a majority of studies in which effects of D are small or absent. It is assumed that homogeneity tests are applied during ENCODING, and that a positive response is initiated if an incongruity is detected.

If homogeneity tests are not adequate for discrimination between target and non-target displays, as when confusable symbols are employed, a feature description of each member of D is placed in the comparison register beside duplicated descriptions of the target. The judgemental process then involves a routine by which features of display items are tested against the duplicated features of the target item. It is again assumed that the routine operates sequentially at the level of individual features, but in parallel at the level of symbols. A 'same' decision can be made when the accumulation of match signals passes a threshold. If this is maintained at a constant level, the time for a 'same' decision will increase with D, because the addition of non-target symbols to the display will raise the proportion of mismatch signals flowing along the single channel to the judgemental accumulators. Typical data were reported by Atkinson, Holmgren & Juola (1969) for a study in which *S*s searched for letter targets within linear arrays of letters. Positive RT was linearly related to D by the function: $\overline{RT} = 444 + 24(D)$ msecs. Thus, 24 msecs might be taken as an estimate of the delay in accumulation of match evidence resulting from presence of a non-target on the display.

Mismatch signals deriving from feature tests on non-targets will add evidence to the 'different' accumulator. In order to avoid premature termination of processing by an erroneous 'different' decision it is desirable that the 'different' threshold should be adjusted to take account of the size of D, being raised as D becomes larger, and lowered as D becomes smaller. This is the same principle as was thought to underlie variation in the 'same' RT in identity judgements. Atkinson, Holmgren & Juola (1969) obtained a linear function for negative RTs, of the form: $\overline{RT} = 474 + 26(D)$ msecs. This function is parallel to the one obtained for positive responses, but has a higher intercept. We could interpret this as indicating that the *S* adjusts his 'different' threshold so as to maintain a 30 msec delay relative to the time for a 'same' decision at each level of D.

In the discussion of identity judgements it was suggested that the executive, MATCH, might localize the source of discrepancy between two arrays, and then focus the feature matching routine. This could also occur in display search tasks if MATCH could determine the approximate source of feature match signals and focus sampling on those locations. An advantage of such a procedure is that it will minimize the flow of mismatch evidence to the 'different' accumulator, and thus reduce the risk of a false 'different' response. Taylor (1976c) obtained results which suggest that a localization procedure of this kind might contribute to the slope of the function relating RT to D. In one condition of his experiment *S*s searched arrays of letters for a target, as in Atkinson's study. The function relating RT to D had a slope of 27 msecs per symbol. In a second condition, the displays consisted of duplicated letters together with a single discrepant letter which might or might not be a target. The slope for this condition was only 13 msecs per symbol. It seems possible that the homogeneity of the background facilitated localization of a candidate target, and thus permitted earlier establishment of a focused sampling routine. However, if such a localization process does operate in display search it appears not to follow a stereotyped spatial pattern since Atkinson, Holmgren & Juola (1969) found no evidence of serial position effects in their data.

The analysis of the COMPARISON stage in memory search experiments can proceed along broadly similar lines. We assume that the symbols making up the memory set are maintained in temporary storage by application of REPRESENTATIONAL functions, and that their descriptions are copied into the comparison register prior to arrival of the probe. The probe symbol is transformed by ENCODING to an internal description which is duplicated in the cells of the comparison register. As previously, the COMPARISON stage is assumed to involve a feature matching routine, operating sequentially at the level of features but in parallel at the level of items, which passes a stream of match and mismatch signals along a single channel to the judgemental accumulators. The sampling time required for a decision that the arrays are 'same' is expected to increase as a function of M, because the addition of items to the memory set leads to occupation of the channel by mismatch signals. The rate of accumulation of mismatch signals from *different* displays is thought to be independent of M, but the threshold of the 'different' accumulator is adjusted upward as M is increased so as to avoid false 'different' responses.

Results of symbol classification experiments reported by Sternberg (1966, 1967, 1975) and by many other researchers are in broad agreement with this account. The RTs for both 'same' and 'different' responses increase as a linear (or logarithmic) function of M, having a slope of perhaps 20–40 msecs per symbol. The 'different' RT is generally greater than the 'same' RT by a constant amount, although this effect may be masked by manipulation of the relative frequencies of positive and negative responses (Sternberg, 1969a). Thus, symbol classification yields basically the same pattern of results as display search.

As is well-known, Sternberg has proposed that these results might be interpreted within the framework of a *serial exhaustive model* of COMPARISON. This theory states that the probe may be matched against the members of the memory set in a seriatim fashion, but that the matching process cannot be terminated when a correspondence is detected. Sternberg assumed that the outcome of the comparison was passed to response processes by a binary decision stage, the transfer occurring more rapidly for a positive than for a negative decision. Such a theory is also applicable to the qualitatively similar results obtained in the display search experiments.

Like the serial self-terminating account of identity judgements, this model cannot readily be distinguished from parallel models which incorporate a limited capacity assumption, or from the feature matching model which has been favoured here. The serial model also gives an unsatisfactory account of the judgemental aspect of COMPARISON, since the assignment of the positive/negative difference to a binary decision stage is entirely *ad hoc*. The model has also been attacked on empirical grounds, chiefly with regard to the shape of the function relating RT to M, and the possibility that COMPARISON may be selective rather than exhaustive.

Some workers, most notably Briggs and his associates, have questioned Sternberg's assumption that the relation between RT and M is strictly linear. Briggs has contended that the RT is a logarithmic function of M, such that $RT = A + B(H_c)$ msecs. H_c is an information theoretic index derived by summing $p_i \log p_i$ values corresponding to the probability of occurrence, p_i, of each of a set of possible states arising during the COMPARISON stage. In general, the relevant states have been considered to be a match against each of the possible memory set items or a failure to match any memory set item. For example, where $M = 2$, the probe may match the first member of M with a probability of 0·25, or the second member of M with a probability of 0·25, or may match neither member with a probability of 0·5. H_c is simply the sum of the $p \log p$ values obtained for each of these probabilities, expressed in bits of information.

Briggs (1974) has surveyed the results of a large number of memory search experiments, and has compared the adequacy of linear and logarithmic functions as descriptions of the effect of M on the RT. He found that the linear function often gave a good fit for experiments using digits as stimuli, but that the logarithmic function was superior in a majority (62 per cent) of experiments where letters, words or pictures were stimuli. This seems sufficient to raise serious questions concerning the linearity of the memory search function, and hence concerning the validity of the serial exhaustive model.

The main assault on Sternberg's position has involved attempts to demonstrate *selectivity* in COMPARISON. It has been felt that a demonstration that certain members of the memory set were processed in preference to others could be taken as contrary to the view that COMPARISON is an exhaustive process. However, such a demonstration is not easily made because symbol classification involves REPRESENTATIONAL processes as well as COMPARISON processes. If we are correct in assuming that the members of the memory set are held in temporary storage and are then transferred to the comparison register, we must accept the possibility that selectivity might occur at either the transfer or the feature matching stages.

Memory search tasks differ from display search in showing effects of the *serial position* of positive probes in the memory set. We have already commented on the boundary effects which occur when M contains a sequence of consecutive digits (DeRosa & Morin, 1970). Serial presentation of items from varied sets, whether in the visual or auditory modality, characteristically produces data in which 'same' RTs show recency effects, and perhaps a smaller primacy effect. This was shown by Corballis (1967) and Morin, DeRosa & Stultz (1967) in studies using fixed sizes of M = 5, and M = 4. In general, the recency effect (tendency for RTs of probes located late in the list to be shorter than RTs for earlier items) is more marked than the primacy effect (speeding of RT to the first item in the list). In other experiments the value of M has been varied and comparable patterns of results have been obtained (Kennedy & Hamilton, 1969; Corballis, Kirby & Miller, 1972; Burrows & Okada, 1971; Wingfield, 1973). Clifton & Birenbaum (1970) and Forrin & Cunningham (1973) have reported studies in which the length of the delay between presentation of the memory set and presentation of the probe has been varied, and have shown that the recency effects are strongest at the shortest delays.

When memory set items are presented as a simultaneous visual display 'same' RT increases as the probed position is shifted from the left across to the right of the display. Ellis & Chase (1971) reported that RT increased at a rate of about 40 msecs per position for memory sets of four visually presented letters. Analogous results were reported by Klatzky & Smith (1972) and Klatzky, Juola & Atkinson (1971).

It will be clear from this brief review that the flat serial position functions predicted by Sternberg's serial exhaustive model are an exception rather than a rule. They probably occur only when a fixed set procedure is used, and the memory set has been stored in a relatively long-term episodic memory (Corballis & Miller, 1973). Experiments using varied set procedures produce data suggestive of a spatially organized left-to-right process for simultaneous visual displays, and of a temporally organized end–start process for sequentially presented visual or auditory lists. Notions of this kind are, of course, at variance with Sternberg's theory, although his position might be defended if it could be demonstrated that the serial position effects relate to a stage of processing other than COMPARISON, such as ENCODING or the transfer of symbol descriptions from the temporary storage registers to the comparison register.

An experiment attempting this type of discrimination was reported by Raeburn (1974). Memory sets of 3–6 items were presented serially under a varied set procedure. As in other experiments, a marked recency effect was obtained. Although RT increased as a function of M for both positive and negative trials, this trend was not apparent for probes of the final position in the list. Thus, the experiment demonstrated a Serial Position × M interaction. This is consistent with the view that serial position affects COMPARISON rather than ENCODING but may also be interpreted by reference to REPRESENTATIONAL processes. Analogous results were reported by Okada & Burrows (1974). A fixed set procedure was used, with M = 2, 3, 4 and 5. Under a control condition all serial positions were probed with equal frequency, but in an experimental condition the first position in the memory set was probed on 60 per cent of positive trials. Under these conditions, the slope of the function relating RT to M was only 5 msecs per item for first position probes, as against 20 msecs per item for the remaining positions. This interaction did not occur under the control condition.

In a related study, Darley, Klatzky & Atkinson (1972) cued a particular member of the memory set on some trials. *S*s were told that the cued item was the only member of the memory set which could be probed on positive trials, although they were required to hold the set in memory and report it back after the trial. The RT function had a slope of 38 msecs per item in absence of a cue, but only 3 msecs per item when the cue was presented. This implies that *S*s may be able to hold a set of symbols in temporary memory by application of REPRESENTATIONAL operations, but that they can elect to consider only one of these during COMPARISON. In other words, these results support the distinction proposed earlier between the temporary storage registers and the comparison register, and suggest that there is scope for selectivity at the stage of transfer. In this case, the selective influence on COMPARISON is somewhat indirect, being related to the codes which are passed to the COMPARISON stage rather than to the events occurring during the stage.

A conclusion, therefore, is that the selective effects demonstrated in these studies are mediated, at least in part, by REPRESENTATIONAL processes distinct from COMPARISON. This account may be extended to a further group of studies in which attempts have been made to find evidence for selective processing of subsets of memory set items. Various bases for internal division of the memory set have been tried, including modality of presentation (Burrows & Solomon, 1975), the categorial distinction between letters and digits (Lively & Sanford, 1972; Sanford, 1972; Kaminsky & DeRosa, 1972;

Krueger, 1975), temporary versus permanent memory representations (Forrin & Morin, 1969), or arbitrary divisions signalled by colour cues (Williams, 1971; Crain & DeRosa, 1974). It does not seem worthwhile to discuss the findings of these studies in detail, since the extent of their contribution to the analysis of the COMPARISON stage is so uncertain.

VII.6 JUDGEMENTS OF CORRESPONDENCE

At the start of the previous section it was pointed out that the display search and memory search tasks are special cases of a larger class of comparison tasks which involve disjunctive definitions of equivalence. In the standard version of such a task the *S* is presented with two arrays of symbols and must indicate whether or not they contain any common items (Nickerson & Pew, 1973). The disjunction may be formulated so as to make correspondence of position part of the definition of equivalence, although this need not be so. Displays may be presented simultaneously or in succession, and their sizes may be equated or allowed to vary independently. As in the case of identity judgements, the factors which may be varied are the lengths of the arrays, M and D, and C, the number of symbols they have in common.

We will consider firstly the disjunctive version of the array comparison task of Bamber (1969). The *S* is presented with two arrays, such that $M = D$, or $D_1 = D_2$, and the number of common symbols varies from $C = 0$ to $C = D$. He is instructed to respond 'same' if there are any same symbols in corresponding positions, and 'different' if there are none. Thus, *same* is defined by the disjunction: (*Same* at P_1) *or* (*Same* at P_2), and so on, and includes disjunctions of conjunctions of same positions, such as ((*Same* at P_1) *and* (*Same* at P_2)).

It will be recalled that in Nickerson & Pew's experiment disjunctive comparison of arrays produced slower RTs than conjunctive comparison, and a tendency for 'different' RT to appear greater than the slowest of the 'same' RTs. An outcome of this kind was also obtained by Silverman & Goldberg (1975) in a study in which *S*s matched simultaneously displayed 4-digit arrays. The 'same' RT increased as C was reduced from $C = 4$ (all positions same) to $C = 1$ (only one same position), and this latter condition produced a large number of errors. 'Different' RT was substantially greater than 'same' RT for the $C = 1$ case. This pattern is also apparent in Taylor's (1976a) experiment in which array size was varied at $M = D = 1 \ldots . 4$.

For each value of D the 'same' RT increased as C became smaller, and RTs and error frequencies were highest when C = 1. The 'different' RT increased with D at about the same rate as the C = 1 'same' RT, and was about equivalent in general level.

These findings can be interpreted within the sampling and decision model in a manner similar to that proposed for array search and memory search. We assume that the two arrays are entered into the cells of the comparison register, and that the executive MATCH then initiates a routine for matching features of symbols occupying corresponding display locations. As before, the tests are supposed to occur sequentially at the level of features, but in parallel at the level of items. The time required for accumulation of match signals will increase as the number of different symbols increases, that is as C becomes smaller, and D – C becomes larger. Avoidance of error on such trials requires that the 'different' threshold should be adjusted to each new value of D, being set at a level which is generally sufficient for completion of a 'same' decision when C = 1.

In tasks of this kind, where correspondence of position is a critical aspect of the definition of equivalence, the MATCH executive must apply a disciplined feature matching routine. Any failures of discipline, resulting in comparison of features of symbols in non-corresponding locations, will delay the accumulation of 'same' evidence due to occupation of the channel by spurious mismatch signals. If the likelihood of this occurring increased as D became larger we might expect to see a small effect of D on the 'same' RT (Taylor 1976a).

It is also possible that feature matching may focus on the locations containing same symbols. An extreme of this kind of selectivity might involve matching of the arrays serially, position by position, in a left-to-right fashion. An example of such serial processing has been described by Bamber, Herder & Tidd (1975) in a study of nominal identity comparisons of letter arrays which differed or contained a single NI match. 'Same' RT increased as a regular function of left–right position, having a slope of 211 msecs per location. The RT to indicate that the arrays were 'different' was related to D by a slope of over 300 msecs, which was about twice as steep as the slope for 'same' RTs. These results provide a classic illustration of the operation of a serial self-terminating process. It is worth noting that such results are only obtained when processing rates are slow enough for the eyes to fixate each display item individually, and are clearly strategically distinct from most of the situations discussed in this chapter. They demonstrate selectivity in INSPECTION rather than in COMPARISON.

Relaxation of the requirement that same symbols occupy corresponding locations will increase the complexity of the feature matching routine. This point can be illustrated by reference back to Nickerson & Pew's (1973) study. If the *S* must respond positively to arrays containing one or more common letters but without regard to position, feature match evidence must be obtained from both corresponding and non-corresponding locations. This could be achieved if MATCH successively tried out various routines, perhaps testing corresponding locations first, and non-corresponding locations somewhat later. In the Nickerson & Pew study, reversal of position added 40 msecs to 'same' RT when there were two same letters, and 73 msecs when there was only one same letter (see Table VII.3.1). It could be that outcomes of tests on corresponding locations are monitored by MATCH, and that a switch to tests on non-corresponding locations occurs if a count of match signals remains below a critical level after a brief delay.

This kind of switching from one sampling routine to another is also likely to be involved in tasks in which M and D vary independently, and a positive response is required if the two sets contain one or more common items. An experiment reported by Nickerson (1966) illustrates the procedure. *S*s were presented with two successive arrays, such that M = 1, 2 or 4, and D = 1, 2 or 4. On positive trials one or more items were common to the two lists. It was found that both 'same' and 'different' RTs were affected by the values of M and D, so that RT was approximately related to the product, $M \times D$. 'Different' RTs were consistently greater than 'same' RTs, and appeared to show greater effects of M and D. An increase in C, the number of items common to the two lists, reduced the level of the 'same' RT. The most frequent errors were positive responses to display sets having only one item in common.

Briggs and his colleagues carried out extensive studies of the situation where M and D vary independently, and positive trials are limited to the case where C = 1. These experiments mostly employed a fixed set procedure and consistent assignment of individual symbols to the positive or negative response. The RT was plotted in relation to H_c, the information theoretic transformation of M. It was shown that the slope value, B, of this function, increased as the display size, D, became larger (Briggs & Swanson, 1970). Subsequently, Briggs & Johnsen (1972) argued that display size might also be represented by an uncertainty measure, referred to as H_d. They then pointed out that B could be expressed as a linear function of H_d, such that: $B = C + E(H_d)$ msecs. By substitution of this expression in place of B, the equation relating RT to M and D can be written as: $RT = A + C(H_c) + E(H_c \times H_d)$ msecs. A is the intercept parameter representing the operations of ENCODING and response RETRIEVAL and EXPRESSION. E is the time constant of a process of uncertainty reduction occurring during COMPARISON. This is related to the product $M \times D$, and thus to the size of the set of disjunctive possibilities which could support a 'same' response. C is related to the size of the memory set, and could correspond to the REPRESENTATIONAL process, and tranfer of symbol descriptions to the comparison register.

The experiments by Briggs, together with varied set studies reported by Nickerson (1966) and others, agree in showing that negative RTs are greater than positives, and more markedly affected by M and D. This was interpreted by Sternberg as evidence for self-termination of the display search process. Briggs, on the other hand, considered that exhaustive processing occurred on both positive and negative trials, but that an additional *rechecking operation* was often applied prior to acceptance of a 'different' decision. It appeared that the function relating 'different' RT to H_c was non-linear, and that this was chiefly due to disproportionate delays on trials where M and D were large (Briggs & Johnsen, 1972). Briggs proposed that 'different' RT might be related to M by the expression: $RT = A + B(H_c)^r$ msecs. This differs from the equation for 'same' RT only in the presence of the exponent, *r*, which was taken by Briggs to be an index of the degree of involvement of rechecking operations. It was shown that *r* increased as a linear function of H_d, the measure of display size.

Although terminologically distinct, the theory about COMPARISON formulated by Briggs has points in common with the sampling and decision theory advanced in this chapter. Both approaches see comparison under disjunctive instructions as a matter of testing for a range of alternative forms of equivalence, and both assume that 'different' decisions may be delayed relative to completion of these tests.

VII.7 CONCLUSIONS

The COMPARISON function has provided cognitive psychologists with an absorbing topic for study, and the consequence has been the emergence of an extensive if confusing experimental literature. Much of this treats of variants of Sternberg's memory search task, which has perhaps received a disproportionate amount of attention. In the hope of redressing this imbalance the present chapter has adopted a broader definition of COMPARISON as a mental function which enters into a variety of symbol processing tasks.

COMPARISON has been viewed as a processing stage which is subject to selective influence by a number of experimental factors, including memory set size, M, display size, D, the number of symbols common to two arrays, C, and the 'same' or 'different' decision taken at termination of the judgemental process. Other relevant factors, such as code congruity and similarity, have been given less detailed treatment in this chapter.

Of critical importance are the instructions by which array equivalence is defined for the *S*, especially the distinction between conjunctive and disjunctive criteria. When given a disjunctive criterion *S*s appear to test out alternative ways of demonstrating equivalence of the arrays, and delay a 'different' decision until sufficient time for these tests has passed. This account, formulated within the terms of the sampling and decision model, appeared reasonably descriptive of results from array search, memory search, and array comparison experiments.

The phenomenon of fast 'same' responses observed when *S*s make judgements of identity under conjunctive instructions posed problems for this, as for other models of COMPARISON. It was suggested that the 'same' decision may be delayed for long enough to allow for detection or localization of a discrepancy between the arrays presented for comparison. Thus, fast reactions to identity may be possible on account of an early responsiveness of the processing system to incongruity. Since fast 'different' responses are not observed in analogous experiments using disjunctive criteria we might conclude that there is no corresponding early responsiveness of the system to congruity. Against this, it did appear that a response to homogeneity facilitated 'same' decisions in display search experiments.

This chapter concludes the discussion of the Symbolic Memory system. The intention has been to explore some of the more fundamental properties of the Symbolic Memory, particularly the representational codes on which it is based, and the operations used to manipulate them. In Part Two a similar approach will be adopted with regard to the larger Lexical Memory system in which a person's vocabulary knowledge is stored.

PART TWO

The Lexical Memory

CHAPTER VIII

The Lexical Memory

DESCRIPTIVE AND PSYCHOLOGICAL ANALYSIS

VIII.1 INTRODUCTION

In Part One a conceptual and experimental analysis of the Symbolic Memory was undertaken. This system was postulated as the psychological basis of that limited area of competence which relates to a knowledge of the letters of the alphabet and the numerals. In Part Two this analysis will be extended to the *Lexical Memory*, which is defined here as a name for the competence exhibited by a literate individual in the more fundamental uses of written language.

This competence may be viewed as an understanding of the spelling system of English combined with a knowledge of English vocabulary and grammar. Its full characterization is a task for workers in the formal disciplines of linguistics and philosophy, and lies outside the scope of the present text. We would, nonetheless, argue that the essential competence of a reader of English is exemplified in his capacity (1) to assign appropriate pronunciation to English words and non-words of regular spelling, and (2) to judge words or sentences by semantic criteria.

In this chapter we shall concentrate initially on an analysis of properties of the spelling system of English, and will consider the implications of such an analysis for the construction of a model of the processing system underlying the Lexical Memory. A general proposal emerging from a number of recent linguistically oriented discussions (see, for example, Klima (1972), N. Chomsky (1970), Gleitman & Rozin (1977)) is that the English spelling system serves two major signalling functions. One of these, which will be called the *non-lexical* function, is the specification of pronunciations without regard for lexical identity, meaning or grammatical significance. The second function is *lexical* in character, and emphasizes morphemic aspects of written language.

These two aspects of spelling are very clearly distinguished in modern Japanese script. In Japanese there are two sets of phonetic symbols, known as the *Kanas* (the Hiragana and the Katakana) which may be used to represent the syllabic components of Japanese and foreign words. There is in addition an ideographic script, consisting of characters borrowed from the Chinese, called *Kanjis*, which specify words and concepts. Japanese children begin by learning to read in the phonetic scripts (which involve very regular grapheme-syllable correspondences), but replace the Kana versions of many content words (nouns, verbs, adjectives) by Kanji ideographs in the course of their schooling. This transition is sometimes helped by printing the Kana version above a newly introduced Kanji (called Furigana). Makita (1968) and Sakomoto & Makita (1974) have maintained that this spelling system minimises the incidence of reading disability in Japan.

VIII.2 GRAPHEME-PHONEME CORRESPONDENCES

The English spelling system corresponds to the non-lexical Japanese Kanas in that alphabetic symbols are used to represent speech sounds. However, the spelling-to-sound relation is formulated at the level of the *syllable* (consonant-vowel combination) in Japanese, but at the level of the *phoneme* in English, and it has been suggested that the requirement for phonemic segmentation of speech is one significant cause of difficulty in learning to read an alphabetic script (Gleitman & Rozin, 1977).

Gibson (1965) referred to the spelling-to-sound relations of English as *grapheme-phoneme correspondences*, and argued that a beginning reader succeeds in isolating the letters and letter groups which map in a reliable and consistent way onto the vocalic and consonantal elements of spoken English. The letter clusters isolated in this way were called *spelling patterns* (SPs). A grasp of the grapheme-phoneme correspondences is demonstrated by a reader's ability to pronounce nonsense words which have been constructed by juxtaposing consonant and vowel spelling patterns, e.g. DINK, GRISP, SPRILK, BLORDS, PRILTHS. These non-words are built around a basic consonant-vowel-consonant (C–V–C) pattern which is also characteristic of many regularly spelled English words (Fries, 1962). Gibson, Pick, Osser & Hammond (1962) noted that many of the consonant SPs are restricted to the initial or terminal position in C–V–C structures, and that the property of pronounceability is lost if these constraints are violated by reversing the positions occupied by the consonant SPs, e.g. NKID, SPIGR, LKISPR, DSORBL, LTHSIPR.

These comments suggest that non-lexical spelling regularity is dependent on constraints operating at the level of orthography (sequencing of symbols in writing). This regularity may be defined in a purely *statistical* fashion by tabulating the frequencies with which letters and letter groups occur in general or in specified positions in English words of a given length. If non-words are constructed which conform to these statistical regularities they appear pronounceable and word-like (Miller, Bruner & Postman, 1954; Mason, 1975). Alternatively, the regularity may be defined orthographically so as to emphasize the status of the vowel and consonant SPs as building blocks which may be assembled in many different combinations to specify the C–V–C, C–V and V–C forms which are possible in spoken English (cf Hansen & Rogers, 1968).

Letter sequences which conform to these statistical and orthographic constraints exemplify the notions of regularity or *legality* in English spelling. In general, regular letter sequences are pronounceable, although some pronounceable sequences may be classified as irregular in their orthography. For example, STODZ and PRAMF appear to be pronounceable non-words, but their terminal consonant SPs are not normally used in English spelling, and might be treated as illegalities on those grounds.

VIII.3 LEXICAL FUNCTIONS OF SPELLING

It is matter of frequent comment that English spelling includes many inconsistencies and seeming anomalies which appear to violate the rules of grapheme-phoneme correspondence. Some words are notoriously irregular in their spelling, such as ONE, LAUGH, TONGUE, BEAUTY, and others, like SWORD and ISLAND, include letters which are not pronounced. We can find cases of words of similar spelling but differing pronunciation, as in the pairs LEMON DEMON, COUCH TOUCH, ROUGH DOUGH, and many instances where changes in pronunciation are not reflected in orthography. Examples are SOW, LEAD and WIND, and the syntactic transformations involved in such pairs as: ANXIOUS ANXIETY, or COURAGE COURAGEOUS (see N. Chomsky (1970)).

These examples indicate that a knowledge of grapheme-phoneme correspondences is not in itself adequate for assignment of correct pronunciations to English words. It is too often necessary to determine the lexical identity or syntactic function of a word in order to know how to pronounce it. This conclusion stands as a major objection to the view that written language is a simple surrogate for spoken language, with SPs corresponding to sounds rather as the dots and dashes of the morse code correspond to the letters of the alphabet. What is implied is that the reader has a knowledge of the lexical identities of the words in his vocabulary, and that it is this knowledge, combined with an understanding of syntactic function, which enables him to pronounce them correctly.

If we follow this argument, which is in line with recent discussions of the relationship between orthography and phonology by Noam Chomsky (Chomsky & Halle, 1968; N. Chomsky, 1970), we are led to the conclusion that recognition of visual words involves consideration of semantics and syntax. Chomsky has suggested that the internal lexicon may represent words as abstract entities which are accessible to the alternative surface variants. NATION, NATIONAL and NATIONALITY might all contact a single lexical entry which corresponds to the essential morphemic unit (nation). This underlying form may be elaborated into its syntactic variants by application of transformational rules, which will automatically introduce the vowel alternation which distinguishes NATIONAL from NATION, or the stress alterations which distinguish TELEGRAPH, TELEGRAPHY and TELEGRAPHIC. Some empirical support for such proposals has been presented by Smith & Baker (1976), who found that considerations of syntactic function and morphemic structure were necessary to account for the pronunciations assigned to C–V–C–V–C non-words embedded in sentence contexts.

These ideas appear to offer a valuable clarification of the nature of the competence achieved in learning to read visual words. It seems that English orthography functions to point to the lexical entry for a word rather than to specify its pronunciation with precision. An implication is that the irregularities of spelling which must distress a grapheme-phoneme translation device may be tolerable and even desirable. It is perhaps more important to indicate that SIGN, SIGNAL and SIGNATURE, or BOMB, BOMBER and BOMBADIER, belong together than to point to the differences in their pronunciation. This has quite important consequences for the teaching of basic reading skills, which have been discussed by Carol Chomsky (1970). By the same arguments, the variations in the spellings of homonyms, such as WEEK and WEAK, SALE and SAIL, RAIN and REIGN, FILE and PHIAL, YOU, EWE and YEW, which are very common in English, may be seen as a device for facilitating access to different lexical entries.

A final point of importance is that Chomsky's interpretation of vocabulary knowledge presupposes a capability for decomposition of visual words into morphemes. Many words may be segmented into a stem or root morpheme, corresponding to the lexical entry in Chomsky's theory, and affixes which perform one of a number of syntactic functions, including negation, pluralization, tense marking, specification of syntactic class, and marking of comparatives and superlatives. Thus, the verb AGREE may be negated by the prefix DIS-, nominalized by the suffix -MENT, made into an adjective or adverb by the suffixes -ABLE and -ABLY, and changed in tense and person by the inflections -S, -ED, -ING. In other cases the word stem and other morphemes cannot be related to spatially distinct segments of the word, as for example the plurals MOUSE/MICE and MAN/MEN, the past forms GO/WENT and TAKE/TOOK, or the comparatives and superlatives GOOD/BETTER/BEST and BAD/WORSE/WORST. Nonetheless, it seems reasonable to assert that these words contain two morphemes, one corresponding to the lexical entry and the other to a syntactic function (Lyons, 1968). There are also many words which have primarily syntactic functions, such as negatives, quantifiers, articles, pronouns, prepositions, demonstratives, and auxiliary verbs.

These comments suggest that the competence of a literate person includes a knowledge of the ways in which visual words specify their lexical entries (stem or root morphemes) and their syntactic functions. It is difficult to avoid the conclusion that this knowledge depends on a detailed acquaintance with the individual characteristics of the words contained in the vocabulary store. If he is to appreciate that DIS- and UN- are prefixes in the words DISAGREE and UNJUST but not in the words DISPLAY and UNDULATE the *S* must presumably be familiar with the meanings of these particular lexical forms. He cannot decompose words into their constituent morphemes by application of a rule stating that DIS- and UN- are prefixes having a negative syntactic function.

VIII.4 TWO-CHANNEL MODEL OF READING

The arguments of the two preceding sections indicate that English spelling contains a phonetic element (the grapheme-phoneme correspondences) and a lexical and grammatical element (concerned with the signalling of lexical identity and syntactic function). This distinction between lexical and non-lexical aspects of spelling can acquire a significance in the psychological analysis of the Lexical Memory if it can be shown that the linguistic distinctions correspond to functional divisions in the processing system. Arguments supporting the existence of such divisions have recently emerged from neuropsychological investigations of cases of *acquired dyslexia*. These are instances of partial breakdown of competence in reading following brain injury or cerebral vascular accidents, and provide evidence of (1) the possibility of selective impairment of the non-lexical grapheme-phoneme translation function, and (2) an impairment in ability to read words of abstract meaning or primarily grammatical function.

Marshall & Newcombe (1973) reviewed a number of studies of acquired dyslexia and suggested a threefold classification into: (1) cases involving impairment of the graphemic processing system (visual dyslexia), (2) cases of impaired lexical processing of spelling, and (3) cases of impaired non-lexical processing of spelling. The first type is marked by the occurrence of errors of visual confusion. The other two types are characterized by errors which are suggestive of either: (1) grapheme-phoneme translation occurring without support of lexical information, or (2) lexical processing operating in the absence of effective grapheme-phoneme translation.

Problems of a primarily visual nature are indexed by the occurrence of visual confusions in the naming of letters (Thomsen & Harmsen, 1968), and in the reading of words (Simmel & Goldschmidt, 1953; Casey & Ettlinger, 1960). The errors may be localized at the beginnings or ends of the words (Warrington & Zangwill, 1957; Kinsbourne & Warrington 1962). Shallice & Warrington (1977) have also recently described what appears to be a disorder of the selective encoding operation. Two *S*s were studied, both of whom could name letters or words presented in isolation, but who had difficulty in naming letters embedded in words or arrays of other letters, and who often made errors of transposition when naming words flanked by other words. The effect did not occur when the target letter was surrounded by numbers. Marshall & Newcombe (1973) described two patients who produced visual errors in reading, such as: DUG→'bug', PEW→'knew', WAS→'wash'. Lexical variables, such as frequency of usage and part of speech, had little effect on performance of one of the *S*s, although the other showed some advantage of nouns over verbs, and words of higher frequency over words of lower frequency.

The second category of patient discussed by Marshall & Newcombe (1973) was characterized by errors in grapheme-phoneme translation, including confusions over phonemically ambiguous consonants, as in: INCENSE→'increase', GUEST→'just', PHASE→'face', LOGIC → 'lugus', REIGN → 'region'. These *S*s also made errors in vowel pronunciation and stress assignment. Their performance was affected by word frequency, and nouns were more easily read than other parts of speech. Errors of this kind would arise if the *S*s were attempting to apply a knowledge of grapheme-phoneme correspondences in the absence of a knowledge of the lexical identities and syntactic functions of the words they were reading. We can note that this interpretation implies that the lexical system for processing of spelling was impaired in these *S*s. Their reading was therefore dependent on the non-lexical grapheme-phoneme translation system. This system is liable to error whenever ambiguous grapheme-phoneme relations are encountered, and may produce neologisms (non-words) as output.

Marshall & Newcombe (1973) identified a third group of patients whose impairment appeared to involve a selective defect in the non-lexical grapheme-phoneme translation system. *S*s in this category cannot read regularly spelled non-words, make occasional semantic errors when reading English words, and show a selective loss of ability to read words which are abstract in meaning or which serve a primarily grammatical function. For example, Patterson & Marcel (1977) described two *S*s who were able to name only 8–10 of the letters of the alphabet and who failed almost entirely in their attempts to read non-words such as DUBE, PLOSH, FILK and WIDGE, although they could repeat these words in imitation of auditory input. Their errors were mostly omissions, or actual words, as in: DAKE → 'drake', SPRADE → 'spade', but never neologisms. A semantic component was evident in some of the error responses: RUD → 'naughty', GLEM → 'jewel'.

Errors in reading which bear a semantic relation to the stimulus word have been viewed as a defining characteristic of this form of dyslexia. Patterson & Marcel (1977), Shallice & Warrington (1975) and Marshall & Newcombe (1966) all reported instances of semantic errors, sometimes called *paralexic errors*, such as FACT → 'truth', AIR → 'fly', CANARY → 'parrot' co-existing with derivational errors, such as BAKER → 'bakery', semantic errors incorporating a visual component, such as DINE → 'wine', and errors of a purely visual nature, such as ORIGIN → 'organ', DEEP → 'deer'. Performance also typically showed a strong effect of frequency of usage, syntactic class, and the imageability of the referent of the stimulus word. The *S* studied by Marshall & Newcombe (1966) read 45 per cent of nouns correctly, 16 per cent of adjectives, and only 6 per cent of verbs. He was virtually unable to read function words, that is prepositions, adverbs, determiners, pronouns (other than 'I'), question markers, or conjunctions (other than 'and'). Shallice & Warrington's *S* demonstrated a similar effect, with 43 per cent of nouns correct, 32 per cent of adjectives, and 7 per cent of verbs, although he was slightly more successful in reading high frequency function words. Gardner & Zurif (1975) commented on a similar part of speech effect in a sample of dyslexic *S*s.

This noun facilitation effect is qualified by effects of *concreteness* and *imageability*. Gardner & Zurif found that the effect was limited to nouns having picturable and manipulable referents, that is to concrete nouns. However, there is dispute concerning the relationship between concreteness and imageability. These may be operationally defined in terms of instructions to *S*s which stress the possibility that the referent can be experienced by the senses or the capacity of the word to evoke a mental image (Paivio, Yuille & Madigan, 1968). Richardson (1975a, 1975b) has presented evidence to support the conclusion that imageability is the more important factor. This issue was also investigated by Shallice & Warrington (1975) and by Patterson & Marcel (1977), who each confirmed the importance of imageability, and suggested that this variable, though correlated with concreteness, provided the better prediction.

In summary, this brief consideration of neuropsychological studies of acquired dyslexia suggests that there are three principal ways in which the Lexical Memory of a literate person might suffer selective damage. A form of *visual dyslexia* arises if the system for graphemic encoding is impaired. This shows itself in errors of visual confusion and problems of spatial selectivity, although performance is not much affected by lexical variables, such as frequency of usage, syntactic class, and imageability. A second category, called *surface dyslexia* by Marshall & Newcombe (1973), arises when visual access to semantic/syntactic information is impaired, and word naming is achieved primarily through mediation of a grapheme-phoneme translation channel. The condition is marked by pronunciation errors and production of neologistic responses, and these have been taken here to be characteristic of a grapheme-phoneme translation system operating without support of lexical knowledge. The third category, called *deep dyslexia* by Marshall & Newcombe (1973), or *phonemic dyslexia* by Shallice and Warrington (1975), occurs when the grapheme-phoneme channel has been disabled. Reading is then achieved by visual access to an internal lexicon, and is affected by the lexical variables of frequency, grammatical function and imageability of referent. Errors tend to be visual or semantic, and neologistic responses are not observed.

The neuropsychological evidence therefore lends support to a *two-channel hypothesis* which states that competence in reading (i.e. in phonological interpretation of written words) normally involves contributions from distinct lexical and non-lexical processing channels. In the next section a schematic model of the Lexical Memory will be outlined which will suggest how the Symbolic Memory discussed in Part One might be extended to incorporate these ideas.

VIII.5 MODEL OF THE LEXICAL MEMORY

The linguistic and neuropsychological evidence discussed above converges on the conclusion that the Lexical Memory of a competent reader of English incorporates two neurologically distinct processing systems, which we will call: (1) the grapheme-phoneme translation channel, and (2) the lexical-semantic channel. Our assumption is that the grapheme-phoneme translation channel is *non-lexical* (in the sense that it applies the rules of grapheme-phoneme correspondence without regard for lexical identity or function) whereas the lexical-semantic channel is *morphemic* (i.e. is concerned with the recognition and interpretation of meaningful elements of written language).

This two-channel theory can be represented in the form of a diagram of the components of the Lexical Memory which is shown in Figure VIII.5.1. The lower part of the diagram incorporates the non-lexical (or pre-lexical) processing systems which are concerned with graphemic and phonemic registration, and translation back and forth between the graphemic and phonemic codes via the Symbolic Memory or grapheme-phoneme translation channel. The upper part shows the lexical and semantic systems which are required for the interpretation of written and spoken language and for the generation of meaningful and grammatically coherent speech.

Grapheme-phoneme translation channel

The pre-lexical part of the Lexical Memory consists of the Symbolic Memory discussed in Part One supported by the addition of a grapheme-phoneme translation channel. The graphemic and phonemic registers are short-term memories for spatial properties of graphemic arrays and temporal properties of phonemic sequences. The *symbolic interface* performs the function of letter-by-letter translation to a speech code which was described in Chapter VI. Non-lexical spelling knowledge is embodied in the *grapheme-phoneme interface* which contains pattern recognizers for the vowel and consonant

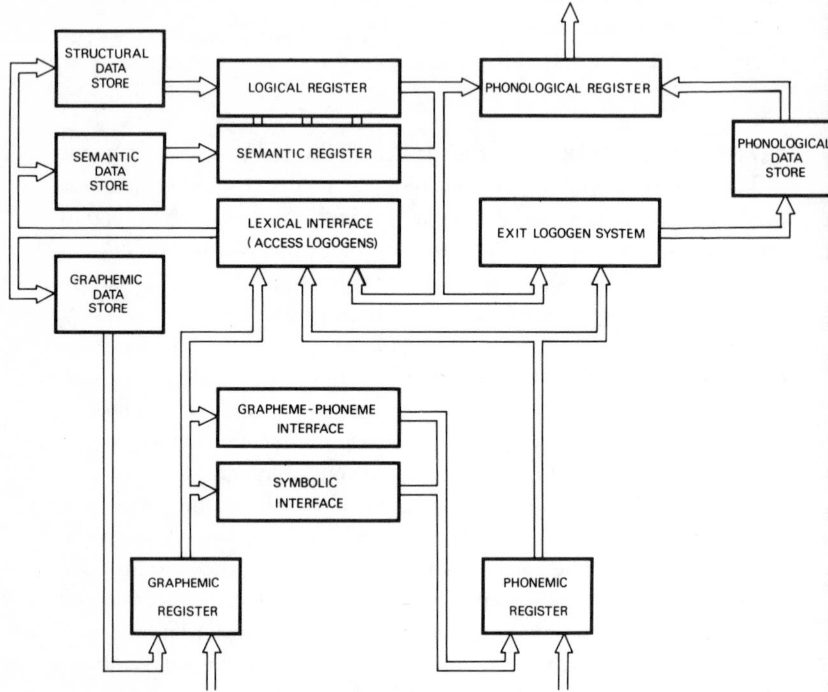

Figure VIII.5.1 Schematic representation of the Lexical Memory system. The lower part of the diagram shows the components mediating grapheme-phoneme translation (the 'symbolic interface' and the 'grapheme-phoneme interface'). The access logogen system ('lexical interface') contains recognizers for graphemic or phonemic representations of words, and may also be affected by semantic input. The system mediates RETRIEVAL of graphemic, semantic and logical codes, which may be copied from the permanent stores into the appropriate temporary storage registers. The exit logogen system accepts phonemic or semantic input, and mediates RETRIEVAL of phonological codes.

spelling patterns of English and facilities for retrieval of their phonemic equivalents from permanent storage.

The overall structure of the grapheme-phoneme translation channel is assumed to be essentially the same as that shown in Figure VI.1.1. The system operates under control of the TASK executive to transform spatially arrayed spelling patterns in the graphemic register into a temporally organized speech code in the phonemic register. It incorporates pattern recognizers for English SPs, and a facility for linking these to elements in a register of addresses of locations in a phonemic data store. Visual representations of the SPs are also retained in a permanent *graphemic data store*, and these may be accessed from the graphemic or phonemic registers during operations of (1) phoneme-grapheme translation, and (2) graphemic representation.

Lexical access systems

In Figure VIII.5.1 knowledge of the lexical and morphemic properties of English spelling is represented in the *lexical interface*. This is viewed as a *logogen system* in the sense of Morton (1968, 1969a) which contains pattern recognizers for the visual words in a reader's 'sight vocabulary'. We will refer to these recognizers as *access logogens*. We assume, following the work of Morton (1969a) and of Broadbent (1967) that the logogens can be represented as evidence accumulators with thresholds, and that they are recognizers for the morphemic elements of written and spoken English (Murrell & Morton, 1974).

Theoretical arguments to support the conclusion that the internal representation of a word may be thought of as an evidence accumulator with a threshold have been presented by Broadbent (1967) and Morton (1969a). These have centred on an analysis of accuracy of report data for visual words presented tachistoscopically or auditory words presented in masking noise. It is well established that performance in such experiments is influenced by frequency of usage, and that it may be modified by procedural variations, such as alterations in the size of the set of stimuli, presence of a linguistic context, and repetition of a word in the experimental setting. Morton and Broadbent have both argued that the frequency effect occurs because thresholds for high frequency words are set lower than thresholds for lower frequency words, and have seen ensemble size and repetition effects as depending on more temporary threshold adjustments. In Morton's account, context effects are attributed to priming

—that is, the addition of semantic input to information accumulating in a logogen.

The essential feature of the theories of Broadbent and Morton is that the probability of correctly reporting a degraded word is considered to depend on independent contributions of the incoming sensory signal and the internal threshold setting or bias of the logogen. By examining the proportions of high and low frequency words occurring as correct and incorrect reports in an auditory recognition experiment, Broadbent was able to conclude that high and low frequency words produced equivalent sensory effects, and that the difference in their recognizability was attributable to variations in internal bias. Morton (1969a) reached the same conclusion on the basis of a reanalysis of an auditory recognition experiment reported by Brown & Rubenstein (1961). In both cases the evidence favouring the threshold theory of word frequency effects depended on algebraic manipulation of expressions defining 'response strengths' of correct and incorrect responses in each of a number of frequency classes.

We will therefore assume that the lexical interface contains an array of logogens whose thresholds vary as a function of frequency of usage. Morton (1968, 1969a) suggested that the mechanism by which a knowledge of lexical frequencies was internalized might be one of threshold adjustment following activation of a logogen unit. He considered that the threshold might be shifted downward when a word was recognized, and that it would then return gradually to a level somewhat below its starting point. An experiment by Murrell & Morton (1974) showed that if *S*s learn a list of words and then participate in a tachistoscopic recognition test they are able to report list words at lower flash durations than other words of equivalent frequency. Also included in the tachistoscopic task were some words which were similar to list words. These were either alternative derivations from the same root morpheme, such as PAINS and PAINED, or structurally similar but morphemically distinct words, such as PAINS and PAINT. Tachistoscopic performance was facilitated by possession of a common root morpheme but not by structural similarity. We may take this as a demonstration that logogens are recognizers for word stems. Gibson & Guinet (1971) have provided additional evidence that inflections, such as ——S, ——ED or ——ING, may function as units in recognition tasks.

The lexical interface may be thought of as being internally differentiated to distinguish between visual and auditory inputs, and between stem morphemes and grammatical morphemes. The distinctions are intended to emphasize that words may be assigned a lexical identity on the basis of either phonemic or graphemic characteristics, and may retrieve semantic information about attributes of their referents while being interpreted with regard to their logical function in a sentence frame. It is likely that the visual/auditory distinction is represented at the level of the pattern recognizers, and that the morphemic distinctions are represented at the level of the addressing systems. Thus, it is assumed that the lexical interface is structurally similar to the grapheme-phoneme interface (i.e. possesses a structure of the kind shown in Figure VI.1.1.). The recognizers for spoken words may be referred to as *auditory access logogens*, and the recognizers for visual words as *visual access logogens*. Either set of recognizers may be linked (by a central switching system controlled by the TASK executive) to address registers specifying locations in permanent stores containing information about attributes and classification of objects (the semantic data store) or about the logical relationships which may be asserted by sentences (the structural data store). A temporary storage register, called the *semantic register*, is provided to hold the products of these semantic and syntactic retrieval operations. For convenience it is proposed that attributes of objects may be listed in the cells of the lower row of this register, and that logical structures may be specified in the upper row.

Lexical exit systems

The other major function of the Lexical Memory is to mediate access to phonological codes which may be used to control articulation in vocal expression. In the theory originally outlined by Morton (1968, 1969a) semantic retrieval and phonological retrieval were viewed as alternative functions of a single monolithic logogen system. He recognized that in practice there might be differences in ease of retrieval of semantic and phonological codes, and cited the paralexic errors of Marshall & Newcombe's (1966) patient as one relevant instance, and the phenomena of 'perceptual defence' and 'discrimination without awareness' as others (Neisser, 1967). In order to accommodate these discrepancies within the monolithic model he suggested that logogens might have two thresholds, with a lower one allowing semantic access and a higher one retrieval of a phonological code.

The position favoured here is that language interpretation (semantic RETRIEVAL) and language production (phonological

RETRIEVAL) are distinct functions of the Lexical Memory. For this reason the unitary logogen system of Morton has been divided into an *access* component and an *exit* component which is required for speech production. This has been labelled as the *exit logogen system* in Figure VIII.5.1. It is assumed that the exit logogens are recognizers for sets of attributes held in the semantic register which are linked to addresses of locations in a phonological data store containing articulatory descriptions of words. The system is also able to accept input of features from the phonemic register which may contain a representation of speech input or a code derived from visual input by grapheme-phoneme translation. Once retrieved, phonological codes may be placed in an output register for control of EXPRESSION in speech or writing. Syntactically motivated modifications of word order, inflection, stress assignment, and insertion of functors might occur at this stage. This requires provision for translation of logical structure in the semantic register to temporal structure in the phonological register, and for recognition of syntactic features in the exit logogen system.

It should be noted that Morton (1977a) has recently revised his position on this issue, and accepted the need for distinct access and exit logogen systems. Relevant evidence is contained in a report of an experiment by Winnick & Daniel (1970) which employed a priming design like that of Murrell & Morton (1974). In a preliminary phase of the experiment *S*s produced names as responses to visual words, pictures of objects, or definitions of objects. These names then occurred in a tachistoscopic recognition test along with control words which had not occurred in the first phase. An obvious prediction of a unitary logogen model is that all three types of priming should have facilitated performance in the recognition task. However, Winnick & Daniel obtained facilitation only for those words which had been visually displayed in the naming task. Morton obtained comparable results in replications and extensions of this experiment.

To summarize, the structural model of the Lexical Memory sketched in Figure VIII.5.1 incorporates two major routes which may be involved in the apparently simple skill of reading aloud visually displayed words. There is firstly the *grapheme-phoneme channel* by which regularly spelled letter arrays may be translated to a phonemic code. This can provide input to the exit logogen system and generate a word or neologism as speech output. There is secondly a *lexical-semantic channel* in which semantic attributes retrieved by input of graphemic features to the access logogen system occur as input to the exit logogens for retrieval of a phonological coding of a word. It is assumed that the two channels operate in conjunction with one another in normal readers, but that the effects of disabling one of them may be observed in cases of acquired dyslexia such as those described by Marshall & Newcombe (1973).

VIII.6 CONCLUSIONS

This chapter has discussed the manner in which the Symbolic Memory system might be expanded to take account of the knowledge a literate person possesses of the language he reads and writes. It was considered that the important additional requirements are for a grapheme-phoneme translation channel, embodying a knowledge of the spelling-to-sound regularities of written English, and a lexical interface through which words may address semantic and syntactic information. A schematic model of the Lexical Memory can be constructed by adding these components to the Symbolic Memory, together with an output system for semantic control over generation of speech.

The model of the Lexical Memory can now be used as a framework for discussion of experimental studies of lexical and semantic information processing. As previously, we assume that the input-output transformations required for lexical naming and comparison tasks depend on operations of ENCODING, REPRESENTATION, RETRIEVAL, COMPARISON and EXPRESSION, which may be vulnerable to selective influence by external factors. In addition to the factors already discussed, it is anticipated that language characteristics, such as letter frequency, orthographic structure, word frequency and semantic or syntactic relations between words will affect processing. Indeed, it will become evident that one of the main preoccupations in the experimental study of the Lexical Memory has been the investigation of the impact of orthographic and lexical knowledge on the different processing stages.

CHAPTER IX

Word Superiority Effects

LEXICAL INFLUENCES ON GRAPHEMIC REPRESENTATION AND COMPARISON

IX.1 INTRODUCTION

One proposal of the previous chapter was that the Lexical Memory shares with the Symbolic Memory a system for analysis and representation of graphemic properties of written language. This shared component includes the higher order executive, called INSPECTION in Chapter IV, and the temporary storage facilities (iconic register and graphemic register) which were taken to underlie the functions of graphemic ENCODING and REPRESENTATION. The additional components contributed by the Lexical Memory include the interface structure (access logogens) which mediates access to semantic and phonological codes, and the grapheme-phoneme translation system, which mediates access to phonemic representations of orthographically regular letter arrays.

The recoding of visual words in terms of speech and meaning will be examined in Chapters X and XI. This chapter will explore the more limited possibility that a literate individual's orthographic and lexical knowledge may have a facilitating influence on the operations of graphemic encoding or representation. A hypothesis of this kind is suggested by the classical studies of Cattell (1885), Pillsbury (1897) and others, who showed that letter arrays which form words are better reported than meaningless arrays in tachistoscopic recognition tasks. More recently it has been demonstrated that this superiority also occurs for regularly spelled non-words, whether regularity is defined in terms of orders of approximation to English (Miller, Bruner & Postman, 1954) or consistencies of English spelling (Gibson, Pick, Osser & Hammond, 1962). These phenomena are well-attested experimentally, and are variously referred to as 'familiarity effects' or 'word superiority effects'.

The interpretation of the word superiority effect has provoked much debate. The reason for this is probably that the tachistoscopic recognition task is not well-adapted to the problem of localizing the effect within a sequence of processing stages. Although the classical experiments leave open the possibility that linguistic knowledge facilitates the preliminary operations of graphemic encoding, they do not establish this point conclusively and do not exclude the possibility that the influence is located during subsequent storage or response retrieval processes. These inadequacies have led to the development of more refined experimental techniques, some of which will be considered in this chapter.

In discussing this topic we shall be looking for experimental evidence to support the proposal that linguistic knowledge has a beneficial influence on *graphemic* encoding and representational processes. We would describe an effect as being graphemic only if its locus could be shown to be the iconic register or the graphemic register (see Figure IV.5.1). A consequence of this restriction is a requirement that stored linguistic information which facilitates graphemic processing should itself be graphemic in character. For this reason the diagram of the Lexical Memory shown in Figure VIII.5.1 includes a *graphemic data store* in which visual descriptions of words in a person's vocabulary are held. We assume that graphemic representational processes could be facilitated if these codes were accessed (via the lexical interface) and used to improve the quality of a description being formed in the graphemic register (Seymour & Jack, 1978).

IX.2 DETECTION AND DISPLAY SEARCH

In the earlier discussion of graphemic encoding (Chapter IV) it was argued that arrays of symbols might be processed in a quasi-parallel fashion up to the point of entry into the iconic register but that the subsequent operations of selective transfer to the graphemic register might well be serial in nature. It appeared that characteristics of the icon formation sub-stage were observable through accuracy and RT measurements taken in forced-choice detection and display search tasks, certain of which yielded results in which performance was unrelated to D, the display size. By using tasks of this kind, therefore, while varying the orthographic regularity or lexical status of the materials, we can test for an effect of linguistic knowledge on the icon formation sub-stage of processing.

The *forced-choice detection* task will be considered first. In a typical experiment two target letters are identified for the *S*, who is instructed to make a forced choice indicating which of the two has occurred on each of a series of trials. The target letters are briefly displayed and masked and may appear in an array of other letters or flanked by non-alphabetic symbols. A test for the occurrence of a word superiority effect can be made by contrasting detection of letters embedded in words with detection of letters presented in isolation or embedded in non-words.

In representative experiments by Bjork & Estes (1973) and Estes, Bjork & Skaar (1974) the letters L and R were used as targets. The experiments incorporated an important control introduced by Reicher (1969). Materials were selected so that both target letters formed a word on word context trials whereas neither made a word on non-word context trials. If, for example, the display contained the letters PRAY, the correct choice would be a report that the letter R had occurred. However, the alternative possibility, L, would also make a word, namely PLAY. Similarly, the non-word YLAP would remain a non-word if the L were to be misperceived as R. The control has the effect of reducing the contribution of a bias in favour of word-forming choices to the accuracy of the *S*'s performance.

Under these conditions the rates of forced choice detection were found to be essentially equivalent for the word and non-word displays, although there was some advantage for single letters when the effectiveness of the masking stimulus was reduced. This result was confirmed by Massaro (1973) in a study in which *S*s discriminated among the letters G, C, R and P when embedded in the words ACE, AGE, ARE and APE, or in non-words formed by replacing the A-E frame by the consonants, V-H.

In a more extensive study, Estes (1975a) explored the effects of persistence of context after offset of the critical letters, and also of relaxation of the Reicher control. The target letters were again L and R, but the incorrect choice changed the lexical status of the four-letter array on some trials, while preserving it on others. For example, an incorrect choice would make a non-word of the word FARM and a word of the non-word PRAN. Estes confirmed that single letters were better detected than letters embedded in arrays of other letters, but again found no effect of linguistic context when Reicher's control was in force. When the control was relaxed, there was a rise in accuracy for cases where the incorrect choice made a non-word, and a decline in accuracy where the incorrect choice made a word. Thus, although accuracy can be influenced by a bias in favour of word-forming choices, it appears that there are no observable influences of linguistic knowledge on detection performance when this tendency is properly taken into account.

The second experimental situation to be considered is the *array search task* in which a single target is identified for the *S* who must make a positive response if it is present in an array of symbols and a negative response if it is not. It will be recalled that this task sometimes produces data in which RT is unrelated to D (Estes, 1972; Egeth, Jonides & Wall, 1972; Jonides & Gleitman, 1972; Egeth, Atkinson, Gilmore & Marcus, 1973), but that this effect is very much dependent on the confusability of the target and background items. When *S*s search for a target letter in arrays of other letters it is typically found that RT increases as a linear function of D having a slope of 10–30 msecs per item (Atkinson, Holmgren & Juola, 1969; Taylor, 1976c). This was taken to imply that array search often involves COMPARISON processes operating subsequent to the icon formation sub-stage. A possible implication is that the display search task taps a slightly deeper level of ENCODING than the detection task of Estes (1975a), and may be correspondingly more likely to show linguistic effects.

James & Smith (1970) described an experiment in which *S*s searched for a verbally designated target in words of 4 or 6 letters. RT was faster for vowel probes than for consonant probes, was slower for 6-letter than for 4-letter words, and tended to increase across serial positions of the target and then to fall at the extreme righthand position. In a second experiment targets were searched for in words or non-words created by scrambling their letters. There was no word/non-word difference in RT, and the vowel/consonant difference did not occur with the non-words. Thus, this study suggests that there is an effect of D in this lexical version of the array search task, but no facilitation attributable to orthographic regularity. Confirmation is provided in a study reported by Sloboda (1976) in which *S*s verified whether or not target letters matched a single letter or the lefthand letter of 4-letter words or non-words. RT was faster for single letters than for letters in words or non-words, but there was no effect attributable to orthographic regularity. This outcome is qualitatively similar to Estes' findings for letter detection, and suggests the reality of an early level of processing at which decisions about individual letters are taken more readily for letters in isolation than for letters in arrays, and at which the orthographic regularity of an array (or its lexical status) has no facilitating effect.

Mason (1975) reported a series of experiments which reveal the emergence of effects of orthographic regularity in letter search tasks. For these experiments she defined orthographic regularity in terms of *spatial frequency redundancy*. This is a measure of the degree to which the letters making up an array occur in the positions which they commonly occupy in words of the same length. She used 6-letter words and non-words as displays, the latter being constructed so as to maximize or minimize spatial frequency redundancy. For example, the letters of the word THEORY may be rearranged to produce the non-words HORTEY and YTERHO. The sum of the positional frequency scores, as given in the normative tables of Mayzner & Tresselt (1965), is maximized in HORTEY but minimized in YTERHO. Her *S*s were American 6th Grade children, classified as good or poor readers on the basis of a standardized reading test. Their task was to determine the presence or absence of target letters in displays of these three types. For negative trials, poor readers showed no effect of spatial frequency redundancy, whereas good readers showed a 117 msec advantage for words and non-words of high redundancy relative to non-words of low redundancy. However, these effects did not occur on trials when the target was present, and were not replicated for negative trials in a second experiment. This latter experiment did nonetheless indicate that good readers responded positively to targets occurring in low frequency positions faster for redundant than for non-redundant arrays. A further study demonstrated that good readers also responded faster to target letters occurring in their probable locations than to targets occurring in less probable locations.

In subsequent experiments, Mason & Katz (1976) utilized non-alphabetic symbols and varied redundancy experimentally. In a control condition, each symbol occurred equally often in each position of a series of 6-symbol arrays. A *distributional redundancy* condition was created by allowing some symbols to occur more often than others, though equally frequently in the six positions of the arrays. In a *spatial redundancy* condition symbols occurred with equal frequency, but with restriction on the positions in which they could occur. RT to respond to the presence of a target symbol was facilitated by redundancy of both types, and this effect combined additively with a serial position effect, RT being faster at the centre than at the ends of the arrays. The experiment was repeated with children classified as good and poor readers and replicated the findings of Mason (1975). Good readers showed facilitation of RT due to spatial redundancy of the arrays, but this effect did not occur for poor readers.

These experiments establish that RT in array search tasks is sensitive to variations in orthographic regularity, although the effect may be demonstrable only in highly skilled readers. Possession of lexical status appears to make no additional contribution, since Mason obtained quite similar RTs for words and regular non-words (Mason, 1975). We conclude that good readers are attuned to statistical properties of written language, and have internalized a model of positional frequencies which assists the formation of a spatially structured graphemic description of a symbol array.

IX.3 PROBED RECOGNITION

The converse of the display search tasks discussed in the preceding section is the memory search task in which a symbol array is followed by a probe stimulus. This procedure has already been described in relation to partial report tachistoscopic tasks (Sperling, 1960), and the symbol classification task of Sternberg (1975). Partial report tasks were taken to reflect the operation of selective encoding by which symbol description may be transferred from the iconic to the graphemic register. Symbol classification provides an index of the operation of COMPARISON of a probe symbol against a memorized array. For purposes of the present discussion we will assume that an array of simultaneously presented symbols is held in the graphemic register prior to this comparison. Hence, variation of orthographic regularity or lexical status within the framework of these tasks will allow us to test for linguistic effects on the processes of forming and maintaining the graphemic code.

Mewhort (1967) described an adaptation of Sperling's experiment in which pairs of non-words were presented followed by an auditory signal indicating which should be reported. The non-words were taken from the list used by Miller, Bruner & Postman (1954), and varied in their orders of approximation to English. Performance was more accurate for regular than for irregular arrays, thus replicating the classic word superiority effect, but was also influenced by the regularity of the row which was not reported. If we make the assumption that both rows were represented in the iconic register, and that the cued row was then selectively transferred to the graphemic register, a plausible conclusion is that orthographic regularity influenced the selective process.

A majority of the experiments to be discussed in this section have tested accuracy of response to probes of a single position in a briefly presented symbol array. The probe may consist of a pair of letters, the *S* being required to make a forced choice as to which occurred in a designated display position (Reicher, 1969; Wheeler, 1970), or can be an instruction to report the identity of the letter occurring in a particular position (Estes, 1975a). Facilitating effects of orthographic regularity have almost always been obtained in this experimental paradigm (Krueger, 1975). These findings stand in contrast to those reported in the detection experiments in showing a superiority for probed recognition of letters in words over letters in irregular non-words or single letters presented in isolation.

In Reicher's (1969) experiment displays containing words, irregular non-words or single letters were tachistoscopically exposed and then masked. The display was followed by a pair of probe letters. For example, WORD, OWRD or D might be followed by:

D
– – –
K

The *S* was instructed to indicate which probe had occurred. Incorrect choices always formed words on word trials, and non-words on non-word trials. Reicher found that accuracy was consistently greater for letters in words than for letters in non-words or letters in isolation.

Wheeler (1970) also contrasted letters in words with letters in isolation, and introduced some procedural modifications, such as variation in delay of the probe and in the absolute and relative position of the critical letter. His words were selected so that two-choice alternatives could be found for each of four positions while preserving lexical status. For example, READ can be tested by R/H at position 1, E/O at position 2, A/N at position 3, and D/L at position 4. Despite these refinements, a 10 per cent advantage for letters in words over letters in isolation was obtained.

This superiority of letters in words has appeared a surprising and somewhat counter-intuitive phenomenon. As already mentioned, single letters yield higher accuracy than letters in words in detection tasks (Massaro, 1973; Estes, 1975a), and also produce faster display search RTs (Johnson, 1975; Sloboda, 1976). Subsequent research suggests that the effect may arise because word displays are typically encoded to a deeper or more durable level of representation. Mezrich (1973) showed that the effect could be reversed by instructing *S*s to vocalize the display during the interval before onset of the response alternatives, and Johnston & McClelland (1973) demonstrated a critical dependency on disruption of the display by pattern masking. When a blank white mask was used the advantage for letters in words disappeared. An implication is that single letters are more vulnerable to masking than words, and that this reduces the likelihood that a graphemic (or phonemic) code will be formed.

Estes (1975a, 1975b) has provided a careful analysis which seems consistent with this view. In an experiment he presented arrays of four symbols for 50 msecs between offset and reappearance of a masking array of dollar signs. The arrays were words or single letters flanked by non-alphabetic symbols, and the *S* was instructed to report the identity of the symbol which had occupied the position marked by an arrow. The frequency of correct reports was higher by 10 per cent or more for letters in words than for single letters. The effect occurred overall, and for a subset of words in which the letters L or R could occur in the probed position without destroying lexical identity. Estes reported an analysis of error responses which showed that, although intrusion errors were about equally frequent for the two types of display, errors of *omission* were more frequent for single letters than for letters in words. This difference in the frequency of omissions was largely responsible for the word superiority effect.

From these results we might conclude that processing of a masked letter often stops at the iconic level, but that letter arrays undergo further processing, through selective encoding and phonemic RETRIEVAL, which leaves a durable trace in the graphemic or phonemic registers. As a test for a visual representational mode Thompson & Massaro (1973) varied the similarity of the probes in a forced choice task. For example, the first position in REAL might be tested by the confusable letters, R and P, or by the non-confusable letters, R and M. If the code consulted in discriminating the probes was primarily visual we would expect to observe a deleterious effect of confusability. However, Thompson & Massaro found no such effect for either letter or word stimuli. Hawkins, Reicher, Rogers & Peterson (1976) used homonyms as alternatives on word trials to test for involvement of phonemic codes. Single letter displays were probed by pairs of letters, and word displays by pairs of words, *S*s being required to make a forced choice. For one group, the word alternatives were predominantly homonyms, such as SENT, CENT. These *S*s showed a word superiority effect, implying that the effect is not critically dependent on formation of a phonemic code. On the other hand, performance of a second group of *S*s, who were presented with homonym alternatives only rarely, did deteriorate on homonym trials. A reasonable conclusion may be that the superiority of words over letters depends on formation of a graphemic code which is often supported by a retrieved phonemic code. It is true that we would expect a graphemic representation to be vulnerable to visual confusability, However, such an effect might not be observable if alternative phonemic and semantic codes were retrieved, and this possibility was not adequately controlled against in the Thompson & Massaro study.

Reicher (1969) also demonstrated that letters embedded in words yielded better performance than letters embedded in irregular non-words. This effect was shown by Aderman & Smith (1971) to extend to a comparison between orthographically regular and irregular non-words, and was confirmed in the position probe experiments of Estes (1975a, 1975b), who found a 6 per cent difference in accuracy between words and irregular non-words. The analysis of errors indicated that the effect was mainly attributable to a difference in frequencies of errors of *transposition*. *S*s were more likely to report a letter which occurred on the display, though not in the cued position, for non-words than for words. This effect was observed in general, and in the subset of displays which controlled for tendencies to produce word-forming guesses. Additional experimental conditions demonstrated that word forming biases were evident when the control was relaxed and the context was displayed after masking of the critical symbol.

Estes' experiment suggests that graphemic descriptions of orthographically regular arrays may differ from those of irregular arrays in having a more stable structure for labelling of the relative spatial locations of graphemes. This is in line with the conclusions of Mason (1975) in emphasizing the contribution of an internalized knowledge of positional frequencies of letters to construction of a graphemic code. The precise nature of this contribution is unclear, but one possibility is that activation of recognizers for word stems and spelling patterns in the lexical and grapheme–phoneme interface structures gives access to a graphemic data store in which visual descriptions of letter sequences are held. This would in effect mean that the graphemic code for a word or regular non-word would include a contribution from permanent storage which would be absent for irregular non-words. One implication of this view is that a reduction in the graphemic regularity of an array, achieved for example by alternating the cases of its letters, should lessen the advantage of orthographically regular arrays. McClelland (1976) has reported a diminution of the word superiority effect due to case alternation, and Coltheart & Freeman (1974) found that case alternation impaired word identification.

Further evidence that the word superiority effect is not dependent on formation of a phonemic code was presented by Baron & Thurston (1973). Their *S*s saw a brief exposure of a word or irregular non-word followed by a forced choice probe. The word alternatives were sometimes homophones (for example, BALL probed by BALL/BAWL), and sometimes non-homophones (BALD probed by BALD and BAWD). There was no deleterious effect of homophony of the alternatives on forced choice performance. Baron & Thurston also contrasted actual words and orthographically regular non-words, and concluded that lexical status made no additional contribution to the word superiority effect. It should be mentioned that this last conclusion of Baron & Thurston's was questioned by Manelis (1974). He pointed out that many of the words used by Baron & Thurston were of low frequency, or were inflected. In a follow-up study he obtained forced choice recognition data for regular non-words and high frequency four-letter words. Some of his *S*s showed effects of lexical status, particularly when the probes used were letter pairs rather than word pairs.

In summary, these experiments on probed recognition provide strong evidence for the occurrence of a word superiority effect at the level of the graphemic register. We have supposed that the advantage for letters in words over letters in isolation arises because words are more effective in gaining access to the register when ENCODING processes are disrupted by masking. The advantage due to orthographic regularity may reflect a difference in the quality of positional coding in graphemic descriptions of random letter arrays and arrays which correspond to lexical entries or English spelling patterns.

IX.4 GRAPHEMIC COMPARISONS

Another situation which has appeared relevant to the study of graphemic representational processes is the 'same'–'different' matching task introduced by Posner & Mitchell (1967). Evidence from symbol matching experiments discussed in Chapters V and VII suggested that physical identity comparisons of letters involve operations on a graphemic code. If linguistic knowledge influences the quality of this code, it follows that word superiority effects should be observable in array matching tasks in which words and non-words are used as stimuli.

Eichelman (1970b) reported an experiment of this kind. He measured 'same' and 'different' RTs for matching of simultaneously presented arrays made up of two words or two orthographically irregular non-words. As has already been pointed out (Chapter VII) performance on this task is affected by the display size, D, and by C, the number of letters common to 'different' arrays. Eichelman confirmed the effect of D, but noted that it interacted strongly with familiarity. The 'same' RT increased at a rate of 60 msecs per letter for the irregular arrays, but at a rate of only 21 msecs per letter for the word displays. 'Different' RT was affected by D and C, and words were classified faster than non-words when both D and C were large.

Subsequent research suggests that these comparisons are genuinely graphemic, and that the word superiority effects are not critically dependent on speech recoding of the arrays. For example, Baron (1975) reported that 'different' RT was no greater for homophonic pairs, such as FORE/FOUR, than for non-homophonic pairs, such as SORE/SOUR. Kleiman (1975) used a variant of the task in which *S*s were required to respond 'same' if two words contained the same letters after the first letter. 'Same' RTs were equivalent for rhyming pairs, such as BLAME/FLAME, and for non-rhyming pairs, such as LEMON/DEMON.

Other experimenters have attempted to determine the relative contributions to the word superiority effect of lexical status and orthographic regularity. Baron (1975) found no difference between regularly spelled non-words and actual words and concluded that lexical status made no contribution beyond that of orthographic regularity. On the other hand, lexical status can produce an effect in the absence of orthographic regularity, since Henderson (1974), Henderson & Chard (1976) and Seymour & Jack (1978) have all shown that orthographically irregular but meaningful abbreviations, such as GPO, IBM, or BBC, are matched faster than control stimuli produced by rearrangement of their letters. Chambers & Forster (1975) contrasted words of high and low frequency of usage with regular and irregular non-words. Unlike Baron, they reported that words were matched faster than non-words, and that high frequency words were matched faster than low frequency words. It seems to be established, therefore, that both lexical status and orthographic regularity facilitate graphemic comparison processes.

A further factor which has been investigated is the visual familiarity of the displays. One approach has been to disrupt the normal configuration by inverting or rotating the displays, or by insertion of spaces between letters. Manipulations of this kind appear to increase the general level of the RT but not to alter the magnitude of the word superiority effect (Schindler, Well & Pollatsek, 1974; Well, Pollatsek & Schindler, 1975). Mixing of upper and lower case letters, on the other hand, has been shown to increase the RT and to reduce the size of the word superiority effect (Pollatsek, Well & Schindler, 1975).

A demonstration that visual familiarity makes a significant contribution to lexically based word superiority effects has been given by Henderson & Chard (1976). They noted that abbreviations like GPO and BBC are normally written in upper case letters and appear unfamiliar when written in lower case, as gpo or bbc. The word superiority effect associated with such stimuli disappeared when they were printed in the unfamiliar case. This finding has been confirmed by Seymour & Jack (1978) for abbreviations classified as normally occurring in upper case. However, the converse of the effect did not occur for abbreviations thought to be familiar in lower case—etc, cwt and lbw, for example.

In order to determine the locus of the familiarity effect we can treat familiarity as a factor and test to see whether it combines additively or interactively with other factors known to influence the ENCODING, COMPARISON or response RETRIEVAL stages. An effect on ENCODING is contra-indicated since familiarity has been found to combine additively with variations in stimulus quality (Henderson & Chard, 1976). An influence on response RETRIEVAL is also unlikely since familiarity adds with effects due to instructions which reverse the normal mapping of 'same' and 'different' decisions onto 'Yes' and 'No' reports (Seymour & Jack, 1978). There is, on the other hand, consistent evidence in the experiments on this topic of interactions of familiarity with factors influencing the COMPARISON stage.

It was argued in Chapter VII that COMPARISON is a complex process involving routines for matching of graphemic (or other) features and for the accumulation of match and mismatch signals by 'same' and 'different' judgemental counters. The overall duration of the stage was thought to be influenced by the factors of array size (D and M), the number of symbols common to the two arrays (C), and, under some circumstances, the array positions of matching or discrepant symbols. In addition, the judgemental aspect of the process is indexed by the 'same' or 'different' outcome of the comparison.

Interactions of familiarity with D, the display size, were reported for 'same' decisions by Eichelman (1970b), Chambers & Forster (1975) and Henderson (1974). In the case of 'different' responses, familiarity interacted with C, the number of common symbols, in the experiments of Eichelman (1970b), Barron & Pittenger (1974), and Chambers & Forster (1975). When 'different' arrays match at all but one position, so that $C = D - 1$, the 'different' RT increases as the single discrepant location is moved from left to right across the array. This effect is also found to interact with familiarity (Chambers & Forster, 1975; Well, Pollatsek & Schindler, 1975; Henderson & Henderson, 1975). Thus, if we accept the earlier conclusion that D, C and location of difference are factors influencing COMPARISON, the logic of the additive factor method will lead to the conclusion that this stage of processing is also considerably influenced by the familiarity of the letter strings and thus, by implication, by the subject's knowledge of written language.

An influence of familiarity on the judgemental phase of COMPARISON is suggested by interactions of familiarity with effects due to decision outcome ('same' versus 'different' decisions). These interactions have taken three main forms. Sometimes familiarity effects occur for both 'same' and 'different' responses, but are larger for 'same' responses. This pattern was found in the studies of Eichelman (1970b), Henderson (1974), and also in the experiments of Schindler, Well & Pollatsek (1974), Well, Pollatsek & Schindler (1975) and Pollatsek, Well & Schindler (1975). In other cases a familiarity effect is obtained for 'same' responses but not for 'different' responses. An outcome of this kind occurred in the experiment by Barron & Pittenger (1974), in the first of the experiments of Chambers & Forster (1975), in some of the experiments of Egeth & Blecker (1971), and for a practised *S* in the study by Henderson (1974). A third type of interaction is sometimes reported, in which familiarity is shown to facilitate 'same' responses while inhibiting 'different' responses. Interactions of this kind were described by Baron (1975), Besner & Jackson (1975), Henderson & Chard (1976), Hershenson (1972) and Seymour & Jack (1978).

This third type of interaction is of particular interest, since it suggests that the coding of the 'same' or 'different' decision formulation may contribute to the familiarity effect. In Besner & Jackson's (1975) study *S*s made physical identity judgements about pairs of words or pairs of irregular non-words. 'Same' RTs showed a typical word superiority effect, but 'different' RT was greater for word than for non-word displays. In Hershenson's (1972) study regular non-words were contrasted with irregular non-words. Orthographic regularity facilitated 'same' RTs, but inhibited 'different' RTs. Seymour & Jack's (1978) experiment involved nominal identity matching of familiar three-letter abbreviations. 'Same' RTs were faster for the abbreviations than for their controls, whereas 'different' RTs were slower for meaningful pairs, such as FBI/BBC, than for the controls, IFB/CBB.

These experiments indicate that lexical status and orthographic regularity are both sufficient for production of a reversed meaningfulness effect on 'different' RTs. The studies all used a procedure in which meaningful and meaningless displays were randomly intermixed, and it seems probable that the interaction is most likely to be observed under these conditions. Seymour & Jack's data also demonstrate a dependence of the interaction on the graphemic regularity of the display, since they found that the effect disappeared when the abbreviations were printed in lower case, as, for example, fbi/bbc.

IX.5 INTERPRETATION OF WORD SUPERIORITY EFFECTS

This chapter has presented evidence that word superiority effects occur in tasks involving display search (Mason, 1975), probed recognition (Reicher, 1969), partial report (Estes, 1975a), and graphemic comparison (Eichelman, 1970b; Chambers & Forster, 1975). We have argued that these experiments demonstrate an influence of a literate person's knowledge of characteristics of written language on the selective phase of graphemic encoding and on the representation and comparison of graphemic codes.

The effects observed in the display search experiments appeared to be attributable to the skilled reader's knowledge of positional frequencies of letters (Mason, 1975). It is not entirely clear how this type of statistical information might be utilized during graphemic processing. However, one possibility is that specification of word length and target identity are sufficient to indicate the high probability display locations, and that this information is taken into account by the INSPECTION executive in its control over the spatially selective phase of ENCODING. A mechanism of this kind could underlie the effects obtained by Mason (1975), and the speeded search for vowels noted by James & Smith (1970).

Results for the probed recognition experiments of Reicher (1969) and Baron & Thurston (1973), and the related partial report experiments of Estes (1975a), seemed most readily interpretable in terms of variations in the quality of spatial coding in the graphemic register. It has been assumed that the register contains graphemic feature descriptions and a higher-order structure for labelling of relative spatial location. The code constructed following brief exposure of a random letter array may be labile and partial in both these respects. A superior description can be formed for a word or regular non-word because the developing graphemic code activates recognizers in the grapheme–phoneme and lexical interface systems. We proposed that this allows access to a graphemic data store in which visual models of spelling patterns and morphemic elements are retained. The contribution from permanent memory adds to stability and fullness in the graphemic code, and retrieval of additional phonemic and semantic codes may assist the representational functions involved in maintenance of the code. Once activated, this system provides a durable basis for responses to forced-choice or partial report probes.

The analysis of the graphemic comparison task suggested that familiarity exerted a selective influence on a COMPARISON stage of processing. In seeking to interpret this influence we can reconsider the sampling and decision model of COMPARISON which was outlined in Chapter VII. It will be recalled that the model assumed that COMPARISON involved a spatially disciplined feature matching process and the accumulation of match/mismatch evidence by 'same' and 'different' counters. Word superiority effects could result from an influence of familiarity on either (1) the *rate* of accumulation of match and mismatch signals, or (2) the *threshold* settings of the 'same' and 'different' counters.

A number of explanations based on variations in the rate of evidence accumulation can be distinguished. One possibility is that semantic and phonemic comparisons co-occur with graphemic comparisons during the matching of meaningful displays. These could provide additional match/mismatch evidence, but this would not affect the rate of accumulation if input to the judgemental stage flowed along a single channel. One could assume the existence of different judgemental devices for the graphemic, phonemic and semantic registers. A familiarity effect might occur if the devices raced against one another, and if the semantic or phonemic comparisons sometimes finished sooner than the graphemic comparison. However, RTs for semantic or phonemic decisions about visual words are substantially greater than RTs for graphemic decisions (Cohen, 1968; Kleiman, 1975), so that it is unlikely that semantic or phonemic codes could be retrieved and set up for comparison rapidly enough to modify an ongoing graphemic comparison. Further, experiments which have reduced the diagnostic value of phonemic or semantic codes, by using homophones or different case versions of the same word as 'different' stimuli (Baron, 1975; Besner & Jackson, 1975), have not shown a diminution of familiarity effects on 'same' RTs.

A more plausible explanation states that enhanced stability of spatial coding facilitates the accumulation of feature match evidence. COMPARISON of symbol arrays under conjunctive instructions involves a feature matching routine which tests for equivalence of components of symbol descriptions occupying corresponding locations in the coded representations of the two arrays. We assumed that this kind of disciplined control over evidence sampling was achieved by the MATCH executive, and that it involved enabling and disabling of links between cells of the comparison register. It is reasonable to argue that the discipline of this sampling process will be best maintained when the spatial labelling of the graphemic codes is stable and detailed, and that it will tend to break down as the quality of the labelling deteriorates. Any failures of discipline will result in matching of features of symbols occupying non-corresponding locations. A main consequence of this should be an increase in the proportion of mismatch signals sampled from 'same' arrays, and this would tend to slow the rate of accumulation of match signals. The converse effect could occur for 'different' displays, provided that they shared some same letters.

This account has the advantage of proposing basically similar explanations for the word superiority effects obtained in the probed recognition and graphemic comparison tasks. It is also consistent with certain of the interactions of familiarity with 'same' and 'different' decisions which have been obtained. If 'different' displays differ at all or a majority of positions occasional lapses of sampling discipline will not reduce the rate of accumulation of feature mismatch signals, although there will be an effect on the rate of accumulation of feature match signals. Thus, one might expect to find larger familiarity effects for 'same' than for 'different' decisions, or an effect on 'same' RT but no effect on 'different' RT, and these two outcomes are evident in many of the studies discussed.

Where the account fails is in the interpretation of experiments showing inhibitory effects of familiarity on the 'different' RT. To accommodate these effects it is necessary to consider the second point at which MATCH intervenes in the comparison process, that is by adjustments to the levels of the 'same' and 'different' thresholds. It was argued in Chapter VII that MATCH may adjust the thresholds in order to take immediate account of display characteristics, or longer term account of task instructions or procedural variations.

The standard and reversed effects of meaningfulness could arise if the occurrence of a familiar display triggered a *reciprocal adjustment* of the 'same' and 'different' thresholds. This reciprocal adjustment principle has previously been discussed in relation to semantic comparison processes (see Schaeffer & Wallace [1970] and Seymour [1975]), and will be considered more fully in Chapter XII. The argument might be that displays presented for matching are assigned a positive (meaningful) or negative (meaningless) coding as a by-product of processing through the lexical or grapheme-phoneme interface systems, and that this code, which can be viewed as a value on a bi-polar dimension of evaluative meaning (see Osgood, Suci & Tannenbaum [1957]), is then placed in the semantic register. If MATCH consulted the register from time to time in order to obtain instructions relating to overall task strategy, the positive or negative codes might occasionally be misread as instructions to effect a reciprocal threshold adjustment. It is assumed that a positive evaluative code triggers a reduction in the 'same' threshold and a rise in the 'different' threshold, and that a negative code has the opposite effect.

However, it must be accepted that there is a dearth of converging evidence which might be cited as support for the occurrence of task-irrelevant threshold adjustments of this type. Seymour & Jack (1978) consequently suggested that the reversed effect of meaningfulness on the 'different' RT might be interpreted as a *semantic conflict* resulting from simultaneous coding of the display with respect to its meaningfulness and its sameness or difference. It was proposed in Chapter VII that the output from the COMPARISON stage consisted of an abstract affirmative or negative code representing the concepts (same) or (different). This code is entered into the semantic register (see Figure VIII.5.1) and subsequently controls the production of a 'Yes' or 'No' response. This can be viewed as an operation of phonological retrieval (see Chapter X) involving the input of semantic features to the exit logogen system. If an abstract coding of meaningfulness was present in the semantic register at the same time as the representation of sameness/difference, and if the values of the two codes differed, one being positive and the other negative, it would be necessary to delay entry to the phonological retrieval stage for long enough to discriminate the irrelevant code from the relevant one. This would result in delays of reaction to meaningless 'same' displays and to meaningful 'different' displays, thus producing the familiarity × decision interaction which occurred in Seymour & Jack's (1978) experiment.

To summarize, the argument of this section has been that the word superiority effects found in graphemic comparison tasks reflect an impact of familiarity on both the feature matching and the judgemental aspects of COMPARISON. The effect occurs because visually familiar stimuli, possessing lexical status or orthographic regularity, access representations in the permanent data stores. Critical importance attaches to the graphemic descriptions of spelling patterns and lexical entries, which contribute to the spatial structure of the graphemic code, and to affirmative evaluative codes which trigger reciprocal adjustments in the 'same' and 'different' thresholds or produce conflict at the stage of response RETRIEVAL. Both of these influences operate in favour of a facilitating effect of familiarity on 'same' decisions. The threshold adjustment principle and the semantic conflict hypothesis argue for a negative effect of meaningfulness on 'different' decisions, and the spatial coding principle argues for a reduction or elimination of the effect. Taken in conjunction, therefore, the two types of influence could well give rise to the full range of familiarity × response interactions which have been observed.

IX.6 CONCLUSIONS

The study of word superiority effects has been central to much of the classic and more recent research into psychological processes underlying reading skill. The contribution of this research has been a demonstration of the changes in the functioning of certain of the processes of the Symbolic Memory which occur as a consequence of addition to the system of the superstructure of the Lexical Memory. In this chapter we have concentrated on the graphemic ENCODING and REPRESENTATIONAL functions. Our main conclusion has been that a reader of English differs from a person who merely knows the alphabet in possession of an accessible store of graphemic information which can be used to modify the selectivity of ENCODING and to add to the stability and durability of the graphemic code. The content of this graphemic data store includes generalized information about positional frequencies of letters as well as structural representations of spelling patterns and morphemes.

We concentrated on experiments on probed recognition and

graphemic comparison because these tasks appeared to be valid procedures for externalization of characteristics of the graphemic register. There is nothing in the tasks which demands that the *S* make use of the resources of his Lexical Memory in taking his decisions. Nonetheless, the occurrence of the various types of word superiority effect establishes that incidental consultation of the lexical superstructure does occur. We interpret this within the framework of the schematic model of Figure VIII.5.1 as being a consequence of the adjacency of the graphemic register and the pattern recognition systems in the lexical and grapheme-phoneme interfaces. These recognizers become active when feature descriptions enter the graphemic register, and RETRIEVAL of stored graphemic, phonemic and semantic codes then occurs. We have argued that word superiority effects depend primarily on graphemic retrieval, but that semantic codes exert some influence on the judgemental aspects of COMPARISON.

CHAPTER X

Recoding to Speech

GRAPHEME-PHONEME TRANSLATION AND PHONOLOGICAL RETRIEVAL

X.1 INTRODUCTION

The essential behavioural demonstration of basic literacy is the ability to pronounce visual words correctly. Part of the argument of Chapter VIII was that this seemingly commonplace achievement is based on a complex and sophisticated Lexical Memory system. We proposed that pronunciation of words might involve concurrent activity in two distinct processing channels, called the grapheme-phoneme translation channel, and the lexical-semantic channel. These have been represented in Figure VIII.5.1 as interface structures which mediate transformations of the graphemic code to a phonemic code or to a semantic code. For speech production to occur, one or both of these sets of retrieved features must be passed to the exit logogen system, which mediates phonological RETRIEVAL. This chapter will concentrate on grapheme-phoneme translation and phonological retrieval, leaving the more detailed discussion of lexical access and semantic retrieval for the two chapters which follow.

The topic of pronunciation of words is closely linked to the issues concerning word superiority effects which were discussed in Chapter IX. A random array of letters (Zero Order Approximation to English) will fail to activate a morpheme recognizer in the lexical interface, or recognizers for vowel and consonant spelling patterns in the grapheme-phoneme interface. Pronunciation cannot be mediated by either of these channels, therefore, unless vowel or consonant symbols are added or deleted in a way which increases the meaningfulness or pronounceability of the array. Naming is most likely to proceed through the interface structure of the Symbolic Memory, using the spatially controlled left-to-right strategy discussed in Chapter VI. If the letters do not form a word, but nonetheless conform to the orthographic regularities of written English, they will again activate no recognizer in the lexical interface, although recognition and retrieval of phonemic codes can occur in the grapheme-phoneme translation channel. Words, on the other hand, will activate morpheme recognizers, and the semantic attributes retrieved can be used to generate speech output through the exit logogen system. If the spelling of the word is regular, processing may also occur in the grapheme-phoneme channel, providing an additional source of evidence for input to the exit logogen system. However, words of irregular spelling will create problems for the grapheme-phoneme channel, which may fail to translate them or may assign an incorrect phonemic description.

These comments suggest that we can study the functioning of the grapheme-phoneme translation channel by restricting our stimulus materials to non-words of varying degrees of orthographic regularity. Three types of experimental task have proved useful for this purpose. There is, firstly, the tachistoscopic task which has already been discussed, using either whole report procedures, as in the classic studies of Miller, Bruner & Postman (1954) and Gibson, Pick, Osser & Hammond (1962), or variants of the probed recognition method of Reicher (Aderman & Smith, 1971; Spoehr & Smith, 1975). Secondly, there is the lexical decision task in which word and non-word stimuli are presented, and the *S* makes a positive response to words and a negative response to non-words. Finally, there is a naming task in which RT to vocalize non-words can be related to structural features, such as length or component spelling patterns (Frederiksen & Kroll, 1976). The additional contribútion of the lexical-semantic channel can be assessed by contrasting these data with comparable findings for word stimuli.

X.2 TACHISTOSCOPIC EXPERIMENTS

The original experiments by Gibson, Pick, Osser & Hammond (1962) demonstrated superior performance, in whole report and probed recognition, for non-words of regular spelling, such as SPRILK and BLORDS. This superiority was achieved relative to control words formed by interchanging the initial and terminal consonant spelling patterns (SPs), to make LKISPR and DSORBL. Hence, one might reasonably conclude that the effect of orthographic regularity is not due merely to the presence of SPs in the array, but to their occurrence in their appropriate positions.

It seems therefore that the interface of the grapheme-phoneme translation channel functions as a device for *parsing* of letter arrays.

By this we mean that it may be programmed to search for and to identify initial and terminal consonant SPs, and medial vowel SPs, and to relate their spatial ordering in the graphemic register to a temporal ordering in the phonemic register. This might require some selectivity in the sampling of information from the graphemic register, and perhaps internal differentiation of the interface into sets of recognizers for SPs occurring in each of the positions of a C–V–C or other type of pronounceable frame. On analogy with the interface of the Symbolic Memory the SP recognizers might be expected to vary in accessibility in a manner reflecting their frequencies of occurrence in written language (Venezky, 1962).

Despite these implications the interpretation of the contribution of the grapheme-phoneme translation channel to word superiority effects remains a matter for dispute. The position canvassed in the last chapter was that SPs contact stored graphemic representations which contribute to the clarity and stability of the graphemic code. An alternative and equally reasonable proposal is that the presence of correctly positioned SPs facilitates the transformation of the letter array to a phonemic code. The first of these accounts emphasizes the graphemic regularity of the array, whereas the second emphasizes its pronounceability.

Experiments by Mewhort and his colleagues have suggested that orthographic regularity, as varied in Orders of Appproximation to English, facilitates a left-to-right selective operation of transfer of information from the iconic register to short-term memory (the graphemic and phonemic registers). This is implied by the effects of regularity of the non-cued row on accuracy of partial report (Mewhort, 1967), by differential effects of delay of masking on report of high and low order approximations (Mewhort, Merikle & Bryden, 1969), and by demonstrations that the effects depend on a left-to-right ordering of letters, irrespective of the order of the overt report (Mewhort & Cornett, 1972). Such findings can be taken as evidence for effects occurring during formation of the graphemic code, including activation of recognizers for visual aspects of SPs in the grapheme-phoneme interface.

Regular arrays may also differ from irregular arrays at the stage at which locations in the phonemic data store are addressed and entries are placed in the phonemic register. It is this process that is likely to show an influence of the pronounceability of the letter sequence. One proposal has been that pronounceable arrays may be chunked with respect to their component SPs, whereas irregular arrays must be named letter-by-letter. If phonemic RETRIEVAL is a serial process, and if the graphemic coding of a tachistoscopic display is often labile and limited in duration, letter-by-letter processing might reasonably be expected to yield a less adequate phonemic description than SP processing. This could occur both because of the greater number of retrieval operations required in letter naming, and because the procedure might be taken up only when attempts at identification of SPs had failed.

Aderman & Smith (1971) argued that letter-by-letter and SP processing were alternative retrieval strategies, subject to executive control, and open to manipulation by influences on the *S*s expectancies regarding the type of letter array he would see. In an experiment *S*s were tested on accuracy of forced choice recognition of non-words. The first fourteen trials were used to develop expectancies, *S*s being presented with a blocked sequence of regular or irregular displays. This expectancy was confirmed on the fifteenth trial, where proportions of correct choices averaged 78 per cent for regular displays as against 56 per cent for irregular displays. On the sixteenth trial the expectancies were disconfirmed, a regular array being presented to *S*s expecting irregular arrays, and an irregular array to *S*s expecting SPs. Probabilities of correct choice were 60 per cent for the unexpected SPs, and 64 per cent for the unexpected irregular letters. This result was taken by Smith as a demonstration that the superiority of regular arrays is dependent on the *S* adopting an SP processing strategy.

The more usual experimental situation involves mixed list presentation of regular and irregular non-words (Gibson, Pick, Osser & Hammond, 1962). Under these conditions the *S* may attempt to apply the SP processing strategy to all letter arrays. Irregularity might then be expected to disrupt performance in at least two ways. Firstly, irregular arrays are likely to contain juxtaposed consonants which are not SPs and which may not be pronounceable. Secondly, the letter sequence may lack appropriately placed vowel elements, or *vocalic centres* (Hansen & Rogers, 1968; Spoehr & Smith, 1973). This will disrupt the process of forming a phonemic description of the letter array, since pronunciation is basically a matter of creating syllabic units, or vocalic centre groups (VCGs), in which a vowel sound is flanked by consonantal structures of varying complexity.

Spoehr & Smith (1975) sought to determine the relative importance of appropriately positioned consonant SPs and a vocalic centre for processing of letter arrays through grapheme-phoneme translation. Their materials consisted of non-words containing regular SPs and a vocalic centre, such as BLOST, regular consonant SPs without a vocalic centre, such as BLST, or irregular consonant groups without a vocalic centre, such as LSTB. Proportions of correct forced choice responses were 78 per cent for regular SPs with a vocalic centre, 70 per cent for SPs without a vocalic centre, and 66 per cent for the irregular arrays. These results suggest that presence of regular SPs and of a vocalic centre both contribute to the word superiority effect, although the vocalic centre is possibly the more important element.

Spoehr & Smith argued that their findings could be accommodated within a two-stage model of the grapheme-phoneme translation stage. A first sub-stage, referred to as *unitization*, imposes a VCG structure upon the letter array. This is an operation on the graphemic code, and may be said to correspond to the pattern recognition phase of RETRIEVAL in the present account. The second, called *translation*, breaks the VCG units down into a sequence of phoneme descriptions which may be used to control production of speech. This may be equated with the second sub-stage of RETRIEVAL, involving the addressing of locations in the phonemic data store, and the formation of a description in the phonemic register.

The valuable suggestion made by Spoehr & Smith is that irregularities of graphemic structure increase the load imposed on grapheme-phoneme translation by requiring the insertion of vocalic elements between illegally juxtaposed consonants. Insertions of this kind are required both where the vocalic centre has been omitted, and where non-permissible initial or terminal consonant clusters occur. For example, the non-word BLST can be rendered pronounceable by inserting a vocalic element, ə, into the illegal consonant sequence to produce BLəST. For a letter sequence like LSTB it would be necessary to modify the illegal LS and TB transitions, giving LəSTəB or əLSTəB. The number of such insertions can be predicted, and can be related to accuracy of performance, although, as Spoehr & Smith showed in a subsidiary experiment, an empirical check on vowel insertion behaviour may be useful.

In summary, Spoehr & Smith have argued that grapheme-phoneme translation involves a parsing process in which graphemic representations of vowel and consonant SPs are isolated, and used to address the phonemic data store. The outcome is the formation of a phonemic description of a syllabic structure in the phonemic register. Irregularity, defined in terms of omission of vocalic elements, affects the process of formation of the phonemic description, chiefly by requiring the insertion of vowels at points which assist construction of a phonologically sensible interpretation of the array. Accuracy declines as the number of such insertions increases, and may also depend on the number of distinct VCG units which must be translated (Spoehr & Smith, 1973).

X.3 LEXICAL DECISIONS

A second experimental situation which has proved valuable in the study of word recognition processes is the *lexical decision task*. The *S* is shown a series of letter arrays, and is instructed to make a positive response to those which form words in his vocabulary, and a negative response to those which do not. Positive RTs to word stimuli provide information about the operation of lexical access, and will be discussed more fully in the next chapter. Here we will be concerned with a consideration of the information about grapheme-phoneme translation which can be obtained from a study of lexical decision RTs.

In lexical decision experiments negative RTs to non-words typically show reversed word superiority effects. Orthographically regular, pronounceable arrays are classified as non-words less rapidly than irregular arrays (Stanners & Forbach, 1973). Further, speed of rejection of irregular non-words is often faster than the RT for positive classification of some words, whereas negative RTs to regular non-words are generally as great or greater than the slowest RTs to real words (Rubenstein, Garfield & Millikan, 1970; Frederiksen & Kroll, 1976; Coltheart, Davelaar, Jonasson & Besner, 1977). Results of this kind suggest that negative decisions about non-words may be delayed until adequate tests for lexical status have been carried out, but that early detection of orthographic illegalities can be a signal to by-pass this process and to make a rapid negative response.

The grapheme-phoneme translation channel provides a mechanism which could be used in the assessment of the orthographic regularity of words and non-words. We will suppose that in lexical decision the graphemic coding of the array is referred simultaneously to the lexical interface and to the grapheme-phoneme interface. The basis for a positive decision could be the accumulation, past a threshold value, of semantic attributes indicative of meaningfulness retrieved as a consequence of activation of an access logogen unit. Following Coltheart, Davelaar, Jonasson & Besner (1977) we will assume that negative decisions are taken by default, that is by waiting until a deadline, which has been set at a value greater than the delay involved in a slow positive decision, has passed. This judgemental structure might be left unchanged whenever concurrent processing in the grapheme-phoneme channel provided evidence of the graphemic regularity and pronounceability of the array. However, violations of these regularities might be detectable by the TASK executive and accepted as an instruction to lower the deadline for a negative decision. This suggestion is somewhat similar to the proposals regarding effects of meaningfulness on RT for graphemic comparisons made in the last chapter.

Given certain assumptions, this theory predicts that negative RT to non-words should decrease as the violations of orthographic regularity become more flagrant or more numerous. The study by Stanners & Forbach (1973) contains data relevant to such a hypothesis. They conducted a lexical decision experiment in which the non-words were five-letter sequences, composed entirely of consonants or of two pairs of consonants flanking a medial vowel. Removal of the vowel reduced the negative RT by 162 msecs. This result is in agreement with Spoehr & Smith's conclusions regarding the importance of vocalic centres, and is consistent with the view that facilitation of the negative RT depends on activities in the grapheme-phoneme translation channel. Stanners & Forbach used consonant SPs as the initial and terminal letter pairs of their non-words, but varied the normative frequency of occurrence of the SPs on the basis of tables provided by Venezky (1962). Inclusion of high frequency SPs delayed the RT by 60 msecs for arrays containing a medial consonant, and by more than 200 msecs for arrays containing a vowel. The direction of this effect was reversed for positive decisions about words, where high frequency SPs facilitated the RT.

Although it is difficult to specify the precise mechanism underlying such effects, we will take them as evidence for a responsiveness in the judgemental component of lexical decision to the degree of penetration of the grapheme-phoneme translation system achieved by a letter array. Rubenstein has argued that this is a matter both of graphemic regularity and of pronounceability. In a study by Rubenstein, Lewis & Rubenstein (1971a) regular non-words, such as STRIG, BARP and PLIND were contrasted with non-words with orthographic irregularity in the final consonant cluster. The consonants were letter pairs which never occur in the final position in written English, and Rubenstein found that their presence facilitated the negative RT by 100 msecs or so. He also suggested that these graphemic irregularities varied in pronounceability, suggesting that non-words like GROVT and CRESF contained illegal clusters which could nonetheless be synthesized by the human vocal system, whereas non-words such as CREPW and SAGM were pronounceable only by separation of the terminal consonants. The pronounceable non-words were classified about 15 msecs less rapidly than the unpronounceable, and Rubenstein treated this result as evidence for phonemic processing in lexical decisions.

Rubenstein's study may be criticized on various counts, including the intuitive assessment of pronounceability, an inadequate matching of the word samples, and a vulnerability to Clark's (1973a) strictures concerning treatment of linguistic distinctions as 'fixed effects' in the analysis of variance. In a subsequent study, reported by Rubenstein, Richter & Kay (1975), graphemically irregular consonant clusters were rated for pronounceability, and clusters of high and low pronounceability were attached to a common word base. For example, the real word, BLAST, provided a base from which the non-words BLASF and BLASV could be formed. *S*s in the rating study agreed on the graphemic irregularity of terminal SF and SV, but thought the former more pronounceable than the latter. Rubenstein again obtained evidence that pronounceability slightly delayed the negative RT. This finding, together with the supporting discussion, emphasizes the force of the logical distinction between the pattern recognition and retrieval phases of grapheme-phoneme translation. Such non-words as TRIUMF, GRABZ and ORDR contain graphemically illegal terminal consonants, but could nonetheless by synthesized acceptably at the stage of construction of a phonemic code or speech output.

Rubenstein has argued that phonemic recoding occurs as an integral part of the word recognition process, and indeed that a primary route for accessing the internal lexicon is through the speech code. In terms of the diagram in Figure VIII.5.1 this view denies the existence of a visual pattern recognition system in the lexical interface and assumes that visual words can only be recognized by undergoing grapheme-phoneme translation and by then influencing recognizers for phonemic characteristics of words (Gough, 1972; Rubenstein, Lewis & Rubenstein, 1971a). As support for this hypothesis, Rubenstein commented that non-words which are homophones of actual words, such as BOTE, BRANE, MUNK and LAIM, are rejected less rapidly than regular non-words whose pronunciation is not identical to that of any English word. This result was also obtained by Coltheart, Davelaar, Jonasson & Besner (1977), who used non-words which were homophones of English homophones, such as GRONE and PORZE, and contrasted these with non-homophonic controls obtained by altering a single letter, as in BRONE and PORCE.

This effect of homophony suggests that phonemic recoding may occur during processing of non-words, and that the resultant phonemic description may activate a word recognizer in the auditory access logogen system. However, there is no strong implication that phonemic recoding is the only route to the internal lexicon. An effect of homophony could be obtained if concurrent grapheme-phoneme processing modified the setting of the deadline for a negative decision in an upward direction by providing evidence of the orthographic regularity and meaningfulness of a non-word. We prefer to assume, therefore, that the lexicon may be accessed from the graphemic register or from the phonemic register via visual and auditory pattern recognition systems, and that the visual route is primary in lexical decisions. This two-channel account is in agreement with evidence discussed in Chapter VIII, and is implicit in Figure VIII.5.1.

If grapheme-phoneme translation is used to evaluate the regularity of incoming stimuli, it follows that both word and non-word stimuli will be processed in this channel even though the main evidence for the meaningfulness of a word may be derived from the process of visual lexical access. An experiment reported by Meyer, Schvaneveldt & Ruddy (1974a) may be cited as being consistent with this expectation. Meyer studied a version of the lexical decision task in which two letter arrays were presented simultaneously, the *S* being instructed to respond positively if both were words, and negatively if one or both were non-words. His intention was to determine whether graphemic and phonemic similarity of the letter arrays would facilitate lexical decisions. Thus, one might ask whether a both-words decision would be made faster for similar pairs, such as BRIBE/TRIBE or FENCE/HENCE, than for their controls, BRIBE/HENCE and FENCE/TRIBE. The same question can be posed for negative decisions about non-word pairs, such as DEACE/MEACE. In practice, Meyer found no effects attributable to graphemic-phonemic similarity on either positive or negative RTs. This was also true of a version of the experiment in which the letter arrays were presented successively, the *S*s being instructed to react to each word as it appeared. However, there was a significant delay of positive RT when the words were graphemically similar but different in pronunciation. Examples are such pairs as COUCH/TOUCH and LEMON/DEMON. The RT for these phonemically dissimilar pairs was greater by 87 msecs than the RT for their controls in the simultaneous presentation experiment, and by 34 msecs in the successive presentation experiment.

This effect of heterophony provides a particularly clear demonstration of the involvement of the grapheme-phoneme translation channel in lexical decisions. If the decision was based entirely on a consideration of graphemic properties the effect would not occur, since the discrepancy in pronunciation would not be represented. We can see that this is so in Kleiman's (1975) study, in which judgements that two words contained the same letters after the first letter were no slower for non-rhyming pairs, such as COUCH/TOUCH, than for rhyming pairs, such as BLAME/FLAME. Thus, discrepancy in pronunciation is important for lexical decisions but not for graphemic comparisons, implying that translation to a phonemic code occurs in the former but not the latter task situation.

The mechanism underlying Meyer's effect is difficult to specify. He suggested that grapheme-phoneme translation may assign rhyming phonemic descriptions to graphemically similar words, thus arriving at an inappropriate description for one of them. For example, if FREAK has been recoded as /fri:k/, and if BREAK is then encountered, it may be represented as /bri:k/. However, the pronunciation of FREAK is regular in terms of English grapheme-phoneme correspondences, whereas that of BREAK is not. Hence, a lexically innocent grapheme-phoneme translation system would tend to mispronounce BREAK whether or not a regular form, such as FREAK, had been processed immediately before. Presence of an inappropriate description in the phonemic register might affect lexical decision RT in one of two ways. Firstly, the description/bri:k/would fail to activate the auditory recognizer for the word 'break', thus depriving the judgemental mechanism of the additional evidence of meaningfulness which might have been available following successful lexical access through the auditory channel. Secondly, the graphemic-semantic recording necessary for the positive lexical decision might lead to incidental activation of units in the exit logogen system. If the phonological code for correct pronunciation of the word retrieved through this system was compared with the phonemic description passed from the grapheme-phoneme translation channel a discrepancy in pronunciation would be detected. It is possible that a mismatch in outputs from the grapheme-phoneme and lexical-semantic channels is coded as a negative event and is disruptive of the judgemental or response phases of lexical decision.

X.4 VOCALIZATION LATENCIES

A study of the whole process of transforming a visual word into a speech output can be undertaken by obtaining RTs for vocal naming responses to words. According to the diagrammatic model in Figure VIII.5.1 naming of a word involves a process of phonological RETRIEVAL in addition to the grapheme-phoneme translation operation already discussed. The naming of a non-word depends on grapheme-phoneme translation followed by input of phonemic features to the exit logogen system. Thus, it is assumed that the exit logogen system may generate any phonotactically acceptable output, including neologisms which have no lexical status. In the naming of a word, phonological RETRIEVAL involves the input of semantic features to the exit logogen system, although this process is supported by input of phonemic features deriving from the grapheme-phoneme translation channel.

A number of predictions can be derived from this two-channel account of word naming. Firstly, the naming of actual words should be faster than the naming of non-words of equivalent structure, because of the addition of the lexical-semantic component in word naming. Secondly, the naming of words should be affected by lexical variables, such as frequency of usage, on account of the involvement of the lexical-semantic channel. Thirdly, irregularity of spelling should delay word naming because of the reduction in relevant phonemic input to the exit logogens.

A study by Frederiksen & Kroll (1976) provides a useful starting point for an evaluation of these predictions. These authors obtained vocal RT data for naming of words and non-words of one or two syllables and 4–6 letters in length. The same materials were also used in a lexical decision experiment. Non-words were derived from actual words by alteration of a single vowel. Thus, CLOAR was derived from CLEAR, PORSON from PERSON, and so on. The word stimuli varied in frequency of usage as defined by the Thorndike–Lorge (1944) count. It was therefore possible to classify the non-words in terms of the frequencies of occurrence of their base words. However, although there was a strong effect of frequency on word naming RT, this did not extend to the non-words. This implies that frequency is not systematically related to orthographic variations which might influence grapheme-phoneme translation, a conclusion already argued by Morton (1969a) but not universally accepted (Landauer & Streeter, 1973).

The vocal RT for naming non-words was affected by D, the display size, and increased at approximately 28 msecs per letter for one- and two-syllable non-words. There was no effect of number of syllables. This is contrary to the findings of Spoehr & Smith (1973), who reported a syllable effect in probed recognition. Spoehr & Smith did, of course, use actual words as stimuli. However, Frederiksen & Kroll's data for words also failed to show any consistent effect of syllabic complexity. This must raise some question about Smith's proposal that grapheme-phoneme translation is influenced by the number of VCG units which must be parsed and translated. The data are more suggestive of a process which operates sequentially on letters or letter groups in construction of a phonemic code.

Frederiksen & Kroll also analysed their results to reveal effects due to complexity of the consonant SPs and the form of the vowel SPs contained in their non-word stimuli. Vocal RT was affected by the size of the initial consonant SP, but not by the size of the terminal cluster. Four-letter non-words with a two-consonant initial SP were named 50 msecs less rapidly than non-words with a single initial consonant. For six-letter non-words a three-letter initial SP delayed the RT by 154 msecs relative to words with a single consonant. It seems, therefore, that the start of articulation is delayed until the initial consonant SP has been translated. Some effects were obtained due to complexity of the vowel SP, which were interpreted in terms of an influence of the vocalic centre on pronunciation of the initial consonants (Liberman, Cooper, Shankweiler & Studdert-Kennedy, 1967).

These findings for naming of non-words may be contrasted with RTs for negative responses to the same stimuli in a lexical decision experiment. A first point to note is that naming RTs are substantially faster than lexical decision RTs, averaging 565 msecs as against 705 msecs. Secondly, lexical decision RT was not influenced by array length, although, as already noted, this was found to be an important variable in naming. This might be thought paradoxical in view of the proposal that non-words may be processed through the grapheme-phoneme translation system in lexical decision tasks. However, the argument of the previous section was that this processing serves to reduce the level of the negative RT when orthographic irregularities are detected. Regular non-words will produce no such effect, and the deadline for the negative response will remain at a level sufficient to allows positive identification of words of low frequency.

A further contrast can be made between naming RTs for non-words and naming RTs for real words of equivalent structure. Frederiksen & Kroll reported that word naming RT was consistently faster than non-word naming RT, but showed an approximately equivalent effect of array length, amounting to about 28 msecs per letter. As already mentioned, there were substantial effects of word frequency on word naming RT. Confirmation of these findings is contained in a study by Cosky (1976), who found a word length effect of about 21 msecs per letter combined with an effect of word frequency. This pattern of results is consistent with the dual-channel model of word naming. The effect of array length indexes an involvement of grapheme-phoneme translation, and the effects of lexical status and word frequency reflect the contribution of the lexical-semantic channel.

If we are correct in assuming a partial dependence of word naming RT on grapheme-phoneme translation it follows that irregularity of spelling should be associated with a delay of response. Baron & Strawson (1976) have offered a preliminary demonstration of this point by showing that *S*s read lists of irregular words more slowly than lists of regular words. In the diagrammatic model of Figure VIII.5.1 naming of an irregular word must depend primarily on processing through the lexical-semantic channel. Access to this channel involves recognition of graphemic properties by units in the visual component of the lexical interface. Baron & Strawson considered the possibility that visual access of this kind might be disrupted by violations of graphemic regularity, achieved, for example, by mixing of upper and lower case letters. They were able to demonstrate that case alternation delayed reading of irregular words, such as OnCe, HoUr and dOeS, to a greater extent than was found for regular words, such as CoRn, ChEaP and hAnD.

If word naming is in part mediated by the lexical-semantic channel we would expect to observe effects of *associative priming*. Evidence of such effects can be taken from studies of tachistoscopic whole report and word naming. Jacobson (1973) utilized a technique in which a word was briefly presented and was then masked by another word. Duration of the first word was 8 msecs, followed, after a variable delay, by a 120 msec exposure of the mask. Jacobson reported that the first word was correctly identified at shorter masking delays when it was an associate of the mask than when the two words were unrelated. In a somewhat similar study, Allport (1977) briefly displayed a target word with a non-target just above it and then masked both words. The damaging effect of the presence of the non-target on accuracy of the report of the target was mitigated when it was an associate of the target. Jacobson (1973) also described a naming experiment in which *S*s vocalized a word preceded by an associated or non-associated word. The semantic association facilitated the naming RT. This effect was confirmed by an experiment described by Meyer, Schvaneveldt & Ruddy (1974b). Their *S*s saw sequences of two successively displayed words. They were instructed to make a lexical decision about the first and to vocalize the second. The naming RT showed a 48 msec facilitation effect when the word was an associate of the word presented for lexical decision immediately before. Meyer's design also varied stimulus quality of the word to be named. Degradation delayed the RT, and also increased the size of the association effect.

These experiments demonstrate that speed and accuracy of word naming are indeed sensitive to priming by an immediate semantic context. According to the dual channel model the effects occur because word naming is in part mediated by the lexical-semantic channel, and because the recognition units in the access and exit logogen systems are defined and inter-related at a semantic level. In themselves the experiments do not allow us to say whether the priming influences the access system, the exit system, or both. However, the occurrence of the effects in tachistoscopic experiments like those of Jacobson (1973) and Allport (1977), and the interactions with stimulus quality noted by Meyer, Schvaneveldt & Ruddy (1974b), are strongly suggestive of effects located in the access logogen system. A further experiment by Jacobson (1976) is perhaps more easily interpreted in terms of effects on the exit system. He found that masking of words by homonyms, for example YOU masked by EWE, was actually disruptive of report accuracy. The most probable locus for such an effect seems to be the stage of phonological RETRIEVAL. Perhaps the exit logogen system cannot easily cope with a situation in which two distinct sets of semantic attributes access a single phonological code.

X.5 PHONOLOGICAL RETRIEVAL

In this chapter we have argued that visual words may be processed concurrently in two channels, leading to RETRIEVAL of semantic and phonemic codes which converge on the recognizers of the exit logogen system at a final stage of speech production. If we are to study the exit logogen system without the confounding due to the involvement of the lexical and grapheme-phoneme channels we must move away from word naming tasks and in the direction of verbal association tasks of various kinds. Two possible approaches are suggested in the study by Winnick & Daniel (1970). Their *S*s produced names as reactions to pictures of objects and definitions of objects as well as to printed words. Only the latter task facilitated subsequent tachistoscopic recognition, suggesting to Morton (1977a) that the access logogens for a word were not modified when that word was generated as output from the exit logogen system. The critical point is that these semantic association tasks allow us to observe the retrieval of the phonological coding of a word without concurrent processing of that same word through the lexical interface and grapheme-phoneme translation channel.

Phonological retrieval tasks may be classified into a group in which name selection depends solely on consideration of semantic attributes, and those in which additional graphemic information is presented. Semantic tasks are picture naming, responses to verbal definitions, and naming of classes or properties of objects and of instances of specified classes. Each of these tasks may be modified by addition of graphemic information bearing a phonemic relation to the required response. We can also distinguish tasks of a purely graphemic or phonemic nature, such as the verbal fluency tests in which *S*s must produce words possessing certain structural characteristics, a particular starting or ending letter, for example.

The classic study of phonological retrieval is the well-known investigation of tip-of-the-tongue (TOT) phenomena conducted by Brown & McNeill (1966). Definitions of low frequency words were read to *S*s, who were instructed to supply an appropriate word. For example, the definition: 'A navigational instrument used in measuring angular distances, especially the altitude of the sun, moon and stars at sea', was read for the target word 'sextant'. *S*s were said to be in a TOT state when they felt that they knew the word which corresponded to the definition even though they could not immediately recall it. Any *S* entering such a state was required to fill in a response sheet on which he indicated how many syllables he thought the word might have, what its initial letter was, and also to give words similar in sound to the target word, and words similar in meaning. These reports were analyzed to indicate the amount and nature of the partial information which the *S* might have about the word he was attempting to retrieve.

It is to be expected that *S*s in this situation will generate some words which approximate the meaning of the target. Comprehension of the definition resolves to selection of sets of semantic features which provide the primary input to the exit logogen system during RETRIEVAL. These features will influence recognizers for a number of semantically related words, some of which will become available as responses. For example, the definition of 'sextant' evoked words such as 'compass', 'astrolabe', 'dividers' and 'protractor'.

The more provocative feature of Brown & McNeill's paper was their suggestion that *S*s may possess *structural* knowledge of a target word they are attempting to retrieve. *S*s were sometimes able to produce words which sounded similar to the target word, such as 'secant', 'sextet' or 'sexton'. They also appeared quite successful in indicating the number of syllables in the target word, the location of primary stress, or the presence of a suffix. Structurally similar words were most likely to match the target in initial or terminal letters, and *S*s were often able to identify the first letter of the target word. It has been suggested that results of this kind may, in part at least, reflect response biases attributable to a generalized knowledge of structural features of words falling within a particular domain or specialization (Koriat & Lieblich, 1974). Nonetheless, the data imply that input of semantic features to the exit logogen system may lead to retrieval of an incomplete phonological representation of a particular low frequency word. If this partial description was copied into the phonemic register it might be used to access speech codes for words bearing a structural resemblance to the target.

There are two types of constrained association task which also appear to test semantically mediated phonological retrieval. In the *instance naming* task the *S* is given a class name and an attribute name, such as FLOWER——YELLOW, and must respond with the name of a class instance possessing that attribute, for example: 'daffodil'. Freedman & Loftus (1971) obtained vocal RTs for a series of such tests, and reported that RT was facilitated when the noun was displayed before the adjective, and that it was affected by the frequency of occurrence of the most frequent available response word, and also the category dominance, as defined by the norms of Battig & Montague (1969), of the most dominant available word. The converse of this task is *superordinate naming* in which an instance name is presented to the *S*, who responds with the name of its class, as in: DAFFODIL ——'flower'. These RTs are also influenced by dominance of the item in its class, though the effect is modifiable by practice (Sanford & Seymour, 1974a). Pollack (1963a) varied the sizes of the instance name sets and class name sets in a serial version of the task. Variation in size of the ensemble of class names was much more important than variation in the size of each ensemble of instance names. We may note that this ensemble size effect is virtually, though not entirely, eliminated in word naming tasks (Pollack, 1963b; Fraisse, 1964a; Gellatly & Gregg, 1974), presumably on account of availability of input from the grapheme-phoneme channel.

Another task involving an exclusively semantic input to the exit logogen is that of *object naming*. The *S* is shown a series of pictures of objects, and must respond to each by producing its most common name, or a more specific or general label which satisfies the experimental instructions. Since the task depends on processes of pictorial encoding and interpretation it will be treated in greater detail in Part Three. However, we can note here that object naming RT has been related to the Thorndike-Lorge frequency of usage of the object's common name (Oldfield & Wingfield, 1965; Oldfield, 1966), to the size of the ensemble of alternative names obtained in normative studies (Lachman, 1973; Lachman, Shaffer & Hennrikus, 1974), and to the dominance of the normatively preferred name over more specific or more general labels (Segui & Fraisse, 1968; Seymour, 1973a). Carroll & White (1973) suggested that the name frequency variable might be reinterpreted in terms of age of acquisition of vocabulary. They compared word frequency and estimates of age of acquisition as predictors of RT in an object naming experiment, and concluded that the two variables, although correlated, were distinguishable, and that age of acquisition was the better predictor.

These studies indicate that phonological RETRIEVAL is probably influenced by associative and semantic factors (dominance), procedural factors (ensemble size and response uncertainty), and lexical factors (frequency of usage or age of acquisition). Similar word frequency effects occur when input to the exit logogens is entirely graphemic-phonemic, as when *S*s name words with a given starting letter, or of a given length (Duncan, 1966, 1970). This type of graphemically based retrieval is also affected by the position of the cue letter. Loftus, Wiksten & Abelson (1974) presented *S*s with a letter and a number indicating serial position. The *S* was to respond with a word containing the cued letter in the designated position. For example, the instruction B–1 might evoke 'boat', whereas the instruction B–3 might evoke 'table'. The RT was fastest when position 1 was specified, increased as a function of serial position, and declined somewhat at the final position.

The semantic and graphemic-phonemic tasks may be combined to produce a situation which is in many respects an analogue of the two-channel model of word naming. For example, Loftus & Suppes (1972) presented *S*s with nouns followed by single letters, instructing them to produce the name of a class instance which began with that letter. Thus, FLOWER——P might evoke the response 'poppy', which is constrained by semantic and graphemic-phonemic specifications. A correlational analysis was employed to relate the RT to a number of lexical-semantic variables, including: frequency of usage of the category noun, and its length in letters; frequency of usage of the most frequently occurring acceptable response word; the dominance ranking of the response having the highest frequency in the Battig & Montague (1969) norms; an estimate of the total number of acceptable responses, again taken from Battig & Montague; and frequency of usage of category name and of most frequent acceptable response from a juvenile word count included in Thorndike & Lorge (1944). A multiple correlation of $R = +0{\cdot}78$ was obtained between the RT and these structural variables. However, certain of the variables, including the adult measures of category and response frequency of usage, contributed little to this relationship. The main contribution came from the dominance measure, and from the category and response frequency measures based on the children's word counts. These scores are probably related to age of acquisition of vocabulary, and are therefore in agreement with the conclusions of Carroll & White (1973) concerning a possible link between early language use and ease of phonological retrieval.

Another method of combining semantic and graphemic-phonemic input to the exit logogens is by superimposing print on pictures presented for naming. This procedure was used with a restricted ensemble of geometric shapes by Seymour (1969b, 1970a), who reported slight facilitation of RT when the shape name was printed inside the shape. More extensive studies have recently been carried out by Rayner & Posnansky (1977) and Posnansky & Rayner (1977). In their experiments *S*s named outline pictures of objects which contained printed words and non-words bearing a variety of graphemic, phonemic and semantic relations to the target name. The experiments have an important relevance to issues relating to lexical access and semantic retrieval which will be discussed in the next chapter. Here we will concentrate on the effects on naming RT of a phonemic congruence between the irrelevant letters and the required vocal response.

Rayner & Posnansky (1977) briefly displayed picture-word combinations of various types. The picture could contain its own name or another name, as for example the printing of *bird* or *meal* inside a picture of a bird. These conditions correspond closely to the Stroop colour naming task which will be discussed in subsequent chapters. Rayner's data confirmed that picture naming was facilitated by presence of a congruent label but inhibited by presence of an incongruent label. RT was 698 msecs for an unlabelled picture, 636 msecs for a congruent label, and 810 msecs for an incongruent label. It was also possible to facilitate the naming response by presenting a non-word, such as *burd* or *byrd*, which was phonemically congruent with the response. The RTs for these conditions averaged about 560 msecs, as against 582 msecs for non-words such as *baid* or *bude* which did not preserve pronunciation.

The facilitation of the naming response could involve both a semantic and a graphemic-phonemic component. A congruent label may be processed in the lexical-semantic channel, thus facilitating retrieval of a semantic description of the picture, and in the grapheme-phoneme channel, thus providing phonemic input to the exit logogens. A phonemically congruent non-word, on the other hand, may influence name retrieval primarily through the grapheme-phoneme channel, although the possibility of lexical access from the phonemic register cannot be excluded. In order to disentangle these influences it is desirable to look at the effects of labelling by incongruent words which are homophones of the required response. A condition of this kind was included in the studies reported by Posnansky & Rayner (1977). They found that labelling by a phonemically congruent non-word led to greater facilitation than labelling by a homophonic word, although the latter were substantially faster than the Stroop conditions of labelling by an incongruent word or non-word. Thus, homophones may contribute to name retrieval through the grapheme-phoneme channel while causing a degree of interference in the lexical-semantic channel. The implication that traditional Stroop effects have a major semantic component will be taken up again in Part Three.

X.6 CONCLUSIONS

The research discussed in this and the preceding chapter appears to support the contention that a basic level of literacy depends on a functional interaction of four major sub-systems of the Lexical Memory. These systems are respectively concerned with: graphemic encoding, grapheme-phoneme translation, lexical-semantic access, and phonological retrieval. An effort has been made to show that the activity of each sub-system can be distinguished through an appropriate choice of experimental tasks and stimuli, even though the systems normally operate in close collaboration.

In these chapters we have been concerned to show how a person's language processing capability may be modified when he learns to read. A non-literate individual possesses the systems necessary for phonemic encoding of speech sounds, lexical access through an auditory recognition system, semantic and syntactic representation of spoken words and sentences, and retrieval of phonological forms through the exit logogen system. The additions attributable to the acquisition of reading skill consist of the graphemic encoding channel, and the interface structures allowing for graphemic-semantic and graphemic-phonemic recoding.

A main contention has been that the literate person's fundamental capability for pronunciation of written words generally involves concurrent activity in the grapheme-phoneme and lexical-semantic channels. We assume that a word is initially transformed to a description in the graphemic register, that access to recognizers in the lexical and grapheme-phoneme interface systems enhances this description, and that retrieval of phonemic and semantic codes follows. The processing channels converge again at the exit logogen system, which accepts semantic and phonemic input in mediating retrieval of a phonological code.

The dual-channel model resolves the long-standing debate between those who have maintained that reading is primarily a matter of phonemic recoding (Gough, 1972), and those who have emphasized direct visual access to meaning (Smith, 1971; Kolers, 1970). The proponents of these positions fail chiefly through over-stating their cases, both views being correct as partial descriptions of the reading process. An educational implication is that reading teachers might continue their current practice of emphasizing both look-and-say and phonic-attack skills with the aim of building an efficient lexical interface and grapheme-phoneme translation system.

CHAPTER XI

Recoding to Meaning

LEXICAL ACCESS AND SEMANTIC RETRIEVAL

XI.1 INTRODUCTION

The two preceding chapters have discussed the graphemic encoding of words, and their transformation to a speech code. Although the grapheme-phoneme translation channel plays a critical role in such recoding, it seemed necessary to argue for the additional involvement of a lexical-semantic channel. The activity of this channel underlies the second major form of competence exhibited by successful readers, that is their ability to provide the behavioural demonstrations which are taken to indicate *understanding* of the referential and semantic functions of printed words. This chapter will focus on the analysis of the operation of semantic RETRIEVAL which occurs when visual words are recoded in terms of meaning.

In the earlier discussions we assumed that semantic retrieval may be achieved by input of graphemic features to morpheme recognizers contained in a lexical interface structure. This retrieval function, like the others which have been described, must incorporate a pattern recognition phase and an addressing phase during which components of a semantic description are located in permanent storage and transferred to the semantic register (see Figure VIII.5.1).

Certain of the factors influencing semantic retrieval have already been identified. These include visual confusability, lexical frequency of usage, recency of occurrence, semantic context, strength of the associative relation between words, and syntactic/semantic factors concerned with morphemic structure, syntactic function, polysemy, and abstractness/concreteness of meaning. In investigating the impact of these variables on the lexical interface it is desirable to avoid situations in which correlated activities occur in the access and exit logogen systems. Although the traditional tachistoscopic word recognition experiment has demonstrated the importance of such factors as frequency, repetition and context (Solomon & Postman, 1951; Morton, 1964b, 1969a; Broadbent & Gregory, 1968, 1971; Tulving & Gold, 1963; Tulving, Mandler & Baumal, 1964), and also of syntactic function and morphemic structure (Holmes, Marshall & Newcombe, 1971; Marshall, Newcombe & Holmes, 1975; Gibson & Guinet, 1971; Murrell & Morton, 1974), the interpretation of these effects has been obscured by the inherent confounding of the contributions of the access and exit systems.

Tasks having a somewhat more certain focus on the access system include the lexical decision experiment, in which a positive judgement arguably depends on the activation of an access logogen unit, and various types of semantic decision task in which successful performance requires word identification and semantic retrieval. The discussion which follows will concentrate on these situations.

XI.2 VISUAL ACCESS

A key proposal of the dual-channel account of word processing has been that lexical access may be achieved from the graphemic register. This conclusion derives from the linguistic and neuropsychological evidence discussed in Chapter VIII, and may be supported by relevant experimental demonstrations.

Firstly, the occurrence of obviously visual confusions in the tachistoscopic reports of normal *S*s and in the protocols of phonemic dyslexic patients (Morton, 1964b; Marshall & Newcombe, 1966; Shallice & Warrington, 1975) implies the involvement of graphemic representations in word recognition. Secondly, Patterson & Marcel (1977) found that *S*s suffering impairment of the grapheme-phoneme translation channel were nonetheless able to make lexical decisions about words. Thirdly, the experiment by Seymour & Jack (1978), described in Chapter IX, indicated that the influence of lexical status of abbreviations on graphemic comparison RT was dependent on visual format.

Further evidence can be obtained from the Stroop experiments of Rayner & Posnansky (1977) and Posnansky & Rayner (1977). In these studies the graphemic similarity of the print imposed on the object to be named and the actual name of the object was systematically varied. For example, a picture of a horse might contain the array *hcnre*, which matches the picture name in shape and first and last letters, *bcnrc*, which matches the overall shape, or *hgple* which preserves the first and last letters, but not the overall shape. These approximations to the picture name were contrasted with control arrays, such as *pynrk*, which differed from it in first and last letters and general shape. Provided that the exposure of the picture was quite brief, at about 100 msecs, the naming RT showed a facilitation effect attributable to the graphemic similarity of the superimposed print and the picture name, averaging 50 msecs in one experiment, and 100 msecs in another. Further experiments demonstrated that the facilitation occurred relative to RTs for pictures presented without print, and that the interference due to presence of an incongruent label was much reduced if the label was visually similar to the picture name.

If we agree that these orthographically irregular and unpronounceable non-words are not likely to be processed through the grapheme-phoneme channel, Rayner's data can be taken as evidence for a *graphemic* influence on phonological retrieval. The assumption made here is that the effect is semantically mediated. Thus, we suppose that the non-word *hcnre* is sufficiently similar in graphemic description to the word *horse* to activate the access logogen for that word, and that this facilitates formation of a semantic description of the picture which then provides input evidence to the exit logogens during name retrieval. It is, of course, entirely consistent with the dual-channel model that these graphemic effects should co-exist with phonemic effects of the kind described in the last chapter. In practice, a phonemic correspondence appears more important than a graphemic one when the two factors are varied together (Rayner & Posnansky, 1977).

Green & Shallice (1976) approached the issue of visual access to the lexicon by examining effects of spelling alterations on RTs for decisions about sounds of words (whether or not two words rhymed) or about meanings of words (whether or not referents of both words were animate, or inanimate). The spelling alterations preserved pronunciation but destroyed lexical status, as in DOAT, DILE, FOLE. This kind of change was found to be much more disruptive of decisions about meanings than of decisions about sound. An additonal study indicated that semantic decisions about category membership were not affected by syllabic complexity, a finding also reported by Beller & Schaeffer (1974). The interaction of spelling with decision task, together with absence of syllabic effects, was taken to imply that meaning was not accessed through the grapheme-phoneme translation channel. However, we might note that Frederiksen & Kroll (1976) did not obtain syllable effects in either naming or lexical decision, so that the occurrence or non-occurrence of such effects may not be useful as an indicator of involvement of phonemic recoding processes.

A somewhat similar approach was followed by Kleiman (1975). His *S*s made graphemic, phonemic or semantic judgements about pairs of words. In the graphemic task they were instructed to indicate whether the two words contained the same letters after the first letter. The 'same' pairs were all heterophones, such as HEARD/BEARD and COUCH/TOUCH, so that the comparison was necessarily based on graphemic rather than phonemic or phonological representations. These words provided the 'different' pairs in the phonemic task in which *S*s indicated if the words sounded alike apart from their first sound, as do BLAME/FLAME. This choice ensured that *S*s based their decisions on consideration of phonemic rather than graphemic codes. The semantic task required positive responses to synonyms, such as MOURN/GRIEVE, and negative responses to words having different meanings. Kleiman obtained RTs for these judgements under normal conditions and when *S*s were engaged on a secondary task of verbal shadowing of a sequence of auditory digit names.

The rationale of Kleiman's experiment derived from the assumption that a decision process including phonemic/phonological recoding as a necessary component would show greater disruption due to shadowing than a process for which recoding was unnecessary or optional. This assumption can be validated against the results for the graphemic and phonemic tasks. The average RTs for these judgements in absence of shadowing were 970 msecs and 1,137 msecs. Imposition of the shadowing task increased the RT for graphemic comparisons by 125 msecs, whereas the increase for the phonemic task was 372 msecs. There is, therefore, a strong implication that shadowing was more disruptive of phonemic than of graphemic comparison processes, although the experiment does not establish whether the effect should be located in the phonemic or phonological registers of Figure VIII.5.1. The RT for the semantic comparison task was 1,118 msecs, and the increment due to shadowing was 120 msecs. Thus, the disruption of a semantic comparison due to occupation of the speech channel was no greater than that observed for graphemic comparisons, and substantially smaller than that observed for phonemic comparisons. The implication is that semantic RETRIEVAL does not depend on formation of a speech code, and that information about meaning can be accessed directly from the graphemic register.

One further piece of evidence relevant to this issue is contained in the paper by Frederiksen & Kroll (1976). As explained in the last chapter, they reported an effect of word length on RT to name non-words which was taken to be an index of the functioning of the grapheme-phoneme translation channel. This effect also occurred when words were named, implying an involvement of the translation process. However, there were no consistent effects of length when *S*s responded positively to the same words in a lexical decision task. The complexity of the initial consonant cluster was also an important factor in the naming experiments, but one which had no effect on lexical decision RT. Some question about these findings is raised by contrary reports of Gough (1972) and Forster & Chambers (1973). However, Frederiksen & Kroll conducted a careful and extensive study, and it seems reasonable to conclude that effects taken to be characteristic of grapheme-phoneme translation need not occur in lexical decision experiments. Again, the implication is that the information needed for a lexical decision can be accessed directly from the graphemic register.

XI.3 LEXICAL DECISIONS—FREQUENCY AND RECENCY

The experimental situation which appears ideally suited to the study of the characteristics of the access logogen system is the *lexical decision task*. It was argued in the last chapter that the judgement that an array of letters forms a word appears to require the activation of a morpheme recognizer and retrieval of minimal evidence of meaningfulness. If this assumption is correct we must anticipate that variables influencing the states of the logogens, through priming or threshold adjustment, will have reliable effects on positive RT in lexical decision tasks. Hence, we would expect to find effects of frequency of usage, recency of immediate prior occurrence, associative priming, and, possibly, syntactic class and morphemic structure.

The occurrence of effects of *word frequency* is well attested in the experiments of Rubenstein, Garfield & Millikan (1970), Rubenstein, Lewis & Rubenstein (1971b), Forster & Chambers (1973) and Frederiksen & Kroll (1976). A word frequency effect also occurs in word naming experiments (Frederiksen & Kroll, 1976) and in recognition and report experiments (Broadbent, 1967; Morton, 1969a), and must be accepted as a basic property of the lexical interface.

Some authors, most particularly Rubenstein, Lewis & Rubenstein (1971) and Forster & Bednall (1976), have interpreted word frequency effects within the framework of a scanning model of lexical access. This is based on the assumption that the *S* forms a representation of the test array which is then sequentially matched against stored lexical entities. A frequency effect is thought to occur because high frequency entries are checked earlier in the scan than low frequency ones. Such a proposal is, of course, radically different from the general theoretical approach which has been preferred here. In adopting Morton's logogen system as a blueprint for the various interface systems contained within the Lexical and Symbolic Memories we have opted for a content-addressable lexicon in which graphemic features may be referred in parallel to all recognizers. In such a system a word frequency effect is interpreted in terms of variations in the evidence requirements of the recognizers, an idea which may quite readily be represented in terms of frequency-related variations in threshold setting (Morton, 1969a).

Coltheart, Davelaar, Jonasson & Besner (1977) have discussed some experimental evidence which they see as potentially useful in discriminating between the scanning and evidence accumulation models of lexical access. The word and regular non-word materials used in a lexical decision experiment were classified with regard to the number of words that could be created by altering one letter. For example, from WOLF one could derive GOLF, ROLF, WILF, WOOF, and WOLD. A count of the words produced in this way provides a crude indication of the *lexical confusability* of an item, that is the number of entries in the internal lexicon to which it is similar. Coltheart points out that the scanning model requires that any delaying effect of lexical confusability on the RT should be observed for both positive and negative responses. In fact, his study indicated that this factor influenced negative responses to non-words while having no effect on positive responses to words.

As mentioned in the last chapter, Coltheart considered that positive lexical decisions might involve evidence accumulation in a content-addressable logogen system whereas negative decisions were taken by default when an adjustable deadline expired. He interpreted the effect of lexical confusability on negative RT as implying that the TASK executive monitored the general level of activity in the access logogens and raised the deadline for the negative decision if this activity appeared substantial. This could yield an effect of confusability on negative RT, although no such effect need occur for positive RTs since the rate at which the logogen for the displayed word approaches its threshold will be independent of the number of other recognizers which may be concurrently active.

From this discussion we can derive a tentative 'processing stage' model of lexical decisions. We assume an initial stage for graphemic ENCODING of the test display which will be subject to selective influence by stimulus quality factors. This is followed by a stage of semantic RETRIEVAL which is influenced by word frequency and other lexical factors which have been mentioned. At a subsequent judgemental stage evidence of meaningfulness is accumulated up to a threshold value at which RETRIEVAL of an affirmative semantic code occurs. There follow stages for RETRIEVAL and EXPRESSION of manual or vocal response codes. These latter stages should be open to influence by variations in response frequency, or the compatibility of the decision-response assignment.

Some experimental evidence which bears on a processing stage account of this kind has been collected within the framework of an additive factor methodology. For example, Stanners, Jastrzembski & Westbrook (1975) combined the factors of word frequency and stimulus quality in a lexical decision experiment. Stimulus quality was varied between *S*s. The two factors were found to be almost perfectly additive, the word frequency effect being 138 msecs for intact stimuli as against 145 msecs for stimuli degraded by imposition of a dot pattern. This additivity is, of course, consistent with the assumption that graphemic ENCODING and semantic RETRIEVAL are distinct processing stages which are selectively influenced by stimulus quality and lexical frequency.

Morton (1969a) proposed that logogen thresholds are reduced whenever a unit is activated, but then drift slowly back to a level slightly below their starting point. If this adjustment to *recency of occurrence* of a word is characteristic of the lexical interface we would anticipate that repetition of words in a lexical decision experiment should be associated with reductions in RT. This prediction finds support in data reported by Forbach, Stanners & Hochhaus (1974), and in a series of experiments by Scarborough, Cortese & Scarborough (1977). In the latter study regular non-words and words of varying frequency were presented for lexical decision. Some stimuli were repeated in the trial sequence, and the lag between one presentation and the next was varied. Scarborough found that positive responses to words were significantly facilitated by repetition, but that this effect was not influenced by lag, and occurred whether the word was printed in the same or different case on its two appearances.

We may therefore argue that frequency of occurrence and recency of occurrence are two factors influencing the semantic RETRIEVAL stage of lexical decision. Where two factors influence the duration of a common stage it is expected, according to the additive factor methodology, that they will produce interactive effects on the RT.

Scarborough's experiment shows evidence of such an interaction, since he found that word frequency effects occurred when words were first presented but not when they were repeated. In a second experiment, incorporating a longer lag between repetitions, the frequency effect was much reduced on the repetition trials.

By the same arguments, a factor such as the relative frequency of response type, which is thought to have a selective influence on the response RETRIEVAL stage, should combine additively with the frequency and recency effects. Scarborough tested two groups of *S*s, one with positive and negative trials about equally frequent and the other with positives almost four times as frequent as negatives. The RT effect of this response bias was almost perfectly additive with the effect for repetition, and appeared not to interact with frequency of usage.

Morton (1968, 1969a) emphasized that the logogens are recognizers for the *morphemic* attributes of written language. One implication of this view is that repetition effects should reflect semantic relatedness rather than physical relatedness (Murrell & Morton, 1974). The finding that the repetition effect in lexical decision is not modified by a change of case is consistent with this position (Scarborough, Cortese & Scarborough, 1977). On the other hand, if we are right in assuming separate interface systems for the visual and auditory modalities, a change from visual to auditory presentation, or *vice versa*, might well be sufficient to eliminate the effect. Kirsner & Smith (1974) tested this by comparing within- and between-modality repetitions at varying lags. Although they obtained some evidence of cross-modal effects these were much smaller in magnitude than those due to repetition within either modality.

Evidence that physical similarity does not in itself give rise to a repetition effect was contained in the paper by Meyer, Schvaneveldt & Ruddy (1974a). They found no facilitation when rhyming words, such as BRIBE and TRIBE, were displayed in succession. On the other hand, Coltheart, Davelaar, Jonasson & Besner (1977) reported some facilitation for decisions about words preceded by homophones, as for example SALE following SAIL. The effect did not extend to non-words, such as FLANE and FLAIN, and indeed repetition effects were slight or absent for non-word stimuli in the studies by Forbach, Stanners & Hochhaus (1974) and Scarborough, Cortese & Scarborough (1977).

This pattern of results seems consistent with the proposal that repetition effects are located within a modality-specific system of morphemically defined recognizers. The effects do not occur for non-words because no recognizers exist for these forms in the lexical interface. They do not occur for rhyming words because they depend on supra-threshold activation of a unit, and this happens in the logogen for the displayed word but not in the logogens for graphemically or phonemically similar words. The effect observed by Coltheart for homophones is probably mediated by the grapheme-phoneme translation channel. In a dual channel system phonemic recoding could lead to activation of the auditory logogen for the alternative sense of a homophone. It follows that non-words which are homophones of actual words should facilitate the immediately subsequent classification of those words, as, for example, when a non-word decision about BRANE is followed by a word decision about BRAIN. Coltheart argued that there was evidence to support this conclusion in his experiments.

XI.4 SEMANTIC PRIMING

A further feature of the logogens which has been central to Morton's (1968, 1969a) theorizing is their susceptibility to *semantic priming*. This idea fits naturally into the analysis of the exit logogen system, since the recognizers mediating phonological RETRIEVAL are, by definition, responsive to input of semantic attributes held in the semantic register. In the case of the access systems, on the other hand, the morphemic status of the recognizers is tied to a capability for retrieval of semantic information, and there is no *a priori* requirement that the recognizers should also be sensitive to input of semantic information. Nonetheless, it appeared to Morton (1964a, 1964b, 1964c) that a mechanism allowing for contextual priming of the word recognition process could have a considerable value for the analysis of skilled reading.

A semantic influence on recognition can be incorporated into the schematic model of the Lexical Memory (see Figure VIII.5.1) if it is allowed that attributes represented in the semantic register may cause a transitory increase in activation in access logogens possessing links to those same attributes in permanent store. If this increment in activation remained at a sub-threshold level its effect would be to decrease the amount of graphemic input required for recognition of an anticipated word. Semantic input beyond the threshold level would result in the retrieval of graphemic or phonemic codes, which might be experienced as visual or auditory verbal imagery of the kind described by the introspective psychologists of the Würzburg and Cornell schools (Humphrey, 1951).

Empirical demonstrations of semantic priming of word recognition can be found in tachistoscopic and lexical decision experiments. In Allport's (1977) study accuracy of report of a masked target word was influenced by its semantic relation to an adjacent word which could not be reported. Another experiment involved brief display and masking of an array of four words at a duration brief enough to ensure that *S*s seldom reported more than one of the words correctly. Performance was affected by word frequency, and showed visual confusions due to mixing of parts of words. When *S*s were told that each display contained an animal name, and that they should bias their reports in favour of this word, there was a marked gain in accuracy for animal names at the expense of some depression of performance on non-animal words, particularly those of low frequency. It is possible that the partial report instructions primed access logogens having animal properties within their sets of defining attributes. This would effectively have reduced the amount of graphemic information required for achievement of lexical access, and could have produced the bias noted by Allport. Of course, similar priming may have occurred in the exit logogen system, providing an alternative source of facilitation.

Warren (1972) adapted the Stroop colour naming task to the study of semantic influences on lexical access. In the traditional Stroop experiment the *S* names the colour of the ink in which words are printed, ignoring the words themselves (Stroop, 1935). The classic finding is that the words disrupt and delay the colour naming response. This effect is greatest when the words are colour names or names of coloured objects, but also occurs to some degree for words having no obvious colour associations (Klein, 1964). Warren contrasted the naming of coloured Xs with the naming of coloured words. Reactions to the words were consistently slower than the reactions to the Xs, and this effect was enhanced if the word was related to a short list held in memory by the *S* during the naming task. For example, the *S* might be given the list OIL GAS COAL, followed by a word for print colour naming, and an instruction to recall the list. Warren's basic finding was that list words and the category name, FUEL, interfered with naming to a greater degree than words which were unrelated to the list in memory.

If presentation of a list of categorially related items is viewed as a method of priming a subset of logogens, Warren's experiment appears to indicate that priming increases the capacity of a word to interfere with print colour naming. However, as matters stand, it is unclear whether the priming effect is occurring in the access logogen system, the exit logogen system, or both. It is also worth emphasizing that the effect of priming is to *increase* the RT in the Stroop experiment, whereas priming is typically found to enhance accuracy in tachistoscopic experiments, and to speed vocalization in naming experiments (Jacobson, 1973; Meyer, Schvaneveldt & Ruddy, 1974b; Sanford, Garrod & Boyle, 1977).

The facilitating effects of semantic priming in lexical decision tasks have been well-documented, particularly by Meyer and his colleagues. Meyer & Schvaneveldt (1971) presented pairs of letter arrays to *S*s, consisting of two words, two non-words, or a word and a non-word. *S*s were instructed to respond positively if both stimuli were words in one experiment, and if both were words or both were non-words in another. The associative relationship between members of the word pairs was varied, so that related pairs, like BREAD/BUTTER or NURSE/DOCTOR could be contrasted with unrelated controls, such as BREAD/NURSE and BUTTER/DOCTOR. Meyer obtained an 85 msec advantage for associated words in the first experiment, and a 117 msec advantage in the second. In a further study, Schvaneveldt & Meyer (1973) presented sets of three stimuli, *S*s being instructed to respond positively if all three were words. Displays which contained two associated words were classified 90 msecs more rapidly than displays containing only unassociated words.

These *association effects* may be contrasted with the absence of effects due to physical similarity reported by Meyer, Schvaneveldt & Ruddy (1974a). They imply that the logogens are morphemic entities which are associated at the level of a higher-order semantic structure. This conclusion can be related to the work on repetition effects by adapting Meyer's experiment to include sequential presentation of the stimuli. Meyer, Schvaneveldt & Ruddy (1974b) obtained RTs for lexical decisions about each member of sequences of two stimuli, and reported that RT to classify the second item was facilitated when it followed an associate. The same point has been demonstrated for sequential presentation of three words (Meyer, Schvaneveldt & Ruddy, 1972).

The three-word procedure was applied rather neatly to the study of lexical ambiguity by Schvaneveldt, Meyer & Becker (1976). *S*s made lexical decisions about each member of a three-item sequence, such as SAVE BANK MONEY or RIVER BANK MONEY. The middle word of these sequences, BANK, is a homograph, having distinct financial and geographical senses. It follows from the assumption that logogens are morphemically defined that separate units exist in the lexical interface for the two senses (Morton, 1968). Prior presentation of SAVE might result in semantic priming of the unit for the financial sense, whereas presentation of RIVER should result in priming of the geographical sense. It is likely that the graphemic form, BANK, will be recognized by the logogen for its primed sense, and that the attributes corresponding to that sense will then be retrieved. Hence, processing of BANK following SAVE may lead to retrieval of semantic attributes which will prime the logogen for MONEY, whereas processing of BANK following RIVER will not do so.

In line with these predictions, Schvaneveldt, Meyer & Becker (1976) found that the RT to classify the third word of the sequence was facilitated when the first word had primed the relevant sense of the second. The RT for MONEY was 505 msecs following SAVE and BANK, as against 558 msecs following RIVER and BANK. This was confirmed in a second experiment in which the stimulus quality of the third word was reduced.

Schuberth & Eimas (1977) have tested for a facilitating effect of a sentence context on lexical decision RT. An incomplete sentence, such as: THE PUPPY CHEWED THE ——, was briefly displayed followed by a word or non-word. Non-words varied in orthographic regularity, and the words were of high or low frequency and appeared congruent or incongruent in the sentence context. The positive RT was facilitated by both frequency and congruence with the sentence frame, and these effects appeared to be additive.

These studies provide strong evidence in support of Morton's contextual priming hypothesis. It should be emphasized that the priming effects are quite transitory, and are thought to alter from moment to moment in a manner which mirrors the changing content of the semantic register. Meyer, Schvaneveldt & Ruddy (1972) have shown that the size of the association effect declines steeply as the delay between the response to the first of two words and the onset of the second is increased to 4 secs. This rapid decay was also noted by Warren (1972) in his Stroop experiments. It stands in marked contrast to the stability of the repetition effects discussed by Scarborough, Cortese & Scarborough (1977), which were generally independent of the lag between successive presentations even to the point of extending from one day of testing to another.

We may take this to mean that supra-threshold activation of a logogen unit by sensory input brings about a long-term alteration in its state whereas internally generated semantic priming produces a transitory rise in activation which decays within an interval of seconds without effecting any permanent change in the unit. Fischler (1977) has argued that priming is an automatic function of the Lexical Memory system which need not involve executive intervention or conscious strategies. In a demonstration of this point he showed that the size of the association effect was independent of the *S*'s expectancies regarding the occurrence of associated words in a two-word lexical decision experiment. Expectancy was manipulated in a design similar to that used by Aderman & Smith (1971), and by instructions emphasizing the inclusion of associated words in the experiment.

These findings suggest, therefore, that *associative context* defines a further set of factors which influence the duration of the semantic RETRIEVAL stage of lexical decision. If this stage is distinct from the preceding graphemic ENCODING stage, semantic association effects should combine additively with effects due to stimulus quality, as was found for word frequency effects (Stanners, Jastrzembski & Westbrook, 1975). However, experiments in which stimulus quality and association between successively displayed words have been varied have suggested that the two factors have interactive effects on the RT (Meyer, Schvaneveldt & Ruddy, 1972, 1974b). Meyer found that stimulus degradation increased the size of the association effect in both naming and lexical decision experiments.

An interaction of this kind can be interpreted as an effect of visual degradation on the rate of accumulation of graphemic information in the access logogens (see Figure VI.2.1). A reduction in input rate will tend to exaggerate the temporal effect of a difference in evidence requirements of primed and unprimed logogens. The main difficulty with this account is that a comparable interaction should occur when stimulus quality is combined with word frequency, since the frequency effect is also supposed to reflect a difference in the evidence requirements of logogens for high and low frequency words. Becker & Killion (1977) have reported a lexical decision experiment in which semantic priming was combined with variations in stimulus intensity. They too reported a priming x quality interaction, but showed in a subsequent experiment that the intensity variation combined additively with word frequency. We might look for an explanation of this discrepancy in the two-phase character of the RETRIEVAL function. Stimulus quality is more likely to interact with factors which influence the pattern recognition phase than with factors which influence the semantic retrieval phase. Perhaps semantic priming is an influence on pattern recognition, whereas frequency of usage is an influence on semantic retrieval.

XI.5 SEMANTIC RETRIEVAL

In the lexical decision task the semantic information retrieved as the basis for the judgement may, in principle, be limited to minimal evidence of lexical status. However, the occurrence of association effects of the kind described by Meyer establishes that retrieval of a more extensive set of semantic attributes typically occurs when *S*s make lexical decisions. This conclusion can be supported by experimental demonstrations of an influence of semantic properties of words on lexical decision RT.

Rubenstein, Garfield & Millikan (1970) emphasized the possibility that the RT might be influenced by the number of distinct senses possessed by a word. They obtained somewhat faster RTs for a sample of homographs than for non-homographs, and interpreted the effect as being consistent with the scanning model of lexical access. Doubt was cast on these results by Clark's (1973a) discussion of statistical treatment of linguistically defined factors. However, Jastrzembski & Stanners (1975) classified words in terms of the number of distinct senses listed in their dictionary definitions, which varied from less than 10 to over 50 in their sample, and found an inverse relation between RT and number of senses.

A further factor, which was clearly important in the studies of phonemic dyslexic patients, is the syntactic function of a word (Marshall, Newcombe & Holmes, 1975). The dyslexic *S*s found nouns much easier to read than verbs or function words. There is some evidence that this noun facilitation effect also occurs in lexical decisions. Scarborough & Springer (1973) required *S*s to make lexical decisions about regular non-words or four-letter nouns, adjectives or verbs. Their data showed a strong word frequency effect which combined additively with a part of speech effect, nouns being classified about 30 msecs faster than verbs.

The performance of phonemic dyslexic patients was influenced by the concreteness or imageability of words (Shallice & Warrington, 1975). James (1975) has shown that this factor is also relevant for lexical decisions. He obtained an interaction of frequency and concreteness of meaning. Concreteness had little effect on RTs for high frequency words, but facilitated reactions to low frequency words.

Some experimental evidence of effects of morphemic structure has also been reported. Snodgrass & Jarvella (1972) found that presence of a prefix or suffix delayed lexical decision RT, as in the contrast between SCHOOL and PRESCHOOL, or HARD and HARDNESS. Such an effect appears consistent with the view that affixes must be stripped off before recognition of the word stem can occur. The corollary of this view is that the access logogens are recognizers for word stems. This has been investigated by Taft & Forster (1975) in a lexical decision experiment in which some non-word stimuli were stems of actual words which happen not to occur in an unaffixed form. For example, REJUVENATE yields the non-word JUVENATE when the prefix is removed. Negative RT to these items was somewhat greater than for controls, such as PERTOIRE derived from the word REPERTOIRE, which appeared not to have the status of word stems. Taft & Forster (1976) also found that negative reactions to bi-syllabic non-words were delayed when the first syllable was a word stem, as in DUSTWORTH or FOOTMILGE.

The interpretation of these effects of polysemy, concreteness of meaning, syntactic function and morphemic structure must remain somewhat tentative. The most likely possibility is that the experiments reflect variations in the impact on the judgemental stage of lexical decision of the semantic attributes retrieved during processing of the test word. As support for this conclusion we can note that the effects can be modified by changes in the non-word stimuli used in the experiment. James (1975) obtained a concreteness effect when he used non-words which were regular in orthography or which were homophones of actual words, but not when the non-words were irregular. Similarly, Shulman & Davison (1977) have shown that the association effect in classification of two-word displays can be much reduced by using irregular non-words. Possibly the use of irregular non-words results in a reduction in the level of the threshold for a positive decision, and this has the effect of curtailing the semantic retrieval process.

A more direct approach to the study of semantic retrieval is possible in tasks which explicitly require that the *S* retrieve and operate on semantic information. These may be referred to as *semantic decision tasks*. One example is the synonymy judgement task used by Kleiman (1975). However, the situation which has been studied most extensively is one in which *S*s are required to make decisions about the class membership of items. In a typical experiment the *S* might be shown a class name, such as BIRD, followed by an instance name, such as CANARY, under instruction to make a positive response if the instance was a member of the specified category, and negative one if it was not.

We will assume that a task of this kind involves a semantic COMPARISON stage in which attributes of the object referenced by the test word are matched against attributes of the class name. Detailed discussion of the COMPARISON process will be deferred until the next chapter. For the present, the principal interest is in the semantic RETRIEVAL operation which is required to make the relevant attributes of the test word available to COMPARISON. It seems well established that this operation is influenced by the strength of the associative relation existing between the class and instance names. For example, Wilkins (1971) found that the positive RT in this task was related to the production frequency of instance names as responses to category names in a normative study (Cohen, Bousfield & Whitmarsh, 1957). Loftus (1973) proposed that a distinction might usefully be made between *instance dominance* (frequency of occurrence of an instance name as a response to a category name) and *category dominance* (frequency of occurrence of a category name as a response to an instance name). By use of appropriate normative tables (Battig & Montague, 1969; Loftus & Scheff, 1971) she was able to construct word pairs which were dominant on both counts, such as TREE–OAK, pairs which were low on both counts, such as CLOTH–ORLON, and pairs which were high on instance but low on category dominance, such as SEAFOOD–SHRIMP, or which were low on instance but high on category dominance, such as INSECT–BUTTERFLY. In an experiment the word pairs were displayed successively, with either the instance name or the category name first. Pairs of high instance and category dominance were classified faster than pairs of low dominance under both orders of presentation. For pairs having high dominance on one count and low dominance on the other, instance dominance facilitated RT when the instance was presented second, whereas category dominance facilitated when the category was presented second.

The localization of these associative effects in the semantic RETRIEVAL stage of processing can be verified by application of the additive factor method. Sanford, Garrod & Boyle (1977) have reported an experiment in which the factors of instance dominance and stimulus quality were combined. There were strong effects due to both factors, but they were almost perfectly additive. This result is in agreement with the findings of Stanners, Jastrzembski & Westbrook (1975) for word frequency but in conflict with Meyer's findings for association effects (Meyer, Schvaneveldt & Ruddy, 1972, 1974b). We could take this to mean that the effect of dominance on category membership judgements is not simply a variant of the semantic priming effect observed in lexical decision and word naming tasks. However, Sanford, Garrod & Boyle demonstrated that priming by a category name facilitated naming of words, and that this effect interacted with stimulus quality. This seems to imply that a category name can prime the recognizers for dominant instances in some task situations, but that it need not do so.

Why a category name should prime recognizers for instance names in naming and lexical decision tasks but not in categorization tasks is at present uncertain. It may be that the critical distinction is between situations in which successively displayed words may be treated as separate events and situations in which they must be assigned an integrated representation for purposes of COMPARISON. In the latter case attributes of the category name might be cleared from the semantic register and transferred to a comparison register, whereas, in the former, the attributes may be left in the semantic register, causing some incidental priming, until the test word is displayed.

A further point is that categorization requires a degree of *selectivity* in semantic retrieval. The judgement that CANARY is an instance of the class of BIRDS depends on identification of a subset of attributes of the concept (canary) which are relevant for determination of class membership. Although there has been dispute over the stage of processing at which this selection might occur, one reasonable hypothesis is that the retrieval process may be programmed to access categorial attributes. This selective retrieval operation might be expected to show an influence of the strength of the associative relation between the instance and class names.

The assumption that dominance is a factor influencing a selective phase of semantic RETRIEVAL allows us to predict that the effect should combine additively with effects due to factors influencing the COMPARISON stage. From earlier discussion we know that one such factor is M, the size of the memory set, and that another is the positive or negative outcome of the decision. This point can be investigated by adapting Sternberg's symbol classification task to the study of lexical and semantic information processing. In a lexical version of the task lists of words are given as memory sets and the

S classifies probe words as members or non-members of each set (Clifton & Tash, 1973). In the semantic version the memory set consists of category names and the probes are instance names. The *S* responds positively if the probe is a member of any of the categories in memory, and negatively if it is not. The introduction of semantic criteria of equivalence typically produces a 'translation effect' of the kind described by Cruse & Clifton (1973) in symbol classification, that is an increase in the slope of the function relating RT to M, but no change in the intercept. For example, Juola & Atkinson (1971) contrasted lexical and semantic comparisons in an experiment in which *S*s indicated whether a probe was a member of a variable word set, or whether it named an instance of a variable number of categories. The obtained equations were $RT = 617 + 26(M)$ msecs for the lexical task, and: $RT = 653 + 111(M)$ msecs for the category task.

These findings suggest that the distinction between lexical and categorial equivalence is a factor influencing COMPARISON rather than ENCODING or semantic RETRIEVAL. If instance dominance also influenced COMPARISON it would be expected to interact with M in the semantic categorization task. However, a relevant study by McFarland, Kellas, Klueger & Juola (1974) provides no evidence of such an interaction. They varied the instance dominance of probe items and the number of category names in memory and found that these factors exerted additive effects on both positive and negative RTs. To illustrate, the equations for negative trials were: $RT = 608 + 202(M)$ msecs for high dominance items, as against: $RT = 708 + 210(M)$ msecs for low dominance items. Further evidence that dominance of an item in its own category may facilitate negative RT has been given by Millward, Rice & Corbett (1975).

These demonstrations provide strong support for the view that dominance effects are localized in a selective phase of semantic RETRIEVAL. A further possibility is that this sub-stage may be modifiable by repetition. If so, we would predict that dominance and repetition should interact. Hopf-Weichel (1977) investigated the effect of repetition on dominance effects at lags of 5–15 trials in a categorization experiment. The positive RT was affected by dominance and repetition, and the interaction of these effects was significant. As with word frequency, the interaction occurred because items of low dominance gained more by repetition than items of high dominance. Dominance effects were also found to interact with practice in a superordinate naming task (Sanford & Seymour, 1974a).

If the dominance effect is localized in the semantic RETRIEVAL stage preceding COMPARISON it would be expected to combine additively with factors influencing the later processes of response RETRIEVAL and EXPRESSION. One such factor is the compatibility of the decision-report relationship. It will be recalled that in Seymour & Jack's (1978) experiment the instruction to report 'No' for 'same' displays and 'Yes' for 'different' displays did not modify the effects of familiarity of letter strings on graphemic COMPARISON. We might anticipate that this additivity should also be obtained with respect to dominance effects. However, Sanford & Seymour (1974b) found that the magnitude of the dominance effect was substantially increased when *S*s were instructed to use a reversed decision-report mapping.

This interaction of dominance and response compatibility is somewhat puzzling. The reversed instruction clearly creates difficulties for *S*s, tending to raise the level of the RT by 500 msecs or so in this study, and by 300 msecs or more in experiments on word-shape comparison (Seymour, 1969b, 1970b, 1971). Logically, the compatibility effect, which is located after COMPARISON, should not influence the size of the dominance effect, which is located before COMPARISON. One possibility is that the instruction to reverse the normal decision-response mapping is rehearsed throughout the experimental sequence and is represented in the semantic register at the outset of each trial. This instructional code might compete with the test word for space in the semantic register, and could in that way influence the semantic RETRIEVAL process. The *S* is, in effect, trying simultaneously to consider the meaning of the experimental instruction and of the words displayed on the current trial.

XI.6 CONCLUSIONS

This chapter has discussed aspects of the processes involved in retrieval of semantic codings of visual words. The main argument has been that retrieval depends on the pattern recognition and addressing capabilities of a lexical interface structure. This interface has been viewed as a logogen system, in the sense described by Morton (1968, 1969a), but as being specialized for recognition of graphemic patterns, and for the achievement of access to a semantic data store.

It seems evident from the experimental findings described in this and the preceding chapter that a semantic RETRIEVAL stage enters in a significant way into tasks requiring reports of briefly displayed words, naming of words, lexical decisions, and semantic decisions. We have argued that semantic RETRIEVAL includes two sub-stages, the first involving recognition of graphemic descriptions of words or word stems, and the second the selective retrieval of a subset of semantic attributes. The review of currently available research suggested that the pattern recognition sub-stage was influenced by visual factors, including word shape and stimulus quality, and by a form of transitory semantic priming. The selective retrieval sub-stage appeared sensitive to word frequency and associative strength, and showed a relatively durable effect of recent processing of a word.

The evidence reviewed supports a general account of the processes involved in recognition and interpretation of words, but leaves a number of matters of substance unresolved. There is firstly the problem of homographs, that is single visual forms which specify a variety of alternative senses. Some mechanism is required which will allow for selective access to the contextually appropriate set of semantic attributes. We have tentatively opted for the view that separate pattern recognizers exist for each distinct sense of a homograph, and that selectivity may be mediated, in part at least, by the mechanism of semantic priming. Secondly, there is the problem of morphemic structure. It is not at present clear to what extent a word must be parsed into morphemic elements, by stripping away of affixes and isolation of its stem, before lexical access can occur. This points to a more general problem of distinguishing between retrieval of semantic attributes of objects or events referenced by a word and retrieval of syntactic attributes defining its logical function in communication. These matters are fundamental to an understanding of the lexical interface, and deserve more extensive experimental analysis.

CHAPTER XII

Verification

SEMANTIC AND LOGICAL COMPARISON

XII.1 INTRODUCTION

The previous chapter considered some aspects of the process of RETRIEVAL of semantic attributes of nouns, chiefly by reference to experiments on categorization. In these studies the *S*s were in effect answering implicit Yes/No questions of the form: 'Is bird a class name for canary?' or 'Is a canary a kind of bird?' We suggested that responses to such questions might depend on the retrieval of attributes linked to 'canary' and 'bird' which are relevant for determination of issues of class membership. Once retrieved these attributes can be passed to a semantic COMPARISON stage during which a judgement of their equivalence can be made.

Decisions about the class membership of nouns are part of a complex process of *verification* which achieves a judgement of the truth or falsity of a sentence. This topic touches on a number of issues in philosophy concerning the analysis of meaning and truth and the logical structure of sentences which lie somewhat outside the scope of the present discussion. In this chapter consideration will be limited to a sub-class of declarative affirmative sentences (and their negative counterparts) which have a simple subject-predicate structure, and which assert that the referents of the subject nouns are contained in a larger class of entities or possess a specified property or attribute. We can call these category statements ('A canary is a bird') and property statements, the latter being divisible into statements about static properties ('A canary is yellow', 'A canary has wings') and statements about more active properties ('A canary can fly').

The determination of the 'truth' or 'falsity' of such sentences depends on the discovery of a correspondence between an interpretation assigned to the sentence and a knowledge of objects which forms part of the permanent content of the Lexical Memory. There appear to be three distinct aspects of this correspondence which may usefully be emphasized. The first of these concerns a partial correspondence which may exist between object descriptions. The nouns 'canary' and 'bird' may each access a description of properties of shape, size, colour, function, capability, location, affective tone, and so forth, which is held in the semantic data store of Figure VIII.5.1. These descriptions may be expected to overlap in certain respects, and discovery of the area of overlap could provide the verification process with the evidence needed to determine the truth of a given assertion.

Object descriptions of this kind must also be highly structured internally. Part of the description of 'bird' is that it is made up of components such as 'beak', 'wings', 'tail', 'legs', just as part of the description of 'canary' is that it is coloured 'yellow'. We might think of the components as being linked into the object description by a structure defining their locations and their status as object parts. Thus, 'beak' is linked to 'bird' by a (has-as-part) relationship, whereas 'yellow' is linked to 'canary' by a (has-as-colour) relationship. Relationships of this type are linguistically expressed by sentence frames of the form: 'A —— has a ——', or 'A —— is ——'. It follows that there are two conditions to be met if a propery statement is to be taken to be 'true'. The predicated attribute must occur as a component of the description of the subject noun, and there must be a correspondence between the logical relation expressed in the sentence and the relation specified in the object description. Violation of the logical requirement can be noted in such 'false' sentences as: 'A canary is a beak', 'A canary has a bird' or 'A canary can tail'.

Logical factors are also involved in the determination of the truth or falsity of category statements. Such statements assert the existence of a particular relationship between a set of entities named by the subject noun and a set of entities named by the predicate noun. This logical structure is specified by the ordering of the nouns in the sentence frame, the determiner or quantifier governing the subject noun, and the affirmative or negative form of the sentence. These aspects combine to give linguistic expression to a relationship between two noun categories, and the sentence is said to be 'true' if a correspondence exists between this relationship and the relationship between the categories which is represented in permanent memory. To illustrate, we can note that the truth value of a sentence may be altered by a change of word order ('All canaries are birds' versus 'All birds are canaries'), a change of quantifier ('All birds are canaries' versus 'Some birds are canaries'), or by the substitution of a negative quantifier ('Some birds are canaries' versus 'No birds are canaries'). It is evident that the determination of the truth of assertions about 'birds' and 'canaries' cannot be based simply on the discovery of a set of shared attributes. The superset-subset relationship existing between these noun categories must be represented in some accessible form which can be matched against the logical structure of the sentence.

These comments suggest that verification is a highly complex mental function which operates on the logical (syntactic) structure of sentences and which makes use of subordinate retrieval and comparison procedures. Determination of truth or falsity may depend on retrieval and matching of selected parts of object descriptions or on retrieval of a logical code specifying a relationship between concepts and the matching of this against the structural interpretation of a sentence. It seems, therefore, that verification may make use of two distinct types of RETRIEVAL operation, involving: (1) retrieval of object descriptions, and (2) the retrieval of relational expressions. A distinction of this kind was represented in the diagram of the Lexical Memory (see Figure VIII.5.1), where a *semantic data store* containing object descriptions was distinguished from a *structural data store* containing relational expressions. The distinction is preserved in the *semantic register* which has an upper level for specification of logical and relational structure and a subordinate level containing slots for object descriptions.

XII.2 SELECTIVE SEMANTIC RETRIEVAL

A discussion of the retrieval processes underlying sentence verification runs immediately into conceptual problems concerning the nature of the semantic codes which may form the output of the RETRIEVAL function. These problems are reflected in theoretical debates between those who view object classes as arrays of exemplars (Meyer, 1970), or bundles of attributes or features (Smith, Shoben & Rips, 1974), and those who have emphasized the preservation of logical structure in memory, either in the form of a network of relational links (Frijda, 1970; Rumelhart, Lindsay & Norman, 1972; Anderson & Bower, 1973) or a structure of logically inter-related semantic markers (Katz, 1972; Glass & Holyoak, 1976). It seems likely that there is merit in all of these suggestions, since it is evident that people have a knowledge of class exemplars, class attributes and logical relationships between classes which they can call on to meet the requirements of a particular task.

The problem for an analysis of sentence verification is one of specifying the type of information which is consulted in reaching a 'true' or 'false' decision. We can illustrate this by considering the verification of the category statement: 'A canary is a bird'. The truth of this assertion could be confirmed by establishing that the relationship between 'canary' and 'bird' expressed in the sentence by the syntactic frame: 'A —— is a ——' corresponds to the relationship between these noun categories which is stored in memory. In terms of Figure VIII.5.1, this would require that the structural data store should be accessed by syntactically significant components of the sentence and that an appropriate logical description should be placed in the upper level of the semantic register. The structural data store must also be accessed by the nouns 'canary' and 'bird' in order to determine the logical relationship between these classes which is represented in permanent memory. It is uncertain whether this type of relational information could be accessed directly from the graphemic register, or whether, as seems more probable, it is accessible only to semantic input. In this case the graphemic forms 'canary' and 'bird' would have to access their object descriptions in the semantic data store before retrieval of relational information could occur. On completion of these activities the logical level of the semantic register would contain two relational descriptions, one derived from analysis of the sentence frame and the other from consideration of the subject and predicate nouns. An executive controlling VERIFICATION could then decide the truth or falsity of the sentence by calling on a COMPARISON operation to determine whether or not the two relational expressions were equivalent. In this case the 'true'–'false' decision would be said to be based on the outcome of a *logical comparison*.

A second and possibly more direct procedure is to make a comparison of the object descriptions of 'canary' and 'bird'. Provided that the logical structure of the test sentences is not varied by changes of word order or quantification, matching of selected attributes of the two concepts might well be sufficient to indicate whether or not it is likely that they are linked by a subset-superset relation. However, the efficient use of this procedure seems to depend on a capability for *selective retrieval* of attributes which are relevant to the inter-concept relationship which has been asserted. To illustrate, the assertions: 'A canary and a crow are birds' and 'A canary and a banana are yellow' are both 'true', whereas the assertions: 'A canary and a banana are birds' and 'A canary and a crow are yellow' are both 'false'. When class membership is at issue bundles of attributes specifying characteristics common to members of the classes of 'birds' and 'fruits' are relevant to the decision process, but other attributes, including those of colour, are not relevant. When colour is at issue this dimension is defined as relevant and the categorial attributes must be treated as irrelevant. It follows that a verification procedure which relies on the matching of object descriptions depends on a subsidiary capability for selective focus on relevant subsets of attributes.

In the model of the Lexical Memory which is under discussion here selective retrieval has been viewed as a property of the lexical interface structure. An executive controlling the interface—called TASK in Chapter VI—makes and unmakes links between pattern recognizers and cells of registers of addresses of locations in permanent storage. If useful selectivity is to be achieved TASK must be able to link the graphemic (or phonemic) pattern recognizers to addresses of significant subsets of attributes, such as categorial attributes, colour attributes, size attributes, and so forth. This control over retrieval could be established in a general way if, for example, all sentences presented for verification conformed to a subset-superset ordering of subject and predicate nouns within a standard syntactic frame of the: 'A —— is a ——' variety. If this condition was not met, or category statements were intermixed with property statements, the control over retrieval might have to depend on the outcome of the logical analysis of each test sentence. For example, discovery that the sentence had the logical structure: 'A —— has a ——' might lead to an instruction to TASK to set the interface for selective retrieval of attributes concerned with component parts of objects.

If this account of selective retrieval is correct an implication is that the relational codes are both contained in the structural data store and built into the system for linking pattern recognizers to address registers in the lexical interface. The existence of this correspondence effectively allows a logical structure in the semantic register to dominate the retrieval of selected attributes from the semantic data store. Once retrieved, these attribute sets can be passed to a COMPARISON stage for matching. The mechanism for comparison is envisaged as being the same as that described in Chapter VII, consisting of a comparison register which holds the feature descriptions, and a judgemental component containing 'same' and 'different' accumulators which respond to feature match/mismatch signals. Provided that attribute retrieval has been adequately selective, and that the test sentence structures are sufficiently restricted, a matching outcome will indicate to the VERIFICATION executive that the sentence is probably 'true', whereas a mismatching outcome will indicate that it is probably 'false'. In this case, the 'true'–'false' decision may be said to depend on the outcome of a *semantic comparison*.

XII.3 SEMANTIC ATTRIBUTES

An important assumption in this discussion has been that the object descriptions contained in the semantic data store are decomposable into more elementary components which have been referred to as attributes or properties. One influential view has been that the attributes are dimensions of variation which are common to the descriptions of many different object classes, so that the object description specifies the values which the object takes on each of a number of dimensions (Osgood, Suci & Tannenbaum, 1957; Smith, Shoben & Rips, 1974). For example, multi-dimensional scaling of ratings of the similarity of members of classes of living creatures (mammals, birds, fishes) has suggested that the important dimensions of variation may be size and ferocity (Henley, 1969; Rips, Shoben & Smith, 1973; Caramazza, Hersh & Torgerson, 1976; Shoben, 1976).

On these grounds we could propose that the semantic data store is internally structured as a set of dimensions, and that the information retrieved from the store consists of a dimension label, which is part of the logical structure of the object description, and a value or range of values on that dimension. Experimental studies designed to explore some consequences of this hypothesis have for the most part concentrated on the *relative judgement task* which was described in Chapter VI as a technique of investigating the structural coding of the number series or alphabet. This is quite appropriate, since semantic attributes appear formally akin to scales of magnitude if they are viewed as specifications of values on dimensions.

It may be recalled that the experiments on the numerals conducted by Moyer & Landauer (1967), Parkman (1971), Banks, Fujii & Kayra-Stuart (1976) and others revealed three important effects. When *S*s were asked to choose the larger (or smaller) of two digits their RTs were affected by the *distance* between the numbers, the *position* of the smaller number in the number series, and the *congruity* of the semantic relation between the end of the size dimension specified in the instruction and the large or small value of the test numerals. There is evidence that qualitatively similar effects occur when *S*s make comparative judgements about semantic dimensions. RTs to indicate the larger of two named animals increase as the size difference between the animals becomes smaller, so that pairs such as ANT/BEE or COW/ELK are judged less rapidly than ANT/COW or BEE/ELK (Moyer, 1973). Paivio (1975b) confirmed this effect for a wider sample of animate and inanimate object names. The names were rated with respect to absolute size in a normative study, and the ratio of the ratings was used to predict the RT for each pair. Semantic judgements also typically show effects of scale position of the items in a series, usually a facilitation of RT for the extreme positions (Banks, 1977). Interactions between the instructions 'Choose larger' or 'Choose smaller' and scale position (semantic congruity effects) were obtained by Jamieson & Petrusic (1975) and Banks & Flora (1977).

These effects of distance, position and semantic congruity also occur when dimensions other than size are tested. Banks & Flora (1977) instructed *S*s to make relative judgements about intelligence levels of animals, the instructions: 'Choose smarter' and 'Choose dumber' being randomly interchanged. The experiment showed a clear semantic congruity effect, with choice of the smarter member of the pair being quicker for intelligent animals, such as APE and DOG, than for unintelligent animals, such as FISH and CHICKEN, whereas the reverse was true for the 'Choose dumber' instruction. There was also a strong distance effect, animals close on the scale being classified less rapidly than animals which were further apart. Friedman (1976) tested a list of abstract nouns which varied on a dimension of evaluative meaning. *S*s were instructed to 'Choose the better' or 'Choose the worse' word of each pair, and a clear distance effect was obtained. Holyoak & Walker (1976) reported data for names of time periods (... year, month, week, day, ... etc), expressions of quality (perfect, excellent ... poor, awful), and temperature terms (hot ... warm ... cold). All three scales yielded evidence of distance effects and semantic congruity effects. As was mentioned in Chapter VI these effects also occur when a temporal series, such as the names of the months of the year, is tested (Seymour, 1976a).

These experiments encourage the view that the semantic representation of an object class may be composed, in part at least, of magnitude specifications on labelled dimensions of variation. Such dimensions are linguistically specified by certain property statements, especially those having adjectival predicates ('A canary is small'), and by comparative statements ('A canary is larger than a wren', 'A canary is nicer than a crow'). The verification of the sentence 'A canary is small' requires that the sentence should be interpreted as having the logical structure of a sentence in which a size value is predicated, and that this structure should control selective retrieval of size attributes linked to 'canary'. This size description and an analogous description retrieved by the adjective 'small' can then be passed to the COMPARISON stage for matching.

The pioneering study of sentence verification by Collins & Quillian (1969) included a mixture of category statements ('A canary is a bird') and property statements asserting possession of parts, qualities and capabilities. A consistent finding was that property statements were verified less rapidly than category statements, the RT difference being approximately 225 msecs. This could indicate that selective retrieval of property information is less rapid than selective retrieval of a bundle of categorial attributes. However, the difference is not evident in studies in which category and property statements have not been mixed in the trial sequence (Glass, Holyoak & O'Dell, 1974), and the implication may be that the procedure used by Collins & Quillian necessitated deeper analysis of the logical structure of property statements for the purpose of identifying the attribute in question.

Although formal distinctions exist between adjectival statements ('A canary is yellow'), possession statements ('A canary has a beak'), and capability statements ('A canary can sing'), there is little evidence of RT differences among these sentence types in verification tasks (Nelson & Kosslyn, 1975; Holyoak, Glass & Mah, 1976). Thus, the 'active' properties ('... can fly', '... can sing') appear no more or less accessible than the 'static' properties ('... is yellow', '... has wings'). Holyoak, Glass & Mah (1976) have commented on linguistic conventions in attribution of static properties. Possession of a part is normally indicated by a 'have' statement ('A canary has feathers') whereas possession of a quality is indicated by an adjectival statement ('A canary is yellow'). Reversal of this convention ('A canary is feathered', 'A canary has yellowness') produces unnatural forms which are associated with a delay of RT in verification tasks. This is consistent with the proposal that verification of a property statement is contingent on an operation of grammatical analysis which guides selective retrieval of relevant attributes of the subject noun.

The verification of comparative sentences ('A canary is larger than a wren') is more complex. The comparative expression ('... is larger than ...', '... is smaller than ...') specifies the relevant dimension of variation (size) and the relative locations of the subject and predicate nouns on that dimension. Interest in this situation has focussed on the possibility that verification RT may be influenced by the direction of ordering of the subject and predicate nouns on the underlying dimension. The statement: 'A canary is larger than a wren' asserts that 'canary' has a greater value on the size dimension than 'wren', whereas the statement: 'A wren is smaller than a canary' asserts that 'wren' has a lower value than 'canary'. Although the two statements are equivalent with respect to truth value, verification RT is typically found to be faster for the '... is larger than ...' comparative than for the '... is smaller than ...' comparative (Gordon, 1976). This effect has been noted for a variety of dimensions, and has been related to a linguistic distinction between unmarked and marked members of antonym pairs (Greenberg, 1966). In general, the unmarked term refers to values on the positive or upper end of a dimension, and is often linguistically close to the name of the dimension, while the marked term is restricted in reference to the negative or lower end of the dimension. For example, the positive end of the dimension of 'depth' is labelled by the unmarked form 'deep' whereas the negative end is labelled by the linguistically unrelated marked form 'shallow'.

Carpenter (1974) conducted a study of verification of comparative sentences in which unmarked and marked expressions relating to several dimensions were tested. She reported that sentences with unmarked comparatives were verified about 240 msecs faster than sentences with marked comparatives. This markedness effect combined additively with the 'true' or 'false' classification of the sentence. It is possible that this is a linguistic effect analogous to the one described by Holyoak, Glass & Mah (1976). Determination of the dimension which is relevant for verification of the sentence may be achieved faster when the comparative is unmarked than when it is marked. Since a linguistic effect of this kind relates to a stage of sentence interpretation which controls selective semantic retrieval and precedes later comparison activities we would expect it to combine additively with 'true'–'false' differences. However, it is also possible that there is a semantic element in the markedness effect which is related to the positive connotation of unmarked terms and the negative connotation of marked terms (Gordon, 1976). This matter will be discussed further in Part Three.

XII.4 PRODUCTION FREQUENCY AND SEMANTIC RELATEDNESS

The argument up to this point has been that verification of a sentence depends in the first instance on an analysis of its logical structure followed by the selective retrieval of semantic attributes which are relevant to the determination of its truth or falsity. On the basis of the experimental evidence presented at the end of the last chapter (Section XI.5) we can anticipate that *associative strength* (as determined by production frequency norms or ratings of semantic proximity) is a factor which is likely to influence the selective RETRIEVAL stage.

There is good evidence to support the conclusion that the associative relationship between the subject and predicate of a sentence affects the verification RT. Collins & Quillian (1969) noted that 'true' RT for category statements increased as the predicate category became more remote from the subject category ('A canary is a bird' versus 'A canary is an animal'). Names of mammals are classified faster when the category 'animal' is used as a predicate than when the category is the technically correct term 'mammal' (Rips, Shoben & Smith, 1973). Glass, Holyoak & O'Dell (1974) obtained normative data on production frequencies of nouns by instructing *S*s to provide predicates for incomplete sentences quantified by 'all', 'many' and 'some'. They also reported that 'true' RT was facilitated when the production frequency of the predicate noun was high.

Comparable associative effects have been observed in verification of property statements. Collins & Quillian (1969) noted that properties which were strongly characteristic of an object ('A canary is yellow') were verified faster than properties which appeared more remote ('A canary has skin'). Nelson & Kosslyn (1975) also found that properties rated as highly salient in the description of an object produced facilitation of the 'true' RT. Conrad (1972) and Glass, Holyoak & O'Dell (1974) obtained production frequency norms for property sentence frames. They too found that predicates of high production frequency were associated with fast 'true' RTs.

These experiments establish that the strength of the subject-predicate relationship can have an important effect on verification RT. Although it seems likely that this effect is related to the operation of selective semantic RETRIEVAL we cannot exclude the possibility that semantic relatedness influences the duration of a subsequent stage of semantic COMPARISON. The effect can be localized in the selective RETRIEVAL stage if production frequency can be shown to combine interactively with other factors thought to influence RETRIEVAL. One such factor is the repetition of items in the experimental series which was found to interact with dominance variations in superordinate naming (Sanford & Seymour, 1974a) and categorization (Hopf-Weichel, 1977). Collins & Quillian (1970b) also found that repetition of the subject nouns of property statements reduced the general level of the RT and the size of the effect due to remoteness of the predicated property from the subject noun. In the experiment by Holyoak, Glass & Mah (1976) the effect of variations in the linguistic form of the predicate interacted with production frequency, being greater for low than for high frequency predicates. Thus, if repetition and linguistic form are taken to be factors influencing RETRIEVAL, we may reasonably conclude that production frequency also influences this stage.

If production frequency were a factor exerting a *selective* influence on semantic RETRIEVAL it would not be expected to interact with factors influencing the COMPARISON and judgemental stages of verification. We will take one such factor to be the 'true' or 'false' outcome of the verification process. The study reported by Glass, Holyoak & O'Dell (1974) allows us to test for an interaction between production frequency and 'true'–'false' decision. Their production task included incomplete sentences quantified by the negatives 'no' and 'few' as well as by the positives 'some', 'all' and 'many'. Predicates which occurred with high frequency in completions of negatively quantified sentences were used as a source of 'false' positive statements. For example, the 'false' assertion: 'All fires are cold' derives from the frequent use of 'cold' as a predicate for the frame: 'No fires are ——'. Instances of this kind were contrasted with 'false' sentences having predicates which never occurred as responses to the negatively quantified frames. A consistent finding was that the RT to reject 'false' sentences with 'all', 'many' and 'some' as quantifiers was greater for examples of high production frequency than for examples of low relatedness. Since this effect is in the opposite direction to that observed for the 'true' sentences we can conclude that production frequency does indeed interact with 'true'–'false' decision.

This inhibitory effect of semantic relatedness on 'false' RT has been reported in a number of categorization and verification experiments. For categorization Wilkins (1971), Collins & Quillian (1970a), Sanford, Garrod & Boyle (1977) and Smith, Shoben & Rips (1974) all reported that negative items which were related to the category name were rejected less rapidly than negatives which were more remote. Analogous findings have been obtained in sentence verification experiments. Collins & Quillian (1970c) noted that semantically confusable 'false' sentences, such as: 'A tiger has a mane', were rejected less rapidly than non-confusable sentences. In an experiment by Rips,

Shoben & Smith (1973) 'false' sentences asserting that a bird or mammal instance was a 'car' were rejected much more rapidly than sentences asserting that a mammal instance was a 'bird' or that a bird instance was a 'mammal'. The latter type of confusion, exemplified in the sentence: 'A pigeon is a mammal', was greater than that observed in sentences such as: 'A dog is a bird' in which the category 'bird' was predicated of a mammal instance.

We can therefore conclude that semantic relatedness interacts with the 'true' or 'false' outcome of the decision process in both categorization and sentence verification experiments. In general, relatedness facilitates 'true' decisions but inhibits 'false' decisions. The interaction parallels the relationship between visual similarity and 'same'–'different' RT found in letter matching experiments (Posner & Mitchell, 1967), and also the interactions with meaningfulness obtained in experiments on graphemic comparison (see Chapter IX). Its occurrence appears sufficient to allow us to reject the view that relatedness effects are limited to a selective facilitation of a semantic RETRIEVAL stage occurring prior to verification. We must also accept that relatedness influences the judgemental phases of verification.

XII.5 SEMANTIC COMPARISON

The occurrence of an inhibitory effect of semantic relatedness on the 'false' RT has an important bearing on an issue which was raised in Section 2 of this chapter. It was noted there that verification of a category statement such as 'A canary is a bird' might involve a *logical comparison* of relational expressions or a *semantic comparison* of selected attributes. If relatedness facilitated retrieval of a logical expression from the structural data store—e.g. the '—— is a ——' relation linking 'canary' and 'bird'—we would expect to observe facilitation for both 'true' and 'false' RTs. In a related negative sentence, such as: 'A canary is a parrot', the co-ordinate relation existing between 'canary' and 'parrot' should be quickly retrieved and found to mismatch the subset relation expressed in the sentence. Hence, related negative sentences should be rejected faster than unrelated negative sentences, such as 'A canary is a hammer'. A semantic comparison, on the other hand, is based on the matching of arrays of categorial attributes. We know from the research discussed in Chapter VII that 'different' decisions are delayed as the correspondence between two arrays is increased. An inhibitory effect of relatedness is therefore consistent with the view that the verification of assertions about objects often involves an operation of comparison of semantic attributes.

Recently formulated models of the semantic comparison process have described various mechanisms which might give rise to facilitatory and inhibitory effects on 'true' and 'false' RT. Schaeffer & Wallace (1970) discussed the possibility that semantic comparison might be a two-stage process. They thought that object descriptions might initially be matched in a global or holistic fashion, and that this stage might then be followed by a more analytic comparison which focused on a relevant subset of attributes. In order to explain the effects of relatedness they argued that the thresholds of 'same' and 'different' decision makers were adjusted following the preliminary comparison. The adjustment was supposed to be reciprocal in nature, with detection of a high degree of similarity resulting in a reduction in the 'same' threshold and a rise in the 'different' threshold, while detection of a low degree of similarity produced the opposite effect.

This threshold adjustment model was suggested as an explanation of results obtained in two-word categorization tasks studied by Schaeffer & Wallace (1969, 1970). In these tasks the *S*s were instructed to respond positively to pairs of words which named members of the same category, and negatively to pairs of words which named members of different categories. In the first experiment a positive response was required if the words were both names of living things or if both were names of non-living things. It was found that 'same' RT was facilitated by semantic similarity in that pairs drawn from the same object class (LION/CAMEL, TULIP/IRIS) were classified faster than different category pairs (LION/TULIP, CAMEL/IRIS) (Schaeffer & Wallace, 1969). In the second study similarity was shown to inhibit 'different' decisions. *S*s responded positively to word pairs which were both trees, both flowers, both mammals, or both birds. The RT to reject related pairs, such as DAISY/CEDAR, was greater by about 100 msecs than the RT to reject less related pairs, such as DAISY/GIRAFFE (Schaeffer & Wallace, 1970).

The attack on this theory initially took the form of a demonstration that it was inadequate as an account of the two-word categorization task. A key prediction of the model is that both 'same' and 'different' RT should reflect the closeness of the semantic relationship existing between the nouns presented for categorization. Rips, Shoben & Smith (1973) obtained ratings of the proximity of mammal and bird instance names to their category names and to one another. They conducted a study in which *S*s responded positively to pairs of bird names in one trial block, and to pairs of mammals in another trial block. A correlational analysis indicated that the 'same' RT was related to the distance between the first instance name and its category, but not to the distance between the two instances. Shoben (1976) reported a further experiment in which *S*s responded positively to pairs of birds, mammals, fruits or vegetables. He confirmed that the relatedness of 'different' pairs produced an inhibitory effect on the RT. However, the magnitude of the effect depended on the order in which the words were read, being greater for a bird-mammal pair than for a mammal-bird pair. This was seen as inconsistent with the Schaeffer & Wallace model since order of reading should not have influenced the global similarity of the concepts passed to the COMPARISON stage.

It seems likely that the *S*s were carrying out Shoben's task by categorizing the upper noun of each pair and by then testing the second noun for membership of that category. Such an account appears consistent with Rips, Shoben & Smith's (1973) finding of a correlation between 'same' RT and distance between the upper word of each pair and its category, and also with their observation that bird instances are more confusable with the category 'mammal' than are mammal instances with the category 'bird'. Shoben (1976) examined the correlation between 'different' RT and measures of rated semantic distance. He was unable to find a correlation between RT and instance-instance distance, although the RT was significantly related to the distance between the first instance and its category and also to the distance of the second instance from that same category. These two effects were approximately additive. Such a pattern of results is clearly contrary to the predictions of the Schaeffer & Wallace model and appears sufficient to lead us to reject the model as an account of the comparison process occurring in the two-word categorization task.

Smith, Shoben & Rips (1974) described an alternative attribute matching model of COMPARISON, also incorporating two substages, the first global or holistic and the second analytic and focused. Their theory differed from that of Schaeffer & Wallace in the suggestion that the second stage might be optional and that its occurrence might be made conditional on the outcome of the first stage. The model derived from a formally similar proposal made by Atkinson and his associates to account for RT data obtained in experiments on old-new judgements about words stored in episodic memory (Juola, Fischler, Wood & Atkinson, 1971; Atkinson & Juola, 1973, 1974). Atkinson proposed that words occurring in a recognition memory task might retrieve an index of familiarity and that an immediate positive or negative decision could be taken if the value of this index was very high or very low. When the value was intermediate a second processing stage was initiated, which involved, in Atkinson's account, a search through a list structure stored in episodic memory. In Smith, Shoben & Rips' (1974) adaptation of this model the first stage of processing was seen as a feature matching procedure which determined the overall similarity of the unedited attribute descriptions of an instance name and category name. If this similarity index exceeded a high criterion a 'true' decision was immediately taken. If the index fell below a low criterion a 'false' decision was taken. Only if the similarity index was found to fall between these criterial values was the second, more analytic stage of processing initiated, which was seen by Smith as a focused comparison of the essential or defining attributes of the two concepts.

The Smith, Shoben & Rips model, therefore, asserts that relatedness affects the RT by varying the probability that the second analytical stage of processing will be required in order to reach a decision about category membership. A 'same' decision will be taken faster for a good member of a category, where goodness is determined by ratings of relatedness or typicality (Rips, Shoben & Smith, 1973; Rosch, 1973, 1975a), than for a poor or atypical member, because good members usually produce a similarity score which exceeds the criterion for a fast positive response. 'Different' decisions will be delayed by relatedness because related negative items will generally produce a similarity score which exceeds the criterion for a fast negative response and thus triggers the second stage of processing.

It will be evident that the Schaeffer & Wallace and Smith, Shoben & Rips models of semantic comparison differ from the approach adopted in this chapter in their handling of the problem of selectivity in retrieval. In both theories it has been assumed that object descriptions are retrieved in an unedited form and that these unedited attribute sets are matched at a first stage of comparison. Both theories also accept that there is a logical requirement for selectivity of focus on particular subsets of attributes, and this selectivity is located in the COMPARISON stage. An alternative, and from the present point of view more reasonable, possibility is that selectivity is a property of a semantic RETRIEVAL stage which passes edited sets of attributes to the COMPARISON stage. This suggestion is highly damaging to the two-stage models. If the information passed to COMPARISON consists of *selected* subsets of relevant attributes the first holistic stage of comparison appears superfluous, and the rationale for explaining the relatedness effects (whether by a mechanism of threshold adjustment or triggering of second stage processing) can be seen to collapse. The models might be defended if there were strong *a priori* reasons for locating semantic selectivity in the COMPARISON stage, or if experimental factors associated with each sub-stage of the comparison could be identified and shown to yield additivity of effects. However, such arguments or demonstrations have not been forthcoming (Glass & Holyoak, 1976).

An explanation of the relatedness effects can be stated within the terms of the sampling and decision model of COMPARISON which was described in Chapter VII. We assume that relevant subsets of attributes are accessed by a selective RETRIEVAL operation and are then transferred to the comparison register (see Figure VII.1.1) for matching. The RETRIEVAL stage is facilitated by relatedness, so that, for example, retrieval of a subset of categorial properties might be expected to occur faster for a good example of a category than for a poor example. The duration of the COMPARISON stage should be sensitive to the sizes of the arrays of attributes (analogous to the factors of memory set size, M, and display set size, D, in the earlier discussion), and also to the degree of correspondence between the arrays (the factor C in Chapter VII). Although we cannot in general know about the size of the arrays of attributes, information about the degree to which they correspond may be captured, to some extent at least, in ratings of typicality and relatedness (Rosch, 1975a; Rips, Shoben & Smith, 1973; Caramazza, Hersh & Torgerson, 1976). The correspondence of attributes of related negatives may often be intuitively obvious. For example, the categorial properties of 'cedar' and 'daisy' are likely to correspond more closely than those of 'cedar' and 'giraffe', or 'cedar' and 'hammer' because their immediately superordinate classes, 'tree' and 'flower', both have 'plant' as a superordinate category (Schaeffer & Wallace, 1970; Collins & Quillian, 1970a).

In the discussion of array comparison in Chapter VII a distinction was proposed between conjunctive definitions of equivalence (arrays containing the same elements in the same positions) and disjunctive definitions which allow various types of partial correspondence between the arrays. It seems unlikely that the array matching procedure required for semantic comparison fits either of these standard cases. If it is to tolerate typicality variations the system must be permitted to classify arrays as 'same' provided they correspond on a majority of attributes. If it is to avoid error with related negatives it must switch to a 'different' classification if only a minority of attributes are found to correspond. A decision rule meeting this requirement is one which responds to a predominance of match or mismatch evidence. An appropriate instruction in a letter matching task would be to classify the arrays as 'same' if a majority of positions contained the same letters, and as 'different' if a majority contained different letters. Although this situation was not examined in Chapter VII, we may confidently anticipate that 'same' RT and error rate would be likely to increase as the value of C was shifted from $C = D$ to $C = \frac{1}{2}D + 1$, and that the 'different' RT and error rate would increase as C was altered from $C = O$ to $C = \frac{1}{2}D - 1$, where D is the array size and C is the number of positions containing same symbols.

These comments illustrate the manner in which the typicality of positive instances and the relatedness of negative instances might influence the duration of a single stage COMPARISON process. A first assumption is that typicality and relatedness index variations in the correspondence, C, of the attribute arrays sent for comparison. It is then assumed that the MATCH executive applies a routine which transforms elements of the two attribute sets to a sequence of binary match/mismatch signals. As in the earlier account, the match/mismatch signals are thought to flow along a single channel from the comparison register to the judgemental accumulators. Reductions in the value of C will slow the rate of accumulation of evidence in the 'same' accumulator on account of occupation of the channel by mismatch signals, thus producing a tendency for RT and error rate to rise when atypical instances are classified. Similarly, the time to reach a 'different' decision will increase as C becomes larger because the channel will be partly occupied by match signals, and this will produce increases in RT and error rate in classification of related negatives.

XII.6 QUANTIFICATION AND SET RELATION

As has been pointed out by Glass & Holyoak (1976), models which rely on matching of attributes as a basis for a 'true' or 'false' decision are in principle inadequate as general accounts of sentence verification. The reason for this is that the attributes specify the internal structure of an object concept but not the logical relationships which may exist between object classes. As was shown in the introduction to this chapter, it is not difficult to find examples which demonstrate that the determination of truth value must often depend on a consideration of these logical relationships. Attribute matching procedures are likely to provide an inadequate guide to truth value under such circumstances, and may be abandoned or supplemented by logical comparison procedures.

Meyer (1970) introduced experimental techniques which may be used to study the effects on verification RT of variations in the logical structure of the test sentence. The truth of a category statement depends on the set relationship existing between the subject and predicate categories, and the quantifier modifying the subject. Set relations are of four types: (1) Set A may be a *proper subset* of Set B, as 'canaries' is a subset of 'birds'; (2) Set A may be a *proper superset* of Set B, as 'birds' is a superset of 'canaries'; (3) Set A may *overlap* Set B, as 'canaries' overlaps 'pets'; (4) Set A may be *disjoint* from Set B, as 'canaries' is disjoint from 'cabbages'. A particular affirmative statement uses the quantifier 'some' to assert that some (and possibly all) members of Set A (specified by the subject of the sentence) are included in Set B (specified in the predicate). Such statements are 'true' when Sets A and B are related by a subset relation ('Some canaries are birds'), a superset relation ('Some birds are canaries') or an overlap relation ('Some canaries are pets'), but are 'false' for a disjoint relation ('Some canaries are cabbages'). The quantifier 'all' is used to make a universal affirmative statement which asserts that every member of Set A is also a member of Set B. These statements are 'true' when Sets A and B are related by a subset relation ('All canaries are birds') but are 'false' when the sets are related by superset, overlap or disjoint relations.

Meyer conducted two experiments in which *S*s classified universal or particular affirmative sentences involving these four types of subject-predicate set relation as 'true' or 'false'. The structure of the sentence materials was such that it was probably possible for *S*s to classify particular affirmatives on the basis of a test of the relatedness of the subject and predicate nouns, that is by an operation of semantic comparison of attributes. The false sentences were anomalous forms, such as: 'Some houses are vacuums', in which the subject and predicate were effectively unrelated, whereas the 'true' sentences involved a subset, superset or overlap relation. If we assume that the overlap statements, such as: 'Some women are writers', were less related than subset or superset statements ('Some chairs are furniture', 'Some stones are rubies'), we can anticipate that 'true' RT should be greater for overlap statements than for subset or superset statements. These expectations were confirmed by Meyer's data which showed a 100 msec difference between overlap and subset or superset statements. The experiment also incorporated a manipulation of the sizes of the subject and predicate sets which may be interpreted as a variation in relatedness. The subject-predicate relatedness of a subset statement may be enhanced by increasing the size of the subject category ('Some chairs are furniture' versus 'Some thrones are furniture') or by reducing the size of the predicate category ('Some alps are mountains' versus 'Some alps are formations'). These relationships reverse for superset statements, relatedness being reduced by an increase in subject category size ('Some solids are rubies' versus 'Some stones are rubies') and by a reduction in predicate category size ('Some vehicles are Buicks' versus 'Some vehicles are autos'). In each case the category size variation which tended to increase relatedness produced significant facilitation of the 'true' RT.

These results for verification of particular affirmatives may be contrasted with data from an independent group of *S*s who classified universal affirmative statements. A semantic comparison of subject and predicate attributes is not in general sufficient to determine the truth of a universal affirmative since these sentences are 'true' only if the subject category is a proper subset of the predicate category. It follows that the *S* must consider the logical relation between the categories in order to decide truth or falsity. If logical comparison was the procedure predominantly used many of the relatedness effects observed in classification of particular affirmatives would be likely to disappear. On the other hand if retrieval and matching of logical codes is relatively difficult or time-consuming, it might be worthwhile to make a comparison of attributes and to check the logical relation only for sentences with highly related subject and predicate nouns. In this case, we might expect to see a persistence of relatedness effects in classification of universal affirmatives.

The data reported by Meyer (1970) suggest that semantic comparison procedures were used by *S*s who judged the truth of universal affirmatives. 'True' RT for subset statements was facilitated by an increase in subject category size and a decrease in predicate category size. However, the effects were somewhat smaller than those observed for particular affirmatives, and the general level of the RT was greater by 184 msecs, suggesting a reduced reliance on semantic comparison and resort to a slower logical comparison procedure. The 'false' RTs showed a negative relatedness effect, being faster for the disjoint relation, intermediate for the overlap relation, and slowest for the superset relation. Meyer noted that 'false' RTs for sentences with disjoint subject and predicate categories were very similar in the two experiments. This again suggests a reliance on semantic comparison procedures in both cases, with the additional involvement of a logical comparison being restricted for the most part to universal affirmatives involving subset or superset relations.

It seems likely that Meyer's (1970) results were to some degree conditioned by the experimental arrangements he adopted. Had the subject and predicate nouns of the disjoint statements been related the utility of semantic comparison procedures in classification of universal affirmative sentences might have been much reduced. The mixing of universal and particular affirmatives in the same trial sequence might have made it more difficult to avoid resort to logical comparison procedures in classifying particular affirmatives. This could explain why Glass, Holyoak & O'Dell (1974) found no consistent differences among RTs for sentences quantified by 'all', 'many' and 'some' in their study of relatedness effects. General confirmation of these points has been provided by Rips (1975). He reported that the use of related disjoint sentences, such as: 'Some fathers are mothers', greatly increased the 'false' RT and also reduced the RT difference between particular and universal affirmatives. Mixing of the two sentence types in the trial sequence effectively eliminated the difference. Rips also noted that the effects of manipulation of subject and predicate category size which were so important in Meyer's experiments were absent when *S*s classified mixed sequences of universal and particular affirmatives, or a series of particular affirmatives containing related disjoint statements. An absence of effects due to subject-predicate relatedness is to be expected if the arrangements of Rips' experiments successfully encouraged *S*s to abandon semantic comparison procedures in favour of logical comparison procedures.

A further logical property of a sentence which affects its truth value is the presence or absence of a negative. If the quantifier 'some' is replaced by the negative quantifier 'no' the truth values of particular affirmative statements are systematically reversed. Sentences containing subset, superset or overlap subject-predicate relations become 'false' ('No canaries are birds', 'No birds are canaries', 'No canaries are pets') whereas disjoint sentences become 'true' ('No canaries are cabbages'). Thus, it is possible that universal negative statements are logically coded as denials of their corresponding particular affirmative statements, that is by a structure of the form: (False (Some —— are ——)) (Glass, Holyoak & O'Dell, 1974). A reasonable strategy in verifying such sentences might be to determine the truth or falsity of the embedded particular affirmative assertion and then to check for the presence of a negative marker. If the logical code is found to contain a negative the output from semantic comparison must be transformed to its opposite before a response is retrieved and sent for expression.

This account of the processing of negative quantifiers leads to some relatively straightforward predictions. We anticipate that responses to negatives should be slower than responses to affirmatives because of the involvement of an additional semantic transformation stage in which a (true) code is replaced by a (false) code or vice versa. The reversal is analogous to the response change involved when *S*s make an affirmative ('Yes') response to 'different' displays and a denying ('No') response to 'same' displays in semantic comparison tasks, and should produce a corresponding increase in RT (Seymour, 1975). It is in fact well established that latencies to verify negative sentences are greater than latencies for affirmative sentences (Wason, 1961; Wason & Johnson-Laird, 1972; Glass, Holyoak & O'Dell, 1974). A further prediction is that subject-predicate relatedness should facilitate 'false' judgements about negative statements while inhibiting responses to 'true' statements. This prediction is opposite in direction to the findings for particular affirmatives where relatedness facilitates 'true' decisions but inhibits 'false' decisions, but follows from the assumption that negation results in a simple reversal of the truth value of an implicit 'some' statement. The data reported by Glass, Holyoak & O'Dell (1974) tend to confirm these conclusions. They found that relatedness delayed 'true' decisions ('No horses are cows' versus 'No horses are bees') but facilitated 'false' decisions ('No horses are fast' versus 'No horses are loved'). The direction of the effects was opposite to the findings for affirmatively quantified sentences.

Meyer (1973) reported a study in which *S*s classified particular affirmative and universal negative statements in separate blocks of trials. The RTs to classify negative statements were about 200 msecs greater than the RTs for affirmative statements. As in the Meyer (1970) experiment, 'true' responses to particular affirmatives were facilitated by set relation (subset and superset statements were faster than overlap statements) and by category size variations which tended to increase subject-predicate noun relatedness. These effects were preserved in the RTs for 'false' responses to the universal negative statements, but with some increase in magnitude. This interaction of negation with relatedness is reminiscent of the interaction of response reversal instructions with dominance reported by Sanford & Seymour

(1974b). It suggests that the effects of negation are not restricted to a response RETRIEVAL stage but that presence of a negative quantifier has some secondary effects on the prior operations of semantic RETRIEVAL or COMPARISON.

In a further study Meyer (1975) contrasted universal affirmative statements with particular negatives of the form: 'Some chairs aren't furniture'. These two sentence types also involve a symmetric reversal of truth values. Universal affirmatives are only 'true' when the subject and predicate categories are linked by a subset relation, whereas particular negatives are 'false' for this relation ('Some canaries aren't birds') but 'true' for the superset, overlap and disjoint relations ('Some birds aren't canaries', 'Some canaries aren't pets', 'Some canaries aren't cabbages'). The RT for the negative sentences was found to be about 400 msecs greater than the RT for the affirmative sentences. As in Meyer's (1970) experiment, 'false' RT for universal affirmatives was fastest for disjoint relations, intermediate for the overlap relation, and slowest for the superset relation. This trend was preserved in the 'true' responses to particular negative statements, although in this case the interaction with negation was not significant. The results are consistent with the proposal that particular negatives are assigned a logical coding of the form: (False (All —— are ——)), and are verified by determining the truth of the embedded proposition and by then reversing the obtained value before responding.

XII.7 CONCLUSIONS

This chapter has discussed the complex processes involved when a sentence is judged to be 'true' or 'false' by reference to information stored in permanent memory. The sentence verification task provides a useful experimental situation in which the integrated functioning of the Lexical Memory system can be observed. Indeed, verification may reasonably be regarded as a form of elementary problem solving in which a higher-order executive—call it the VERIFICATION executive—dominates the more local activities of the INSPECTION, TASK and MATCH executives in order to schedule a smooth and intelligent flow of encoding, retrieval, comparison and expression operations. In this respect the verification task exemplifies the hierarchical structure of mental control functions which was emphasized by Miller, Galanter & Pribram (1960) and more recently by Broadbent (1977).

The above discussion of the experimental analysis of verification was based on the assumption that the determination of the truth value of an assertion about the superordinate class membership or characteristics of members of an object class might involve the retrieval and matching of two distinct types of mental code. We have referred to these as the *semantic code*, which has been viewed as a description of object characteristics, and the *logical code*, which specifies a relationship between classes and such logical functions as quantification and negation. The experimental findings suggest that *S*s are likely to use semantic codes in verifying sentences whenever procedural arrangements and choice of materials allow them to do so without undue risk of error. Conditions encouraging semantic comparison procedures are those in which the logical structure of the test sentences is held constant and the discovery of a high degree of subject-predicate relatedness can generally be taken as a reliable indication that the response 'true' is appropriate. Since these conditions have been met in a majority of the studies of categorization and sentence verification which have been published the interpretations of their results have properly emphasized semantic retrieval and comparison processes.

Considerations of this kind are helpful in clarifying some of the misgivings expressed by Glass & Holyoak (1976) in their critique of the Smith, Shoben & Rips (1974) model of semantic comparison. As they point out, theoretical analyses of the semantic memory system have of necessity emphasized its logical function in representing relationships between classes as well as properties of entailment or contradiction existing within a marker structure of the kind described by Katz (1972). Since sentence verification tasks appear, on the face of it, to require *S*s to retrieve and evaluate relational information of this kind, they have been viewed as a technique for investigation of logical structure in memory. If they have failed in this aim it is because their methodology has permitted *S*s to use an alternative strategy—the retrieval and matching of components of object descriptions—which is not dependent on consultation of the logical structure. Thus, although attribute comparison models can never support a fully sufficient theory of the verification of sentences, they may well offer an adequate account of the processing which occurs in many experimental studies.

According to this view the experiments on categorization and sentence verification which have been discussed in this and the preceding chapter are chiefly of value for the insights which they may have provided into the nature of the codes used to represent object concepts, and the processes by which components of such codes are retrieved and compared. It appears that the important factors influencing these processes are: (1) strength of associative relation, which facilitates selective retrieval; and (2) number of shared attributes, which affects the semantic comparison operation. The assumption that semantic RETRIEVAL often focuses on a selected subset of attributes appeared to imply an availability of relational information to the RETRIEVAL function, and this was treated as part of the addressing capability of the lexical interface structure. However, this involvement appeared distinct from the RETRIEVAL of logical codes from the structural data store. Relatively little information about RETRIEVAL and COMPARISON of logical codes has been provided by the experiments on sentence verification, and it seems unwise to treat 'true' and 'false' RT data as empirical justifications for sketches of the interior of the structural data store.

PART THREE

The Pictorial Memory

CHAPTER XIII

The Pictorial Memory

STRUCTURE AND CONTENT

XIII.1 INTRODUCTION

Up to this point the discussion has focused on the processing of visual symbols, that is the letters and digits (Part One) and words and simple sentences (Part Two). A view expressed from time to time has been that the visual components of the Symbolic and Lexical Memory systems have developed specifically for the purpose of recognition of the elements of written language and their mapping onto the alternative symbolism of spoken language and its interpretative (semantic and syntactic) superstructure. However, it was evident in Chapter XII that the discussion of this superstructure merges easily into a consideration of the representation of objects and classes. In the topic framework of this book knowledge of a three-dimensional world of objects is treated as a distinct area of competence, to be called the *Pictorial Memory*, and it is the nature of this competence, or certain aspects of it, that will be explored in this chapter.

The expression *Pictorial Memory* is in the first instance a name for a collection of behavioural dispositions. These include the seemingly commonplace skills which a person displays when he finds his way about in his environment, appreciates the spatial distribution of objects in that environment, and shows his understanding of the functions of objects, their classification into taxonomies and hierarchies, and their perceptual and other characteristics. Such capabilities are so mundane as to excite little comment except when neurological damage produces severe disruption of spatial orientation or failures to recognize familiar faces, colours or objects (Hécaen, 1972; Luria, 1973). Nonetheless, they represent a fundamental component of human intelligence, and have received a corresponding emphasis in the Piagetian theory of intellectual development (Piaget, 1936; Inhelder & Piaget, 1954; Flavell, 1963).

At a psychological level *Pictorial Memory* is taken to be a name for the neurological system which underlies successful performance in everyday tasks which involve the identification and use of objects, and the construction and interpretation of spatial configurations of objects. These include tasks of diagnostic significance, some of which tap input-output transformations occurring within the *Pictorial Memory* system alone, whereas others involve interactions with the *Lexical Memory*. An example of the first type is a 'same'–'different' judgemental task in which objects (or pictures or photographs of objects) are matched on physical or semantic criteria. Interactions with the Lexical Memory occur in tasks requiring a pictorial-verbal transformation (the naming of objects or description of scenes), a verbal-pictorial transformation (drawing, construction, or visual search for a verbally designated object), and also in judgements of the truth or falsity of statements which make reference to physically present object configurations.

The Pictorial Memory functions in the initial registration of pictorial events, and also in their subsequent categorization and interpretation. The registration functions include the ENCODING and REPRESENTATION of pictorial input, and extend to certain phenomena of imaging, and also the brief retention and mental manipulation of pictorial information. Categorization and interpretation are involved when pictorial stimuli are assigned to classes or judged with regard to their positions in space or values on dimensions of size, shape, colour, function and affective tone. This can be seen as a matter of RETRIEVAL of semantic codes (object descriptions), selective access to dimensional codes (attributes), and also RETRIEVAL of structural codes giving logical expression to spatial and other relations between objects.

It seems likely that the Lexical Memory and the Pictorial Memory are closely related at the level of interpretative structure. We found in Chapter XII that it was difficult to discuss sentence verification without consideration of attributes of object classes. It will become apparent in this chapter that it is equally difficult to discuss the representation of categorial and spatial attributes of objects without reference to linguistic evidence. This suggests that there may be merit in the proposal that the Lexical and Pictorial Memories share a common interpretative domain, an idea which will be explored further in this and the following chapters.

XIII.2 STRUCTURAL MODEL OF THE PICTORIAL MEMORY

It will be convenient to assume that the Pictorial Memory supports the mental functions of ENCODING, REPRESENTATION, RETRIEVAL, COMPARISON and EXPRESSION which have already been discussed in relation to the Symbolic and Lexical Memories. These functions must depend on the availability of facilities for permanent and temporary storage of pictorial information, and on the presence of an interface containing pattern recognition and addressing components for mediation of the recoding involved in REPRESENTATION and RETRIEVAL. These ideas are represented diagrammatically in Figure XIII.2.1. As with the previous diagrams, this is intended to illustrate relations among certain functionally necessary parts of the memory system, and should not be taken as having an anatomical reference.

We assume that the input to the Pictorial Memory takes the form of neural signals arising from the projection of luminance variations from surfaces of objects (or pictures) to the retinal receptors. The information necessary for perception of a three-dimensional world is contained in this input (Gibson, 1963, 1966), which is transformed, by application of a pictorial encoding function, to an internal description which we will call the *pictorial code*. The pictorial encoding function is presumably analogous to the graphemic encoding operation described in Chapter IV, incorporating provision for very brief temporary storage in an *iconic register*, and for selective transfer of information to a more durable level of temporary storage labelled as the *pictorial register* in Figure XIII.2.1.

It seems likely that iconic registration and control over selective encoding and eye-movements by the INSPECTION executive are facilities which are shared by the Symbolic and Pictorial Memories. However, the memory systems are differentiated at the level of the durable storage registers, and the pictorial register is considered to be distinct from the graphemic register. Experiments by Sanders & Schroots (1969) and by Henderson (1972b) were cited in Chapter IV as empirical support for a separation of this kind.

Following theoretical treatments of pattern recognition by Sutherland (1968, 1973) and others, it will be supposed that the *pictorial code* takes the form of a descriptive structure in which the elementary components of an object and their spatial inter-relationships are specified. Attempts by specialists in artificial intelligence to pro-

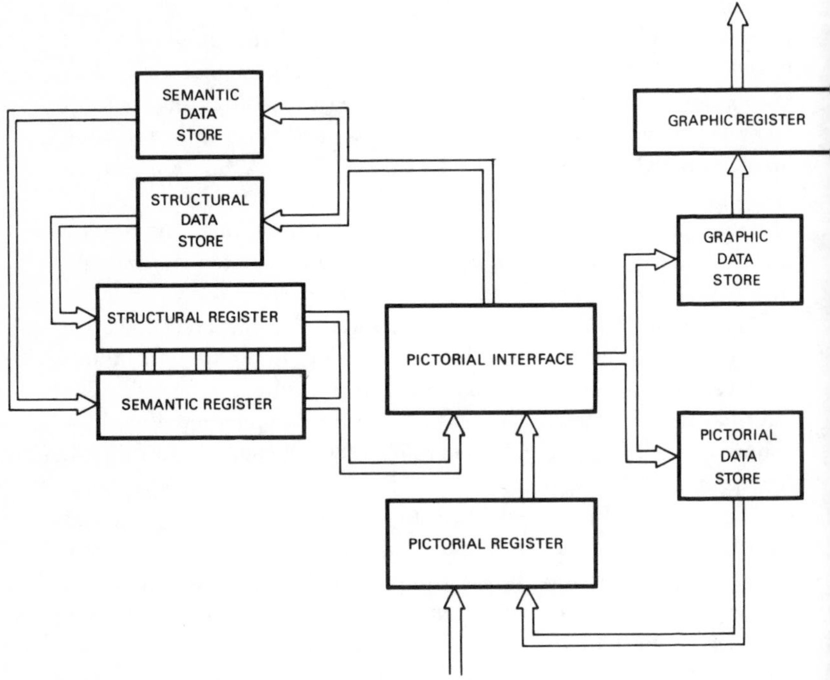

Figure XIII.2.1 Schematic representation of the Pictorial Memory system. A pictorial register holds the products of pictorial encoding and also codes retrieved from the pictorial data store following input of pictorial or semantic information to recognizers in the pictorial interface structure. The interface also mediates access to semantic and logical representations of objects and scenes, and to plans for drawing and other forms of graphic output.

gramme computers to carry out this pictorial encoding function have demonstrated that it must be a process of considerable complexity (Minsky & Papert, 1972). There are problems of distinguishing objects from shadows, of interpreting a two-dimensional projection in three-dimensional terms, and of isolating objects despite overlap and concealment of surfaces. Such analyses suggest that the pictorial code formed during the initial encoding of an object or picture should include a two-dimensional interpretation (a statement about points, lines, bounded regions, and properties of brightness, size, colour, orientation and two-dimensional shape) and a three-dimensional interpretation which is descriptive of relations among surfaces, edges, and elementary forms, such as cubes, wedges and cylinders.

A further assumption is that pictorial descriptions of familiar objects are held in a permanent store, labelled as the *pictorial data store* in Figure XIII.2.1. This store can be thought of as containing descriptions of standard pictorial exemplars of the object classes which a person knows. We will refer to these descriptions as *prototypes*. They approximate a person's 'image' of an object class, and may well represent an average of the appearances of those class members which are regarded as typical instances when viewed in a standard orientation. For example, Rosch, Mervis, Gray, Johnson & Boyes-Braem (1976) reported that *S*s imagined items of furniture as seen from the front whereas vehicles and living creatures were imagined from a side viewpoint.

These permanently stored prototypical descriptions may be accessed by input of information to a *pictorial interface* structure. This is thought to have the same internal organization as the analogous structures in the Symbolic and Lexical Memories. A pictorial address register may be linked, by intervention of the TASK executive (see Chapter VI), to banks of pattern recognizers which are responsive to the pictorial codes held in the pictorial register, or to object descriptions held in the semantic register. This arrangement is analogous to the scheme proposed for representation of graphemic codes in Chapter V. It provides a mechanism by which the pictorial code may be maintained in the pictorial register, or retrieved when an object concept is represented at the more abstract level of the semantic register. These processes of retrieval and representation of the pictorial code are taken to underlie the phenomena of imagery and visualization. The system also allows for a contribution of permanently stored knowledge of objects to their recognition under conditions of degraded sensory input, again paralleling the proposal made for graphemic codes during the discussion of word superiority effects (Chapter IX).

On the output side it has been assumed that the Pictorial Memory possesses capabilities for externalization of object descriptions by drawing and construction. Drawing involves a spatially structured sequence of movements, and must presumably depend on a permanent storage facility to hold the relevant motor programmes and a temporary storage register in which they can be placed immediately prior to expression as observable output. These have been labelled as the *graphic data store* and *graphic register* in Figure XIII.2.1. The drawing of an object requires that a description should be maintained in the pictorial register and used to locate motor codes in the graphic data store, and this retrieval function is dependent on the linking of the pictorial pattern recognizers to the graphic address register. In copying, the input to the pictorial register is derived by application of the encoding function to an external stimulus. In drawing from memory the code must first be obtained from the pictorial data store by input of semantic attributes to the pictorial interface.

The motor programmes held in the graphic data store mediate manual reactions other than drawing, including the key press responses which have been utilized in numerous experimental studies. These situations presumably involve the formation of arbitrary associations linking the semantic coding of a truth value (or other categorization) with the spatial designation of a response (left key or right key). Spatial codes of this kind might be pictorial in nature, but could also be logical structures which are held in the structural data store and placed at the logical level of the semantic register when retrieved. A decision to press a left or right key might be assigned a semantic coding, therefore, which could control EXPRESSION directly if semantic pattern recognizers were linked to the graphic address register.

We must also assume the existence of a semantic level of representation at which the attributes and categorial assignments of objects are coded. In Figure XIII.2.1 information of this kind, which is descriptive of the colours of objects, their sizes, spatial attributes, and functional and affective properties, is held in a *semantic data store*. These codes may be accessed from the pictorial register, and are placed at the lower level of the *semantic register* when they are retrieved. The semantic component of the Pictorial Memory also contains provision for specification of *relationships* between objects.

These include assertions of their similarity or difference with respect to class membership or values on particular attributes, and also statements concerning spatial locations of objects relative to one another. Such relationships are expressed linguistically by equative, comparative and locative constructions of various types. In the discussion of the Lexical Memory these logical codes were viewed as part of the content of a *structural data store* to be entered into the upper (logical) level of the semantic register following retrieval. A similar arrangement is proposed for the Pictorial Memory in Figure XIII.2.1.

The diagram leaves open the question of whether or not the semantic register and its associated semantic and structural data stores are the same as the equivalent components in the diagram of the Lexical Memory (Figure VIII.5.1). The assumption that the two Memories share a semantic and logical resource has substantial explanatory value, since it suggests that the two systems operate in a common code at the conceptual level (Pylyshyn, 1973; Clark & Chase, 1972). The existence of a common code of this kind is helpful in discussing the lexical-pictorial transformations which occur when people talk about the things they see, or imagine or draw the things they hear or read about. However, the assumption that the Lexical and Pictorial Memories use the same type of conceptual representation need not imply that the semantic registers of Figures VIII.5.1 and XIII.2.1 are one and the same mechanism. We could equally. well imagine that semantic registration functions are duplicated in the two Memories, but that there is provision for transfer of information from one register to the other. There is similar uncertainty concerning the permanent storage registers. Although it is reasonable to suppose that the attributes of an object, such as 'canary', or the logical definition of a relationship, such as: 'X above Y', are retrieved from a common storage facility irrespective of the form of the input (words or pictures), this need not be so. It could be that the Lexical and Pictorial Memories have developed independent storage facilities for attribute and relational descriptions.

XIII.3 BREAKDOWN OF THE PICTORIAL MEMORY IN OBJECT AGNOSIA

In the discussion of the Lexical Memory in Chapter VIII it proved valuable to consider evidence from neuropsychological studies of the breakdown of reading skill in cases of acquired dyslexia. This kind of evidence is also helpful in the discussion of the Pictorial Memory.

We might look to neuropsychological evidence for confirmation of the proposed distinction between pictorial and semantic levels of object recognition, and also of the role of semantic codes in mediating the lexical-pictorial transformations involved in drawing a named object or in naming a pictured object.

Luria (1973) has commented that, whereas damage to the optic system or primary areas of the occipital cortex may lead to partial blindness (hemianopia), damage at a deeper level can leave basic visual functions intact while impairing the patient's ability to integrate components of complex patterns or to recognize objects which have been degraded by visual noise. For example, when attempting to copy pictures of objects, patients in this group draw some of the parts correctly but fail to place them in their proper spatial relation to one another. It seems likely that this reflects disruption of the pictorial encoding function by which two- and three-dimensional descriptions of objects are formed. Luria suggests that object processing at this level is primarily a function of the right hemisphere of the brain. This conclusion is supported by Warrington & Taylor (1973), DeRenzi, Scotti & Spinnler (1969), Warrington (1973) and others, who have shown that right hemisphere damage may be associated with failures in identification of degraded pictures or unfamiliar views of objects, or in making 'same'–'different' judgements of a perceptual nature.

There is a relatively rare neurological condition, known as *object agnosia* (Hécaen, 1972), in which the pictorial encoding function is preserved but a deficit is observable at the higher level of semantic interpretation of pictures. Taylor & Warrington (1971) provided a detailed description of a single patient who appears to fall into this category. This patient was quite successful in copying a picture of an object which was placed before him, but very poor at drawing named objects from memory. A similar case, involving a marked difference between copying and drawing, was described by Luria (1973). In the structural model of the Pictorial Memory (Figure XIII.2.1) copying is achieved by the operation of pictorial encoding followed by retrieval of graphic plans. In drawing a named object there is no pictorial input and retrieval of graphic (or pictorial) information is dependent on input of semantic attributes to the pictorial interface. Hence, an impairment at the level of semantic coding of object attributes could disrupt drawing from memory while leaving copying intact.

If this interpretation is correct patients in this group should perform normally on tasks which tap the pictorial encoding function (such as perceptual 'same'–'different' judgements) while showing a deficit in tasks involving the semantic representational function (classification, semantic comparison, naming). These expectations have been confirmed for the single patient studied by Taylor & Warrington (1971) and for three further patients whose performance was analysed in some depth by Warrington (1975). The *S*s were quite successful in perceptual matching tasks, including the matching of different viewpoints of the same object, suggesting that the pictorial encoding function was intact. However, they were confused about the functions of objects, and had difficulty in naming and categorizing. Taylor & Warrington's *S* did not know what to do with a folded umbrella which was handed to him while he was standing in the rain. He performed poorly on semantic matching tasks, such as matching colours to objects, or determining that two different objects were members of the same class.

A relationship between a deficit in drawing objects from memory and a deficit in the naming of objects has been demonstrated by Tsvetkova (1975). She gave *S*s who had shown object naming difficulties the tasks of drawing objects in response to verbal command or filling in details on incomplete drawings. Although the drawing technique of these *S*s was not impaired they proved unable to give the drawings a correct set of differentiating features, and complained that they were unable to visualize what should be drawn. Warrington's (1975) group of *S*s also exhibited a defect in object naming. This occurred when the input was pictorial, and also when the input was verbal (a description of the object to be named). The semantic basis of the failure is well-illustrated by one of the *S*s who commented, on being shown a second photograph of a table tennis bat, that he had already seen a photograph of that object taken from another angle and had said then that he had no idea what it was. Warrington's patients were also impaired on the task of matching a spoken name against an array of pictures of objects (Peabody Picture Vocabulary Test), and in describing an object in response to a picture or name.

One aspect which is common to the reports of Tsvetkova (1975) and Warrington (1975) is the tendency for the patients to lose information about properties which serve to differentiate members of perceptually homogeneous classes, such as the classes of 'flowers' or 'birds', while preserving some competence at a more general level of categorization. Warrington presented her *S*s with sets of three objects, asking them to indicate which one possessed a named property. Discrimination of animals from non-animals, or birds from non-birds (a superordinate classification) was superior to discrimination based on more narrowly defined properties, such as habitual location (English or foreign), ferocity, size or colour. Comparable results were obtained when the *S*s responded to single pictures (or object names) with answers to questions like: 'Is it an animal?' or 'Is it larger than a cat?' Again, the general categorization produced better performance than queries about object identity or properties of location and size.

It is of interest to note that the pattern of disability observed in these *S*s is in some respects the converse of that found in the cases of phonemic dyslexia which were discussed in Chapter VIII. Those *S*s demonstrated an inability to read nouns of abstract meaning and words having a primarily syntactic function. By contrast, the agnosic patient described by Taylor & Warrington (1971) was able to understand relational expressions, such as 'on top of', 'behind' and 'beside', although he did not know the meanings of familiar concrete nouns. One of Warrington's (1975) *S*s was able to give very adequate definitions of abstract nouns (for example, 'pact' was defined as 'a friendly agreement') while complaining that he had forgotten the meanings of words like 'hay', 'needle', 'acorn' and 'poster'.

A reasonable conclusion is that these *S*s reveal the consequences of a selective impairment of the central system for representation of the semantic attributes of objects. The failures might be expected to occur if the *semantic data store* shown in Figures VIII.5.1 and XIII.2.1 had suffered selective damage. The information about attributes and functions of objects would then not be available to retrieval operations initiated in the Lexical or Pictorial Memory, and confusions concerning the categorization of objects and the interpretation of concrete nouns would follow. There is some suggestion that such failures may be peculiar to certain classes of pictorial stimuli. For example, Warrington's (1975) patients showed deficits in recognition of objects and faces, but not in recognition of colour. The neuropsychological literature contains reports of selective deficits in the processing of facial stimuli (prosopagnosia) and also selective loss of knowledge of the colours of objects (Hécaen, 1972).

XIII.4 OBJECT CLASSES

This discussion of neuropsychological evidence for a condition of agnosia for objects brings us back to certain problems concerning the nature of object classes which were initially raised in Chapter XII.

The proposal made there was that object classes may be defined in terms of attribute structures, that is by configurations of spatial and logical relationships among labelled dimensions on which particular values are specified. The approach to the identification of these attributes was relatively indirect, relying chiefly on similarity ratings and multi-dimensional scaling procedures (Rips, Shoben & Smith, 1973; Caramazza, Hersh & Torgerson, 1976).

A more direct approach has been suggested by Rosch, Mervis, Gray, Johnson & Boyes-Braem (1976). These authors instructed *S*s to list attributes of members of nine object classes, and also to describe the movements involved in a typical interaction with the objects. The stimuli were drawn from three biological taxonomies (trees, fishes, and birds), and six non-biological taxonomies (fruits, musical instruments, tools, clothing, furniture, vehicles). These were taken to be the major categories of objects used in Western culture, excluding 'animals', which was considered to be ambiguous as between a technical sense and popular sense (broadly equivalent to 'mammals'), and categories which cut across a number of other classifications, such as 'foods' and 'toys'. Each category was represented by names selected as lying at one of three levels in a hierarchical classification scheme. We may refer to these as the *superordinate level*, initially equated with the class names mentioned above, the *basic object level*, equated with class instances, such as 'oak', 'trout', 'canary', 'apple', 'trumpet', 'hammer', and a *subordinate level* which involved differentiation of the basic object names, as in the examples 'golden eagle', 'rainbow trout', 'claw hammer'.

Rosch conducted this study with the aim of examining the changes in the content of the attribute lists which occurred as the level of generality of the object class name was altered. *Superordinate names* appear to label somewhat heterogeneous collections of objects which have certain functional properties in common. *Basic object names*, on the other hand, generally label perceptually homogeneous classes of entities, whereas *subordinate names* point to minor distinctions which can be used to differentiate the members of these classes. It follows that relatively few attributes or typical movements should be identifiable for superordinate names, but that a large set of characteristics, many of them perceptual in nature, should be available for basic object names. Subordinate names might be expected to add little to this list beyond a few differentiating features.

These expectations were quite well supported in the case of names taken from non-biological taxonomies. For example, the superordinate name 'tool' elicited a restricted set of attributes (to make things, to fix things, made of metal) and a description of a grasping movement. A basic object name, such as 'saw', evoked a more detailed attribute list, including: (has(handle, teeth, blade, edge)), (is(sharp)), (can(cut)), and an account of the activity of manipulating a saw. The subordinate name 'cross-cutting hand saw' produced little in the way of additional attributes or movement descriptions. This tends to confirm that superordinate names are associated with a small number of attributes, chiefly descriptive of function, and that basic object and subordinate names typically evoke a much more extensive set in which statements about physical characteristics predominate.

The three level analysis was less successful in the case of the biological taxonomies. The problem here is that the class names 'bird', 'fish' and 'tree' appear to be superordinates but in practice produce data which allocate them to the basic object level. A conclusion of this kind is evident in earlier studies by Segui & Fraisse (1968) and Seymour (1973a) which were concerned with the naming of pictures of objects. Segui & Fraisse found that the question: 'What is this?' tended to be answered by a class name rather than a specific name when the picture was taken from a biological taxonomy (birds, flowers, fishes, trees and dogs) but by a specific name in preference to a class name when it was taken from a non-biological taxonomy (clothing, furniture, vegetable, weapon or musical instrument). Thus, *S*s were more likely to respond 'fish' than 'trout' to a picture of a trout, and more likely to respond 'hammer' than 'tool' to a picture of a hammer. Segui & Fraisse suggested that a distinction might be made between perceptual classes, in which members were characterized by strong similarity of appearance, and functional classes, in which membership was determined by similarity of function. It seemed that objects drawn from perceptual classes evoked a class name rather than a specific name, and that the reverse was true of objects drawn from functional classes.

Seymour (1973a) argued that Segui & Fraisse's findings could be rationalized by assuming that a picture of an object preferentially evokes a category name which labels a class of perceptually homogeneous entities, although names of greater generality or specificity can be produced if necessary. In his study, the category level was exemplified by 'flower', 'dog', 'table', 'bed', 'glove' and 'hat'. It can be seen that this corresponds directly to the basic object level in Rosch's analysis. The implication is that biological class names may often be located at the basic object level rather than at the superordinate level. A conclusion of this kind is supported by the analyses of attribute lists and movement descriptions reported by Rosch, Mervis, Gray, Johnson & Boyes-Braem (1976). A biological class name, such as 'bird', was shown to elicit an extensive set of attributes, many of them perceptual in nature: (has(feathers, wings, beak, legs, feet, eyes, tail, head, claws)), (can(lay eggs, fly, chirp, eat worms)). The movement associated with the class was one of following the flight of a bird by rotation of the head and eyes. The names of class members, such as 'sparrow', elicited this same list and description plus a small number of differentiating features: (is(small, brown)). Names at a more specific level, like 'song sparrow' or 'field sparrow', elicited no additional features.

These results are consistent with the view that pictorial encoding of an object (or picture of an object) leads preferentially to retrieval of a set of attributes which allocate the object to membership of what Rosch has called a *basic object* class. She confirmed that names from this level predominate overwhelmingly as spontaneous responses in picture naming. They also have a much greater frequency of occurrence than superordinate or subordinate names in the early stages of language development. An important aspect of this approach to categorization is the proposal that basic object classes may be defined in terms of shared *perceptual* attributes. Basic object classes are taken to reflect those divisions of the environment which group together entities having a maximum number of attributes in common with one another and a minimum number in common with members of other classes. It follows from this that objects grouped at the level of a basic object class should be characterized by much greater similarity of appearance than objects which are grouped at the level of a superordinate class.

Rosch, Mervis, Gray, Johnson & Boyes-Braem (1976) used outline pictures of objects from the superordinate classes of clothing, vehicles, animals and furniture to validate this hypothesis. The pictures were normalized with respect to size and orientation and a measure of area of overlap was taken. Not surprisingly, pictures which were equivalent at the basic level (for example, two fish or two cars) were shown to be more similar than pictures which were equivalent at the superordinate level only (a car and an aeroplane, or a fish and a dog). It was also established that if the outlines of two objects from the same basic level class were averaged the identity of the class was preserved. This was not true of pictures produced by averaging outlines of members of a superordinate class.

Objects which are categorized at either the basic level or the superordinate level may vary in the degree to which they approximate an idealized representation of a class, earlier referred to as a *prototype*. At the basic level the class prototype may be pictorially defined, either as a configuration of perceptual attributes or as a description of a standardized form which is held in the pictorial data store. At the superordinate level, on the other hand, the prototype is presumably more abstract in nature, perhaps consisting of a configuration of functional attributes.

Rosch has demonstrated in various studies that *S*s can rate the prototypicality of pictorial and lexical instances of basic object and superordinate classes with a high degree of reliability (Rosch, 1973, 1975a). She has sought to explain these ratings by recourse to Wittgenstein's (1953) principle of 'family resemblance'. Wittgenstein noted that inclusion in a superordinate class, such as the class of 'games', was not reducible to possession of a set of criterial attributes. Class membership seemed to be conferred on entities which had at least some attributes which were characteristic of some other class members. This claim was investigated empirically by Rosch & Mervis (1975) in a study involving the listing of attributes of members of superordinate classes. This confirmed that the class members evoked a range of attribute names, each appearing in the definitions of some exemplars even though there were no criterial attributes which occurred in the definitions of all exemplars. A measure of 'family resemblance' was computed by weighting each attribute listed in response to an item to reflect the number of other items of which it was characteristic. This measure was found to correlate highly with Rosch's (1975a) ratings of typicality of class instances.

This principle also appears applicable to the basic object classes. Rosch & Mervis (1975) obtained attribute listings for pictures of objects from basic level classes. They found that the pictures evoked a core of essential attributes which occurred for all class members together with other attributes which occurred for some members but not for others. A 'family resemblance' measure based on these additional attributes correlated strongly with ratings of the typicality of the pictures.

It may be useful to refer back at this point to the comments on verification of category statements which were made in the last chapter. When category membership is determined by a semantic comparison, that is by matching of attributes of a class prototype and a class instance, it seems reasonable to say that class membership varies on a scale of prototypicality, that is in terms of the degree of correspondence of the two attribute sets. This has been taken by some, for example Lakoff (1972), to imply a potential for variation in the degrees of truth value which may be associated with category statements. Thus, a consequence of the intuition that a sparrow is a more typical bird than a penguin is the proposal that the assertion: 'A sparrow is a bird' may be regarded as more 'true' than the assertion: 'A penguin is a bird'. Oden (1977) has recently shown that *S*s can sensibly make judgements about degrees of truth of this kind, and that their performance is quite well predicted by ratings of typicality.

XIII.5 PERCEPTUAL AND SPATIAL ATTRIBUTES

The discussion of the possible nature of object classes has tended to confirm that objects, whether pictorially or verbally designated, may be assigned a semantic coding which takes the form of a structure of attributes. It was suggested in the last chapter that this structure might include a logical component (a specification of the relations of attributes to one another and to the object taken as a whole) and also a dimensional component (a specification of the values taken by an object on a number of scales of variation). Bierwisch (1969) has noted that this attribute structure may be viewed as an elaboration of the concept (physical object) which appears as a semantic marker in the theory of Katz & Fodor (1963). We can identify certain attributes which appear necessarily to be part of the description of an object—that it has colour, for example, brightness, shape, size, extension in two or three dimensions, texture and consistency.

In the case of *colour* it is likely that we are dealing with a structure not unlike the one proposed for object classes. The label 'colour' might be viewed as a superordinate which groups together a set of basic object classes, each corresponding to one of the major colour categories. On the basis of cross-cultural data Berlin & Kay (1969) proposed the existence of eight basic chromatic categories (red, yellow, green, blue, orange, brown, pink and purple) and three achromatic categories (black, white and grey). There are of course many additional terms which function as subordinate names for alternative versions of the basic categories (crimson, scarlet, maroon and so forth), and also for colours lying at the boundaries between categories (reddish brown, greenish blue). Rosch has presented evidence to suggest that the basic level colour categories are structured around prototypical exemplars, much as was proposed for the basic object classes discussed in the last section (Heider, 1971, 1972; Rosch, 1973;

Mervis, Catlin & Rosch, 1975). Thus, each basic colour term might be thought of as specifying a space within the colour solid (defined by variations in hue, saturation and brightness) and as pointing to a focal region within that space.

In the structural model of the Pictorial Memory (see Figure XIII.2.1) colour attributes may be specified in abstract terms at the level of the semantic register, and in more concrete terms at the level of the pictorial register. Thus, the lexical item 'canary' may retrieve from the semantic data store an attribute structure which includes the assertion: (has-as-colour(yellow)). We can view (yellow) as a label for a dimension of variation which is defined in terms of a range of values of hue, saturation and brightness. If the components of this were to be isolated by a selective retrieval operation and transmitted to the exit logogen system the colour name 'yellow' would be likely to be evoked. Transmission of the same components to the pictorial interface would result in retrieval of a chromatic code from the pictorial data store and its entry into the pictorial register, possibly resulting in visual experience of colour.

The achromatic dimension of brightness might be thought of as a scale of continuous variation extending from an extreme of darkness through intervening gradations to an extreme of brightness. In saying that the dimension extends from one extreme to another we imply a possibility of polarization or inherent directionality. For example, we might think of blackness as representing a zero point (or origin) on a scale which extends upward in the direction of increasing values of brightness. We could then say that the scale is polarized in a dark-light direction. We might also say that the scale measures a property of brightness, and that its dark end represents an absence of that property, so that 'dark' is in a sense the negation of brightness.

Questions of this kind also arise in relation to scales which define variations on dimensions of size ('large'–'small', 'big'–'little'), shape ('rounded'–'angular'), horizontal extent ('compact'–'elongated', 'long'–'short'), vertical extent ('tall'–'short', 'high'–'low'), and breadth and depth ('broad'–'narrow', 'deep'–'shallow'). Linguistic analyses of the pairs of antonymous adjectives which label the poles of these dimensions have focused on issues concerning their 'conditions of application' (that is, the contextual requirements underlying use of an adjective in description of an object), and the matter of polarization. In discussing German adjectives Bierwisch (1967, 1970) noted that choice of an acceptable adjective is dependent on the dimensional structure of the object qualified (whether it is characterized by one, two or three dimensions), and whether its maximal extension is horizontal or vertical (see also Teller (1969) and Clark, (1973b, 1974)). Thus, we say that a cigarette is 'long' whereas a tower is 'tall', that a giraffe is 'tall' whereas its neck is 'long', and that the sea is 'deep', but the fisherman's line is 'long'. If these adjectives are interchanged, statements of doubtful acceptability result. It seems inappropriate to speak of a 'long tower' or a 'long giraffe', or of a 'tall cigarette' or 'tall fishing line'.

The detailed specification of these 'conditions of application' represents a topic in linguistics which lies outside the scope of the present discussion. However, we can note that the applicability of adjectives is related to the intrinsic horizontality or verticality of the object described. To use the adjective 'tall' we require a substantial three-dimensional object having a vertical orientation which extends upward from ground level, such as a tower or a giraffe. The orientation may be canonical rather than actual. We could, for example, say: 'The tall girl's long body basked in the Mediterranean sunlight', allowing 'tall' to refer to her canonical upright extent and 'long' to her current recumbent extent. Similarly, the adjective 'long' appears to be applicable to objects having horizontal extent, such as lorries, trains, snakes and crocodiles. However, this constraint is weak, since 'long' is used for parts of objects irrespective of orientation, as in the giraffe's 'long legs' and 'long neck', the kite's 'long string', or the fisherman's 'long line'. Equally, although 'deep' has a sense of downward verticality in a 'deep well' or 'deep pool', this is relaxed in expressions like 'deep thicket' or 'deep wound'. The conditions of application of the spatial adjectives are, therefore, extremely complex, and Bierwisch's analysis serves to emphasize the responsiveness of the recognition units in the exit logogen system to subtle variations in semantic input.

Bierwisch (1967) also commented on the intrinsic directionality of spatial dimensions. Dimensions which are descriptive of the sizes of objects, including their extent in each of three dimensions, characteristically have a low end, representing absence of extent or small extent, and a higher end representing large extent. We can think of the dimension of 'size' as defining an increase in extent from those values which we call 'small' towards the greater values which we call 'large'. Thus, the dimension is thought of as extending from 'small' to 'large' rather than vice versa. Bierwisch noted that an asymmetry exists in the manner in which the adjectives labelling polarized dimensions of this kind can be combined with measurement terms and expressions like 'half as' and 'twice as'. These expressions generally modify the positive member of the adjectival pair, as in: 'The tower is fifty feet tall', or 'The mother giraffe is twice as tall as the baby giraffe'. Sentences like 'The tower is fifty feet short' and 'The baby giraffe is half as short as the mother giraffe' appear deviant, except in special cases where shortness appears to function as a dimension, as in: 'The mother's mini-skirt was twice as short as the daughter's' (Teller, 1969). On these grounds we may think of the scales of height, depth, size and the like as involving measurement from an origin in the direction of increased extent. The scales therefore have the characteristics of ratio scales in the sense of Stevens (1951). They will be referred to here as *unidirectional scales* or directionally polarized dimensions.

This matter of polarity of dimensions is closely related to the notion of lexical marking which was briefly considered in the last chapter. On scales involving unidirectional measurement from a zero point the adjective expressing lack of extent is generally said to be *marked* whereas adjective expressing greater extent is said to be *unmarked*. The unmarked adjective is taken to be the more common form, representing the occurrence of positive values on the dimension in question, while the marked form is a relatively unusual usage referring to a restricted range of very low values. It has been noted by Greenberg (1966) and by Clark (1969, 1973b) that the unmarked adjective is often linguistically close to the name of the dimension, as in 'deep' and 'depth', 'high' and 'height', 'wide' and 'width', 'long' and 'length'. This is not true of the marked adjectives 'shallow', 'low', 'narrow' and 'short'. Related to this is the observation that the unmarked adjective can function both as a name for the dimension (its *nominal* sense) and as a name for the positive pole of the dimension (its *contrastive* sense). We can ask: 'How deep is the pool?' without any presupposition about an expected range of values on a depth dimension. However, if we ask: 'How shallow is the pool?', the question appears to presuppose a range of very small values of depth.

Bierwisch (1970) has remarked that contrastive usages of spatial adjectives are often based on an implicit comparative structure (see also Sapir [1944]). If we say: 'That table is high' we mean that the table takes a value on a scale of height which is greater than the value which is normal for tables (assuming that 'high' is used as a statement of vertical extent rather than of position). Had the value fallen below this norm we could have asserted: 'That table is low'. The same considerations apply for the other antonymous pairs we have considered—'large'–'small', 'big'–'little', 'deep'–'shallow', 'tall'–'short', 'thick'–'thin', 'wide'–'narrow'. It seems that the unidirectional scales labelled by these adjectives possess two points of reference. The first of these is the zero position or origin from which measurement is made. The second is a normatively specified region around which values which are to be called 'low' shade into values which are to be called 'high' (Clark, 1973b). This norm is not fixed, but may vary as the class of object being measured changes. The adjective 'large' might be applied to 'eagles', 'elephants', and 'churches', just as 'small' might be applied to 'wrens', 'ants' and 'huts', although the absolute sizes of these objects vary greatly.

In the case of unidirectional spatial attributes, therefore, we can equate the lexically marked member of each antonymous adjectival pair with a restricted region of the dimension which extends from a variable norm downward (that is against the polarized orientation of the dimension) to locate a zero value expressing absence of the property in question. It is sometimes suggested that the marked adjective possesses a *negative valence* of some kind, possibly because it expresses absence or lack of the dimensional property (Gordon, 1976; Huttenlocher & Higgins, 1971). However, it is unclear whether this negativity is to be thought of as being logical in character (for example, a coding of 'low' as 'not-high'), or as having an affective or evaluative component. The latter possibility was stressed by Hamilton & Deese (1971). They gave *S*s a pair of adjectives to use as standards, 'deep' and 'shallow' for example, and asked them to place other adjectives with whichever standard they belonged. The *S*s showed a reliable tendency to sort on the basis of a marked/unmarked distinction. When questioned, a majority mentioned evaluative characteristics as the basis for their choices.

It seems, therefore, that certain spatial dimensions may be polarized both with regard to direction and with regard to affect. This negative-positive polarization probably relates to the evaluative dimension of connotative meaning which emerged as a consistent factor in Osgood's studies of the semantic differential (Osgood, Suci & Tannenbaum, 1957). There are certain attributes of objects which are primarily evaluative, and which are labelled by adjective pairs such as 'good'–'bad', 'happy'–'sad', 'beautiful'–'ugly', 'kind'–'cruel', 'strong'–'weak'. Huttenlocher & Higgins (1971) noted that these evaluative dimensions differ from the spatial dimensions in that they lack a single zero point or origin from which measurement can proceed unidirectionally. They are better viewed as independent scales of goodness and badness which emerge in contrary directions from a central area of neutrality. In recognition of this point they might be referred to as *bidirectional* scales. The dark-bright dimension is possibly of the same type (independent scales emerging from greyness towards blackness or whiteness), as are the horizontal left-right and front-back dimensions, and also a dimension of verticality viewed as extending upward in the direction of increasing height and downward in the direction of increasing depth.

The applicability of the marked/unmarked distinction to adjectives which label bidirectional dimensions is a matter of some uncertainty. Dimensions defining the major spatial co-ordinates of the perceptual world (left-right horizontal, front-back horizontal, up-down vertical) are either queried by an entirely open question of the: 'Where is X?' variety, or by questions which specify a particular half dimension—'How far up is he?', or 'How far down?', 'How far to the left (or right)?', 'How far ahead (or behind)?'. These cases do not satisfy Greenberg's (1966) criteria of lexical equivalence of a dimension name and positive polar adjective, or of nominal usage of the positive adjective. For this reason, arguments such as those of Clark (1973b) in favour of the proposal that 'deep' is marked relative to 'high', that the locative preposition 'below' is marked relative to 'above', or that 'behind' is marked relative to 'ahead' or 'in front' are difficult to accept. In the case of 'high'–'deep', for example, we would have to agree that 'deep' can simultaneously be of positive polarity relative to 'shallow' and of negative polarity relative to 'high'.

Nonetheless, other bidirectional dimensions could be said to exhibit some characteristics of markedness. We might say that 'bright' is lexically close to the dimension name 'brightness', and that the question: 'How bright is it?' is neutral whereas the question: 'How dark is it?' is restrictive. The dimensions of goodness, happiness, beauty, kindness and strength are lexically close to the positive adjectives 'good', 'happy', 'beautiful', 'kind' and 'strong', and it is arguable that these may be used in a neutral nominal sense. Thus, the question: 'How beautiful is she?' is possibly open to some form of denial that she is beautiful, whereas the reverse is not true of the question: 'How ugly is she?' There is an evident positive-negative polarization in these scales which parallels that of the unidirectional dimensions. Rather as 'low' can be taken to mean 'not-high', so 'ugly' might be taken to be an emphatic form of 'not-beautiful', and 'cruel' an emphatic form of 'unkind'. We cannot reasonably reverse this positive-negative polarization. It would not be correct to assert that 'beautiful' is definable as 'emphatically not-ugly', or that 'kind' is 'emphatically not-cruel'.

These comments illustrate that bidirectionality on certain dimensions may be combined with a unidirectional positive-negative polarization. A further possibility, partially considered in Clark's (1973b) discussion, is that movement in a forward and upward direction may be characterized as being inherently positive, whereas movement in a backward or downward direction is treated as inherently negative. While difficult to justify, these claims appear intuitively acceptable, and are also reflected in metaphorical uses of spatial terms. We commiserate with the person who is 'behind in his work' or 'down on his luck', and admire (or envy) the one who is 'ahead', 'on top of things', or 'on the up and up'. These evaluative connotations extend to the marked and unmarked adjectives labelling the unidirectional spatial dimensions. It is better to be a 'deep' personality than a 'shallow' one, better to have a 'broad' than a 'narrow' education, and so forth.

XIII.6 CONCLUSIONS

This chapter has undertaken a preliminary examination of the Pictorial Memory system. A main conclusion has been that the Pictorial Memory is primarily a system for the *interpretation* and categorization of objects. It seemed reasonable to distinguish between a level of picture processing which is broadly perceptual in character, being concerned with the construction of a two- or three-dimensional description of an object, and a level which is more obviously semantic, involving isolation of attributes of objects, their assignment to classes, and the specification of logical and locative relations between objects.

The distinction between perceptual and semantic levels in the analysis of objects appeared to be supported by the neuropsychological evidence which was considered. In particular, the condition of agnosia for objects seems to reflect a selective disruption of a system in which a knowledge of attributes of objects is permanently maintained. An experimental approach to this issue can be made using 'same'–'different' judgemental tasks in which pictures of objects are matched on the basis of pictorial or semantic criteria. Some relevant research will be discussed in the next three chapters.

A further conclusion was that the semantic coding of an object may be viewed as a logical structure in which values on attributes or dimensions are specified. These attribute structures were seen as a basis for the assignment of objects to basic level and superordinate classes, and thus for the naming of objects at different levels of abstraction, and also for the description and comparison of objects with regard to particular attributes. The linguistic analyses of antonymous adjective pairs suggested that certain spatial dimensions were directionally polarized, and that this was often associated with a positive-negative evaluative connotation. One problem for the experimental analysis of the Pictorial Memory (Chapters XIV, XV and XVI) will be to determine the impact on information processing indices of these properties of object descriptions (levels of classification, prototypicality, and lexical marking of adjectives).

As background to this discussion there remains the question of the relationship between the Lexical and Pictorial Memories. Although a topical division between these two systems has appeared useful in the present context this should not be taken to imply acceptance of a dual memory position of the kind proposed by Paivio (1972, 1975a) in his analyses of mnemonic effects of pictorial imagery. When Paivio speaks of verbal and imaginal systems he appears to be concerned with relatively concrete representations, that is with graphemic or phonemic codings of words on the one hand and pictorial (image-like) codings of objects on the other. The present proposal accepts this separation, since it has been assumed that graphemic, phonemic and pictorial registration are distinct processes. However, the codes held in the graphemic, phonemic and pictorial registers are regarded as no more than the substrate of the interpretative structures which are essential and significant parts of the Lexical and Pictorial Memories. The question we might seek to resolve by experiment, therefore, is whether the Lexical and Pictorial systems share the same interpretative structure, or whether these structures are to a greater or lesser extent distinct.

CHAPTER XIV

The Pictorial Code

REPRESENTATION AND MANIPULATION OF GESTALTS

XIV.1 INTRODUCTION

The preceding chapter outlined a structural model of the Pictorial Memory and considered its role in the representation of categorial and dimensional properties of objects. Attributes of this kind were assigned to a semantic and logical level of registration which was considered to be distinct from a pictorial level of registration. A problem for the experimental analysis of the pictorial memory is to determine whether these two levels can indeed be distinguished from one another. Conceptually, the distinction is between a representation which has the characteristics of a literal, image-like gestalt, and one which is in the form of a logical structure specifying relationships among labelled dimensions. We may think of a simple shape, say a red triangle of a certain size, as an entity which may be directly apprehended or which may be analysed into its component attributes and defined as a logical conjunction of values on dimensions of form, colour, size, brightness, and location.

It seems clear that the pictorial and semantic representations of an object may often be referentially synonymous. They differ primarily in emphasis, with the pictorial description tending to emphasize global or gestalt properties, while the logical and semantic description emphasizes the analysis of the object into its component dimensions. The intuitive plausibility of these two approaches has led to much dispute, with some authors arguing that all aspects of object appearance in perception and imagery can be captured by an abstract propositional code (Pylyshyn, 1973; Anderson & Bower, 1973), whereas others maintain that the pictorial code is a literal representation which is different in kind from the semantic or logical code (Cooper & Shepard, 1976; Kosslyn & Pomerantz, 1977; Paivio, 1976; Shepard & Podgorny, 1977).

The present discussion will start from the position that the distinction between holistic and dimensional codes is conceptually well-founded and that it relates to the *level* (pictorial or semantic) at which information is coded. A characteristic of the pictorial code is that it emphasizes gestalt properties of shapes rather than component dimensions. In addition, if we assume a direct analogy between the pictorial code and the graphemic code discussed in Chapters IV and V, we would anticipate that pictorial representations of objects should be capable of being transformed by quasi-spatial operations, such as mental rotation, and that these codes should be available for relatively direct matching against the products of pictorial encoding.

XIV.2 DURABLE PICTORIAL STORAGE

An initial assumption which requires validation is the proposal, embodied in Figure XIII.2.1, that a *pictorial register* exists which is functionally equivalent to the graphemic register. This issue can most readily be addressed by examining performance in tasks involving the short term retention of briefly displayed novel and unnameable visual forms. By using shapes which are unfamiliar we can reduce the likelihood that semantic recoding or naming will occur, and thus improve the chances of selectively examining characteristics of the pictorial register.

A relevant series of experiments was reported by Phillips (1974). The stimuli were patterns generated by lighting randomly selected cells in 4×4, 5×5, 6×6 or 8×8 matrices. The computer used to control the experiment created a novel pattern on each trial. This was displayed for 1 sec and was followed by a variable inter-stimulus interval (ISI) at the end of which a second pattern was displayed. The second pattern was either identical to the first or differed from it by addition or removal of one illuminated cell. The *S* was required to make a 'same' or 'different' response. Phillips found that a very short ISI of 20 msecs produced extremely accurate and fast responses which were unaffected by variations in the complexity of the patterns. At longer ISIs, falling in the range 1–9 secs, accuracy and RT showed substantial effects of pattern complexity. Accuracy declined somewhat as the ISI increased, but remained well above chance for the 4×4 and 5×5 matrices.

Phillips proposed that this experiment tapped two levels of pictorial encoding. The first level, which he called the sensory representation, exists only briefly but is unaffected by variations in pattern complexity. The second level, called the schematic representation, is limited with regard to complexity while being relatively durable. We may equate the first of these levels with the iconic register (see Chapter IV), and the second with the pictorial register. In subsequent experiments Phillips demonstrated that the sensory (iconic) component could be eliminated by visual masking of the first pattern or by a spatial displacement of the second pattern relative to the first. This last factor appeared to be effective because displacement prevented the *S* from basing his judgement on an awareness of movement or its absence as the second display replaced the first.

A further series of experiments, described by Phillips & Christie (1977), suggested that the schematic (pictorial) code has a capacity of only one pattern. In these studies, a sequence of 4×4 matrices was presented and followed after a short delay by a reverse order sequence of probes. The *S* was instructed to indicate for each probe whether or not it was identical to one of the patterns presented in the series. Phillips found that responses were accurate and rapid for the probe of the last pattern, whereas probes of other patterns produced a uniformly lower level of accuracy. This recency effect was preserved when the final pattern was masked, when the delay before presentation of the probe was extended to several seconds, and when length of the lists varied unpredictably. These results were taken to imply that schematic memory for patterns was divisible into two components, one defined by the recency effect (here equated with representation of a single pattern in the pictorial register), and the other by the poorer retention of other patterns in the series. In Figure XIII.2.1 this second type of storage might be located in the pictorial data store, or in a pictorial episodic memory system which is not represented in the diagram.

Podgorny & Shepard (1977) have recently described a series of experiments which clarify some additional properties of the pictorial coding of matrix patterns. The stimuli were 5×5 and 3×3 matrices, with some cells filled and some left unfilled. Podgorny used a probe task to compare the processing of a physically present matrix with the processing of one which the *S* visualized in response to instructions. In the latter case the cells of a 3×3 matrix were assigned number codes, 1–9, and the patterns were specified by a sequence of two, three or four digits which told the *S* which cells should be imagined as being darkened. An empty matrix was available to the *S* during this preparatory phase. The visualization condition was contrasted with a perceptual condition in which the matrix containing darkened squares was displayed on the screen. When the *S* indicated that he was ready a probe was presented, consisting of a single dot or of a set of dots, equal in number to the cells of the matrix which were filled or which were imagined as being filled. The *S* was instructed to indicate rapidly whether the probe or probes were 'on' the real or imagined pattern, or 'off' the pattern. The multiple probes were always all on the pattern or all off the pattern.

This experiment allows us to observe whether the pictorial coding of a matrix pattern which has been generated by an internal imaginative process differs, in terms of processing time measures, from a code which is formed as a product of perception. Podgorny's data suggest that reactions to probes may be slightly faster when the darkened matrix is physically present than when it is represented only in imagination. However, the effect was small, amounting to a non-significant 25 msecs for multiple probes and to about 50 msecs for single dot probes. In general, positive responses to multiple probes were faster than positive responses to single probes. This indicates that reactions are faster to a probe which shares the gestalt properties of the current pictorial representation than to a probe which corresponds to it only partially. This effect did not occur for 'off' responses, presumably because the undarkened squares of the matrix do not possess gestalt qualities, being merely a background against which the darkened figure is seen or imagined.

The gestalt quality of the pictorial code was confirmed by more detailed analyses of the relationship between RT and the compactness of the pattern on the matrix. Podgorny found that an index of compactness, defined as the square root of the area of the figure divided by its perimeter, successfully predicted the RT for single and multiple probes, and for perceived and imagined patterns. In the single probe conditions this effect occurred primarily for 'on' responses, the 'off' responses being relatively uninfluenced by the compactness of the figure. However, if the background to the figure was more compact than the figure itself, there was evidence of reversal of this figure-ground relationship. In these cases RTs for 'off' responses were predicted by the completeness of the background squares, and the 'off' RT was faster than the 'on' RT.

Podgorny's experiment indicates, therefore, that the RT to respond to a probe of a matrix pattern is influenced by a gestalt property—figural compactness—irrespective of whether the pattern is available directly to perception or has been generated by the imagination. This supports the proposal that the pictorial register can contain gestalt-like pattern descriptions which may be formed by the pictorial encoding process or by an internal generative process of pictorial retrieval. It is also worth noting that negative RTs in this situation are characterized by a distance function, RT tending to increase with proximity of the probe to the filled squares which make up the figure.

XIV.3 SIZE SCALING AND ROTATION

If the pictorial code is formally analogous to the graphemic code we would anticipate that a shape representation established at this level should be transformable by quasi-spatial operations, such as expansion or contraction of the figure, or rotation in two-dimensional space. A further proposal, which derives from the assumption that pictorial codes are relatively literal representations of perceptual gestalts, is that these transformation processes should appear analogous to changes of state which are encountered in perception. An alteration of size normally involves a process of expansion or contraction, as when an object approaches or retreats into the distance. When an object is tilted its axis rotates from one orientation to another. A consistent proposal of Shepard and his co-workers has been that mental transformations are analogues of these types of continuous change (Cooper & Shepard, 1976). Hence, we anticipate that RT to solve problems which require that stimuli should undergo transformations of size or orientation will relate directly to the amount of change which is necessary.

Size transformations have been examined in the context of 'same'–'different' judgement tasks in which *S*s have been instructed to indicate whether or not pairs of shapes are identical apart from a difference in size. The ratio of the sizes of the two shapes is varied. It is assumed that the judgement that the shapes are identical depends on a prior judgement which equates their sizes, and that the time to make this adjustment will reflect the magnitude of the size difference. Sekuler & Nash (1972) presented *S*s with two rectangles in succession on each trial of an experiment. The instruction was to classify the rectangles as 'same' if they had the same height-to-width ratio while disregarding differences in size or orientation (on half of the trials the second rectangle was rotated 90° relative to the first). It was found that 'same' RT increased as a regular function of the difference in size between the rectangles, with a halving or doubling of size each costing about 70 msecs of processing time. The function was preserved when one rectangle was rotated relative to the other, although this also added about 70 msecs to the RT. Thus, the experiment suggests that size transformation and rotation might be independent 'normalization' procedures which can precede a shape comparison.

A difficulty with this theory is posed by experiments which show interactions of effects due to size discrepancy and 'same' versus 'different' responses. If rescaling of size occurs before the judgemental process is initiated we must anticipate that the effect will be observed for both 'same' and 'different' responses. Evidence to support this view was presented by Bundesen & Larsen (1975). They described an experiment in which *S*s matched blacked-in polygons which differed in size by ratios ranging from 1:1 to 1:5. The RTs for 'same' and 'different' responses were found to increase as an approximately linear function of the size ratio. However, the 'different' pairs in this experiment were made up by inverting one member of each 'same' pair. Besner & Coltheart (1977) have since shown that this additivity of the size ratio and 'same'–'different' effects breaks down when different forms are presented on the 'different' trials. In one such study, Besner & Coltheart (1976) used articulated line segments as stimuli, and found that a size difference affected 'same' RT but not 'different' RT. Thus, if the size ratio effect does index a normalization process, we must conclude that this process does not precede comparison of the shapes. Rather, it seems likely that the *S* starts with a global test of the similarity of the forms and by-passes the size adjustment stage if this provides adequate evidence that the shapes are 'different'.

Application of rotation functions to pictorial codes can be investigated in a task in which *S*s judge whether or not patterns are symmetrical about an axis which varies in its orientation. For example, Corballis & Roldan (1975) used arrangements of dots placed either side of a line as stimuli. The patterns were either exact repetitions or mirror images, and the *S*s were instructed to classify the mirror images as being symmetrical and the repetitions as non-symmetrical. The RT for both types of judgement increased markedly when the axis of the figure was rotated from the vertical. However, this effect could be offset by tilting the observer's head. If the *S* tilted his head through 45° he responded to patterns tilted at the same angle as though they were vertical. Thus, the two-dimensional co-ordinate system involved in spatial structuring of pictorial representations appears, in this instance, to be defined relative to the retina. This contrasts with findings for symbols, since Corballis, Zbrodoff & Roldan (1976) reported no effect of head tilt on speed of discrimination of normal and reflected symbols in the Cooper & Shepard (1973) task.

A relatively direct adaptation of the procedures used by Cooper & Shepard to the study of the pictorial code was described by Cooper (1975). The stimuli were black polygons generated by a procedure for construction of nonsense shapes (see Attneave & Arnoult, 1956) and varied in complexity with regard to the number of angles on their perimeters of the form (6–24). In a preliminary phase of the experiment the *S*s learned to discriminate arbitrarily chosen standard forms from their mirror-image reflections. During this phase the forms were presented in a particular orientation, defined as upright for that shape, although the particular orientation used varied from one *S* to another. A reaction time experiment was then conducted in which standard and reflected forms were presented in the standard orientation or tilted 60°, 120°, 180°, 240° or 300° clockwise from the vertical. The *S*s were required to respond positively to the standard forms and negatively to their reflections. It was found that the RT increased as a linear function of the angle of rotation of the form (measured clockwise or anti-clockwise from the vertical), and was well described by the equations: $\overline{\text{RT}} = 754 + 2{\cdot}16(\text{d})$ msecs for positive responses, and $\text{RT} = 812 + 2{\cdot}15(\text{d})$ msecs for negative responses, d being defined as one degree of angle from the vertical. The response effect of about 60 msecs combined additively with the effect due to orientation of the test shape. However, Cooper was unable to find any effect of the complexity of the shapes on either the intercept or the slope of the RT functions.

Cooper (1975) conducted a second experiment which tested for the occurrence of preparatory rotation of a code held in the pictorial register. The *S* was shown a standard form for 3 secs followed by an arrow indicating the orientation in which the test figure would be presented. Duration of the arrow was controlled by the *S*, who closed a switch to indicate when he had completed the preparatory rotation of the form held in memory. The test form was then presented in the expected orientation, and the *S* classified it as a standard or mirror-image form. Cooper reported that preparation effectively eliminated the relationship between RT and orientation of the test form. This result, which corresponds to the findings of Cooper & Shepard (1973) for rotation of symbols, confirms that the pictorial coding of a shape can be transformed by an operation of mental rotation, and that the product of this rotation is available for direct matching against an incoming stimulus.

The experiment also provided a measure of the time elapsing before the *S* closed the switch to indicate that he had completed rotation of the form. *S*s were instructed to rotate clockwise under some conditions, and anti-clockwise under others. A consequence of this was that rotation sometimes had to proceed through more than 180° in order to reach the required orientation. When Cooper plotted this preparation RT in relation to the angle of rotation, which now extended by 60° steps over the range 0°–300°, she obtained a linear function described by the equation: $\overline{\text{RT}} = 569 + 2{\cdot}71(\text{d})$ msecs. The intercept was somewhere lower than that found for discriminative RTs in the first experiment, but the rotation rate was approximately the same.

These findings are consistent with the view that pictorial codings of patterns may undergo a transformation of orientation which mimics the perceptual consequences of viewing an object rotating clockwise or anti-clockwise in two-dimensional space. However, since Cooper restricted her observations to a subset of only six orientations, we cannot confidently prefer a theory which states that rotation is an analogue of *continuous* change to one which states that it is an analogue of jerky change. Cooper & Shepard (1976) report some additional evidence on this point. *S*s imagined a polygon rotating in two-dimensional space. A test version of the form was presented during this activity for classification as standard or reflected. Using an estimate of the *S*'s rotation rate, Cooper arranged that the orientation of the test form should coincide with the orientation of the imagined form on some trials, and diverge from it by a greater or lesser amount on other trials. In agreement with Cooper & Shepard (1973), she found that RT was independent of test stimulus orientation when actual and imagined orientation coincided but that RT was an increasing function of the angular discrepancy in orientation when the two did not coincide. On certain trials *S*s were probed at orientations which were intermediate between the 60° points which were normally tested. Performance on probes occurring at these unexpected and unusual orientations was no different from that observed at the familiar 60° points. Cooper took this to imply that the trajectory of the rotation process passed through the orientations falling between each 60° position.

A further important feature of Cooper's (1975) experiment is the absence of an effect of figural complexity on rotation rate. This finding appears to run counter to the results reported by Phillips (1974) for short-term retention of pictorial information, since the complexity of matrix patterns was clearly important in his experimental situation. On the other hand, an absence of complexity effects is consistent with the proposal that the pictorial coding of a form is a unified, gestalt-like entity. A possible objection to Cooper's (1975) experiment is that *S*s may have coded the shapes in a somewhat reduced or schematic form, perhaps opting for one distinctive component which could be rotated and used to make the discrimination. However, Cooper & Podgorny (1975) have since demonstrated that complexity affects neither the time to complete preparatory rotation nor the time for a discriminative reaction even under conditions where retention of detail of the shapes is necessary. This was achieved by requiring *S*s to discriminate standard forms from their reflections and from various rather subtle topographic transformations. Cooper & Shephard (1976) argue that these findings are difficult to reconcile with a propositional account of pattern representation, and see them as favouring the view that the rotation operates on a gestalt which may incorporate considerable complexity of detail.

XIV.4 BLOB PROCESSING

The proposal that the pictorial code possesses the qualities of a gestalt has important implications for theories about the processing of multi-attribute stimuli. This term is applicable to stimulus sets which are generated by systematically combining variations on two or more dimensions or attributes. For example, an experimenter might form a stimulus set by taking all combinations of two shapes (square or circle), two colours (red or green) and two sizes (large or small), giving a set of eight stimuli which are distinguishable on attributes of form, colour and size. Much effort has been devoted to attempts to determine whether the attributes of such stimuli are processed serially or in parallel (see, for example, Egeth [1966], Hawkins [1969], Saraga & Shallice [1973]). However, we can note that this question is meaningful only if the stimuli are decomposed into their attributes at an early point in processing, and that this is a proposal which conflicts with our assumptions about the unanalysed nature of the pictorial code.

Garner (1970) and Garner & Fefoldy (1970) argued that stimulus attributes might be classified as *integral* or *separable*. The distinction was based in part on the results of studies of the subjective similarity of multi-attribute forms. If we think of a set of forms which vary in terms of two attributes—say 'size' and 'colour'—we can represent each stimulus as a point on a two-dimensional surface (having variation in size as one dimension, and variation in colour as the other). In judging the similarity of pairs of shapes, *S*s might proceed in one or other of two ways. If the shapes were perceived in terms of values on the component dimensions the judgement of similarity would be expected to reflect their separation on each dimension, producing what has been called a city block metric (Shepard, 1964). If, on the other hand, the dimensions underlying construction of the stimulus set were merged in perception, the judgements would reflect the global similarity of shapes as represented by the direct distances between points on the two-dimensional surface (known as a Euclidean metric). Garner proposed that attributes yielding a city block metric could be described as *separable*, and that those which yielded a Euclidean metric could be described as *integral*. He subsequently noted that physically distinct attributes might fuse to form a gestalt, in which case the component dimensions were said to *configure*.

The integrality-separability distinction was related to performance in speeded classification tasks by Garner & Fefoldy (1970). *S*s sorted cards containing stimuli created by combining values on two attributes into sets determined by the value taken on one of the attributes. The second attribute was defined as irrelevant to the classification, and its value was either held constant (control condition) or was allowed to vary independently of the value on the target dimension (orthogonal condition), or to co-vary with the value on the target dimension (correlated condition). Integral dimensions, such as the value and chroma of a colour chip, produced a gain in classification speed in the correlated condition and a delay in the orthogonal condition. When value and chroma were represented at spatially distinct locations these effects disappeared. It was argued that the spatial separation enhanced the separability of the dimensions, and thus eliminated the effects on classification speed which were taken to be characteristic of integral dimensions.

The position adopted here is that integrality of dimensions and configuring of parts of forms are properties of the pictorial level of coding, whereas separability of dimensions is a property of the semantic level of coding. Thus, integrality and separability are not viewed as characteristics of certain stimuli or dimensions, but as characteristics of the different *levels* at which the stimuli may be processed. A viewpoint of this kind has recently been expressed by Lockhead (1972). He argued that perceptual processing of shapes involved two stages, the first being global, holistic and obligatory, and the second analytic and optional. He has used the expression *blob processing* to refer to the first stage (here equated with pictorial encoding), and defined it as an operation which locates an unanalysed configuration at a point in a multi-dimensional stimulus space.

Lockhead has used stimulus identification tasks to demonstrate the distinction between the blob processing and dimension processing accounts of pictorial encoding. In such tasks the *S* makes a unique identifying response to each member of a set of stimuli. There are severe limitations on the ability of *S*s to make such judgements when the stimuli vary on only one dimension (Miller, 1956). However, improvements occur if variation on the target dimension is correlated with variation on a second irrelevant dimension. Lockhead (1972) noted that correlation of the values taken by stimuli on two dimensions may be arranged in a number of different ways. A positive linear correlation pairs increasing values on one dimension with increasing values on the other, whereas a negative correlation pairs increasing values on one dimension with decreasing values on the other. An alternative procedure, called a 'sawtooth correlation', enhances the scatter of points on the two-dimensional surface, as in the series: A_1B_2, A_2B_4, A_3B_1, A_4B_3, in which A and B are dimensions each taking four values of increasing magnitude. A procedure of this kind maximizes the Euclidean distances between the stimuli while the linear correlations tend to minimize those distances.

According to the blob processing theory the critical factor governing speed and accuracy in identification is *discriminability*, that is, the distances separating the stimuli in the multi-dimensional stimulus space. Hence, it is expected that the sawtooth correlational procedure, which maximizes inter-stimulus distance, will lead to faster and more accurate performance than the linear correlational procedures, which minimize inter-stimulus distances. Such a prediction does not follow from a theory which assumes decomposition of the stimulus into its component dimensions and independent processing of each segregated dimension. According to the dimension processing theory correlated dimensions yield gains in speed and accuracy because they add to the number of independent decision processes which are functioning to categorize the stimulus. If processing time for each dimension varies randomly, and if processing terminates as soon as one or the other dimension specifies the identity of the stimulus, an RT gain can be anticipated because an increase in the number of active dimensions increases the probability that one will terminuate with a below average decision time. Such an interpretation requires that the dimensions should be correlated (so that each response category is uniquely specified by a value on each of two dimensions), but is indifferent to the form of the correlation (Lockhead, 1972).

Monahan & Lockhead (1977) have demonstrated that a theory of this kind cannot be correct. In one experiment they used rectangular stimuli which varied on dimensions of height and width. Absolute identification of members of a series of six rectangles (indicated by pressing one of six keys) was both faster and more accurate when the height/width combinations reflected a sawtooth correlational scheme than when they reflected a linear correlational scheme. An effect of this kind would not be expected to occur if identification involved parallel evaluation of segregated dimensions of height and width. It is, however, consistent with the blob processing theory, since the sawtooth correlation of dimensions enhances the discriminability of the stimuli, and this is viewed as the dominant factor influencing speed of identification. In a further experiment the stimuli were pairs of lines whose lengths varied independently. Performance on a series created by positive linear correlation of the line lengths was radically different from performance on series created by sawtooth correlation or negative linear correlation. Once again, therefore, logically equivalent procedures for combining stimulus dimensions yielded divergent results, and the similarity of the stimuli, viewed as blobs or gestalts, appeared to be the major determinant of identification RT.

XIV.5 SENTENCE–PICTURE COMPARISON

As was mentioned at the beginning of the last section, much of the research which has been concerned with the processing of multi-attribute stimuli has, ostensibly, been addressed to questions about the serial or parallel processing of segregated dimensions. Garner (1970) argued that the serial versus parallel issue was logically sub-ordinate to the integrality-separability distinction, being applicable to separable dimensions but not to integral dimensions. If we are right to equate integrality of dimensions with the pictorial code and separability of dimensions with the semantic code, we are led to the conclusion that the serial-parallel issue is not relevant to comparisons of stimuli occurring at the pictorial level, although it may be relevant for comparisons occurring at the semantic level.

It happens that the tasks which have most often been used to investigate the serial versus parallel issue are precisely those which seem most likely to tap processing at the pictorial level. These include a *categorization task*, in which the *S* is given a description of a class of target shapes and responds positively to stimuli which match the description and negatively to those which do not, and a *comparison task* in which pairs of forms are displayed to be classified as 'same' or 'different'. It seems likely that a comparison procedure operating on pictorial codes could support successful performance on both of these tasks.

In the 'same'–'different' judgement task, pairs of shapes are presented to the *S*, simultaneously and side by side, and he is instructed to make a positive response if they are physically identical and a negative response if they are discrepant. This situation is formally analogous to the task of matching symbol arrays under conjunctive instructions which was discussed in Chapter VII. The number of attributes defined as relevant to the 'same' or 'different' decision is a variable which is equivalent to the display size factor, D, in the earlier discussion and the number of attributes taking the same value may be equated with the factor, C, the array correspondence.

A prediction of the blob processing account is that the 'same' RT should be independent of the number of attributes defined as relevant, although the 'different' RT is expected to increase as the number of attributes taking the same values increases. Results consistent with these expectations have been reported by Nickerson (1967b) and Hawkins (1969). In the latter study the stimuli varied on dimensions of form, colour, and size of an inscribed circle, and stimulus sets were constructed which varied on one, two or all three of these dimensions. There was no evidence of any tendency for 'same' RT to increase as a function of the number of relevant dimensions. Indeed, in Hawkins' first experiment, RTs in the two and three-dimensional conditions were generally faster than RTs for the slowest of their single component dimensions. This outcome is clearly contrary to the predictions of the serial or parallel dimension processing models, but was shown by Hawkins to be due in part to a speed-accuracy trade-off. When this was properly controlled it was found that RTs in the two-dimensional conditions were essentially equivalent to RTs for the slower of their component dimensions in the one-dimensional conditions.

Experiments on categorization were reported by Nickerson (1967a) and Marcel (1970b). In Nickerson's study the *S*s verified conjunctive definitions of shapes which specified values on one, two or three attributes. The shapes varied on dimensions of form (circle, square, triangle), colour (red, yellow, blue), and size (large, medium, small). Marcel's (1970b) experiment also involved variations in form and colour, but the third attribute was the orientation of stripes within each figure (horizontal, vertical or oblique). In both studies *S*s verified three-attribute descriptions ('large red circle', for example), and the positive and negative RTs were contrasted with the two-attribute and single attribute descriptions which can be formed from these values. In Nickerson's study the single attribute descriptions were 'large', 'red' and 'circle', and the two-attribute descriptions were 'large circle', 'red circle' and 'large and red'.

If *S*s transform these descriptions to a pictorial code against which incoming test shapes are matched we would expect that the positive RT should be independent of the number of attributes mentioned. This is because pictorial codes are viewed as blobs and not as values on segregated dimensions. The data reported by Nickerson (1967a) and Marcel (1970b) are generally in agreement with this prediction. In neither study did the RT increase as a function of the number of attributes specified in the criterion. This finding is consistent with blob processing theory but counter to dimension processing models which assume serial evaluation of the dimensions or parallel evaluation with variable decision times on each dimension. In both cases the logical requirement that the decision should be delayed until processing has been completed on all dimensions leads to the prediction that RT will increase with the number of relevant dimensions, either because there are more dimensions to be processed in series, or because there is an increased likelihood that one of the component dimensions will return a slower than average decision time on any given trial (Nickerson, 1967a).

A blob processing interpretation of this task might state that the description given to the *S* specifies a point in a multi-dimensional stimulus space and that a positive response is made if the incoming stimulus is assigned to approximately the same location. The problem for the judgemental process is to discriminate small discrepancies between description location and stimulus location which are attributable merely to random perturbations from larger discrepancies which are properly indicative of a mismatch between the stimulus and description. Since speed of discrimination is dependent on proximity in the stimulus space (Lockhead & King, 1977; Monahan & Lockhead, 1977) we would expect negative RT to vary as a function of the similarity of non-target shapes to the target concept. We have already noted that spatial proximity affects negative RT in a probe task of the kind described by Podgorny & Shepard (1977). This is also true of the categorization task, since both Nickerson (1967a) and Marcel (1970b) reported increases in RT and error rate for reactions to negative stimuli which mismatched the target description on only one attribute.

A detailed analysis of the confusability effects which occur on negative trials in the shape categorization task was undertaken by Saraga & Shallice (1973). They contrasted a two-attribute condition, in which the target was 'red square', with the single-attribute conditions using 'red' and 'square' as targets. The negative instances were rectangles or triangles, coloured orange or blue. The data from the unidimensional conditions confirmed that a rectangle was discriminated as a non-instance of 'square' less rapidly than a triangle, and that an orange patch was classified as a non-instance of 'red' less rapidly than a blue patch. The confusion effect was greater on the colour dimension, where blue patches were rejected 128 msecs faster than orange patches, than on the form dimension, where triangles were rejected 42 msecs faster than rectangles.

This pattern was also apparent in the two-attribute condition. The slowest negative RTs were obtained for the stimuli which were closest to 'red square' on a two-dimensional surface representing a variation in form and a variation in colour. Average negative RT for this subset was about 520 msecs. The orange square, which matched the target in form and was confusable in colour, was rejected less rapidly than the red rectangle, which matched in colour and was confusable in shape (569 versus 508 msecs). The RT for the orange rectangle was slightly lower than this, at 488 msecs. These RTs were somewhat greater than those obtained for stimuli which were remote from the target in shape (red or orange triangle), which averaged 472 msecs, or those which were remote in colour (blue square or rectangle), which averaged 437 msecs. Finally, blue triangle, which was remote on both dimensions, produced the lowest negative RT of 428 msecs.

Saraga & Shallice elected to discuss these RTs in relation to issues concerning serial and parallel processing of values on segregated dimensions, and were able to present careful arguments to demonstrate the inapplicability of serial models or parallel models which assume a limitation on processing capacity (Corcoran, 1971). Although they favoured a parallel processing account, there seems to be a reasonable case for arguing that their results are consistent with a blob processing interpretation in which negative RT is considered to be directly dependent on the Euclidean distances between negative instances and the target concept in a multi-dimensional stimulus space. A proposal of this kind could be validated by a demonstration that judgements of the similarity of the stimuli used successfully predicted negative RT in the two-attribute condition.

The categorization task has been represented in the above discussion as a situation in which the *S* transforms a verbal description to a pictorial code which then provides a basis for a 'same' or 'different' judgement about a probe shape. If the description presented to the *S* varies from trial to trial this situation becomes a *sentence-picture comparison task.* Sentence-picture comparison is a type of verification task in which the truth or falsity of a sentence is determined by reference to an external situation rather than by a consideration of semantic information stored in permanent memory (see Chapter XII). It has been extensively used in psycholinguistically oriented studies of sentence processing which have investigated the effects of syntactic factors, such as negation and active or passive voice, on the verification RT (see Gough [1965], Glucksberg, Trabasso & Wald [1973], Olson & Filby [1972], Clark & Chase [1972], and Carpenter & Just [1975]).

An assumption underlying the 'constituent comparison' models of sentence verification formulated by Clark & Chase (1972) and Carpenter & Just (1975) was that a sentence-picture comparison occurs at the level of the semantic or logical registration systems in the Lexical or Pictorial Memories (see Figures VIII.5.1 and XIII.2.1). This proposal is supported by demonstrations that linguistic effects occur, especially when the sentence and picture against which it is to be verified are presented simultaneously (Clark & Chase, 1972; Carpenter & Just, 1975).

Nonetheless, the analysis of the pictorial retrieval function proposed here clearly allows that the simple locative sentences used in the verification experiments (e.g. 'The circle is above the square') could be transformed to a pictorial code which could provide a reliable basis for the 'true' or 'false' judgement. If this did happen, the linguistic effects would be expected to disappear, and RTs for sentence-picture comparisons would be expected to be similar to RTs for picture-picture comparisons. This latter prediction was tested by Seymour (1974c, 1974d). The displays were combinations of square and circle outlines, drawn one inside the other, and descriptions of the form: 'Square inside circle' or 'The circle is outside the square'. Under simultaneous presentation conditions the RTs for sentence-picture comparisons were substantially greater than the RTs for picture-picture comparisons, but this difference was completely eliminated under a successive presentation condition in which the sentence preceded the test picture.

The more critical prediction of the pictorial recoding account of sentence-picture comparison is that linguistic effects which occur in the simultaneous presentation condition should disappear under conditions of successive presentation. In fact, this prediction has often been shown not to hold. Gough (1966) reported effects of negation and passive voice in an experiment in which the probe pictures were presented 3 secs after presentation of a spoken sentence. Seymour (1974c) presented square-circle pictures 1 sec following display of sentences of the form: 'The square is inside the circle', 'The circle has the square inside', or 'Outside the square is the circle'. These sentences are referentially synonymous and thus differences between them noted in the simultaneous condition might be expected to disappear in the successive condition. However, it was found that the sentence structure effect occurred under both conditions, and that it co-existed with the converge of the picture-picture and sentence-picture RTs found in the successive condition. Further evidence of survival of linguistic or logical effects in successive sentence-picture comparison has been given by Trabasso, Rollins & Shaughnessy (1971) and by Carpenter & Just (1975).

It is likely that these studies failed to provide evidence for pictorial recoding in sentence-picture comparison because the *S*s were not allowed long enough to achieve a well-formed pictorial representation, or because they were not encouraged to adopt this strategy. Tversky (1975) has shown that effects of negation can be eliminated in a sentence-picture comparison task of the kind studied by Clark & Chase (1972) if the sentence is presented for 5 secs and there is then a 5 sec ISI before presentation of the probe picture. A thorough study of the conditions allowing for pictorial recoding has recently been undertaken by Glushko & Cooper (1978). They presented *S*s with sentences asserting the relative spatial locations (above, below, left or right) of simple geometric forms. The number of relational assertions varied from one to three. The factors of linguistic complexity (number of assertions) and markedness of the spatial prepositions (see Chapter XV) influenced the RT when the sentences and pictures were simultaneously displayed. However, these effects were eliminated when the *S* was allowed as much time as he required to study the sentence and prepare a pictorial representation.

It seems reasonable to conclude from these results that 'same'—'different' judgements about shapes, the categorization of shapes by reference to a target description, and the verification of sentences about simple pictures, may all be based on matching procedures applied at the level of the pictorial code. We have argued that this code possesses the properties of a *gestalt*, and that it is for this reason that pictorially based judgements are not affected by variations in the complexity of the dimensional description of a target shape (Hawkins, 1969) or of locative sentence structures (Glushko & Cooper, 1978).

XIV.6 CONCLUSIONS

This chapter has concentrated on the experimental investigation of the pictorial level of representation. It appeared that this level could be tapped by using simple non-symbolic forms in tasks involving responses to visual probes, physical identity matching, or preparation for spatially transformed stimuli. In many respects, the ground covered here is similar to that explored in relation to the graphemic code. We have shown that pictorial codes can be formed by operations on sensory input (pictorial ENCODING) or by internal generative activities (pictorial RETRIEVAL), and that these codes may be maintained in temporary storage (pictorial REPRESENTATION) and transformed by the quasi-spatial operations of mental size scaling and rotation.

Much of the experimental evidence derives from tasks which involve comparison of retained or generated pictorial codes. It has been assumed that the data reflect characteristics of the pictorial code and also the judgemental activities which underlie 'same' and 'different' decisions. The judgemental aspect has not been pursued in this context since it has already been discussed quite extensively elsewhere. However, it seems likely that pictorial comparisons are similar to graphemic identity judgements, depending on the accumulation of homogeneity evidence by counters whose thresholds can be adjusted by intervention of a control programme (the MATCH executive).

So far as the pictorial code itself is concerned the major conflict seems to be between accounts which emphasize the gestalt qualities of the encoded stimulus and those which emphasize the separability of its component dimensions. The position adopted here has been that both of these views have merit, but that the gestalt emphasis is the more appropriate at the pictorial level of coding. We can say, therefore, that the pictorial code is characterized by figure-ground properties (compactness) (Podgorny & Shepard, 1977), an absence of dimensionality (Lockhead, 1972), and an absence, within reason, of effects of descriptive or logical complexity (Glushko & Cooper, 1978).

CHAPTER XV

Coding of Attributes

COLOUR, SIZE AND LOCATION

XV.1 INTRODUCTION

The argument of the two preceding chapters has been that objects and their attributes may be represented at two distinct levels of processing, which we have called the *pictorial code* and the *semantic code*. The last chapter considered some aspects of the pictorial code, especially its *gestalt* and manipulable qualities. In this and the next chapter we will turn to an examination of the semantic code. An assumption underlying much of the preceding discussion has been that objects are represented in the semantic register as *configurations of attributes* in which dimensions of variation, many of them perceptual in nature, are specified and assigned values. In this chapter, experiments relating to the processing of attributes will be discussed. We will concentrate on a perceptual characteristic (colour), and two relational characteristics (location and size). The aim will be to demonstrate that semantic representations of attributes differ from the pictorial codes discussed in the last chapter, and also to explore the hypothesis that pictures of objects and names of qualities access a central semantic system in which attribute information is coded.

There are three experimental tasks which have proved valuable in the study of attribute codes. The first of these is an identification or *naming task* in which the *S* is required to label the value which an object takes on a specified attribute. The second is the *relative judgement task* in which the *S* indicates which of two stimuli has the greater (or lesser) value on an attribute. The third is a *comparison task* in which the *S* decides whether objects have the same value on an attribute, or, more usually, whether a verbal label correctly names the value taken by a particular object.

The following discussion will consider the attributes of colour, location and size, and will draw on evidence from the three types of experimental task where appropriate. In the case of *colour* the experiments have, for the most part, involved comparison tasks and naming tasks, and particular interest has attached to situations in which semantic conflicts are induced by simultaneous specification of relevant and irrelevant attribute values (Stroop effects).

The principal method of studying the coding of *spatial location* has been a verbal-pictorial comparison task in which the *S* verifies a verbal statement about the relative locations of objects by referring to a picture. Aside from attempts to model the control structure of the sentence-picture verification process (see Clark & Chase (1972) and Carpenter & Just (1975)) the main value of this type of experiment has been in the study of the relationship between 'lexical marking' and spatial decision making.

With regard to *size*, the focus has been on tasks involving relative judgements of magnitude. The effects of distance, scale position and semantic congruity which are obtained in relative judgement tasks have already been mentioned (Chapters VI and XII). One issue to be examined here is the relationship between these effects and the modality (pictures or words) of the test stimuli. If size attributes are coded in a central semantic system, the effects should be identical for pictures and words apart from a possible difference of access time in favour of one class of stimulus or the other. There are, in addition, questions relating to the 'conditions of application' and bi-polar structure of spatial dimensions which can be investigated empirically in the context of the relative judgement task (Clark, Carpenter & Just, 1973).

XV.2 PICTORIAL AND SEMANTIC CODING OF COLOUR

The brightness and colouring of an object are visible characteristics which are encoded by the human perceptual system and incorporated into a gestalt-like representation called the pictorial code. In the discussion of this level of representation in Chapter XIV it was argued that pictorial codes could contain information that was diagnostic for response selection in certain types of comparison task, but that in other situations it might be necessary to isolate a particular attribute and to assign it a value at a semantic level of coding.

The distinction between pictorial and semantic representations of colour can be supported by reference to experiments conducted by Rosch (1975b). *S*s made physical identity judgements about pairs of colour chips which had been selected as focal or peripheral examples of their categories. On alternate trials the *S* was primed by presentation of a colour name spoken 2 secs before the patches were displayed.

This procedure is directly comparable to the one followed by Rosch (1975a, Experiment 5) in a study of physical identity comparisons of pictures of objects. Rosch found that such comparisons were not affected by the typicality of the objects within their superordinate classes, or by priming with the superordinate name. On the other hand, priming by a basic level name did affect physical comparisons of pictures (Rosch, Mervis, Gray, Johnson & Boyes-Braem, 1976, Experiment 6). The experiment with colours demonstrated that a priming effect occurred, and that it took the form of a typicality × priming interaction. Priming facilitated 'same' decisions about focal colours, inhibited 'same' decisions about peripheral colours, and produced no effect on 'different' responses.

The experiment by Rosch (1975b) suggests that colour names retrieve pictorial representations of their focal hues, and that the presence of this code in the pictorial register influences the process of judging physical identity of colour. In a further experiment, *S*s made nominal identity comparisons of colour patches, classifying as 'same' those pairs which were physically identical or which were physically different although from the same colour category. The physically identical pairs again showed a typicality × priming interaction whereas the nominally identical pairs showed additive effects of priming and typicality. It is likely that the categorial comparisons depended on retrieval of semantic codes, and that this process was facilitated by typicality and by priming. If so, Rosch's experiment successfully demonstrates that pictorial and semantic representations of colour possess distinct characteristics.

Rosch's technique has not, as yet, been applied to the study of the colours of objects. However, a reasonable assumption is that names of objects having characteristic colours (e.g. blood, lemon, leaf) are capable of retrieving pictorial representations of their colours from the pictorial data store. If such words were used as priming stimuli, we would expect to find that physical identity comparisons were facilitated for patches of colour which corresponded closely to the colour of the named object, even though the colours were not focal examples of their categories. This prediction depends on the assumption that *S*s store in memory fairly exact representations of the colours of objects. An empirical evaluation of this kind of memory for object colour might usefully be undertaken in the future.

The effect of priming on physical identity comparisons of colour is only observed when the colour name precedes the display by an adequate interval of time. This interval was found by Rosch (1975b) to be about 500 msecs. When the colour name was spoken simultaneously with the display there was no effect on physical identity comparisons, although the effect on nominal comparisons was preserved. An implication is that colours and colour names access the semantic register (the presumed locus of the nominal comparison) at approximately similar rates. A situation in which colours and irrelevant colour names are simultaneously presented for processing is in fact characteristic of experiments on Stroop effects. In Stroop experiments the irrelevant verbal information is presented visually in the form of a word whose print colour forms the primary focus for attention (Stroop, 1935). These experiments have most usually been conducted as studies of interference with colour naming by irrelevant and incongruent colour names (see Section XV.3 of this chapter). However, the Stroop procedure can also be applied to 'same'–'different' judgement tasks, and it is this application which is relevant to the distinction between pictorial and semantic levels of colour representation.

Egeth, Blecker & Kamlet (1969) presented evidence to suggest that physical identity comparisons of colour are not vulnerable to interference by irrelevant colour names. In a serial response task their *S*s classified pairs of rows of Xs as 'same' or 'different' in colour. Performance on this task was not affected when the Xs were replaced by colour names which often conflicted in meaning with their print colours. A similar test was made by Morton & Chambers (1973), using a card sorting task. Their *S*s sorted cards into 'same' or 'different' piles on the basis of a match or mismatch of the print colours of two sets of Xs or two colour names. In this case there was a small effect due to the presence of the irrelevant words. Similarly, physical identity (and nominal identity) matching of pairs of words was carried out slightly faster when both were printed in black than when they were printed in incongruent colours. It is likely that these effects are analogous to the other demonstrations of an influence of irrelevant physical variations on 'same'–'different' judgements of letters and shapes (see Chapters V and XIV). This could be verified by experiments in which RTs for colour matching were obtained, and there was a more precise control over the nature of the irrelevant information.

If colour is processed at the semantic level vulnerability to interference by irrelevant colour names should be much increased. Thus, we would expect to observe Stroop effects if *S*s made *nominal* comparisons of the print colours of incongruent colour names, or if they made a semantic comparison between a colour name and a colour patch. The second of these predictions was initially examined by Treisman & Fearnley (1969). Their *S*s sorted cards into a 'same' pile if a colour name matched the colour of a row of Xs, and into a 'different' pile if there was a mismatch. A Stroop condition was introduced by replacing the Xs by incongruently coloured colour names. When *S*s matched colour names against the print colour of the irrelevant colour names substantial Stroop interference effects occurred. This result was confirmed by Morton & Chambers (1973), and may be taken as a demonstration that the semantic coding of colour can be disrupted by the presence in the attentional field of an inconguent colour name.

Dyer (1973) reported an experiment in which 'same' and 'different' RTs were measured in a word-colour comparison task analogous to the one used by Treisman & Fearnley. *S*s compared a colour name, printed in white, with the print colour of a row of Xs or a colour name. The irrelevant colour name could be congruent with its own print colour, or incongruent. Relative to the control condition (the row of Xs), the 'same' RT was facilitated by congruity and substantially delayed by incongruity. The facilitation effect, amounting to about 50 msecs, is probably analogous to the priming effect on nominal comparisons noted by Rosch (1975b). Thus, the semantic coding of colour is facilitated by presence of the written name of that colour, but inhibited by the presence of the name of any other colour. In Dyer's experiment the inhibitory effect amounted to about 180 msecs. However, it would probably be wrong to conclude that these effects are localized within a processing stage concerned solely with the representation of colour. The 'different' RTs showed a general delay due to presence of an irrelevant colour name, and this effect was greater for congruent names than for incongruent names. An interaction of this kind could occur if the irrelevant word was sometimes compared with its own print colour, and if the outcome of this comparison intruded on the main 'same'–'different' judgemental process.

A further possibility to be considered is that the chromatic interpretation of a colour name may be affected by the colour in which the word is printed. Such effects have been called 'reverse Stroop effects' (see, for example, Uleman & Reeves [1971]), since they depend on interference with word processing by colour (as opposed to the verbal interference with colour processing which occurs in the classic Stroop effect). Treisman & Fearnley's (1969) experiment included a condition in which *S*s matched a colour name against the colour of a row of Xs, ignoring the colour in which the word was printed. There was an interference effect due to the irrelevant colour which appeared to be of similar magnitude to the verbal interference effect obtained in their study. Morton & Chambers (1973) reported a similar result, but established in addition that the relative magnitudes of the verbal and chromatic interference effects depended on the order in which the colour name and colour components of the display were processed. Dyer's (1973) study included a comparable condition in which a colour name, printed in white or in a congruent or incongruent colour, was matched against the colour of a row of Xs. 'Same' RTs were facilitated by congruity of colour and retarded by incongruity, and the effects were very similar in size to those observed with verbal distractors. The main point of difference was the absence of a reversed congruity effect on the 'different RTs. Thus, although variations in print colour generally produce only slight effects on speed of reading words, colour does have an effect on the process of interpreting a word in terms of the colour it denotes.

These experiments provide a general validation for the proposed distinction between the pictorial and semantic levels of colour representation. Judgements which are made at the pictorial level are not vulnerable to Stroop effects although they are influenced by advance priming by a colour name. Semantic judgements, by contrast, show a strong susceptibility to Stroop effects. The interpretation of a colour or a colour name is facilitated by congruent irrelevant information and disrupted by incongruent irrelevant information. It seems that we are dealing with a central semantic system which is accessible to word stimuli and to colour stimuli. Indeed, these demonstrations of the capacity of words to interfere with the coding of colour, and of colours to interfere with the interpretation of words, provide evidence in support of the view that the Lexical and Pictorial Memories share a common semantic resource.

XV.3 STROOP INTERFERENCE WITH COLOUR NAMING

Stroop (1935) measured the times which *S*s took to read lists of colour names and to name a series of colours. The words were printed in black or in incongruent colours. The colours were attributes of non-verbal symbols (squares or swastikas) or of incongruent colour names. The average time required to read 100 colour names printed in black was 41 secs. Varying the print colour of the words added just over 2 secs to this time, but this effect was not statistically significant. Naming 100 colours took longer than reading the names of the colours, averaging just over 63 secs. Colour naming suffered massive interference when the *S*s named the print colour of incongruent colour names, with the average naming time increasing to 110 secs. It is this delay in naming the print colour of incongruent colour names which constitutes the classic Stroop effect.

A notable feature of Stroop's results was the asymmetry in the interference effects noted in the naming and reading tasks. Irrelevant words interfered with colour naming but irrelevant colour did not interfere with word reading. It is very likely that this asymmetry is dependent on the differing speeds of the reading and naming processes. As soon as the basic skills are acquired, reading becomes a more rapid operation than naming (Lund, 1927), and a susceptibility to Stroop interference effects emerges (Schiller, 1966). This reading-naming difference is a general phenomenon which applies to objects and other spatial attributes in addition to colour (see Fraisse [1964, 1969]). Similarly, Stroop interference effects are not limited to colour, but are also found in the naming of quantity and location (Morton, 1969b; Fox, Shor & Steinman, 1971), and in the naming of objects (Rosinski, Golinkoff & Kukish, 1975; Rayner & Posnansky, 1977; Posnansky & Rayner, 1977).

The reading-naming difference and the asymmetry in the direction of the Stroop effect may be discussed within the context of the dual channel model or word naming (see Chapter X). It was argued that a visual word accesses its phonological representation via concurrent activity in a lexical-semantic channel and a grapheme-phoneme translation channel. The naming of a colour, object, or other spatial attribute occurs in a pictorial-semantic channel only (Seymour, 1973a, 1976b). Thus, in *naming* the input to the exit logogen system of Figure VIII.5.1 consists of semantic attributes alone, whereas in *reading* it consists of semantic attributes supported by phonemic attributes. The phonemic attributes appear to become available soon enough and in sufficent quantity to discount the possibility that semantic coding of an irrelevant perceptual attribute will interfere with reading. This is not because perceptual attributes cannot give rise to interference. It was shown in the last section that print colour produces congruity and incongruity effects when *S*s are required to interpret a word in terms of the colour it denotes. Further, when word processing is delayed by visual masking, reading rate is affected by print colour (Gumenik & Glass, 1970).

The interfering effect of irrelevant words on the naming of colours (or other spatial attributes) may also be interpreted within the framework of the models of the Pictorial and Lexical Memories (Figures VIII.5.1 and XIII.2.1). The naming of print colour involves stages of (1) pictorial encoding of colour; (2) retrieval of a semantic representation of colour; and (3) retrieval of a phonological representation of a colour name. The translation of an input to the Pictorial Memory into an output from the Lexical Memory is achieved via the semantic register which, according to the unitary memory theory, is common to the two systems. Stroop congruity and interference effects could occur at any or all of these stages. An irrelevant colour name might retrieve a chromatic code which disrupted the pictorial coding of colour, or a semantic code which interfered at the central semantic stage, or a phonological code which conflicted with the production of the colour name in speech. However, the evidence cited in the last section suggests that pictorial disruption is probably not a significant factor. Egeth, Blecker & Kamlet (1969) did not obtain Stroop effects when *S*s made physical comparisons of colour, and Rosch (1975b) found no priming effect when a colour name was presented simultaneously with physically identical colour patches. We will therefore concentrate on semantic retrieval and phonological retrieval as the most probable loci of the interference effects.

Although Stroop effects have frequently been viewed as a form of 'response competition' the available evidence does not favour the view that the sole locus of the interference is to be found in a peripheral output channel concerned with articulatory expression. If this were so we would not expect to find Stroop effects in the comparison tasks described in the last section, or in a memory search version of the task reported by Hock & Egeth (1970). Further, if the effect arose simply because grapheme-phoneme translation of a word resulted in pre-emptive occupation of the articulatory channel we would expect the interference to occur in equal measure for any pronounceable letter array. However, the magnitude of the Stroop effect varies according to a 'semantic gradient' defining the proximity in meaning of the irrelevant words to the domain of the naming task. This gradient was first demonstrated by Klein (1964). He used as distractors (1) names of the print colours, (2) names of other colours, (3) object names with strong colour associations (lemon, grass, fire and sky), (4) high frequency words unrelated to colour, (5) low frequency words unrelated to colour, and (6) orthographically irregular non-words. The interference with colour naming was greatest for the colour names, intermediate for the associates, and lowest for the words unrelated to colour. The gradient has been reported for other domains by Fox, Shor & Steinman (1971), and is evident in the performance of children as soon as they have learned to read (Schiller, 1966).

Morton (1969b) and Warren (1972) argued that the magnitude of the interference effect might depend on *priming* of logogen units. If the unit for a word is primed, either because it is semantically related to the domain of the task or, in the case of Warren's study, because the word or one of its associates is currently represented in short-term memory, this will increase the likelihood that a phonological representation will be retrieved, and that articulatory conflicts will occur. However, on this theory we would anticipate that words related to colour would produce interference irrespective of their relation to the colour of their print. The word 'blood' printed in red ink would evoke the response 'blood' and this would interfere with the production of the response 'red'. In fact, it is found that interference effects are eliminated when the stimuli are congruently coloured colour associates (Dalrymple-Alford, 1972).

For these reasons it seems improbable that articulatory conflicts constitute the primary or sole cause of the Stroop effect. A more likely possibility is that a conflict arises during the semantic processing stage, and that it reflects interpretative problems which are encountered when alternative colour attributes are simultaneously activated. Evidence consistent with such a view was presented by Seymour (1977) in a report of a series of experiments concerned with the colour associations of month and season names. It was found in normative studies that the seasons and their associated months attracted consistent colour responses, with green predominating for 'spring', yellow for 'summer', brown for 'autumn' and white for 'winter' (Seymour, 1976a). These colour associations appeared to derive from a rich set of scenic, vegetative, climatic and social associations which are provoked by the month and season names. In addition, the names are linked in a formal structure, specifying the cyclic ordering of the months and seasons, the allocation of months to seasons, and relations of opposition between 'winter' and 'summer' and between 'spring' and 'autumn'.

The co-existence of these chromatically toned associative fields and the formal structure of seasonal oppositions permitted the design of an experiment in which contributions of Stroop interference and congruity effects to input and output stages of processing could be evaluated. Season names were printed in green, yellow, brown and white and were displayed one at a time to *S*s who were instructed to respond by naming the season associated with the print colour (direct naming condition) or by naming the season opposite to the one associated with the colour (opposite naming condition). Direct naming was facilitated when the word on the display was the name of the season associated with the print colour, and this effect also occurred when the word was a month name related to that season. Thus, the response 'spring' to green print was facilitated when the display contained the word 'spring' or the name of a spring month. The question of interest related to the fate of this facilitation effect in the opposite naming task. In this case the *S* must appreciate that green signifies spring, determine that autumn is opposite to spring, and then respond by saying the word 'autumn'. If Stroop facilitation and interference effects related to response processes we would expect these reactions to be facilitated when the word 'autumn' appeared in green. If, alternatively, they relate to an input stage of encoding and semantic retrieval we would expect the response 'autumn' to green ink to be facilitated by the word 'spring' or by the name of a spring month. It was this latter result which consistently occurred in Seymour's experiments, none of which showed evidence for response-related facilitation effects.

The experiments with the season names also demonstrate that print colour can affect the latency of verbal *associative* responses to words provided that the task requires representation of colour at a semantic level. When *S*s responded to season names by naming their opposites, or to month names by naming their seasons, the colour in which the word was printed had no effect on the RT. However, when *S*s responded to season names by naming their associated colours, or by naming the colours of their opposites, a congruity effect was obtained. This again depended on the relation between the colour and season name displayed, and not on the relation between the colour and the response that was made. Thus, printing the word 'spring' in green ink facilitated the response 'green' in the direct naming task and the response 'brown' in the opposite naming task.

Seymour (1977) argued that these results were consistent with a 'conceptual encoding' interpretation of Stroop effects. The *S* initially forms a semantic coding of the relevant stimulus attribute, and this operation can be assisted by irrelevant but congruent information. If incongruent irrelevant information is present, two distinct semantic codes will be constructed. In order to proceed to the next stage of processing (which may involve phonological retrieval, transformation to an opposite, or comparison against a memory set), the *S* must discriminate the relevant code from the irrelevant one. The time required to make this discrimination is related to semantic proximity, and is analogous to the other distance effects which have been observed in semantic comparison tasks and relative judgements.

Although it seems likely that a semantic ambiguity of this kind lies at the basis of the Stroop effect, the model of the Lexical Memory developed in Part Two clearly allows for subsidiary phonological effects which are mediated by the grapheme-phoneme channel. Effects of variation in the *phonemic* relationship between non-word distractors and naming responses (see Rayner & Posnansky (1977) and Posnansky & Rayner (1977)) establish that grapheme-phoneme translation occurs and that it produces an effect on phonological retrieval (see Chapter X). Posnansky & Rayner (1977) also included an experimental condition in which an irrelevant word printed on a picture was a homophone of the picture name. A display of this kind might be expected to induce a semantic conflict while facilitating phonological retrieval. In agreement with this expectation, Posnansky & Rayner found that the homophone displays were named less rapidly than pictures containing congruent labels or phonemically congruent non-words (where there is no semantic conflict) but more rapidly than the Stroop displays (which involve semantic conflict and phonological conflict).

In conclusion, it seems that the Stroop interference effects observed in naming tasks reflect somewhat complex disruptive influences. Grapheme-phoneme translation results in the input of incongruent phonemic properties into the exit logogen system. There is at the same time a processing block in the semantic register which is attributable to the simultaneous activation of alternative codes, and the input of task-relevant semantic attributes to the exit logogens is held back while this ambiguity is resolved.

XV.4 POSITION AND DIRECTION

The second class of attribute to be considered concerns the coding of the *spatial location* of an object, defined relative to a surrounding frame or adjacent object. We assume that location, like colour, is represented in an unanalysed form at the pictorial level. However, the pictorial code cannot be used to express the essentially *relational* character of locative information. This is a property of the semantic level at which arrangements of objects may be assigned one or more of a large number of alternative spatial interpretations. For example, a pair of shapes might be represented as 'A above B' or 'B below A', or 'A near B', illustrating some of the many relational descriptions which could be applied to a single picture.

In the case of colour, the existence of a central semantic code which is accessible to pictorial and lexical inputs was suggested by the occurrence of Stroop effects of various types. The proposal that an analogous system exists for the coding of spatial location can be supported by demonstrations that spatial terms give rise to Stroop interference phenomena analogous to those obtained with colour. When *S*s respond to spatial aspects of displays their perfomance is disrupted if irrelevant words specify incongruent spatial information (Fox, Shor & Steinman, 1971; Morton, 1969b; Shor, Hatch, Hudson, Landrigan & Shaffer, 1972; Beller, 1975).

In addition to standard Stroop effects, the experiments have demonstrated the occurrence of *perceptual* effects, in which coding of one spatial aspect interferes with coding of another, and *lexical* effects, in which a word interferes with the spatial interpretation of another word. Perceptual effects have been demonstrated by Clark & Brownell (1975, 1976). *S*s were required to indicate whether an arrow was pointing up or down. The position of the arrow in a rectangular frame was varied as an irrelevant perceptual attribute. Clark & Brownell reported that the RT to indicate the direction of the arrow was affected by its position. The response to up-pointing arrows was made faster when the arrow was located high in the rectangle than when it was located low in the rectangle, and this trend was reversed for responses to down-pointing arrows. In a further study *S*s read a directional term ('up' or 'down') and then determined whether or not it was descriptive of the direction of an arrow located at any one of six positions in a rectangle. This comparison task also produced a congruity effect which was independent of the directional term being verified and the 'same' or 'different' outcome of the decision. The additivity of these effects suggests that the effect of arrow position on the coding of arrow direction may be localized within a conceptual encoding stage during which a direction code is formed and discriminated from a position code.

Seymour (1974a) described an experiment which demonstrated the occurrence of a *lexical* interference effect. *S*s saw displays on which the preposition 'above' or 'below' was located inside a square. In a control condition, a row of Xs was printed above or below the square, and, in the Stroop conditions, the word 'up' or 'down' replaced the Xs. The task for the *S* was to determine whether a set of symbols (a word or a row of Xs) appeared in the position named by the preposition, and to make a 'Yes' response if it did and a 'No' response if it did not. The reaction was delayed when the irrelevant word ('up' or 'down') conflicted in meaning with the simultaneously displayed preposition ('above' or 'below'). In this instance, therefore, an irrelevant spatial term interfered with the spatial interpretation of the word, but appeared not to affect the coding of the location it occupied.

If the *S* is required to *name* the location of a word a verbal interference effect can be obtained. For example, Seymour (1973c) presented *S*s with displays consisting of the word 'above', 'below', 'left' or 'right' printed above, below, left of or right of a small dot. Vocal RT for naming of the location of the word was affected by its meaning, being facilitated by congruity and delayed by an incongruity. The interference was most marked when the target location and distractor represented opposed values on the same spatial dimension (for example, 'above' written in the lower location), and showed some asymmetries ('above' interfered more with the naming of the lower location than did 'below' with the naming of the upper location).

It seems likely that this asymmetry within the vertical dimension is related to the directional polarization of spatial dimensions which was discussed in Chapter XIII. The argument of Clark (1974) was that the perceptual world is structured in an inherently asymmetric fashion, with the directions 'forward' and 'up' being coded as positive, and directions 'backward' and 'down' as negative. The horizontal directions 'left' and 'right' were, on the other hand, considered by Clark to be inherently symmetric. The asymmetry of the vertical dimension is reflected in linguistic usage, and underlies the distinction between marked and unmarked spatial adjectives. According to the arguments developed in Chapter XIII, asymmetric dimensions tend also to be affectively polarized, with the unmarked expression having a positive valence, and the marked expression a negative valence. Hence, we might expect to find that the coding of one object as 'higher than' or 'above' another object is in some sense positive or natural, whereas the coding of its location as 'lower than' or 'below' a reference point will be negative or unnatural.

Evidence relating to these considerations has come from studies of locative comparisons, such as those reported by Seymour (1974a) and Clark & Brownell (1975). In these experiments the unmarked expressions 'up', 'high' and 'above' are frequently found to be associated with faster RTs and lower error rates than their marked counterparts. Thus, Seymour (1969a, 1973c) reported that positive responses to 'above' displays were faster by 60–100 msecs than positive responses to 'below' displays, although there was little evidence of an effect of markedness on negative responses. Olson & Laxar (1973) contrasted the horizontal terms 'right' and 'left', and found, despite the theoretical symmetry of these terms, that 'right' was processed consistently faster than 'left'.

The markedness effect appears to be a property of the semantic level of coding of location. If *S*s are permitted to base their decisions on a pictorial coding of a display the effect does not occur. For example, Chase & Clark (1971) printed upward or downward pointing arrows in a square and instructed *S*s to indicate whether the arrow pointed to the location occupied by a dot. No 'above'–'below' difference was obtained. When Olson & Laxar (1973) conducted a similar experiment with left and right pointing arrows the advantage for the right location over the left was eliminated. We assume that a pictorial aspect of these displays (the proximity of the arrow head to the dot) provided the *S*s with sufficient information for choice of a positive or negative response. Thus, the absence of effects in these studies implies that markedness, in common with other lexical and semantic factors, does not influence processing at the pictorial level of representation.

An experiment described by Clark & Chase (1972, Experiment 4) suggests that the occurrence of a semantic comparison may also be a precondition for the observation of markedness effects. *S*s were presented with the words 'above' and 'below' beside a display consisting of a star above or below a plus sign. The task was to indicate which of the two shapes appeared in the location specified by the preposition. There was only slight evidence of an 'above'–'below' difference in this case, implying that the effect is not reducible to variations in speed of conceptual encoding of 'above' and 'below' statements (although this was the explanation favoured by Clark & Chase [1972]), but is in some way dependent on the occurrence of a semantic comparison of lexically and pictorially derived spatial codes.

Confirmation that 'above'–'below' differences are not attributable to a lexical-semantic retrieval stage of processing has been provided by Just & Carpenter (1975). Their displays consisted of three Vs, upright or inverted, beside two vertically positioned letters, one a vowel and the other a consonant. *S*s were instructed to interpret the Vs as upward or downward pointing arrows, and to respond positively if the arrow direction correctly specified the position of the vowel, and negatively if it did not. Positive RTs were about 56 msecs faster for the 'up' than for the 'down' displays. Thus, a markedness effect occurs when an abstract comparison of locations is made, even though marked and unmarked lexical items are not presented.

We can also exclude the possibility that markedness effects are localized within the stage of pictorial encoding and interpretation. The experiments by Just & Carpenter (1975) showed no advantage for encoding of information from upper locations of matrix displays. Further, Seymour (1974b) obtained RTs for matching the prepositions 'above' and 'below' against the location of a dot defined relative to a horizontally oriented face. In this case the critical spatial information was on the left or right of the display, so that contributions attributable to top-down scanning tendencies were eliminated. Nonetheless, positive responses to 'above' displays were about 66 msecs faster than positive responses to 'below' displays. In their experiments on 'right' and 'left', Olson & Laxar (1973) included conditions in which the left-right distinction was defined relative to the viewpoint of the observer and relative to the viewpoint of someone facing the observer. An advantage for 'right' over 'left' was found in both cases implying that this effect is also independent of directional scanning tendencies.

It seems likely, therefore, that the markedness effects observed in judgements of spatial location occur during a COMPARISON stage of processing. There may in addition be an influence on the 'same'–'different' judgemental process or a subsequent operation of response retrieval. An influence on response processes is suggested by the finding of interactions with the affirmative or negative nature of the response used by the *S*. A markedness effect occurs when *S*s respond 'Yes' to 'same' displays but not when they reverse their decision-report assignment, and respond 'No' (Seymour, 1971, 1973d). The effect also interacts with 'same' versus 'different' decisions, being primarily a characteristic of 'same' RTs (Seymour, 1969a; Chase & Clark, 1971). In this respect, the markedness effect is analogous to the word superiority effect observed in graphemic comparison tasks (see Chapter IX).

In discussing the word superiority effects we argued that familiarity × decision interactions might be attributed to two distinct types of influence on a judgemental stage of processing. The first related to the *quality* of the codes passed to the COMPARISON stage, the argument being that retrieval of stored graphemic information enhanced the spatial structure of codes formed as descriptions of familiar letter arrays. The second related to the possibility that familiar entities might retrieve positive or negative semantic codes which affected the judgemental phase of processing (Seymour & Jack, 1978). It seems likely that these two explanations are also relevant to the interpretation of markedness effects.

Just & Carpenter (1975) argued that presentation of a marked term in a verbal-pictorial comparison task induced the *S* to assign an atypical coding to the picture. Thus, although it may be natural to represent two vertically arranged objects by a structure of the form: 'A above B' (Clark & Chase, 1974), the task of verifying a sentence containing the marked preposition 'below' leads the *S* to adopt the structure: 'B below A' (see Clark & Chase (1972) for demonstrations that *contingent encoding* of this kind occurs in sentence-picture comparison tasks). It is possible that logical codes which incorporate a marked relational expression are structurally unstable, and that this has an adverse effect on the comparison process.

An argument of this kind can be supported by reference to experiments reported by Seymour (1974c). These studies contrasted the verification of locative sentences with the construction (by drawing) of the arrangements of shapes which they described. The sentences contained the prepositions 'inside' and 'outside' and specified a relationship between two geometric forms (a square and a circle). A standard sentence, such as 'The square is inside the circle', was verified against a square-circle picture faster than referentially synonymous non-standard sentences, such as 'Inside the circle is the square' or 'The square has the circle outside', both for simultaneous and for successive presentation of the sentence and picture. When *S*s drew the shapes described the order of construction was constrained by the preposition of the sentence in the standard case, but was variable in the non-standard cases. It was proposed that the *S* interpreted the sentence as a procedure for verification (or drawing), and that this procedural code was unstable or inherently ambiguous when non-standard sentences were encoded. If we view unmarked terms as standard, and marked terms as non-standard, an explanation of this kind can be seen to be equally applicable to the discussion of markedness effects.

The instability of marked logical codes could depend on the *logical negativity* of marked expressions (see Huttenlocher & Higgins [1971]). Evidence favouring the possibility that 'below' is coded as 'not-above' was provided by Chase & Clark (1971). *S*s were presented with the preposition 'above' or 'below' printed inside a square, and were instructed to verify whether or not the preposition correctly specified the position of a dot located above or below the square. The *S*s were told that one of the two possible positions was masked within a block of trials, but that the occurrence of a dot in that position could be inferred from its absence in the other position. Thus, when the lower location was masked, the absence of a dot above the square implied that it was present (though not visible) below the square. When the upper location was masked, absence of the dot in the lower position implied presence above the square. The first of these conditions produced data which were very similar to those obtained in the standard experiment involving masking of neither location. However, the second condition produced a substantial delay of RT for those displays on which absence of a dot in the lower location implied its presence in the upper location. Hence, it seems that *S*s can readily accept that 'not-above' means 'below', but have difficulty in interpreting 'not-below' to mean 'above'.

Logical negativity of this kind could contribute to the instability of the semantic code and produce adverse effects during the COMPARISON stage of processing. It seems likely, however, that we must also accept the involvement of affective codes which influence the process of transforming a 'same'–'different' decision to a 'Yes' or 'No' response. This conclusion is encouraged by results of experiments in which markedness has been found to facilitate a negative response. In the Stroop experiment reported by Seymour (1974a) the presence of the word 'down' on a 'different' display containing the preposition 'below' led to faster 'No' RTs than were obtained in the control condition. A facilitation effect also occurred in a study described by Seymour (1974b) in which the prepositions 'above' and 'below' were matched against the position of a dot defined relative to a normally oriented or inverted face. Negative responses to 'below' displays were made faster when the face was inverted than when it was normally oriented. It was suggested that this was because inversion of the face increased the overall negativity of the display, and that such negativity facilitated the 'No' response.

These results suggest that markedness effects, like word superiority effects and Stroop effects, are the outcome of a number of complex interactions occurring during the central stages of processing. Use of a marked code probably creates difficulties for a COMPARISON stage which are related to the logical negativity of the marked forms. At the same time, the retrieval of an affirmative response is facilitated by the affectively positive code associated with unmarked representations and inhibited by the affectively negative code associated with marked representations. The converse relationship is assumed to hold with regard to retrieval of negative responses. Positive and negative affective codes may affect the RT by triggering reciprocal adjustments in the 'same' and 'different' thresholds (Seymour, 1975), or by creating a Stroop conflict at the stage at which the display is categorized as 'same' or 'different'. It is likely that the 'same'–'different' codes are affectively polarized, and that a problem of discrimination can arise if affirmative or negative codes associated with the markedness of the display are active at the point when the 'same' or 'different' code is used to retrieve a positive or negative response.

XV.5 SIZE AND EXTENSION

A further set of attributes which have received some experimental investigation are those which concern the *sizes* of two- or three-dimensional forms. The most frequently used task has been the *relative judgement task* in which the *S* is required to indicate which of two objects has the greater (or lesser) extent on a particular attribute. We can anticipate that the size attribute will show evidence of the same distinction between pictorial and semantic levels of coding as was apparent in the cases of colour and location.

If the *S* is presented with pairs of stimuli (such as lines of differing length, or geometric forms of differing size) and is asked to indicate which is physically larger (or smaller) it is likely that the information which is diagnostic for choice of response will be available in the pictorial register. The two shapes may 'configure' to form a wedge-like gestalt whose thicker (or thinner) end specifies the key which must be pressed. When such experiments are conducted the discrimination RT is found to be related to the difference in magnitude between stimuli, that is to their discriminability within a multi-dimensional stimulus space (Henmon, 1906; Crossman, 1955; Curtis, Paulos & Rule, 1973). However, we do not expect such judgements to show effects which are characteristic of the semantic level, such as the markedness effects described in the last section, or the Stroop conflicts which have been discussed throughout this chapter.

These expectations are confirmed by the results of studies which have explicitly set out to contrast pictorial judgements with judgements based on semantic codes. For example, Moyer & Bayer (1976) conducted an experiment in which *S*s chose the larger of two circles.

The stimulus set consisted of four circles, separated by increments of 2 mm of diameter for one group and 4 mm of diameter for the other. Comparisons of physically present circles showed a distance effect and faster RTs for the 4 mm set, but no effect due to the position in the series of the circles displayed. *S*s in a second group learned to associate nonsense names with the circles. They were then presented with pairs of names under instruction to indicate which denoted the larger circle. The RT was again affected by the difference between the stimuli in the series, and *S*s who had learned the 4 mm series reacted somewhat faster than those who had learned the 2 mm series. However, these effects were both much greater in magnitude than those obtained with physically present circles, and there was also an effect of the position of the referenced circles in the series, RTs being faster for names of large circles than for names of small circles.

Moyer's experiment demonstrates that the results obtained for mental comparisons of size are qualitatively similar to those obtained for physical comparisons, but very far from being identical. The critical distinction is perhaps that the memorial comparisons give rise to a *semantic congruity effect*, whereas physical comparisons do not. As has already been mentioned, the congruity effect reflects a tendency for large values of an attribute to be discriminated faster under 'Choose larger' than under 'Choose smaller' instructions, and for small values to be discriminated faster under 'Choose smaller' than under 'Choose larger' instructions (see Audley & Wallis, 1964; Banks, Clark & Lucy, 1975; Banks, 1977). This position × instruction interaction cannot be clearly seen in Moyer & Bayer's (1976) study since they did not use a 'Choose smaller' instruction. However, in a replication of the experiment described by Banks (1977) both instructions were used, and a congruity effect was obtained for the memorial comparisons but not for the physical comparisons.

Effects which appear to be semantic in nature also occur when *S*s compare objects with respect to a particular spatial dimension. If the *S* must decide which object is the taller, or which is the wider, he must isolate the relevant attribute from others which are inherent in the gestalt-like pictorial code. According to the viewpoint developed in Chapter XIV this is an abstractive process by which a selected aspect of the appearance of an object is assigned a semantic coding. Clark, Carpenter & Just (1973) have described a number of experiments, all using relative judgement tasks, which explore the possibility that retrieval of such codes is affected by the 'conditions of application' of spatial descriptions and the distinction between lexically marked and unmarked poles of spatial dimensions (see Chapter XIII). It was found that judgements of size were made faster for squares than for rectangles, but that judgements of height and width were made faster for rectangles than for squares. No markedness effect was obtained for the size judgements, but judgements of vertical and horizontal extent were faster when the question was unmarked ('Which is taller/wider?') than when it was marked ('Which is shorter/narrower?').

Further experiments by Clark, Carpenter & Just (1973) were designed to clarify the conditions of application of adjectives of height ('tall' and 'short') and adjectives of depth ('deep' and 'shallow'). A description of height may appropriately be applied to an object which is vertically elongated relative to a fixed base or origin. Depth, on the other hand, is appropriately predicated of objects having a surface from which distance into an interior can be measured. Clark confirmed that vertical rectangles were compared with respect to height faster than they were compared with respect to depth. If the base of the rectangles was placed at the top of the picture rather than at the bottom the judgements of height were delayed. When pictures of containers were used as stimuli, height judgements were faster than depth judgements for side views, but this relationship reversed when the containers were tilted so as to show their interiors. Markedness effects occurred in some of these experiments, but appeared not to be a consistent propery of judgements of this kind.

There seems to be considerable scope for future extensions of this line of research. It was noted in Chapter XIII that the conditions determining the application of adjectives to members of particular object classes are extremely subtle and complex. These conditions could be examined empirically in experiments employing pictures of objects in place of the schematic forms used by Clark, Carpenter & Just. As a preliminary step in this direction, Banks, Clark & Lucy (1975) obtained relative judgements of height for pairs of small circles attached to downward-going or upward-going lines. *S*s were instructed to interpret the circles at the tops of their lines as balloons on strings and the circles at the bottom of their lines as yo-yos hanging from strings. *S*s selected the higher of the two balloons faster than the lower, whereas with yo-yos, they selected the lower one faster than the higher one. This is a form of semantic congruity effect, and implies that the balloons were implicitly coded with respect to height whereas the yo-yos were implicitly coded with respect to lowness. Further studies are required to determine whether these interactions depended on the displays used or whether the instruction to view them as balloons or yo-yos contributed significantly to the effect.

Paivio (1975b) argued that judgements of the relative sizes of real objects, whether verbally or pictorially designated, were based on the processing of image-like representations, that is on pictorial codes. He commented that *S*s reported using imagery while carrying out the task, and has since shown that high imagery ability correlates with fast and accurate performance in relative judgement experiments (Paivio, 1977). Nonetheless, the arguments already presented make it highly unlikely that the larger-smaller judgement derives directly from a consideration of pictorial codes. If the *S* is to compare the real-world sizes of two pictured objects, say a cathedral and an aeroplane, he cannot normally rely on physical properties of the display to determine his choice. Information about size must somehow be retrieved from memory and set up for processing by a comparison routine. We assume that the coding of size is abstracted from among other possible attributes of these objects, and that it takes the form of a logical structure in which the objects are coded as (large) or (small) relative to a norm (see Banks, [1977]). It is, of course, in principle possible that *S*s could generate image-like pictorial representations from a semantic structure of this kind, and that the relative judgement could then be based on a pictorial code (see Chapter XIV). However, when Holyoak (1977) explicitly instructed *S*s to use an image comparison strategy in making size judgements he found that this led to a substantial increase in RT, implying that pictorial codes are not the normal representational mode in memorial comparisons of size.

In the present discussion the occurrence or non-occurrence of a semantic congruity effect has been viewed as the principal indicator of the level of coding employed in a relative judgement task. If there is an interaction between object size and the 'Choose larger' versus 'Choose smaller' instructions this implies that the objects have been assigned an abstract size code which may be congruent or incongruent with an instructional code. Hence, the finding, reported by Banks & Flora (1977), that memorial comparisons of sizes of named and pictured objects produce large semantic congruity effects, may be taken as evidence against Paivio's image processing theory and in favour of the semantic coding hypothesis.

Paivio (1975b) contrasted pictures and words as stimuli in the relative judgement task. He found that responses to pairs of pictures were 180–190 msecs faster than responses to pairs of words. This *pictorial superiority effect* suggested to him that size judgements were made in a system which was more directly accessible to pictures of objects than to printed names of objects. Banks & Flora (1977) conducted a similar experiment, and obtained a picture-word difference of 221 msecs. They noted that the effect combined additively with effects due to the size separation of the objects (the distance effect) and with the interaction of object size and 'Choose larger' versus 'Choose smaller' instructions (the semantic congruity effect). This additivity implies that the code utilized in the comparative judgement is accessed faster by a picture than by a word (a difference in 'conceptual encoding' time), but that thereafter the judgemental processes are equivalent for the two types of stimuli (see Banks, (1977).

These findings could be reconciled with a 'dual memory' theory of the kind proposed by Paivio (1975b, 1976, 1977) by arguing that there are certain *perceptual* attributes ('size' being one example) which are represented in the semantic superstructure of the Pictorial Memory, but that there are other attributes of a more *conceptual* nature which are represented in the semantic superstructure of the Lexical Memory. A prediction from this 'dual-memory' theory is that picture-word differences will diminish or reverse as the attribute being judged by the *S* is shifted along a perceptual-conceptual continuum. As a test of this prediction, Banks & Flora (1977) obtained RTs for judgements of the relative *intelligence* of a series of named or pictured animals. They considered that intelligence was a conceptual rather than perceptual attribute. However, contrary to the predictions of the dual-memory theory, they obtained a pictorial superiority effect of 289 msecs, and this combined additively with a distance effect and a semantic congruity effect. Paivio (1977) extended this design to judgements of the pleasantness and monetary value of objects, and also found that these non-perceptual attributes produced a distance effect and a pictorial superiority effect. Friedman & Bourne (1976) may be consulted for additional evidence that picture-word differences are independent of the attribute being processed.

Although these issues merit further study, the available data encourage the conclusion that attributes of objects are coded in a central semantic system which is accessible from the interface structures of the Lexical and Pictorial Memories. Indeed, as has already been argued, the Stroop interference effects noted in the experiments on colour and spatial location imply the existence of just such a central representational system. There has not been much effort to demonstrate the occurrence of Stroop effects in the domain of size. However, Paivio (1975b) presented *S*s with pairs of pictures whose relative sizes were congruent with their actual sizes (a zebra drawn larger than a lamp) or which conflicted with the actual size relation (a lamp drawn larger than a zebra). The incongruent condition produced a delay in the relative judgement RT. This effect was specific to picture stimuli, and did not occur when the sizes of word stimuli were varied (Paivio, 1975b). We might view this as a perceptual Stroop effect analogous to the one demonstrated by Clark & Brownell (1975, 1976) in their studies of effects of position on judgements of direction.

Banks (1977) has argued that the data obtained in the relative judgement experiments can be interpreted within the framework of a three-stage processing model of the kind developed to handle judgements of the relative magnitudes of digits (Banks, Fujii & Kayra-Stuart, 1976). The model distinguishes stages of (1) conceptual encoding, (2) comparison, and (3) response retrieval and expression. The encoding stage involves the operations of pictorial (or graphemic) encoding followed by a semantic retrieval stage which represents the stimuli in terms of the values they take on a size attribute. Banks proposes that this stage is the locus of the pictorial superiority effects. The stage is also at least partly responsible for Stroop interference effects (see Seymour, 1977), and is probably the main locus of Paivio's (1975b) size congruity effect. In the comparison stage the *S* discriminates the size codes formed for the two stimuli and relates the outcome of the discrimination to the instruction he has been given. The discrimination process is assumed to give rise to the symbolic distance effect, while the semantic congruity effect occurs when the decision about the stimuli is related to the instruction.

General support for this processing stage model has been provided by demonstrations of the additivity of the picture-word difference and the symbolic distance and semantic congruity effects (Banks & Flora, 1977). Banks (1977) has also reported that size congruity effects combine additively with distance effects, but interact with the semantic congruity effects. A pattern of this type might be obtained if the irrelevant size relations present in the picture delayed onset of the discrimination stage, and also left information in the semantic register which affected the matching of the stimulus codes against the instruction.

The critical theoretical question posed by these experiments concerns the nature of the representation of size which is operated on during the comparison stage. The contrast here is between the proposal that the code is some kind of analogue of continuous variation in size, and the proposal that the codes are more akin to discrete linguistic entities expressing concepts like (large), (small), (average). Support for the analogue theory might be obtained if it could be shown that symbolic distance effects reflected real size differences between stimuli. Moyer & Bayer (1976) provided some relevant evidence, since they found that RT was affected by the diameter difference between referenced circles in both the perceptual and memorial conditions of their experiment. However, Banks (1977) reports that he has twice attempted without success to replicate this effect. Further experiments, using series of animal names arranged at differing degrees of size separation, failed to support the conclusion that real size determines the observed RT effects. It appeared rather that *S*s constructed a list representation for use in the experiment (perhaps analogous to the month and weekday structures in permanent memory), and that ordinal and positional relations within this structure gave rise to the effects.

The linguistic theory, which has been favoured by Banks (1977), states that memorial representations of size consist of only a small number of discrete categories, and that the initial coding of a stimulus may be extremely general, defining it simply as (large) or (small). If the stimuli are very remote from one another in size, as in the example MOUSE CATHEDRAL, the codes (small) and (large) will be sufficient for the discrimination. However, other pairs, such as MOUSE ANT and CATHEDRAL AEROPLANE, may be coded as both (small) or both (large), and it is then that the additional processing which underlies the symbolic distance effect becomes essential. The extra processing might be viewed as a search of memory for additional information which can help to discriminate the sizes of the stimuli. As this information becomes available a point is approached at which the stimuli can successfully be located either side of the neutral region of a size dimension.

In order to accommodate the semantic congruity effect it is probably necessary to assume that the initial global coding of the stimuli determines the sub-dimension in terms of which they are discriminated. If the coding for both stimuli is (large) the additional processing serves to determine which member of the pair is greater in size than the other. When the instructions are 'Choose larger' the location of this item on the display can be passed directly to the response stage. With 'Choose smaller' instructions, on the other hand, it is the other location which must control the response, and this involves some time-consuming rearrangement prior to the response stage. For pairs classified as (small) we assume that the discriminative process serves to identify the item which is the more extreme on a sub-dimension of smallness. The outcome of this discrimination matches the instruction 'Choose smaller' but not the instruction 'Choose larger'.

XV.6 CONCLUSIONS

This chapter has explored the distinction between pictorial and semantic levels of coding of attributes of objects. We have concentrated on experiments relating to a perceptual quality (colour), and to two relational attributes (spatial location, and size). In each case it has been possible to show that the semantic level of coding is characterized by certain experimental effects which do not occur when circumstances allow the *S* to base his decision on diagnostic properties of the pictorial code.

The effects which appear to be distinctively semantic in nature are those relating to the typicality of colours, the markedness and conditions of application of spatial terms, and the congruity of object size and instructions in relative judgement tasks. It has been proposed that the semantic codes are maintained in a central system (the semantic and structural registers of Figures VIII.5.1 and XIII.2.1) in which attributes of objects may be labelled and assigned values. This central code is accessible to linguistic and pictorial stimuli, and defines a locus at which Stroop interference effects can occur, sentences and pictures can be judged to match or mismatch, and relative values of stimuli on a given attribute can be determined.

While the experiments provide good evidence for the existence of a central system for representation of attributes, they are much less clear on the fundamental question of the nature of the attribute codes. Much of the difficulty arises from the problem of distinguishing between a representation which codes continuous variation on an attribute and one which is formulated in terms of a few ordered categories. A tentative resolution of this uncertainty is the proposal that coding of continuous variation is characteristic of the pictorial level of representation, but that the semantic code is normally formulated in terms of discrete categories or relationships, many of which possess direct linguistic counterparts.

An important characteristic of the semantic code is its susceptibility to Stroop interference effects. It has been shown that these effects are not restricted to the verbal interference originally demonstrated by

Stroop (1935), but that they occur whenever conflicting attribute values are simultaneously specified. Thus, the coding of a spatial or perceptual attribute is affected by concurrent processing of words or other perceptual aspects, and interpretation of a lexical input can be affected by processing of irrelevant perceptual aspects, or by irrelevant words. The semantic aspect of these effects can be explained by assuming that completion of a conceptual encoding stage is delayed while the relevant attribute code is discriminated from the irrelevant code (Seymour, 1977). This seems to be a general property of semantic processing which can also give an account of the relationship between affectively polarized codes (such as those representing variations of familiarity or markedness) and the 'same'–'different' judgemental process (Seymour & Jack, 1978).

CHAPTER XVI

Object Classes

CODING AND CATEGORIZATION OF OBJECTS

XVI.1 INTRODUCTION

The last chapter developed the view that attributes of objects may be coded in a central semantic system which is accessible to the objects themselves and also to the names of qualities and relationships (colour adjectives, size adjectives and locative prepositions). In this chapter this general viewpoint will be extended to a consideration of *object concepts*. We assume that objects, like attributes, may be represented in an unanalysed and uninterpreted form in the pictorial register, but that they may also be assigned an interpretative code at the level of the semantic register. This semantic code is viewed as a *configuration of attributes*, that is as a logical structure in which the salient attributes of the members of an object class are identified, interrelated, and assigned values.

The assumption that objects may be coded in the pictorial register can be validated by experimental demonstrations that visual descriptions of objects can be retained in temporary storage and retrieved from permanent memory. Such demonstrations depend on the extension of the methodology of Posner, Boies, Eichelman & Taylor (1969) to the study of pictorial codes, and some relevant experiments will be given brief consideration in this chapter. An additional question is posed by the three-dimensional character of solid objects. Although the drawings or photographs which are typically used as stimuli in experiments on pictorial information processing are objectively two-dimensional, they are taken to represent three-dimensional structures, and are frequently perceived as possessing extension in depth. It will be argued that the three-dimensional interpretation of an object is an achievement of the pictorial level of representation, and that the object representations held in the pictorial data store are three-dimensional in character.

The semantic coding of an object permits the segregation and examination of its component attributes, and also its assignment to a class or category. The view which will be argued in this chapter is that *categorization* is a matter of isolation of a subset of attributes which is relevant to the object's classification at a particular level of abstraction. The research by Rosch and her associates which was discussed in Chapter XIII suggested the existence of three principal levels of classification, referred to as the *basic* level, the *superordinate* level, and the *subordinate* level (see Rosch, Mervis, Gray, Johnson & Boyes-Braem, 1976). The basic level of categorization is one at which sets of objects which share perceptual and other attributes may be grouped together and readily differentiated from other perceptually homogeneous classes. Categorization at this level is supposed to be natural and direct, and may therefore correspond closely to the attribute configuration which is established when the pictorial representation of an object is assigned a semantic description. The superordinate and subordinate levels, being more general or more specific, require isolation of special subsets of attributes which are related to superordinate class membership or which differentiate between members of a basic object class. It follows from these comments that decisions about basic object class membership should generally be taken faster than decisions about superordinate or subordinate class membership, and experiments relating to this prediction will be discussed later in this chapter.

There remains the question, raised towards the end of the last chapter, of the distinction between dual and unitary models of the semantic structures of the Lexical and Pictorial Memories. The evidence already cited favours the view that object concepts are coded in a central system which is more rapidly accessed by pictures than by words. This leads to the expectation that decisions about category membership will also be taken faster for pictures of objects than for their names, but that semantic effects, such as those due to the typicality of class instances or the relatedness of negative instances, will be independent of the modality of the test stimulus. Experimental studies relating to this prediction will be considered at the end of the chapter.

XVI.2 PICTORIAL CODING OF OBJECTS

The existence of a level for pictorial representation of solid objects can be verified by demonstrations that physical identity comparisons of pictures of objects are not influenced by factors which are known to be important at the semantic or phonological levels of coding.

Relevant factors include the *typicality* of objects as instances of superordinate classes, which affects the speed of class membership decisions (Rosch, 1975a), and the *frequency of occurrence* of the basic level name of an object, which affects speed of object naming (Oldfield, 1966).

Rosch (1975a, Experiment 5) obtained RTs for physical identity comparisons of pairs of simultaneously displayed pictures of objects. The typicality of the objects as instances of their superordinate classes was varied, but produced no observable effect on the 'same' or 'different' RT. Rosch also employed a priming procedure analogous to the one followed in the studies of comparisons of colour which were described in the last chapter (Rosch, 1975b). On alternate trials the superordinate name of the objects was spoken 2 secs before the display was presented. No effect of priming was obtained. We may note that this result contrasts with Rosch's findings for colours, which indicated that priming by a colour name facilitated physical identity comparisons of focal hues (Rosch, 1975b). The implication is that superordinate names retrieve attributes which are too few in number or too abstract in character to exert much influence on the pictorial level of coding.

A basic level name, on the other hand, is thought to correlate with a configuration of essentially perceptual attributes which should be readily transformable into a pictorial representation. The presence of such a representation in the pictorial register might well exert a facilitating effect on a physical identity comparison of structurally congruent pictures. Confirmation of this prediction has been given by Rosch, Mervis, Gray, Johnson & Boyes-Braem (1976, Experiment 6). Presentation of a basic or subordinate name 2 secs before display of pairs of same or different pictures led to a 50 msec reduction in 'same' RT. Priming by superordinate names had no such effect.

Absence of an effect of name frequency on picture comparisons was demonstrated by Wingfield (1968). The pictures were successively displayed at an inter-stimulus interval (ISI) of 5 secs. The RT to indicate whether the second picture was same as the first was unrelated to the Thorndike–Lorge frequency of the basic level name of either picture, although this variable had been shown to produce very substantial effects in the object naming experiment reported by Oldfield & Wingfield (1965). The same result was obtained when the test picture was matched against an object name, implying that the name retrieved a pictorial representation from storage.

A similar experiment was conducted by Bartram (1976), using somewhat shorter ISIs (250 msecs and 2,000 msecs). The stimuli were photographs of objects having names of high or low frequency of occurrence. *S*s were instructed to respond 'same' to pictures which had the same name and 'different' to pictures taken from different basic level classes. The 'same' trials included pairs of physically identical pictures, photographs of the same object taken from different viewpoints, and photographs of different objects drawn from the same basic level class. Picture matching was unaffected by name frequency except in the case of matching of differing viewpoints of the same object. For objects having high frequency names these comparisons were made as fast as physical identity comparisons, whereas, for objects having low frequency names, the different viewpoints were matched no faster than pairs of different objects belonging to the same class.

A general demonstration that *S*s are able to retain and generate pictorial representations of objects has been given by Scheerer-Neumann (1974). The experiment was a direct adaptation of the procedures used by Posner, Boies, Eichelman & Taylor (1969), and examined physical identity comparisons (word to word, and picture to picture) and semantic comparisons (word to picture, and picture to word) at ISIs falling in the range 50–2,000 msecs using 'pure list' and 'mixed list' experimental designs. Under 'pure list' arrangements, where ISI and modality of the memory and test stimulus were held constant in each block of trials, the RT for physical identity comparisons remained approximately constant as ISI varied, and RTs for semantic comparisons decreased as a function of ISI, being no slower than the physical identity comparisons at intervals greater than 500 msecs. These results are suggestive of the retention and generation of pictorial and graphemic codes. An experiment by Tversky (1969), involving the comparison of schematic faces and learned nonsense names, also indicated that *S*s have an option to retain or generate pictorial and graphemic codes.

The experiments reported by Bartram (1976) are relevant to questions concerning the level at which the three-dimensional (3D) structure of an object is represented. If different viewpoints of a single object are alternative instantiations of a 3D pictorial code we might expect them to be matched more rapidly than pictures of different objects from the same class, since the latter possess distinct 3D structures. In Bartram's study of matching of photographs this prediction was supported for objects having names of high frequency, but not for objects having names of low frequency. It seems possible, however, that this interaction occurred because the low frequency objects used were pictorially and semantically confusable, being for the most part tools and instruments of various kinds. Klatzky & Stoy (1974) presented pairs of drawings for matching at ISIs of 100–4,000 msecs, and found that physical identity comparisons were made faster than name identity comparisons over this range of intervals, and that comparisons of mirror-image pictures were no slower than comparisons of identical pictures. On the other hand, Bartram (1976) conducted a study in which line drawings of objects were displayed at an ISI of 500 msecs, and reported that different viewpoints of the same objects were matched more rapidly than different objects from the same class, but less rapidly than identical pictures. Similarity or difference of viewpoint had no effect on 'same' or 'different' judgements about different objects.

These experiments support the conclusion that objects may be represented by a pictorial code which is unaffected by variations in name frequency or strength of superordinate class membership. It seems likely that this code represents the three-dimensional structure of individual objects, and that it is accessible to at least some of the alternative views which are formed as an object is rotated in space.

XVI.3 OBJECT NAMING

The semantic level of coding of object concepts can be studied in the context of an *object naming* task. Object naming is a complex function which involves the transformation of an input to the Pictorial Memory to an output from the Lexical Memory. It may be assumed to depend upon a series of processing stages, involving (1) pictorial ENCODING of the presented object; (2) the RETRIEVAL of a semantic code in which attributes of the object are specified; (3) the RETRIEVAL of a phonological representation of an object name (selected at a level of abstraction appropriate to the task); and (4) the EXPRESSION of the name as audible speech. The function is impaired when the system for semantic coding of objects is defective (termed *agnosia for objects*) and when the system for phonological retrieval is defective (termed *nominal aphasia*) (Oldfield, 1966; Warrington, 1975).

We have already noted that object naming, like colour naming, is vulnerable to Stroop interference effects (Rayner & Posnansky, 1977). These effects are presumably located in the two major stages of object naming, that is in the semantic coding stage and in the phonological retrieval stage. Variables of a lexical nature which probably have their main impact on the phonological stage were briefly considered in Chapter X. These include the frequency of occurrence of the object name (Oldfield & Wingfield, 1965; Oldfield, 1966), the age at which that name was first acquired (Carroll & White, 1973), and the size of the set of alternative names which may be associated with an object (Lachman, 1973; Lachman, Shaffer & Hennrikus, 1974; Lachman & Mistler-Lachman, 1976).

Oldfield (1966) interpreted the effect of name frequency on object naming RT in terms of an activity of lexical search. This view has been rejected as contrary to the assumption that phonological retrieval is achieved via a content-addressable logogen system. Threshold variations related to frequency of usage might be expected to produce some frequency effects at the phonological retrieval stage of naming. However, it is also likely that name frequency and age of name acquisition are correlated with the object's familiarity as a visible and manipulable entity, and that familiarity of this kind affects the semantic stages of naming. Such a conclusion is supported by the results of a study described by Bartram (1973). A frequency effect obtained in the naming of objects disappeared when the same names were used to label arbitrarily associated nonsense shapes. Bartram considered that this result was contrary to the view that frequency effects were localized in a phonological retrieval stage, and that it favoured the view that frequency influenced a prior semantic coding stage.

A technique for the investigation of the stages of processing which precede phonological retrieval was suggested by Bartram (1974). He capitalized on the observation, made by Oldfield & Wingfield (1965), that object naming RT declines as a function of practice with a particular set of stimuli. The experiments were constructed as a series of trial blocks, each involving presentation of 16 photographs of objects for naming. Some of the objects were novel stimuli whose names had not occurred in previous blocks (non-repetitions). Others showed objects whose names had occurred in previous blocks, and these included pictures of a new object from classes already used (name repetitions), different viewpoints of objects already presented (object repetition with variation of viewpoint), and repeats of pictures already shown (identical repetitions). All three types of repetition produced substantial practice effects which were quite absent in the naming of novel objects. However, the identical repetitions were associated with faster RTs than the name repetitions or object repetitions with variation of viewpoint.

The occurrence of these repetition effects enabled Bartram to examine the impact of practice in naming a particular instance of an object class on the naming of an alternative view of that same object or a new object from the same class. *S*s went through a series of 6 blocks of trials and were presented with the same pictures for naming in each block (identical repetition condition). In the seventh and eighth trial blocks they encountered either the objects they had already seen photographed from a different viewpoint or new objects from the same basic level classes. Presentation of a new object resulted in a dramatic increase in naming RT to approximately the level observed for non-repeated objects at the same stage of practice. These RTs were considerably greater than those obtained following practice with different objects from the same class, and further practice did not eliminate this disadvantage. This indicates that practice with a particular picture impaired performance on the naming of new exemplars from the same class. Quite different results were obtained for *S*s who transferred from identical repetitions to the naming of new views of the same objects. Only a small increase in the naming RT occurred, and the reactions quickly stabilized at a level equivalent to that observed for practised performance with variation of viewpoint.

It is difficult to specify the mechanism underlying the repetition and transfer effects reported by Bartram (1974). However, the experiments indicate that pictorial and semantic coding stages contribute in a major way to the object naming RT and that these stages are modifiable by practice in dealing with particular objects or particular object classes. The first of these repetition effects could reflect a contribution from the pictorial data store to the coding of repeated objects. If repetition of an object, with or without variation of viewpoint, resulted in the construction of a 3D pictorial model, and this was retrieved during formation of the pictorial code (see Chapter IX for a similar proposal for the graphemic encoding of words and familiar abbreviations), the effect could be to facilitate retrieval of a semantic code which could then be used for efficient addressing of the common name of the object. Since large repetition effects occur when *S*s practice with different objects from the same class we cannot assume that a pictorial contribution of this kind is the major determinant of the repetition effect. Possibly a similar modification occurs in the semantic data store as a consequence of repetition of objects from a particular basic level class, and these codes also facilitate categorization of an object and retrieval of its name. The deleterious effect of practice with a specific object on the naming of another object from the same class could occur because the *S* tests for a match with a stored pictorial code and classifies the object as new when he fails to find one. The absence of such an effect when transfer is made to a novel viewpoint of a familiar object can be taken as confirmation of the proposal that stored pictorial codes represent the three-dimensional structure of objects.

Rosch, Mervis, Gray, Johnson & Boyes-Braem (1976) argued that there is a naturally determined level of abstraction which is fundamental in human categorization, referred to as the *basic object* level. We assume that this level is realized as a semantic coding of predominantly perceptual attributes of an object, and that this code maps onto a single name or small set of names when its components occur as input to the exit logogen system. It follows that the naming of objects at the basic level utilizes the most direct available link between pictorial and phonological codes. Naming at other levels of abstraction (the subordinate and superordinate levels) probably depends on a modification of this semantic stage of naming. While the exact nature of this modification remains obscure, it is possible that superordinate naming involves a rearrangement of the semantic description of the object which has the effect of increasing the salience of those attributes which are linked to a superordinate class name. Subordinate naming, on the other hand, might involve a selective focus on the perceptual attributes which are useful for discrimination within a basic level class (see Seymour (1973a) for a discussion of these possibilities). The assumption that editing of the object description is necessary for superordinate and subordinate naming but not for basic level naming leads to the prediction that evocation of superordinate and subordinate names should always be less rapid than evocation of basic level names.

Various experiments may be cited as support for this prediction. Wingfield (1967) presented pictures of objects having names of varying frequency of occurrence for classification into the superordinate classes of 'furniture', 'clothing', 'musical instrument' and 'medical instrument'. The superordinate naming RTs were contrasted with basic level naming RTs obtained for the same pictures by Oldfield & Wingfield (1965). For objects having basic names of high or moderate frequency superordinate naming RT was greater than basic level RT and unrelated to basic name frequency. However, this trend reversed for medical and musical instruments having names of low frequency of occurrence, such as 'xylophone', 'stethoscope' and 'syringe', which were named faster by their superordinates than by the specific labels. We cannot make very much of this result, since

Wingfield used a small sample of objects and also confounded basic name frequency and superordinate categories. Nonetheless, it seems possible that the basic level of categorization is pitched somewhat higher for manmade objects of low familiarity than for more frequently encountered objects. Thus, terms like 'stethoscope' and 'syringe' probably form part of a specialized vocabulary of subordinate names used to differentiate the basic level class of 'instruments'.

Other studies have consistently indicated that superordinate naming RT is greater than basic level RT by 200 msecs or so. Segui & Fraisse (1968) used items from the superordinate classes of 'furniture', 'clothing', 'vegetables', 'weapons' and 'musical instruments', and reported that superordinate naming RT averaged 872 msecs as against 710 msecs for basic level naming. Seymour (1973a), citing data obtained by Hutcheon (1970), contrasted basic level and superordinate naming RTs for 'table', 'bed', 'glove' and 'hat', and found a difference of 238 msecs (620 msecs versus 858 msecs). Gellatly & Gregg (1975) used a wider range of objects from the classes of 'animals', 'fruit', 'furniture', 'clothing', 'musical instruments' and 'tools', and obtained a basic level naming RT of 755 msecs and a superordinate naming RT of 947 msecs, a difference of 192 msecs. The exact size of the difference obtained in a particular study will depend on the frequency of occurrence of the basic level names of the objects sampled, the sizes of the sets of superordinate and basic names which are used, and the typicality relationship existing between an object and its superordinate. For example, the studies by Wingfield (1967) and Seymour (1973a) indicate that the basic-superordinate difference is substantially greater when 'bed' is named as 'furniture' than when 'chair' or 'table' are named as 'furniture'.

The studies mentioned also provide evidence that subordinate names are evoked less rapidly than basic level names, although the basic-subordinate difference tends to be rather smaller than the basic-superordinate difference. Segui & Fraisse (1968) obtained naming RTs for instances of the basic level biological classes 'bird', 'fish', 'flower', 'tree' and 'dog' and contrasted these with subordinate naming RTs for specific names, such as 'sparrow', 'iris' and 'bulldog'. The basic level naming RT averaged 681 msecs as against 836 msecs for subordinate naming. In Seymour's (1973a) study basic level naming of 'flower' and 'dog' produced an RT of 684 msecs whereas the RT for subordinate naming of objects from these classes was 764 msecs. This basic-subordinate difference of 80 msecs appeared much smaller than the basic-superordinate difference of more than

200 msecs. However, the contrast is confounded with the types of categories which have been sampled, since biological categories contribute to the basic-subordinate distinction while non-biological categories contribute to the basic-superordinate distinction. There are also the relevant factors of name frequency of occurrence, size of response set, and prototypicality of object concepts and their pictorial instantiations, which have not as yet been satisfactorily controlled in naming experiments of this type. Nonetheless, we can reasonably conclude that the basic-subordinate and basic-superordinate RT differences which are predicted by the semantic editing hypothesis have been demonstrated.

XVI.4 CATEGORIZATION OF OBJECTS

Certain of the problems associated with the naming task can be avoided by using a *categorization task* in which the *S* classifies probe pictures as members or non-members of previous specified classes. In an experiment of this kind Gellatly & Gregg (1975) tested for a basic-superordinate RT difference. They found that 'Yes' responses were made less rapidly when a picture was matched against a superordinate name than when it was matched against a basic level name. However, the effect was rather small, amounting to 22 msecs for one group of *S*s and 63 msecs for another (the groups were differentiated in terms of the 'relatedness' of negative instances to the target category). Seymour (1973a) examined RTs to match simultaneously displayed basic, subordinate or superordinate names and pictures. Basic names were matched faster than subordinate or superordinate names, but the effects were no more than about 40 msecs in each case. In a similar study, Hock, Gordon & Corcoran (1976) displayed basic level or subordinate names together with pictures of objects which were normally oriented or inverted. There was a small effect due to name level which combined additively with an effect for orientation of the picture. The paper by Rosch, Mervis, Gray, Johnson & Boyes-Braem (1976) included a report of an experiment in which pictures were matched against spoken basic level, subordinate or superordinate names. There was a basic-superordinate difference of 52 msecs, and a basic-subordinate difference of 124 msecs for positive RT. The effects for negative RT were 52 msecs and 64 msecs. Gellatly & Gregg also obtained a name levels effect on negative RT.

It seems evident from these studies that there are reliable basic-superordinate and basic-subordinate RT differences in categorization and word-picture comparison experiments. However, the effects are smaller than those observed in the naming experiments, especially in the case of the basic-superordinate difference. Since the effects combine additively with a perceptual manipulation (inversion of the picture) and a judgemental factor ('Yes' versus 'No' decision and response) it is likely that they are located at a semantic retrieval stage of processing which follows pictorial encoding and precedes semantic comparison. To make the comparison the *S* must isolate a subset of attributes which are appropriate to the level of the target category, and must then compare these with attributes derived from the name. Thus, if the target category is 'furniture', and a picture of a chair is presented, we assume that superordinate attributes must be selectively retrieved before the comparison stage can be entered upon. It appears that this selective operation occupies an interval which is small by contrast with the time required to select a set of attributes and to use them to evoke the name 'furniture' (Seymour, 1973a).

A categorization experiment has recently been reported by Smith, Balzano & Walker (1977) in which the factors of name level and instance typicality were varied. Typicality, as assessed in Rosch's (1975a) study, is a measure of the relationship between a basic class and its superordinate. For this reason we would expect typicality to be more important when pictures are matched against superordinate names than when they are matched against basic level names, although variations in the typicality of the pictures might well be important at the basic level. This expectation was supported by Smith's results, which indicated that typicality effects were substantially greater for superordinate than for basic names. It seems likely, therefore, that the selective semantic retrieval operation which precedes superordinate categorization is facilitated by typicality.

In the discussion of lexical categorization tasks (see Chapters XI and XII) it was established that semantic relatedness has a facilitatory effect on positive decisions and an inhibitory effect on negative decisions. Effects of semantic relatedness are also observed in picture categorization experiments. For example, Seymour (1973a) reported that unrelated name-picture combinations, such as 'furniture'–'tulip', were classified as 'different' faster than combinations which shared a superordinate ('glove'–'hat') or which shared a basic level name ('spaniel'–'greyhound'). Relatedness effects were also obtained by Gellatly & Gregg (1975) and by Smith, Balzano & Walker (1977). In these experiments the negative RT increased when the name and picture shared a higher order property, such as 'living' or 'non-living', and the effect was consistently greater for superordinate categorization than for basic level categorization. Thus, the effects of typicality and relatedness which were earlier shown to be characteristic of semantic comparisons of categorial attributes of words can be seen to be equally important when pictures are classified at a superordinate level.

XVI.5 PICTORIAL SUPERIORITY EFFECTS

In the last chapter we noted that relative judgements of size and other attributes were made faster when object concepts were designated by pictures than when they were designated by names (Paivio, 1975b; Banks & Flora, 1977). This *pictorial superiority effect* was taken to imply that the central system in which attributes of objects are coded can be accessed more rapidly from the pictorial interface than from the lexical interface. In the present chapter it has been assumed that the categorization of an object depends on the formation of a semantic code in which values on certain salient attributes are specified. It follows that we expect to observe comparable pictorial superiority effects when words and pictures are contrasted in categorization tasks.

Potter & Faulconer (1975) obtained 'Yes' and 'No' RTs for superordinate categorization of pictures of objects and names of objects. They reported the occurrence of a 50 msec pictorial superiority effect for both positive and negative responses. In a similar study, involving categorization of pictures and words as animate or inanimate, Pellegrino, Rosinski, Chiesi & Siegel (1977) reported a 70 msec effect.

The size of the pictorial superiority effect increases substantially when pairs of pictures or pairs of names are presented for classification. Pellegrino, Rosinski, Chiesi & Siegel (1977) reported that the RT for superordinate classification of pairs of pictures was 715 msecs, whereas the RT for pairs of words averaged 900 msecs. The superiority effect of 185 msecs is similar in magnitude to the one obtained by Paivio (1975b) for relative judgements of size. Pellegrino also included mixed modality pairs consisting of an object name and a picture. The RTs were 810 msecs when the picture was on the left and 851 msecs when the picture was on the right. It was argued that this result was not consistent with a dual-memory model which assumes distinct semantic systems for the Lexical and Pictorial Memories. In a dual system classification of mixed modality pairs will involve an additional operation of transfer of information from one memory system to the other. This leads to the prediction that the mean RT for mixed modality displays should be greater than the mean RT for same modality displays. However, the relevant comparisons all yielded non-significant results.

Large pictorial superiority effects were obtained by Rosch (1975a) in an extended series of experiments on superordinate classification. *S*s were presented with pairs of pictures or pairs of names and were required to respond positively if both belonged to the same superordinate class and negatively if they belonged to different classes. Picture-word differences were not explicitly analysed, but it seems evident from the data that decisions about pictures were taken consistently faster than decisions about words, and that the differences ranged from about 100 msecs to 300 msecs in the various experiments.

Rosch also conducted a study involving physical identity matching of pictures or words. These comparisons were probably based on pictorial and graphemic codes, but nonetheless gave evidence of a pictorial superiority effect of 100 msecs or so. This suggests that the effect is mediated, at least in part, by differences in speed of visual information processing in the pictorial and lexical channels. Further studies might usefully be carried out to determine the extent of this contribution more precisely.

According to the unitary memory theory the attribute descriptions accessed by pictures of objects and names of objects are held in a common storage system (the semantic data stores of Figures VIII.5.1 and XIII.2.1), and are placed, following retrieval, in a central system for registration of meaning, called the semantic register. If the attribute configurations retrieved by words and pictures are strictly equivalent we would expect to find that the pictorial superiority effect combined additively with effects which relate to the semantic comparison stage. The experiments on relative judgements of size and intelligence reported by Banks & Flora (1977) provided evidence which was consistent with this view. Distance effects and semantic congruity effects were each found to be of approximately equal magnitude for picture and word stimuli.

Rosch (1975a) studied the effects of typicality and priming on speed of superordinate classification of pairs of pictures and pairs of words. The stimuli were either physically identical or denoted different objects from the same superordinate class, or from different superordinate classes, and had been selected to represent three levels of typicality within their respective classes. On alternate trials the name of the superordinate category of the stimuli was spoken 2 secs before onset of the display. Rosch found that physically identical displays were classified faster than categorially identical displays, and that this effect occurred for word and picture stimuli. There were in addition effects of typicality on speed of same category judgements for the physically identical and categorially identical pairs. Prior presentation of a superordinate name reduced the RT for same category decisions, and this effect combined additively with the typicality effect. In the case of the physically identical displays, priming facilitated classification of typical category members but delayed classification of atypical instances. These effects occurred for both words and pictures.

Unfortunately Rosch did not explicitly test for interactions of the priming and typicality effects with the picture-word difference. However, it seems clear from the graphs included in her paper that these effects were similar in form and magnitude for pictures and words. This conclusion is strengthened by the results of a test for effects of semantic similarity on 'same' decisions in the experiment described by Pellegrino, Rosinski, Chiesi & Siegel (1977). Decisions that pairs of items were 'both living' were taken faster if they belonged to the same category of living creatures (both birds, both fish, both mammals, or both insects) than if they came from different categories. Similarly, decisions about articles of clothing were taken faster when the two items were worn close to one another on the body than when they were worn further apart. The effect of semantic proximity occurred for word, picture and mixed modality pairs, and did not interact with the pictorial superiority effect.

The unitary memory model does not require that the semantic effects obtained with picture and word stimuli in categorization tasks should be identical. Since the two classes of stimulus access the semantic codes through independent interface structures it is quite possible that the attribute descriptions retrieved will differ somewhat in detail. For example, Seymour (1973b) conducted an experiment involving comparisons of geometric forms which were designated by pairs of shapes, a name and a shape, or pairs of names. The 'different' RT was sensitive to the similarity of the shape concepts, as defined in terms of values on dimensions of contour and elongation, but the exact pattern of the confusion effects depended on the type of display presented. The same conclusion follows from a recent study reported by Guenther & Klatzky (1977). *S*s classified pairs of picture or name stimuli as 'same' if both belonged to a target category, and as 'different' if they did not. The 'different' RTs showed evidence of a negative relatedness effect, but the effect was substantially greater for picture stimuli than for word stimuli.

A further experiment described by Guenther & Klatzky (1977) suggests that this modality × relatedness interaction reflects an option to code attributes of pictures differently from the attributes of object names. When mixed modality word-picture combinations were presented for superordinate classification in addition to same modality picture pairs and word pairs the modality × relatedness interaction disappeared. It was argued that the inclusion of the mixed modality pairs encouraged the *S*s to retrieve comparable attribute descriptions for the word and picture stimuli. The results for the 'same' trials supported this interpretation. Stimuli which were same at the basic level were classified faster than stimuli which were same at the superordinate level, and this effect occurred for the mixed modality displays as well as for the same modality displays.

The experiments by Rosch (1975a) provide some additional evidence on these issues. It will be recalled that she obtained an interaction of priming and typicality when *S*s classified physically identical word or picture displays as belonging to the same superordinate category. It seems unlikely that these comparisons were made at the levels of the peripheral graphemic or pictorial registers, since we would not then have expected priming and typicality to have influenced the RT. A more probable interpretation is that these displays were matched at a semantic level, and that their equivalence was determined by consideration of basic object descriptions. If so, the observed priming × typicality interaction implies that a superordinate name retrieves attributes which are descriptive of the class prototype, and that the presence of these attributes in the semantic register facilitates matching of descriptions of typical class members while disrupting the matching of atypical class members.

Rosch conducted experiments in which the interval between the priming stimulus and the onset of the display was varied. As in the experiments on colour matching (Rosch, 1975b), she found that simultaneous presentation of the priming stimulus and display eliminated the priming × typicality interaction observed with the physically identical displays, although the additive effects of priming and typicality were preserved in classification of different objects from the same superordinate class. The priming × typicality interaction was reinstated for picture displays when the interval was greater than 200 msecs, and for word displays when it was greater than 300 msecs. If picture and word pairs were intermixed in the trial sequence an interval of 400–500 msecs was necessary to re-establish the interaction for pictures, but this delay was apparently not sufficient for words.

Intervals greater than 500 msecs were not tested, but Rosch verified in another experiment that the interaction occurred for both words and pictures in a mixed presentation design using a 2 sec interval.

These results may be taken to imply that the attribute descriptions retrieved by pictures of objects differ in certain respects from those retrieved by names of objects. The configuration of prototypical attributes evoked by a superordinate name must apparently exist in the semantic register for somewhat longer if it is to affect the classification of names than if it is to affect the classification of pictures. An effect of this kind could occur if the prototypical description initially approximated the pictorially based code but was progressively extended to include an approximation to the lexically based code.

In summary, the experiments which have contrasted pictures of objects and names of objects as stimuli in categorization tasks have provided further support for the existence of a central system for description of attributes of objects which is accessible to word and picture stimuli. However, it seems that access to this central code is often achieved more rapidly by pictorial representations of objects than by their names, and that the codes retrieved by pictures may differ in some respects from those retrieved by words.

XVI.6 CONCLUSIONS

This chapter has concentrated on the coding and categorization of familiar objects. The main argument has been that objects may be represented within the Pictorial Memory at two distinct levels, one pictorial and the other semantic. Pictorial codes may be formed by encoding operations or by retrieval of information from the pictorial data store, and are assumed to represent the three-dimensional structure of a solid object in a global, undifferentiated form (see Chapter XIV). The pictorial code is therefore descriptive of the physical appearance of an object but does not isolate its component attributes or provide a basis for decisions about class membership.

The semantic coding of an object has been viewed as a structure in which perceptual and functional attributes are labelled and assigned values. It has been assumed that different configurations of attributes may be isolated and used to support judgements about class membership. The research on categorization conducted by Rosch and her colleagues suggested that objects are naturally classified at three levels, called the subordinate level, the basic object level and the superordinate level. Experimental evidence appeared to confirm that the pictorial coding of an object maps relatively directly onto a basic level semantic description, and that additional editing or retrieval operations may be necessary for successful isolation of subordinate or superordinate attribute configurations.

Conclusion

CHAPTER XVII

Experimental Cognitive Psychology

AN EVALUATION OF THE APPROACH

XVII.1 INTRODUCTION

This book has considered a substantial amount of recent experimental cognitive research which has been conducted with the aim of analyzing fundamental processes involved in the interpretation of visual language and visual objects. The impression gained is that this is a well-structured area of enquiry, possessing its own theoretical goals and experimental methodology, and that, contrary to the views of Newell (1973), the past ten to fifteen years have seen a significant advance in understanding and technique, combined with an accumulation of knowledge about visual cognitive functions.

It appeared from the outset that the *conceptual framework* utilized in categorizing and interpreting experiments was a major determinant of the cumulative or fragmentary appearance of experimental research. In the absence of an appropriate framework worthwhile judgements of the value and significance of research cannot be formulated. For this reason, the development of a structure within which a wide range of cognitive experiments might be classified and discussed was assigned a high priority during the preparation of the text.

The conceptual structure which is represented in the headings given to the parts, chapters and sub-sections of the book was based, in the first instance, on a distinction between three major areas of competence which were labelled as the *Symbolic Memory*, the *Lexical Memory*, and the *Pictorial Memory*. These labels were considered to refer to three educationally and culturally significant domains of human intellectual achievement, concerned with (1) symbolic problem solving in science, mathematics and logic, (2) the understanding of text and the acquisition of new information by reading, and (3) solving of spatial problems and interpretation of a world of objects. These forms of competence are, of course, themselves significant topics for study in cognitive psychology (Neisser, 1976). However, for reasons to be developed below, they have been judged to lie outside the scope of this book, which has been directed at the analysis of the mental processes underlying the exercise of competence.

XVII.2 EXECUTIVE FUNCTIONS OF INTELLIGENCE

The research described in this book has been concerned with the derivation of inferences about *mental functions* and *mental codes* from a study of the impact of experimental variations on speed and accuracy of response in simple tasks involving the identification, naming and comparison of visual stimuli. Information of this kind has value if we wish to make empirically well-grounded statements about mental activities which are formulated at this particular level of specificity. Discussions of educational failure of a fundamental nature, of loss of competence following brain injury or of factors influencing efficiency of man-machine interaction may all benefit from an experimental analysis of mental processes of the kind which has been undertaken.

We can avoid unnecessary argument if the proper sphere of application of the experimental method can be defined and differentiated from domains which form the territory of other cognitive sciences. A differentiation of this kind can be based on a consideration of the units of analysis employed and the aspect of cognitive functioning which is to be modelled. The experimental method is appropriate for the development of descriptions of mental functions and mental codes and their interactions in simple information processing tasks. However, the formulation of such descriptions constitutes only one among a number of goals which might be set up by cognitive scientists. We might, for example, assert that our study of the *Symbolic Memory* should concentrate on logical problem solving procedures, that the analysis of the *Lexical Memory* should focus on the comprehension of real texts, and that the topic of the *Pictorial Memory* should be about procedures in spatial problem solving, or abilities to find one's way around in a complex environment. These are all ambitious but reasonable goals for cognitive science, although they are, in general, not goals which can be approached directly by applications of the experimental method.

One reason for this is that the experimental approach, as defined here, does not represent a sensible procedure for investigation of the *executive functions* of human intelligence. It has from time to time been necessary in this book to postulate the existence of a superordinate executive and of subordinate executives which control processing during the activity of a particular mental function. However, these executives were introduced on logical grounds, and the experimentally obtained data contributed little to the analysis of their activities. Since the experiments typically involve tasks which are simple and fundamental in character they are of relatively little help to us if we wish to understand the complex achievements of intelligence which are evident in problem solving activities and in processing of natural language. The performance of these complex tasks is extended in time, and involves a purposeful chain of cognitive, perceptual and overt activities (Miller, Galanter & Pribram, 1960). Thus, the critical component which must be modelled in a description of complex behaviour consists in the dynamic activity of the executive function.

A research procedure which is appropriate for the description of the executive functions has been developed within the field of 'artificial intelligence' (Boden, 1977). This approach involves descriptive and intuitive analysis of complex intellectual achievements supported by the development of dynamic theories which are expressed as programmes which may be run on a digital computer. Hence, theories about the *competence* labelled by the terms *Symbolic Memory*, *Lexical Memory* and *Pictorial Memory* are most likely to emerge from research in 'artificial intelligence' (as exemplified in the work of Newell & Simon (1972), Winograd (1972), Minsky (1975) and many others), and the more global and descriptive approaches which are evident in differential psychology (Guilford, 1967) or in qualitative discussions of the kind provided by Bartlett (1932, 1958), Miller, Galanter & Pribram (1960) or Neisser (1976).

We can, therefore, identify two distinctively different approaches to the study of cognitive processes. There is an *experimental method* which has been developed for the purpose of empirical validation of assumptions about mental concepts, and there is a *descriptive method* which supports intuitive speculations about complex mental activities and the dynamic processing theories of 'artificial intelligence'. It is possible that a beneficial merging of these two lines of enquiry will eventually occur. However, they appear at present to be distinct with regard to goals and methodology. The experimental literature can be examined without reference to findings emerging from 'artificial intelligence' (as has been done in this text), and books on 'artificial intelligence' can be written without consideration of research in experimental cognitive psychology (see, for example, Boden, 1977, and Raphael, 1975). Thus, although the programme written by Winograd (1972) deals directly with the comprehension of referential relationships between sentences and arrangements of objects, it is difficult to see how the dynamic processes he has modelled can be translated into experimentally testable consequences, or how the findings and interpretations of the experiments described in Parts Two and Three of this book can have any bearing on the decisions taken during the development of his programme.

XVII.3 THE EXPERIMENTAL METHOD

The experimental method has been characterized in this text as a procedure which allows us to formulate inferences about mental functions and also the logical structure of human information processing systems. The significant contribution of the method is that it provides a rationale for the *empirical* validation of mental concepts. In Chapter II it was proposed that the *additive factor method* of Sternberg (1969a) provides a methodology for the investigation of mental concepts. The method is based on the assumption of *selective influence*, which states that each of the major mental functions is sensitive to the influence of members of a set of experimental factors. Sternberg's argument was that factors exerting selective influences on distinct 'stages of processing' yield additivity of effects, whereas factors influencing a common stage yield an interaction of effects.

Many instances of applications of this method have been described in this book. These studies have helped to validate the existence of *mental functions* concerned with ENCODING, REPRESENTATION, RETRIEVAL and COMPARISON of *mental codes* which represent stimuli in terms of their visual, auditory or semantic attributes. It has, nonetheless, been rare to find systematic and complete applications of the additive factor method to the analysis of a particular task. More usually the logic of the method is invoked at the stage of interpretation of data as a justification for proposals concerning the localization of particular effects within the processing sequence.

The additive factor method is vulnerable to a number of criticisms which may explain why its adoption has not been more wholehearted. Sternberg emphasized the independent and successive nature of the 'processing stages' and thus placed great stress on demonstrations of additivity of effects. However, additivity is defined as the absence of a significant interaction, and the conclusion in favour of additivity is therefore based on acceptance of a null hypothesis (Pachella, 1974). Sternberg also supposed that the method might be used as a procedure for the *discovery* of 'processing stages'. An approach of this kind seems to point in the direction of a somewhat arid operationalism, in which various *ad hoc* combinations of factors are tried out, and attempts are made to interpret the pattern of interactions and non-interactions which emerges.

There is also an uncertainty about the strength of the conclusions which may be drawn when instances of additivity or interaction are obtained. If the stages are to some degree mutually dependent or overlapping, factors which exert selective influences on successive stages may also produce effects which extend across stages. The interactions obtained in such cases do not represent a failure of selectivity or a major convergence of influence on a single stage. It is also possible that factors which do influence a common stage will have additive effects on the duration of that stage, and, in such a case, additivity would not imply genuine selectivity of influence.

These remarks indicate that the additive factor method cannot be used in any purely mechanical way as a procedure for identifying 'processing stages'. Nonetheless, the method appears to have considerable potential if it is applied intelligently and in conjunction with an adequately developed *a priori* conceptualization of the sequence of mental functions required for performance on a particular task. If this analysis is extended to include a specification of the experimental factors which are likely to be related to each function, it then becomes possible to design experiments which test for theoretically interesting instances of additivity or interaction.

By requiring that 'processing stages' should correspond to significant mental functions we can avoid the proliferation of stages which is likely to result from an uncritical interpretation of additivity of effects. We would not, for example, agree that 'binary decision', as defined in Sternberg's (1969a, 1975) accounts of symbol classification, enjoys the status of a processing stage. Similar objections apply to other *ad hoc* stages, such as the 'truth index' switching operation which appears in certain models of sentence-picture comparison (Clark & Chase, 1972; Glucksberg, Trabasso & Wald, 1973; Carpenter & Just, 1975).

XVII.4 MICRO-STRUCTURE OF PROCESSING STAGES

Much of the experimental research which has been discussed in this book has been directed at the analysis of the *mental functions* which are required for the formation, maintenance and transformation of the internal representations which we have called the mental codes.

The experimental studies have helped to validate the assumption that the mental functions correspond to time-consuming activities of the neurological systems underlying each domain of competence, and have supported the division of certain of them into sub-stages. They have also extended our ideas about each function by indicating which factors exert an influence on its duration, and the manner in which these influences combine.

Although this advance in our ability to make empirically based statements about otherwise unobservable mental processes might be viewed as a modest achievement, many investigators have assumed that the experimental method will also support much more precise analyses of the *micro-structure* of individual processing stages. Endeavours of this kind are exemplified in Sternberg's (1975) serial exhaustive model of COMPARISON, counting models of arithmetical operations (Parkman & Groen, 1972; Parkman, 1973), scanning models of lexical access (Rubenstein, Lewis & Rubenstein, 1971b), phonological retrieval (Oldfield, 1966), or determination of category membership (Meyer, 1970; Landauer & Meyer, 1973), and also in models of the verification process which incorporate operations of 'constituent comparison' and 'truth index switching' (Clark & Chase, 1972; Glucksberg, Trabasso & Wald, 1973; Carpenter & Just, 1975). These models all depend on the assumption that the duration of a particular stage of processing may be the sum of the durations of a number of mini-operations, so that its overall duration is directly determined by the occurrence or non-occurrence of these component activities.

We can refer to such models as *computational models* since they seek to specify the micro-structure of a processing stage in terms of the programme of operations which is required for the transformation of input to output. It has been noted by Sternberg (1969a) that such models depend on an assumption of *pure insertion* which states that component processes may be added to or subtracted from the sequence of events making up a stage without altering the nature of the remaining events. It is perhaps surprising that Sternberg rejected this subtractive method as a procedure for investigation of the major processing stages, but then resorted to it in formulating a model of the micro-structure of the COMPARISON stage.

From the present viewpoint the major difficulty with the computational models is that they are based on postulated elementary operations whose existence cannot be validated by the experimental procedures which have been outlined. Theories which are formulated in terms of unverifiable mental entities are themselves likely to be unverifiable, and it is for this reason that many of the debates about serial and parallel processing models appear in retrospect to have been futile (Townsend, 1972). The computational models have the status, therefore, of procedural representations, often presented as flow-charts incorporating operations, tests and branches, which could be realized as short computer programmes. As such, they constitute attempts to model simple executive functions in the same format as has appeared appropriate for the dynamic description of the complex functions of intelligence, and could be represented as an intrusion of the 'artificial intelligence' approach into the domain of the experimental approach.

The position adopted in this text has been that the computational models of the micro-structure of individual processing stages are probably incorrect as statements about the manner in which experimental factors influence the durations of the stages. They also appear to be inappropriate as theoretical statements in an empirically based analysis of mental concepts, since they propose unverifiable theories which are formulated in terms of elements which are too small to allow for validation by the experimental method.

XVII.5 LOGICAL STRUCTURE OF MENTAL CODES

The second type of entity which has been analysed by the experimental method is the *mental code*. This has been defined as an internal representation of visible, acoustic or semantic attributes of stimuli, which may be formed as a consequence of input to the sensory systems or following retrieval of information from the permanent data stores. The argument that congruity and similarity of codes are factors which influence a COMPARISON stage of processing has enabled us to use the additive factor method to validate the existence of codes of different types.

In the course of these discussions relatively little has been said about the precise nature and logical structure of the mental codes. It seemed that the peripheral graphemic and pictorial codes were gestalt-like and that they were manipulable by the quasi-spatial operations of rotation and size scaling. The central semantic and logical codes, on the other hand, appeared to involve the analysis of the stimulus into its attributes, and to be formulated in discrete or categorial terms which included relational and logical components. These are somewhat global and descriptive statements about the mental codes, and we may question whether the experimental method will support a more detailed or formal analysis.

Various instances can be identified in the literature in which attempts have been made to specify the structure of the semantic and logical codes. These include the model of category judgements developed by Smith, Shoben & Rips (1974), which incorporates a distinction between characteristic and defining features, and the models of sentence-picture comparison outlined by Clark & Chase (1972), Glucksberg, Trabasso & Wald (1973) and Carpenter & Just (1975), which include assumptions about logical structure in sentence representations.

The specification of the logical structure of mental representations is undoubtedly a legitimate goal for cognitive scientists, and one which is central to the study of syntax, semantics and logic, and also to the development of theories in 'artificial intelligence'. However, the relationship between formal descriptions of the kind developed within these disciplines and observations made in experimental investigations is obscure. If we wished to use the experimental method to confirm or refute the existence of a specific logical structure in a mental code it would be necessary that we should be capable both of defining the logical structure and of detailing the nature of its influence on a particular stage of processing. It is by no means obvious that a rationale for developing arguments of this kind is presently available.

What we tend to find, therefore, is that speculative statements about mental codes are combined with equally speculative statements about the micro-structure of a processing stage to yield a solution which is in apparent conformity with observed reaction time data. It is then asserted that the reaction times have been 'predicted' and that the assumptions about coding and processing have been validated. However, this mode of theorizing is exceedingly insecure, because, as has already been noted, we lack procedures for empirical validation of assumptions about the micro-structure of processing stages or for discrimination between alternative forms of code description.

In the model formulated by Smith, Shoben & Rips (1974) a set of assumptions about processing (global comparison at a first stage, and an option for focused comparison at a second stage) was related to an assumption about coding (the distinction between defining and characteristic features) to provide an overall statement about the manner in which semantic similarity influenced the RT. However, as was noted in the discussion in Chapter XII, the model is critically dependent on the assumption that selective focus on subsets of relevant attributes is achieved during the COMPARISON stage of processing. If this assumption is rejected, the two-stage model of COMPARISON collapses, and it is no longer possible to maintain that the RT data offer any kind of empirical validation of the proposed distinction between characteristic and defining features.

The sentence-picture comparison model of Carpenter & Just (1975) is based on assumptions about the micro-structure of a 'constituent comparison' stage of processing and further assumptions about the propositional format of affirmative and negative sentences. If the two sets of assumptions are combined in a particular way it can be shown that the data obtained in sentence-picture comparison experiments are consistent with a model which postulates a cyclic process of 'constituent comparison' which is reinitialized each time a mismatch is encountered. The previously formulated model of Clark & Chase (1972) did not incorporate this proposed reinitialization operation. Their model did, on the other hand, postulate an operation of 'truth index switching', which was triggered whenever constituents were found to mismatch. Carpenter & Just retained this idea, but assumed that truth index switching occupied a negligible interval of time.

It can be seen that the processing assumptions underlying these models are based on a set of non-verifiable entities, including 'constituent comparison', 'truth index switching' and 'reinitialization'. Since we cannot know whether the assumptions are correct we cannot treat a good fit between the model and the RT data as a validation of the parallel set of assumptions concerning the structure of the logical codes. Equally, if the proposal concerning code structure is changed, and the fit of the model is then worsened (see Tannenhaus, Carroll & Bever, 1976), we cannot feel confident that this is because the new proposal is in some sense less adequate.

These comments suggest that an experimental psycholinguistics in which conceptually justified proposals about code structure are supposedly submitted to empirical validation by applications of the experimental method may well not be a viable endeavour at the present time. The experimental approach lacks the power to resolve questions about logical structure, and is indeed inappropriate as a method of approaching such questions.

XVII.6 SCHEMATIC MODELS OF THE MEMORY SYSTEMS

In view of these limitations on the analytic power of the experimental method it has not seemed worthwhile to undertake a detailed examination of computational or other models which purport to give accounts of the processing occurring at the level of the micro-structure of individual stages. It seems that we should for the time being be content with a somewhat grosser level of description of cognitive processes, and the argument of this book has been that the processing stages and sub-stages together with the mental codes provide the elementary units in terms of which such descriptions might be formulated. These are considered to be valid units for consideration in experimental cognitive psychology, since questions about their existence or general characteristics can be investigated by appropriate applications of the experimental method.

Adoption of this approach has led to the development of two types of descriptive model. The first of these, which can be called a *stage model*, diagrams a sequence of major processing stages each of which is associated with a listing of the factors which influence its duration. Models of this kind were outlined for the tasks of symbol naming and symbol classification in Chapter II (Figures II.3.2 and II.4.2). These diagrams can be useful as summaries of the research findings relating to particular tasks, but are limited to situations which have been extensively studied within the framework of the additive factor method, and for which it is reasonable to propose a linear sequence of more or less independent stages.

The second type of model is exemplified in the diagrams of the components of the *Symbolic*, *Lexical* and *Pictorial Memories* (see Figures III.3.1, VIII.5.1 and XIII.2.1), and also in the diagrams of the components underlying the activities of the mental functions of ENCODING, RETRIEVAL and COMPARISON (Figures IV.5.1, V.1.1, VI.1.1 and VII.1.1). These diagrammatic models are conceptual in origin, and are introduced with the aim of clarifying what appear to be necessary assumptions concerning the components and structure of the processing systems. They provide a form of description which is global enough to avoid being task specific while being at the same time readily related to models which have been formulated in terms of processing stages or sub-stages.

These *diagrammatic models* can function as organizing frameworks for discussion of experimental tasks which involve different types of input-output transformation, or which focus on codes formed at different stages of processing. As such they provide a basis for categorization of experiments, and for interpretation of their outcomes. By mapping the experimental results onto the component systems represented in the diagrams we can specify the characteristics of each system which are found in normal *S*s whose symbolic, lexical and pictorial processing systems are intact. A descriptive framework of this kind may readily be transferred to clinical and educational contexts in which failures of basic competence within these domains are the principal concern.

The diagrammatic models should not be viewed, therefore, as discoveries emerging from empirical research or, indeed, as theoretical statements which may be falsified by resort to experimental data. There are, nonetheless, many ways in which such diagrams might be formulated, and evidence from experimental or neuropsychological studies can be helpful in deciding in favour of one alternative or another. The decision to represent the pictorial and graphemic registers as separate systems, or to subdivide Morton's (1968, 1969a) monolithic logogen system into input and output lexicons, provide cases in point, as does the conclusion that the semantic registers of the *Lexical* and *Pictorial Memories* can probably be represented as a unitary system.

According to this view, the goals of experimental cognitive psychology are primarily descriptive. The research starts from certain *a priori* conceptualizations of mental processes and the overall structure of mental systems. As the data obtained by the application of the experimental method are assimilated, the researcher seeks to extend the structure, revise its logic, and fill in the details of certain of its regions. The enterprise seems more obviously concerned with the achievement of a progressive clarification of structure than with a game of setting up and knocking down tightly formulated theories.

XVII.7 CONCLUSIONS

This final chapter has examined some more general issues concerning the place of experimental cognitive psychology within the wider field of cognitive science. The conclusion has been that the experimental approach is distinct, in terms both of aims and methods, from other approaches to the study of cognition, such as those of 'artificial intelligence' or linguistics, which are directed at the modelling of complex forms of human intellectual competence. It seems that the experimental method has little to contribute to these disciplines, since it is not well adapted to the study of complex intentional behaviour or to the investigation of logical structure in mental codes.

The experimental method was seen as a procedure for the empirical validation of assumptions concerning the structure of human information processing systems, and for the study of the mental operations and codes implied by the activities and achievements of such systems. In this respect, the discipline of experimental cognitive psychology appears to share a number of objectives with fields of clinical application in neurology and education. There is in both cases a commitment to the analysis of *fundamental* forms of intellectual competence.

It seems likely, therefore, that the contributions to educational practice which, it is to be hoped, will be made by contemporary research in cognitive science, will take two distinct forms. A clarification of the nature of the achievements underlying success in mathematics, science and language arts will probably depend on the development of dynamic models of problem solving and text comprehension of the kind which are emerging from research in 'artificial intelligence'. Experimental cognitive psychology may contribute an understanding of the basic cognitive functions which are established during primary schooling, and which form the foundation of later educational achievements.

Bibliography

Bibliography

ADERMAN, D. & SMITH, E. E. (1971). Expectancy as a determinant of functional units in perceptual recognition. *Cognitive Psychology*, **2**, 117–129.

ALLPORT, D. A. (1975). The state of cognitive psychology: a critical notice of Chase, W. G. (ed.), *Visual Information Processing*. New York: Academic Press. *Quarterly Journal of Experimental Psychology*, **27**, 141–152.

ALLPORT, D. A. (1977). On knowing the meaning of words we are unable to report: the effects of visual masking. In DORNIC, S. (ed.), *Attention and Performance VI*. Hillsdale: Erlbaum.

ALLUISI, E. A., MULLER, P. F. & FITTS, P. M. (1957). An information analysis of verbal and motor responses in a forced-pace serial task. *Journal of Experimental Psychology*, **53**, 153–158.

AMBLER, B. A. & PROCTOR, J. D. (1976). The familiarity effect for single-letter pairs. *Journal of Experimental Psychology: Human Perception and Performance*, **2**, 222–234.

ANDERSON, J. R. & BOWER, G. H. (1973). *Human Associative Memory*. Washington: Winston.

ASSO, D. & WYKE, M. (1967). Experimental study of the effect of letter reversals on reading. *British Journal of Psychology*, **58**, 413–419.

ATKINSON, R. C., HOLMGREN, J. E. & JUOLA, J. F. (1969). Processing time as influenced by the number of elements in a visual display. *Perception & Psychophysics*, **6**, 321–326.

ATKINSON, R. C. & JUOLA, J. F. (1973). Factors influencing speed and accuracy of word recognition. In KORNBLUM, S. (ed.), *Attention and Performance, IV*. New York: Academic Press.

ATKINSON, R. C. & JUOLA, J. F. (1974). Search and decision processes in recognition memory. In ATKINSON, R. C., KRANTZ, D. H. and SUPPES, P. (eds.), *Contemporary Developments in Mathematical Psychology*. San Francisco: Freeman.

ATTNEAVE, F. & ARNOULT, M. D. (1956). The quantitative study of shape and pattern perception. *Psychological Bulletin*, **53**, 452–471.

AUDLEY, R. J. & WALLIS, C. P. (1964). Response instructions and the speed of relative judgements. I. Some experiments on brightness discrimination. *British Journal of Psychology*, **55**, 59–73.

AVERBACH, E. & CORIELL, A. S. (1961). Short-term memory in vision. *Bell Systems Technical Journal*, **40**, 309–328.

BAMBER, D. (1969). Reaction times and error rates for 'same'–'different' judgments of multidimensional stimuli. *Perception & Psychophysics*, **6**, 169–174.

BAMBER, D. (1972). Reaction times and error rates for judging nominal identity of letter strings. *Perception & Psychophysics*, **12**, 321–326.

BAMBER, D., HERDER, J. & TIDD, K. (1975). Reaction times in a task analogous to 'same'–'different' judgment. *Perception & Psychophysics*, **18**, 321–327.

BAMBER, D. & PAINE, S. (1973). Information retrieval processes in 'same'–'different' judgments of letter strings. In KORNBLUM, S. (ed.), *Attention & Performance, IV*. London: Academic Press.

BANKS, W. P. (1977). Encoding and processing of symbolic information in comparative judgements. In BOWER. G. H. (ed), *The Psychology of Learning and Motivation, 11*, New York: Academic Press.

BANKS, W. P., CLARK, H. H. & LUCY, P. (1975). The locus of the semantic congruity effect in comparative judgments. *Journal of Experimental Psychology: Human Perception and Performance*, **1**, 35–47.

BANKS, W. P. & FLORA, J. (1976). Semantic and perceptual processes in symbolic comparisons. *Journal of Experimental Psychology: Human Perception and Performance*, **3**, 278–290.

BANKS, W. P., FUJII, M. & KAYRA-STUART, F. (1976). Semantic congruity effects in comparative judgments of magnitudes of digits. *Journal of Experimental Psychology: Human Perception and Performance*, **2**, 435–447.

BARON, J. (1975). Successive stages in word recognition. In RABBITT, P. M. A. and DORNIC, S. (eds.), *Attention and Performance, V.* London: Academic Press.

BARON, J. & STRAWSON, C. (1976). Use of orthographic and word-specific knowledge in reading words aloud. *Journal of Experimental Psychology: Human Perception and Performance*, **2**, 386–393.

BARON, J. & THURSTON, I. (1973). An analysis of the word-superiority effect. *Cognitive Psychology*, **4**, 207–228.

BARRON, R. W. & PITTENGER, J. B. (1974). The effect of orthographic structure and lexical meaning on 'same'–'different judgments. *Quarterly Journal of Experimental Psychology*, **26**, 566–581.

BARTLETT, F. C. (1932). *Remembering.* Cambridge: Cambridge University Press.

BARTLETT, F. C. (1958). *Thinking: An Experimental and Social Study.* London: George Allen & Unwin.

BARTRAM, D. J. (1973). The effects of familiarity and practice on naming pictures of objects. *Memory & Cognition*, **1**, 101–105.

BARTRAM. D. J. (1974). The role of visual and semantic codes in object naming. *Cognitive Psychology*, **6**, 325–356.

BARTRAM, D. J. (1976). Levels of coding in picture–picture comparison tasks. *Memory & Cognition*, **4**, 593–602.

BATTIG, W. F. & MONTAGUE, W. E. (1969). Category norms for verbal items in 56 categories: a replication and extension of the Connecticut category norms. *Journal of Experimental Pschology Monograph*, **80** (3, Part 2).

BECKER, C. A. & KILLION, T. H. (1977). Interaction of visual and cognitive effects in word recognition. *Journal of Experimental Psychology: Human Perception and Performance*, **3**, 389–401.

BELLER, H. K. (1970). Parallel and serial stages in matching. *Journal of Experimental Psychology*, **84**, 213–219.

BELLER, H. K. (1971). Priming: effects of advance information on matching. *Journal of Experimental Psychology*, **87,** 176–182.

BELLER, H. K. (1975). Naming, reading and executing directions. *Journal of Experimental Psychology: Human Perception and Performance*, **1**, 154–160.

BELLER, H. K. & SCHAEFFER, B. (1974). On matching words: syllabification and priming. Unpublished paper, State University of New York.

BERLIN, B. & KAY, P. (1969). *Basic Colour Terms: Their Universality and Evolution.* Berkeley: University of California Press.

BESNER, D. & COLTHEART, M. (1976). Mental size scaling examined. *Memory & Cognition*, **4**, 525–531.

BESNER, D. & COLTHEART, M. (1977). Visual operations in the recognition of different size forms. Unpublished paper, University of Reading.

BESNER, D. & JACKSON, A. (1975). Same–different judgments with words and nonwords: a word superiority/inferiority effect. *Bulletin of the Psychonomic Society*, **6**, 578–580.

BIERWISCH, M. (1967). Some semantic universals of German adjectivals. *Foundations of Language*, **3**, 1–36.

BIERWISCH, M. (1969). On certain problems of semantic representations. *Foundations of Language*, **5**, 153–184.

BIERWISCH, M. (1970). Semantics. In LYONS, J. (ed.), *New Horizons in Linguistics*. Harmondsworth: Penguin Books.

BJORK, E. L. & ESTES, W. K. (1973). Letter identification in relation to linguistic context and masking conditions. *Memory & Cognition*, **1**, 217–223.

BODEN, M. A. (1977). *Artificial Intelligence and Natural Man*. Hassocks: Harvester.

BOIES, S. J. (1969). Retention of visual information from a single letter. Unpublished M.A. Thesis, University of Oregon.

BOIES, S. J. (1971). Memory codes in a speeded classification task. Unpublished Doctoral Dissertation, University of Oregon.

BRACEY, G. W. (1969). Two operations in character recognition: a partial replication. *Perception and Psychophysics*, **6**, 357–360.

BRAINARD, R. W., IRBY, T. S., FITTS, P. M. & ALLUISI, E. A. (1962). Some variables influencing the rate of gain of information. *Journal of Experimental Psychology*, **63**, 105–110.

BRAND, J. (1971). Classification without identification in visual search. *Quarterly Journal of Experimental Psychology*, **23**, 178–186.

BRIGGS, G. E. (1974). On the predictor variable for choice reaction time. *Memory & Cognition*, **2**, 575–580.

BRIGGS, G. E. & JOHNSEN, A. M. (1972). On the nature of the central processing in choice reactions. *Memory & Cognition*, **1**, 91–100.

BRIGGS, G. E. & SWANSON, J. M. (1970). Encoding, decoding and central functions in human information processing. *Journal of Experimental Psychology*, **86**, 296–308.

BROADBENT, D. E. (1967). Word frequency effect and response bias. *Psychological Review*, **74**, 1–15.

BROADBENT, D. E. (1977). Levels, hierarchies and the locus of control. *Quarterly Journal of Experimental Psychology*, **29**, 181–201.

BROADBENT, D. E. & GREGORY, M. (1968). Visual perception of words differing in letter diagram frequency. *Journal of Verbal Learning and Verbal Behaviour*, **7**, 569–571.

BROADBENT, D. E. & GREGORY, M. H. P. (1970). Effects on tachistoscopic perception from independent variation of word probability and of letter probability. *Acta Psychologica*, **35**, 1–14.

BROOKS, L. R. (1968). Spatial and verbal components of the act of recall. *Canadian Journal of Psychology*, **22**, 349–368.

BROWN, C. R. & RUBENSTEIN, H. (1961). Test of response bias explanation of word frequency effect. *Science*, **133**, 280–281.

BROWN, R. & MCNEILL, D. (1966) The 'tip of the tongue' phenomenon. *Journal of Verbal Learning & Verbal Behaviour*, **5**, 325–337.

BRYDEN, M. P. (1960). Tachistoscopic recognition of non-alphabetical material. *Canadian Journal of Psychology*, **14**, 78–86.

BRYDEN, M. P. (1966). Accuracy and order of report in tachistoscopic recognition. *Canadian Journal of Psychology*, **20**, 37–56.

BRYDEN, M. P. (1967). A model for the sequential organization of behavior. *Canadian Journal of Psychology*, **21**, 262–272.

BUGGIE, S. E. (1970). Stimulus preprocessing and abstraction in the recognition of disoriented forms. Unpublished M.A. thesis, University of Oregon.

BUNDESEN, C. & LARSEN, A. (1975). Visual transformation of size. *Journal of Experimental Psychology: Human Perception and Performance*, **1**, 214–220.

BURROWS, D. & OKADA, R. (1971). Serial position effects in high-speed memory search. *Perception & Psychophysics*, **10**, 305–308.

BURROWS, D. & SOLOMON, B. A. (1975). Parallel scanning of auditory and visual information. *Memory & Cognition*, **3**, 416–420.

CARAMAZZA, A., HERSH, H. & TORGERSON, W. A. (1976). Subjective structures and operations in semantic memory. *Journal of Verbal Learning and Verbal Behavior*, **15**, 103–117.

CARPENTER, P. A. (1974). On the comprehension, storage, and retrieval of comparative sentences. *Journal of Verbal Learning and Verbal Behavior*, **13**, 401–411.

CARPENTER, P. A. & JUST, M. A. (1975). Sentence comprehension: a psycholinguistic processing model of verification. *Psychological Review*, **82**, 45–73.

CARROLL, J. B. & WHITE, M. N. (1973). Word frequency and age of acquisition as determiners of picture-naming latency. *Quarterly Journal of Experimental Psychology*, **25**, 85–95.

CASEY, T. & ETTLINGER, G. (1960). The occasional independence of dyslexia and dysgraphia from dysphasia. *Journal of Neurology, Neurosurgery and Psychiatry*, **25**, 339–344.

CATTELL, J. MCK. (1886). The time taken up by cerebral operations. *Mind*, **11**, 524–538.

CHAMBERS, S. M. & FORSTER, K. I. (1975). Evidence for lexical access in a simultaneous matching task. *Memory & Cognition*, **3**, 549–559.

CHASE, W. G. & CALFEE, R. C. (1969). Modality and similarity effects in short-term recognition memory. *Journal of Experimental Psychology*, **81**, 510–514.

CHASE, W. G. & CLARK, H. H. (1971). Semantics in the perception of verticality. *British Journal of Psychology*, **62**, 311–326.

CHOMSKY, C. (1970). Reading, writing, and phonology. *Harvard Educational Review*, **40**, 287–309.

CHOMSKY, N. (1970). Phonology and reading. In LEVIN, H. and WILLIAMS, J. P. (eds.), *Basic Studies on Reading*. New York: Basic Books.

CHOMSKY, N. & HALLE, M. (1968). *The Sound Pattern of English*. New York: Harper & Row.

CLARK, H. H. (1969). Linguistic processes in deductive reasoning. *Psychological Review*, **76**. 387–404.

CLARK, H. H. (1973a). The language-as-fixed-effect fallacy: A critique of language statistics in psychological research. *Journal of Verbal Learning and Verbal Behavior*, **12**, 335–359.

CLARK, H. H. (1973b). Space, time, semantics and the child. In MOORE, T. E. (ed.), *Cognitive Development and the Acquisition of Language*. New York: Academic Press.

CLARK, H. H. (1974). Semantics and comprehension. In SEBEOK, T. A. (ed.), *Current Trends in Linguistics. XII: Linguistics and Adjacent Arts and Sciences*. The Hague: Mouton.

CLARK, H. H. & BROWNELL, H. H. (1975). Judging up and down. *Journal of Experimental Psychology: Human Perception & Performance*, **1**, 339–352.

CLARK, H. H. & BROWNELL, H. H. (1976). Position, direction, and their perceptual integrality. *Perception & Psychophysics*, **19**, 328–334.

CLARK, H. H., CARPENTER, P. A. & JUST, M. A. (1973). On the meeting of semantics and perception. In CHASE, W. G. (ed.), *Visual Information Processing*. New York: Academic Press.

CLARK, H. H. & CHASE, W. G. (1972). On the process of comparing sentences against pictures. *Cognitive Psychology*, **3**, 472–517.

CLARK, H. H. & CHASE, W. G. (1974). Perceptual coding strategies in the formation and verification of descriptions. *Memory & Cognition*, **2**, 101–111.

CLIFTON, C. & BIRENBAUM, S. (1970). Effects of serial position and delay of probe in a memory scan task. *Journal of Experimental Psychology*, **86**, 69–76.

CLIFTON, C. & TASH, J. (1973). Effect of syllabic word length on memory-search rate. *Journal of Experimental Psychology*, **99**, 231–235.

COHEN, B. H., BOUSFIELD, W. A. & WHITMARSH, G. A. (1957). Cultural norms for verbal items in 43 categories. Technical Report, University of Connecticut.

COHEN, G. (1968). A comparison of semantic, acoustic and visual criteria for matching of word pairs. *Perception & Psychophysics*, **4**, 203–204.

COHEN, G. (1969). Some evidence for parallel comparisons in a letter recognition task. *Quarterly Journal of Experimental Psychology*, **21**, 272–279.

COLLINS, A. M. & QUILLIAN, M. R. (1969). Retrieval time from semantic memory. *Journal of Verbal Learning and Verbal Behavior*, **8**, 240–247.

COLLINS, A. M. & QUILLIAN, M. R. (1970a). Does category size affect categorization time? *Journal of Verbal Learning & Verbal Behavior*, **9**, 432–438.

COLLINS, A. M. & QUILLIAN, M. R. (1970b). Facilitating retrieval from semantic memory: the effect of repeating part of an inference. *Acta Psychologica*, **33**, 304–314.

COLLINS, A. M. & QUILLIAN, M. R. (1970c). Experiments on semantic memory and language comprehension. In GREGG, L. W. (ed.), *Cognition in Learning and Memory*. New York: Wiley.

COLTHEART, M. (1972). Visual information processing. In DODWELL, P. C. (ed.), *New Horizons in Psychology, 2*. Harmondsworth: Penguin Books.

COLTHEART, M. (1976). Iconic storage and visual masking. In HAMILTON, V. and VERNON, M. D. (eds.), *The Development of Cognitive Processes*. London: Academic Press.

COLTHEART, M., DAVELAAR, E., JONASSON, J. T. & BESNER, D. (1977). Access to the internal lexicon. In DORNIC, S. (ed.), *Attention and Performance VI*. Hillsdale: Erlbaum.

COLTHEART, M. & FREEMAN, R. (1974). Case alternation impairs word identification. *Bulletin of the Psychonomic Society*, **3**, 102–104.

CONNOR, J. M. (1972). Effects of increased processing load on parallel processing of visual displays. *Perception & Psychophysics*, **12**, 121–128.

CONRAD, C. (1972). Cognitive economy in semantic memory. *Journal of Experimental Psychology*, **92**, 149–154.

COOPER, L. A. (1975). Mental rotation of random two-dimensional shapes. *Cognitive Psychology*, **7**, 20–43.

COOPER, L. A. & PODGORNY, P. (1975). Mental transformations and visual comparison processes: Effects of complexity and similarity. Technical Report, University of California, San Diego.

COOPER, L. A. & SHEPARD, R. N. (1973). Chronometric studies of the rotation of mental images. In CHASE, W. G. (ed.), *Visual Information Processing*. New York: Academic Press.

COOPER, L. A. & SHEPARD, R. N. (1976). Transformation on representations of objects in space. In CARTERETTE, E. C. and FRIEDMAN, M. (eds), *Handbook of Perception, VIII. Space and Object Perception*. New York: Academic Press.

CORBALLIS, M. C. (1967). Serial order in recognition and recall. *Journal of Experimental Psychology*, **74**, 99–105.

CORBALLIS, M. C., KIRBY, J. & MILLER, A. (1972). Access to elements of a memorized list. *Journal of Experimental Psychology*, **94**, 185–190.

CORBALLIS, M. C. & MILLER, A. (1973). Scanning and decision processes in recognition memory. *Journal of Experimental Psychology*, **98**, 379–386.

CORBALLIS, M. C. & ROLDAN, C. E. (1975). Detection of symmetry as a function of angular orientation. *Journal of Experimental Psychology: Human Perception and Performance*, **1**, 221–230.

CORBALLIS, M. C., ZBRODOFF, J. & ROLDAN, C. E. (1976). What's up in mental rotation? *Perception & Psychophysics*, **19**, 525–530.

CORCORAN, D. W. J. (1971). *Pattern Recognition*. Harmondsworth: Penguin Books.

CORCORAN, D. W. J. & BESNER, D. (1975). Application of the Posner technique to the study of size and brightness irrelevancies in letter pairs. In RABBITT, P. M. A. and DORNIC, S. (eds.), *Attention and Performance V*. London: Academic Press.

COSKY, M. J. (1976). The role of letter recognition in word recognition. *Memory & Cognition*, **4**, 207–214.

CROSSMAN, E. R. F. W. (1955). The measurement of discriminability. *Quarterly Journal of Experimental Psychology*, **7**, 176–195.

CRUSE, D. & CLIFTON, C. (1973). Recoding strategies and the retrieval of information from memory. *Cognitive Psychology*, **4**, 157–193.

CURTIS, D. W., PAULOS, M. A. & RULE, S. J. (1973). Relation between disjunctive reaction time and stimulus difference. *Journal of Experimental Psychology*, **99**, 167–173.

DAINOFF, M. J. (1970). Time course of visual and auditory encoding. *Journal of Experimental Psychology*, **86**, 214–224.

DAINOFF, M. J. & HABER, R. N. (1970). Effect of acoustic confusability on levels of information processing. *Canadian Journal of Psychology*, **24**, 98–108.

DALRYMPLE-ALFORD, E. C. (1972). Associative facilitation and interference in the Stroop color-word task. *Perception & Psychophysics*, **11**, 274–276.

DARLEY, C. F., KLATZKY, R. L. & ATKINSON, R. C. (1972). Effects of memory load on reaction time. *Journal of Experimental Psychology*, **96**, 232–234.

DE RENZI, E., SCOTTI, G. & SPINNLER, H. (1969). Perceptual and associative disorders of visual recognition: relationship to the site of cerebral lesion. *Neurology*, **19**, 634–642.

DEROSA, D. V. & MORIN, R. E. (1970). Recognition and reaction time for digits in consecutive and nonconsecutive memorized sets. *Journal of Experimental Psychology*, **83**, 472–479.

DUNCAN, C. P. (1966). Effect of word frequency on thinking of a word. *Journal of Verbal Learning and Verbal Behavior*, **5**, 434–440.

DUNCAN, C. P. (1970). Thinking of a word under different retrieval constraints. *Journal of Verbal Learning and Verbal Behavior*, **9**, 356–361.

DYER, F. N. (1973). Same and different judgments for word–color pairs with 'irrelevant' words or colors: evidence for word code comparisons. *Journal of Experimental Psychology*, **98**, 102–108.

EGAN, J. P. & CLARK, F. R. (1966). Psychophysics and signal detection. In SIDOWSKI, J. B. (ed.), *Experimental Methods and Instrumentation in Psychology*. New York: McGraw-Hill.

EGETH, H. E. (1966). Parallel versus serial processes in multidimensional stimulus discrimination. *Perception & Psychophysics*, **1**, 245–252.

EGETH, H., ATKINSON, J., GILMORE, G. & MARCUS, N. (1973). Factors affecting processing mode in visual search. *Perception & Psychophysics*, **13**, 394–402.

EGETH, H. & BLECKER, D. (1971). Differential effects of familiarity on judgments of sameness and difference. *Perception & Psychophysics*, **9**, 321–326.

EGETH, H. E., BLECKER, D. L. & KAMLET, A. S. (1969). Verbal interference in a perceptual comparison task. *Perception & Psychophysics*, **6**, 355–356.

EGETH, H., JONIDES, J. & WALL, S. (1972). Parallel processing of multi-element displays. *Cognitive Psychology*, **3**, 674–698.

EICHELMAN, W. H. (1970a). Stimulus and response repetition effects for naming letters at two response–stimulus intervals. *Perception & Psychophysics*, **7**, 94–96.

EICHELMAN, W. H. (1970b). Familiarity effects in the simultaneous matching task. *Journal of Experimental Psychology*, **86**, 275–282.

ELLIS, S. H. & CHASE, W. G. (1971). Parallel processing in item recognition. *Perception & Psychophysics*, **10**, 379–384.

ERIKSEN, C. W. (1966). Temporal luminance summation effects in backward and forward masking. *Perception & Psychophysics*, **1**, 87–92.

ERIKSEN, C. W. & COLLINS, J. F. (1967). Some temporal characteristics of visual pattern perception. *Journal of Experimental Psychology*, **74**, 476–484.

ERIKSEN, C. W. & COLLINS, J. F. (1968). Sensory traces versus the psychological moment in the temporal organization of form. *Journal of Experimental Psychology*, **77**, 376–382.

ERIKSEN, C. W. & COLLINS, J. F. (1969). Visual perceptual rate under two conditions of search. *Journal of Experimental Psychology*, **80**, 489–492.

ERIKSEN, C. W. & SPENCER, T. (1969). Rate of information processing in visual perception: some results and methodological considerations. *Journal of Experimental Psychology Monograph*, **79** (2, Part 2).

ESTES, W. K. (1972). Interactions of signal and background variables in visual processing. *Perception & Psychophysics*, **12**, 278–286.

ESTES, W. K. (1975a). The locus of inferential and perceptual processes in letter identification. *Journal of Experimental Psychology: General*, **104**, 122–145.

ESTES, W. K. (1975b). Memory, perception, and decision in letter identification. In SOLSO, R. L. (ed.), *Information Processing and Cognition: The Loyola Symposium*. Potomac: Erlbaum.

ESTES, W. K., BJORK, E. L. & SKAAR, E. (1974). Detection of single letters and letters in words with changing vs unchanging mask characters. *Bulletin of the Psychonomic Society*, **3**, 201–203.

FISCHLER, I. (1977). Associative facilitation without expectancy in a lexical decision task. *Journal of Experimental Psychology: Human Perception and Performance*, **3**, 18–26.

FITTS, P. M. & SWITZER, G. (1962). Cognitive aspects of information processing: I. The familiarity of S-R sets and subsets. *Journal of Experimental Psychology*, **63**, 321–329.

FLAVELL, J. H. (1963). *The Developmental Psychology of Jean Piaget*. Princeton: Van Nostrand.

FORBACH, G. B., STANNERS, R. F. & HOCHHAUS, L. (1974). Repetition and practice effects in a lexical decision task. *Memory & Cognition*, **2**, 337–339.

FORRIN, B. & CUNNINGHAM, K. (1973). Recognition time and serial position of probed item in short-term memory. *Journal of Experimental Psychology*, **99**, 272–279.

FORRIN, B., KUMLER, M. L. & MORIN, R. E. (1966). The effects of response code and signal probability in a numeral-naming task. *Canadian Journal of Psychology*, **20**, 115–124.

FORSTER, K. I. & BEDNALL, E. S. (1976). Terminating and exhaustive search in lexical access. *Memory & Cognition*, **4**, 53–61.

FORSTER, K. I. & CHAMBERS, S. M. (1973). Lexical access and naming time. *Journal of Verbal Learning and Verbal Behavior*, **12**, 627–635.

FOX, J. (1975). The use of structural diagnostics in recognition. *Journal of Experimental Psychology: Human Perception and Performance*, **1**, 57–67.

FOX, L. A., SHOR, R. E. & STEINMAN, R. J. (1971). Semantic gradients and interference in naming color, spatial direction, and numerosity. *Journal of Experimental Psychology*, **91**, 59–65.

FRAISSE, P. (1964). Le temps de réaction verbale: I. Dénomination et lecture. *L'Année Psychologique*, **64**, 21–46.

FRAISSE, P. (1967). Latency of different verbal responses to the same stimulus. *Quarterly Journal of Experimental Psychology*, **19**, 353–355.

FRAISSE, P. (1969). Why is naming longer than reading? *Acta Psychologica*, **30**, 96–103.

FREDERIKSEN, J. R. & KROLL, J. F. (1976). Spelling and sound: approaches to the internal lexicon. *Journal of Experimental Psychology: Human Perception and Performance*, **2**, 361–379.

FREEBURNE, C. M. & GOLDMAN, R. D. (1969). Left–right differences in tachistoscopic recognition as a function of order of report, expectancy, and training. *Journal of Experimental Psychology*, **79**, 570–572.

FREEDMAN, J. L. & LOFTUS, E. F. (1971). Retrieval of words from long-term memory. *Journal of Verbal Learning and Verbal Behavior*, **10**, 107–115.

FRIEDMAN, A. (1976). Comparing words: an 'internal psychophysics' for a non-physical dimension. Paper presented at the XXIst International Congress of Psychology, Paris.

FRIEDMAN, A. & BOURNE, L. E. (1976). Encoding the levels of information in pictures and words. *Journal of Experimental Psychology: General*, **105**, 169–190.

FRIES, C. C. (1962). *Linguistics and Reading*. New York: Holt, Rinehart and Winston.

FRIJDA, N. H. (1970). The simulation of human long-term memory. *Psychological Bulletin*, **77**, 1–31.

GARDNER, H. & ZURIF, E. (1975). *Bee* but not *be*: oral reading of single words in aphasia and alexia. *Neuropsychologia*, **13**, 181–190.

GARNER, W. R. (1970). The stimulus in information processing. *American Psychologist*, **25**, 350–358.

GARNER, W. R. & FELFOLDY, G. L. (1970). Integrality of stimulus dimensions in various types of information processing. *Cognitive Psychology*, **1**, 225–241.

GELLATLY. A. R. H. & GREGG, V. H. (1974). The effect of set size on the latency to name words. *Acta Psychologica*, **38**, 93–99.

GELLATLY, A. R. H. & GREGG, V. H. (1975). The effects of negative relatedness upon word–picture and word–word comparisons and subsequent recall. *British Journal of Psychology*, **66**, 311–323.

GIBSON, E. J. (1965). Learning to read. *Science*, **148**, 1066–1072.

GIBSON, E. J. (1970). The ontogeny of reading. *American Psychologist*, **25**, 136–143.

GIBSON, E. J., GIBSON, J. J. PICK, A. D. & OSSER, H. (1962). A developmental study of the discrimination of letter-like forms. *Journal of Comparative and Physiological Psychology*, **55**, 897–906.

GIBSON, E. J. & GUINET, L. (1971). Perception of inflections in brief visual presentations of words. *Journal of Verbal Learning and Verbal Behavior*, **10**, 182–189.

GIBSON, E. J., PICK, A., OSSER, H. & HAMMOND, M. (1962). The role of grapheme–phoneme correspondence in the perception of words. *American Journal of Psychology*, **75**, 554–570.

GIBSON, J. J. (1963). The useful dimensions of sensitivity, *American Psychologist*, **18**, 1–15.

GIBSON, J. J. (1966). *The Senses Considered as Perceptual Systems*. Boston: Houghton Mifflin.

GLASS, A. L. & HOLYOAK, K. J. (1976). Alternative conceptions of semantic theory. *Cognition*, **3**, 313–339.

GLASS, A. L., HOLYOAK, K. J. & O'DELL, C. (1974). Production frequency and the verification of quantified statements. *Journal of Verbal Learning and Verbal Behavior*, **13**, 237–254.

GLEITMAN, L. R. & ROZIN, P. (1977). The structure and acquisition of reading, I: Relations between orthographies and the structure of language. In REBER, A. S. and SCARBOROUGH, D. (eds.), *Toward a Psychology of Reading*. Hillsdale, N. J.: Erlbaum.

GLUCKSBERG, S., TRABASSO, T. & WALD, J. (1973). Linguistic structures and mental operations. *Cognitive Psychology*, **5**, 338–370.

GLUSHKO, R. J. & COOPER, L. A. (1978). Spatial comprehension and comparison processes in verification tasks, *Cognitive Psychology*, **10**, 391–421.

GORDON, J. F. (1976). The underlying negativity of comparative sentences and semantically marked forms. Paper presented at the N.A.T.O. Conference on the Psychology of Language, Stirling, 1976.

GOUGH, P. B. (1965). Grammatical transformations and speed of understanding. *Journal of Verbal Learning and Verbal Behavior*, **4**, 107–111.

GOUGH, P. B. (1966). The verification of sentences: the effects of delay of evidence and sentence length. *Journal of Verbal Learning and Verbal Behavior*, **5**, 492–496.

GOUGH, P. B. (1972). One second of reading. In KAVANAGH, J. F. and MATTINGLY, I. G. (eds.), *Language by Ear and by Eye: The Relationship between Speech and Reading*. Cambridge, Mass.: MIT Press.

GREEN, D. W. & SHALLICE, T. (1976). Direct visual access in reading for meaning. *Memory & Cognition*, **4**, 753–758.

GREENBERG, J. (1966). *Language Universals*. The Hague: Mouton.

GROEN, G. J. & PARKMAN, J. M. (1972). A chronometric analysis of simple addition. *Psychological Review*, **79**, 329–343.

GUENTHER, R. K. & KLATZKY, R. L. (1977). Semantic classification of pictures and words. *Journal of Experimental Psychology: Human Learning and Memory*, **3**, 498–514.

GUILFORD, J. P. (1967). *The Nature of Human Intelligence*. New York: McGraw-Hill.

GUMENIK, W. E. & GLASS, R. (1970). Effects of reducing the readability of the words in the Stroop color–word test. *Psychonomic Science*, **20**, 247–248.

HABER, R. N. & STANDING, L. (1969). Location of errors with a post-stimulus indicator. *Psychonomic Science*, **17**, 345–346.

HAMILTON, H. W. & DEESE, J. (1971). Does linguistic marking have a psychological correlate? *Journal of Verbal Learning and Verbal Behavior*, **10**, 707–714.

HANSEN, D. & ROGERS, T. (1968). An exploration of psycholinguistic units in initial reading. In GOODMAN, K. S. (ed.), *The Psycholinguistic Nature of the Reading Process*. Detroit: Wayne State University Press.

HARCUM, E. R. & FILION, R. D. (1963). Effects of stimulus reversals on lateral dominance in word recognition. *Perceptual and Motor Skills*, **17**, 779–794.

HARCUM, E. R. & SMITH, N. F. (1963). Effect of pre-known stimulus-reversals on apparent cerebral dominance in word recognition. *Perceptual and Motor Skills*, **17**, 799–810.

HAWKINS, H. L. (1969). Parallel processing in complex visual discrimination. *Perception & Psychophysics*, **5**, 56–64.

HAWKINS, H. L., REICHER, G. M., ROGERS, M. & PETERSON, L. (1976). Flexible coding in word recognition. *Journal of Experimental Psychology: Human Perception and Performance*, **2**, 380–385.

HÉCAEN, H. (1972). *Introduction à la Neuropsychologie*. Paris: Librairie Larousse.

HEIDER, E. R. (1971). 'Focal' color areas and the development of color names. *Developmental Psychology*, **4**, 447–455.

HEIDER, E. R. (1972). Universals in color naming and memory. *Journal of Experimental Psychology*, **93**, 10–20.

HENDERSON, L. (1972a). Visual and verbal codes: spatial information survives the icon. *Quarterly Journal of Experimental Psychology*, **24**, 439–447.

HENDERSON, L. (1972b). Spatial and verbal codes and the capacity of STM. *Quarterly Journal of Experimental Psychology*, **24**, 485–495.

HENDERSON, L. (1974). A word superiority effect without orthographic assistance. *Quarterly Journal of Experimental Psychology*, **26**, 301–311.

HENDERSON, L. & CHARD, J. (1976). On the nature of the facilitation of visual comparisons by lexical membership. *Bulletin of the Psychonomic Society*, **7**, 432–434.

HENDERSON, L. & HENDERSON, S. E. (1975). Visual comparison of words and random letter strings: effects of number and position of letters different. *Memory & Cognition*, **3**, 97–101.

HENLEY, N. M. (1969). A psychological study of the semantics of animal terms. *Journal of Verbal Learning and Verbal Behavior*, **8**, 176–184

HENMON, V. A. (1906). The time of perception as a measure of differences in sensation. *Archives of Philosophy, Psychology and Scientific Method*, **8**.

HERON, W. (1957). Perception as a function of retinal locus and attention. *American Journal of Psychology*, **70**, 38–48.

HERSHENSON, M. (1972). Verbal report and visual matching latency as a function of the pronounceability of letter arrays. *Journal of Experimental Psychology*, **96**, 104–109.

HOCK, H. S. & EGETH, H. E. (1970). Verbal interference with encoding in a perceptual classification task. *Journal of Experimental Psychology*, **83**, 299–303.

HOCK, H. S., GORDON, G. P. & CORCORAN, S. K. (1976). Alternative processes in the identification of familiar pictures. *Memory & Cognition*, **4**, 265–271.

HOLMES, J. M., MARSHALL, J. C. & NEWCOMBE, F. (1971). Syntactic class as a determinant of word-retrieval in normal and dyslexic subjects *Nature*, **234**, 416.

HOLYOAK, K. J. (1977). The form of analog size information in memory. *Cognitive Psychology*, **9**, 31–51.

HOLYOAK, K. J., GLASS, A. L. & MAH, W. A. (1976). Morphological structure and semantic retrieval. *Journal of Verbal Learning and Verbal Behavior*, **15**, 235–247.

HOLYOAK, K. J. & WALKER, J. H. (1976). Subjective magnitude information in semantic orderings. *Journal of Verbal Learning and Verbal Behavior*, **15**, 287–299.

HOPF-WEICHEL, R. E. (1977). Reorganization in semantic memory: an interpretation of the facilitation effect. *Journal of Verbal Learning and Verbal Behavior*, **16**, 261–275.

HOVANCIK, J. R. (1975). Reaction times for naming the first next and second next letters of the alphabet. *American Journal of Psychology*, **88**, 643–647.

HUMPHREY, G. (1951). *Thinking: An Introduction to its Experimental Psychology*. London: Methuen.

HUTCHEON, E. G. (1970). An investigation into stimulus classification under varying instructions. Unpublished M.A. Thesis, Dundee University.

HUTTENLOCHER, J. & HIGGINS, E. T. (1971). Adjectives, comparatives, and syllogism. *Psychological Review*, **78**, 487–504.

INHELDER, B. & PIAGET, J. (1958). *The Growth of Logical Thinking from Childhood to Adolescence*. London: Routledge & Kegan Paul.

JACOBSON, J. Z. (1973). Effects of association upon masking and reading latency. *Canadian Journal of Psychology*, **27**, 58–69.

JACOBSON, J. Z. (1976). Visual masking by homonyms. *Canadian Journal of Psychology*, **30**, 174–177.

JAMES, C. T. (1975). The role of semantic information in lexical decisions. *Journal of Experimental Psychology: Human Perception and Performance*, **1**, 130–136.

JAMES, C. T. & SMITH, E. E. (1970). Sequential dependencies in letter search. *Journal of Experimental Psychology*, **85**, 56–60.

JAMIESON, D. G. & PETRUSIC, W. M. (1975). Relational judgements with remembered stimuli. *Perception & Psychophysics*, **18**, 373–378.

JASTRZEMBSKI, J. E. & STANNERS, R. F. (1975). Multiple word meanings and lexical search speed. *Journal of Verbal Learning and Verbal Behavior*, **14**, 534–537.

JOHNSEN, A. M. & BRIGGS, G. E. (1973). On the locus of the display load effects in choice reactions. *Journal of Experimental Psychology*, **99**, 266–271.

JOHNSON, N. F. (1975). On the function of letters in word identification: some data and a preliminary model. *Journal of Verbal Learning and Verbal Behavior*, **14**, 17–29.

JOHNSTON, J. C. & MCCLELLAND, J. L. (1973). Visual factors in word perception. *Perception & Psychophysics*, **14**, 365–370.

JONIDES, J. & GLEITMAN, H. (1972). Conceptual category effect in visual search: O as a letter or as digit. *Perception & Psychophysics*, **12**, 457–460.

JUOLA, J. F. & ATKINSON, R. C. (1971). Memory scanning for words versus categories. *Journal of Verbal Learning and Verbal Behavior*, **10**, 552–527.

JUOLA, J. F., FISCHLER, I., WOOD, C. T. & ATKINSON, R. C. (1971). Recognition time for information stored in long-term memory. *Perception & Psychophysics*, **10**, 8–14.

JUST, M. A. & CARPENTER, P. A. (1975). The semantics of locative information in pictures and mental images. *British Journal of Psychology*, **66**, 427–441.

KAMINSKY, D. A. & DEROSA, D. V. (1972). Influence of retrieval cues and set organization on short-term recognition memory. *Journal of Experimental Psychology*, **96**, 449–454.

KATZ, J. J. (1972). *Semantic Theory*. New York: Harper & Row.

KATZ, J. J. & FODOR, J. A. (1963). The structure of a semantic theory. *Language*, **39**, 170–210.

KEELE, S. W. & CHASE, W. G. (1967). Short-term visual storage. *Perception & Psychophysics*, **2**, 383–386.

KELLICUTT, M. H., PARKS, T. E., KROLL, N. E. A. & SALZBERG, P. M. (1973). Visual memory as indicated by latency of recognition for normal and reversed letters. *Journal of Experimental Psychology*, **97**, 387–390.

KENNEDY, R. A. & HAMILTON, D. (1969). Time to locate probe items in short lists of digits. *American Journal of Psychology*, **82**, 272–275.

KINSBOURNE, M. & WARRINGTON, E. K. (1962). A variety of reading disability associated with right hemisphere lesions. *Journal of Neurology, Neurosurgery and Psychiatry*, **25**, 339–344.

KIRSNER, K. & SMITH, M. C. (1974). Modality effects in word identification. *Memory & Cognition*, **2**, 637–640.

KLATZKY, R. L., JUOLA, J. F. & ATKINSON, R. C. (1971). Test stimulus representation and experimental context effects in memory scanning. *Journal of Experimental Psychology*, **87**, 281–288.

KLATZKY, R. L. & SMITH, E. E. (1972). Stimulus expectancy and retrieval from short-term memory. *Journal of Experimental Psychology*, **94**, 101–107.

KLATZKY, R. L. & STOY, A. M. (1974), Using visual codes for comparisons of pictures. *Memory & Cognition*, **2**, 727–736.

KLEIMAN, G. M. (1975). Speech recoding in reading. *Journal of Verbal Learning and Verbal Behavior*, **14**, 323–339.

KLEIN, G. S. (1964). Semantic power measured through the interference of words with colour-naming. *American Journal of Psychology*, **77**, 576–588.

KOLERS, P. A. (1970). Three stages of reading. In LEVIN, H. and WILLIAMS, J. P. (eds.), *Basic Studies on Reading*. New York: Basic Books.

KORIAT, A. & LIEBLICH, I. (1974). What does a person in a 'TOT' state know that a person in a 'don't know' state doesn't know? *Memory & Cognition*, **2**, 647–655.

KOSSLYN, S. M. & POMERANTZ, J. R. (1977). Imagery, propositions, and the form of internal representations. *Cognitive Psychology*, **9**, 52–76.

KROLL, N. E. A. (1977). Effects of irrelevant colour changes on speed of name decisions. *Quarterly Journal of Experimental Psychology*, **29**, 277–281.

KROLL, N. E., KELLICUTT, M. H., BERRIAN, R. W. & KREISLER, A. F. (1974). Effects of irrelevant color changes on speed of visual recognition following short retention intervals. *Journal of Experimental Psychology*, **103**, 97–106.

KRUEGER, L. E. (1970). Effect of bracketing lines of speed of 'same' 'different' judgment of two adjacent letters. *Journal of Experimental Psychology*, **84**, 324–330.

KRUEGER, L. E. (1973a). Effect of irrelevant surrounding material on speed of *same–different* judgment of two adjacent letters. *Journal of Experimental Psychology*, **98**, 252–259.

KREUGER, L. E. (1973b). Effect of stimulus frequency on speed of 'same'–'different' judgments. In KORNBLUM, S. (ed.), *Attention and Performance, IV*. London: Academic Press.

LABERGE, D. & SAMUELS, S. J. (1974). Toward a theory of automatic information processing in reading. *Cognitive Psychology*, **6**, 293–323.

LAKOFF, G. (1972). Hedges: a study in meaning criteria and the logic of fuzzy concepts. *Papers from the eighth regional meeting, Chicago Linguistics Society*. Chicago: University of Chicago Linguistics Department.

LACHMAN, R. (1973). Uncertainty effects on time to access the internal lexicon. *Journal of Experimental Psychology*, **99**, 199–208.

LACHMAN, R. & MISTLER-LACHMAN, J. L. (1976). Internal code activation in picture naming. Paper presented at XXIst International Congress of Psychology, Paris, 1976.

LACHMAN, R., SHAFFER, J. P. & HENNRIKUS, D. (1974). Language and cognition: effects of stimulus codability, name-word frequency, and age of acquisition on lexical reaction time. *Journal of Verbal Learning and Verbal Behavior*, **13**, 613–625.

LANDAUER, T. K. (1962), Rate of implicit speech. *Perceptual and Motor Skills*, **15**, 646.

LANDAUER, T. K. & MEYER, D. E. (1972). Category size and semantic memory retrieval. *Journal of Verbal Learning and Verbal Behavior*, **11**, 539–549.

LANDAUER, T. K. & STREETER, L. A. (1973). Structural differences between common and rare words: failure of equivalence assumptions for theories of word recognition. *Journal of Verbal Learning and Verbal Behavior*, **12**, 119–131.

LIBERMAN, A. M., COOPER, F. S., SHANKWEILER, D. P. & STUDDERT-KENNEDY, M. (1967). Perception of the speech code. *Psychological Review*, **74**, 431–461.

LIVELY, B. L. (1972). Speed/accuracy trade off and practice as determinants of stage durations in a memory-search task. *Journal of Experimental Psychology*, **96**, 97–103.

LIVELY, B. L. & SANFORD, B. J. (1972). The use of category information in a memory-search task. *Journal of Experimental Psychology*, **93**, 379–385.

LOCKHEAD, G. R. (1972). Processing dimensional stimuli: a note. *Psychological Review*, **79**, 410–419.

LOCKHEAD, G. R. & KING, M. C. (1977). Classifying integral stimuli. *Journal of Experimental Psychology: Human Perception and Performance*, **3**, 436–443.

LOFTUS, E. F. (1973). Category dominance, instance dominance, and categorization time. *Journal of Experimental Psychology*, **97**, 70–74.

LOFTUS, E. F. & SCHEFF, R. W. (1971). Categorization norms for 50 representative instances. *Journal of Experimental Psychology*, **91**, 355–364.

LOFTUS, E. F. & SUPPES, P. (1972). Structural variables that determine the speed of retrieving words from long-term memory. *Journal of Verbal Learning and Verbal Behavior*, **11**, 770–777.

LOFTUS, E. F., WILKSTEN, S. & ABELSON, R. P. (1974) Using semantic memory to find vs create a mood. *Memory & Cognition* **3**, 479–483.

LOVELACE, E. A. & SNODGRASS, R. D. (1971). Decision times for alphabetic order of letter pairs. *Journal of Experimental Psychology*, **88**, 258–264.

LUND, R. H. (1927). The role of practice in the speed of association. *Journal of Experimental Pscyhology*, **10**, 424–433.

LURIA, A. R. (1973). *The Working Brain: and Introduction to Neuropsychology*. Harmondsworth: Penguin Books.

LYONS, J. (1968). *Introduction to Theoretical Linguistics*. Cambridge: Cambridge University Press.

LYONS, J. J. & BRIGGS, G. E. (1971). Speed-accuracy trade-off with different types of stimuli. *Journal of Experimental Psychology*, **91**, 115–119.

MCCLELLAND, J. L. (1976). Preliminary letter identification in the perception of words and nonwords. *Journal of Experimental Psychology*, **2**, 80–91.

MCFARLAND, C. E. KELLAS, G., KLUEGER, K. & JUOLA, J. F. (1974). Category similarity, instance dominance, and categorization time. *Journal of Verbal Learning and Verbal Behavior*, **13**, 698–708.

MAKITA, K. (1968). The rarity of reading disability in Japanese children. *American Journal of Orthopsychiatry*, **38**, 599–614.

MANELIS, L. (1974). The effect of meaningfulness on tachistoscopic word perception. *Perception & Psychophysics*, **16**, 182–192.

MARCEL, A. J. (1970a). Some constraints on sequential and parallel processing and the limits of attention. *Acta Psychologica*, **33**, 77–92.

MARCEL, A. J. (1970b). Sequential and parallel processing and the nature of the decisions in pattern recognition and classification. Unpublished paper, University of Sussex.

MARCEL, A. J. & FORRIN, B. (1974). Naming latency and the repetition of stimulus categories. *Journal of Experimental Psychology*, **103**, 450–460.

MARSHALL, J. C. & NEWCOMBE, F. (1966). Syntactic and semantic errors in paralexia. *Neuropsychologia*, **4**, 169–176.

MARSHALL, J. C. & NEWCOMBE, F. (1973). Patterns of paralexia: a psycholinguistic approach. *Journal of Psycholinguistic Research*, **2**, 175–199.

MARSHALL, J. C., NEWCOMBE, F. & HOLMES, J. M. (1975). Lexical memory: a linguistic approach. In KENNEDY, R. A. and WILKES, A. L. (eds.), *Studies in Long Term Memory*. London: Wiley.

MASON, M. (1975). Reading ability and letter search time: effects of orthographic structure defined by single-letter positional frequency. *Journal of Experimental Psychology: General*, **104**, 146–166.

MASON, M. & KATZ, L. (1976). Visual processing of nonlinguistic strings: redundancy effects and reading ability. *Journal of Experimental Psychology*, **105**, 338–348.

MASSARO, D. W. (1973). Perception of letters, words, and nonwords. *Journal of Experimental Psychology*, **100**, 349–353.

MAYZNER, M. S. & TRESSELT, M. E. (1965). Tables of single letter and digram frequency counts for various word-length and letter-position combinations. *Psychonomic Monograph Supplements*, **1**(2).

MERIKLE, P. M. (1976). On the disruption of visual memory: interference produced by visual report cues. *Quarterly Journal of Experimental Psychology*, **28**, 193–202.

MERIKLE, P. M. & COLTHEART, M. (1972). Selective forward masking. *Canadian Journal of Psychology*, **26**, 296–302.

MERIKLE, P. M., COLTHEART, M. & LOWE, D. G. (1971). On the selective effects of a patterned masking stimulus. *Canadian Journal of Psychology*, **25**, 264–279.

MERIKLE, P. M., LOWE, D. G. & COLTHEART, M. (1971). Familiarity and method of report as determinants of tachistoscopic performance. *Canadian Journal of Psychology*, **25**, 167–174.

MERVIS, C. B., CATLIN, J. & ROSCH, E. (1975). Development of the structure of color categories. *Developmental Psychology*, **11**, 54–60.

MEWHORT, D. J. (1967). Familiarity of letter sequences, response uncertainty and the tachistoscopic recognition experiment. *Canadian Journal of Psychology*, **21**, 309–321.

MEWHORT, D. J. & CORNETT, S. (1972). Scanning and the familiarity effect in tachistoscopic recognition. *Canadian Journal of Psychology*, **26**, 181–189.

MEWHORT, D. J., MERIKLE, P. M. & BRYDEN, M. (1969). On the transfer from iconic to short-term memory. *Journal of Experimental Psychology*, **81**, 89–94.

MEYER, D. E. (1970). On the representation and retrieval of stored semantic information. *Cognitive Psychology*, **1**, 242–300.

MEYER, D. E. (1973). Verifying affirmative and negative propositions: Effects of negation on memory retrieval. In KORNBLUM, S. (ed.) *Attention and Performance IV*. New York: Academic Press.

MEYER, D. E. (1975). Long-term memory retrieval during the comprehension of affirmative and negative sentences. In KENNEDY, R. A. and WILKES, A. L. (eds.), *Studies in Long Term Memory*. London: Wiley.

MEYER, D. E. & SCHVANEVELDT, R. W. (1971). Facilitation in recognizing pairs of words: evidence of a dependence between retrieval operations. *Journal of Experimental Psychology*, **90**, 227–234.

MEYER, D. E., SCHVANEVELDT, R. W. & RUDDY, M. G. (1972). Activation of lexical memory. Paper presented at the meeting of the Psychonomic Society, St. Louis, 1972.

MEYER, D. E., SCHVANEVELDT, R. W. & RUDDY, M. G. (1974a). Functions of graphemic and phonemic codes in visual word-recognition. *Memory & Cognition*, **2**, 309–321.

MEYER, D. E., SCHVANEVELDT, R. W. & RUDDY, M. G. (1974b). Loci of contextual effects on visual word recognition. In RABBITT, P. M. A. and DORNIC, S. (eds.), *Attention and Performance V*. London: Academic Press.

MEZRICH, J. J. (1973). The word superiority effect in brief visual displays: elimination by vocalization. *Perception & Psychophysics*, **13**, 45–48.

MILLER, G. A. (1956). The magical number seven, plus or minus two: some limits on our capacity for processing information. *Psychological Review*, **63**, 81–97.

MILLER, G. A., BRUNER, J. S. & POSTMAN, L. (1954). Familiarity of letter sequences and tachistoscopic identification. *Journal of General Psychology*, **50**, 129–139.

MILLER, G. A., GALANTER, E. & PRIBRAM, K. H. (1960). *Plans and the Structure of Behaviour*. New York: Holt, Rinehart & Winston.

MILLWARD, R. B., RICE, G. & CORBETT, A. (1975). Category production measures and verification times. In KENNEDY, R. A. and WILKES, A. L. (eds.), *Studies in Long Term Memory*. London: Wiley.

MINSKY, M. (1975). A framework for representing knowledge. In WINSTON, P. H. (ed.), *The Psychology of Computer Vision*. New York: McGraw-Hill.

MINSKY, M. & PAPERT, S. (1972). Artifical intelligence: current progress report of the Artificial Intelligence Laboratory. Progress report, Massachusetts Institute of Technology.

MITCHELL, D. C. (1972). Short-term visual memory and pattern masking. *Quarterly Journal of Experimental Psychology*, **24**, 394–405.

MONAHAN, J. S. & LOCKHEAD, G. R. (1977). Identification of integral stimuli. *Journal of Experimental Psychology: General*, **106**, 94–110.

MORIN, R. E. & FORRIN, B. (1962). Mixing of two types of S-R associations in a choice reaction time task. *Journal of Experimental Psychology*, **64**, 137–141.

MORIN, R. E., DEROSA, D. V. & STULZ, V. (1967). Recognition memory and reaction time. *Acta Psychologica*, **27**, 298–305.

MORTON, J. (1964a). The effects of context upon speed of reading, eye movements and eye-voice span. *Quarterly Journal of Experimental Psychology*, **16**, 340–354.

MORTON, J. (1964b). The effects of context on the visual duration threshold for words. *British Journal of Psychology*, **55**, 165–180.

MORTON, J. (1964c). A model for continuous language behaviour. *Language & Speech*, **7**, 40–70.

MORTON, J. (1968). Grammar and computation in language behavior. Progress Report No. 6, Center for Research in Language and Language Behavior, University of Michigan, May 1968.

MORTON, J. (1969a). Interaction of information in word recognition. *Psychological Review*, **76**, 165–178.

MORTON, J. (1969b). Categories of interference: verbal mediation and conflict in card sorting. *British Journal of Psychology*, **60**, 329–346.

MORTON, J. (1977a). Some experiments on facilitation in word and picture recognition and their relevance for the evolution of a theoretical position. Unpublished paper, MRC Applied Psychology Unit, Cambridge.

MORTON, J. (1977b). In-depth study of a phonemic dyslexic. Paper presented at a symposium on 'The application of human experimental psychology to the study of brain damage', Oxford, 1977.

MORTON, J. & CHAMBERS, S. M. (1973). Selective attention to words and colours. *Quarterly Journal of Experimental Psychology*, **25**, 387–397.

MOYER, R. S. (1973). Comparing objects in memory: evidence suggesting an internal psychophysics. *Perception & Psychophysics*, **13**, 180–184.

MOYER, R. S. & BAYER, R. H. (1976). Mental comparison and the symbolic distance effect. *Cognitive Psychology*, **8**, 228–246.

MOYER, R. S. & LAUNDAUER, T. K. (1967). Time required for judgments of numerical inequality. *Nature*, **215**, 1519–1520.

MURRELL, G. A. & MORTON, J. (1974). Word recognition and morphemic structure. *Journal of Experimental Psychology*, **102**, 963–968.

NEISSER, U. (1963). Decision time without reaction time: experiments in visual scanning. *American Journal of Psychology*, **76**, 376–385.

NEISSER, U. (1967). *Cognitive Psychology*. New York: Appleton-Century-Crofts.

NEISSER, U. (1969). Selective reading: a method for the study of visual attention. Paper presented at the XIXth International Congress of Psychology, London, 1969.

NEISSER, U. (1976). *Cognition and Reality: Principles and Implications of Cognitive Psychology*. San Francisco: Freeman.

NELSON, K. E. & KOSSLYN, S. M. (1975). Semantic retrieval in children and adults. *Developmental Psychology*, **11**, 807–813.

NEWELL, A. (1973). You can't play twenty questions with nature and win. In CHASE, W. G. (ed.), *Visual Information Processing*. New York: Academic Press.

NEWELL, A. & SIMON, H. A. (1972). *Human Problem Solving*. Engelwood Cliffs: Prentice Hall.

NICKERSON, R. S. (1966). Response times with a memory dependent decision task. *Journal of Experimental Psychology*, **98**, 36–43.

NICKERSON, R. S. (1967a). Categorization time with categories defined by disjunctions and conjunctions of stimulus attributes. *Journal of Experimental Psychology*, **73**, 211–219.

NICKERSON, R. S. (1967b). 'Same'–'different' response times with multi-attribute stimulus differences. *Perceptual and Motor Skills*, **24**, 543–554.

NICKERSON, R. S. & PEW, R. W. (1973). Visual pattern matching: an investigation of some effects of decision task, auditory codability, and spatial correspondence. *Journal of Experimental Psychology*, **98**, 36–43.

ODEN, G. C. (1977). Fuzziness in semantic memory: choosing examplars of subjective categories. *Memory & Cognition*, **5**, 198–204.

OKADA, R. & BURROWS, D. (1974). Divided attention and high-speed memory search. *Journal of Experimental Psychology*, **103**, 191–195.

OLDFIELD, R. C. (1966). Things, words and the brain. *Quarterly Journal of Experimental Psychology*, **18**, 3–16.

OLDFIELD, R. C. & WINGFIELD, A. (1965). Response latencies in naming objects. *Quarterly Journal of Experimental Psychology*, **17**, 273–281.

OLSON, D. R. & FILBY, N. (1972). On the comprehension of active and passive sentences. *Cognitive Psychology*, **3**, 361–381.

OLSON, G. M. & LAXAR, K. (1973). Asymmetries in processing the terms 'right' and 'left'. *Journal of Experimental Psycholgy*, **100**, 284–290.

OSGOOD, C. E., SUCI, G. J. & TANNEBAUM, P. H. (1957). *The Measurement of Meaning*. Urbana: University of Illinois Press.

PACHELLA, R. G. (1974). The interpretation of reaction time in information-processing research. In KANTOWITZ, B. (ed.), *Human Information Processing: Tutorials in Performance and Cognition*. Hillsdale: Erlbaum.

PACHELLA, R. G. & MILLER, J. O. (1976). Stimulus probability and same–different classification. *Perception & Psychophysics*, **19**, 29–34.

PAIVIO, A. (1972). *Imagery and Verbal Processes*. New York: Holt, Rinehart & Winston.

PAIVIO. A. (1975a). Imagery and long-term memory. In KENNEDY, R. A. & WILKES, A. L. (eds.), *Studies in Long Term Memory*. London: Wiley.

PAIVIO, A. (1975b). Perceptual comparisons through the mind's eye. *Memory & Cognition*, **3**, 635–647.

PAIVIO, A. (1976). Imagery, language and semantic memory. Paper presented at XXIst International Congress of Psychology, Paris, 1976.

PAIVIO, A. (1977). Mental comparisons involving abstract attributes. unpublished paper, University of Western Ontario.

PAIVIO, A., YUILLE, J. C. & MADIGAN, S. (1968). Concreteness, imagery and meaningfulness values for 925 nouns. *Journal of Experimental Psychology Monograph*, **76**, (1, Pt. 2).

PARKMAN, J. M. (1971). Temporal aspects of digit and letter inequality judgments. *Journal of Experimental Psychology*, **91**, 191–205.

PARKMAN, J. M. (1972). Temporal aspects of simple multiplication and comparison. *Journal of Experimental Psychology*, **95**, 437–444.

PARKMAN, J. M. & GROEN, G. J. (1971). Temporal aspects of simple addition and comparison. *Journal of Experimental Psychology*, **89**, 335–342.

PARKS, T. E., KROLL, N. E. A., SALZBERG, P. M. & PARKINSON, S. R. (1972). Persistence of visual memory as indicated by decision time in a matching task. *Journal of Experimental Psychology*, **92**, 437–438.

PATTERSON, K. E. & MARCEL, A. J. (1977). Aphasia, dyslexia and the phonological coding of written words. *Quarterly Journal of Experimental Psychology*, **29**, 307–318.

PELLEGRINO, J. W., ROSINSKI, R. R., CHIESI, H. L. & SIEGEL, A. (1977). Picture–word differences in decision latency: an analysis of single and dual memory models. *Memory and Cognition*, **5**, 383–396.

PHILLIPS, W. A. (1974). On the distinction between sensory storage and short-term visual memory. *Perception & Psychophysics*, **16**, 283–290.

PHILLIPS, W. A. & CHRISTIE, D. F. (1977). Components of visual memory *Quarterly Journal of Experimental Psychology*, **29**, 117–133.

PIAGET, J. (1936). *The Origin of Intelligence in the Child.* London: Routledge & Kegan Paul.

PILLSBURY, W. B. (1897). A study in apperception. *American Journal of Psychology*, **8**, 315–393.

PODGORNY, P. & SHEPARD, R. N. (1977). Reaction time to spatial probes of patterns that are imagined, remembered or seen. Unpublished paper, Stanford University.

POLLACK, I. (1963a). Speed of classification of words into superordinate categories. *Journal of Verbal Learning and Verbal Behavior*, **2**, 159–165.

POLLACK, I. (1963b). Verbal reaction times to briefly presented words. *Perceptual & Motor Skills*, **17**, 137–138.

POLLATSEK, A., WELL, A. D. & SCHINDLER, R. M. (1975). Familiarity affects visual processing of words. *Journal of Experimental Psychology: Human Perception and Performance*, **1**, 328–338.

POSNANSKY, C. J. & RAYNER, K. (1977). Visual-feature and response components in a picture-word interference task with beginning and skilled readers. *Journal of Experimental Child Psychology*, **24**, 440–460.

POSNER, M. I. (1970). On the relationship between letter names and superordinate categories. *Quarterly Journal of Experimental Psychology*, **22**, 279–287.

POSNER, M. I. (1973). Co-ordination of internal codes. In CHASE, W. G. (ed.), *Visual Information Processing.* New York: Academic Press.

POSNER, M. I., BOIES, S. J., EICHELMAN, W. H. & TAYLOR, R. L. (1969). Retention of visual and name codes of single letters. *Journal of Experimental Psychology Monograph*, **79**, 1–16.

POSNER, M. I. & MITCHELL, R. F. (1967). Chronometric analysis of classification. *Psychological Review*, **74**, 392–409.

POTTER, M. C. & FAULCONER, B. A. (1975). Time to understand pictures and words. *Nature*, **253**, 437–438.

PYLYSHYN, Z. W. (1973). What the mind's eye tells the mind's brain: a critique of mental imagery. *Psychological Bulletin*, **80**, 1–24.

RAEBURN, V. P. (1975). Priorities in item recognition. *Memory & Cognition*, **2**, 663–669.

RAPHAEL, B. (1975). *The Thinking Computer: Mind inside Matter.* San Francisco: Freeman.

RAYNER, J. & POSNANSKY, C. J. (1977). Stages of processing in word identification. *Journal of Experimental Psychology: General*, **24**, 440–460.

REICHER, G. M. (1969). Perceptual recognition as a function of meaningfulness of stimulus material. *Journal of Experimental Psychology*, **81**, 275–280.

RICHARDSON, J. T. (1975a). The effect of word imageability in acquired dyslexia. *Neuropsychologia*, **13**, 281–288.

RICHARDSON, J. T. (1975b). Further evidence on the effect of word imageability in dyslexia. *Quarterly Journal of Experimental Psychology*, **27**, 445–449.

RIPS, L. J. (1975). Quantification and semantic memory. *Cognitive Psychology*, **7**, 307–340.

RIPS, L. J., SHOBEN, E. J. & SMITH, E. E. (1973). Semantic distance and the verification of semantic relations. *Journal of Verbal Learning and Verbal Behavior*, **12**, 1–20.

ROSCH, E. (1973). On the internal structure of perceptual and semantic categories. In

MOORE, T. E. (ed.), *Cognitive Development and the Acquisition of Language*. New York: Academic Press.

ROSCH, E. (1975a). Cognitive representations of semantic categories. *Journal of Experimental Psychology: General*, **104**, 192–233.

ROSCH, E. (1975b). The nature of mental codes for color categories. *Journal of Experimental Psychology: Human Perception and Performance*, **1**, 303–322.

ROSCH, E. & MERVIS, C. B. (1975). Family resemblance: studies in the internal structure of categories. *Cognitive Psychology*, **7**, 573–605.

ROSCH, E., MERVIS, C. B., GRAY, W., JOHNSON, D. & BOYES-BRAEM, P. (1976). Basic objects in natural categories. *Cognitive Psychology*, **8**, 382–439.

ROSINSKI, R. R., GOLINKOFF, R. M. & KUKISH, K. S. (1975). Automatic semantic processing in a picture–word interference task. *Child Development*, **46**, 247–253.

RUBENSTEIN, H., GARFIELD, L. & MILLIKAN, J. A. (1970). Homographic entries in the internal lexicon. *Journal of Verbal Learning and Verbal Behavior*, **9**, 487–494.

RUBENSTEIN, H., LEWIS, S. S. & RUBENSTEIN, M. A. (1971a). Evidence for phonemic recording in visual word recognition. *Journal of Verbal Learning and Verbal Behaviour*, **10**, 645–657.

RUBENSTEIN, H., LEWIS, S. S. & RUBENSTEIN, M. A. (1971b). Homographic entries in the internal lexicon: effects of systematicity and relative frequency of meanings. *Journal of Verbal Learning and Verbal Behavior*, **10**, 57–62.

RUBENSTEIN, H., RICHTER, M. L. & KAY, E. J. (1975). Pronounceability and the visual recognition of nonsense words. *Journal of Verbal Learning and Verbal Behavior*, **14**, 651–657.

RUMELHART, D. E., LINDSAY, P. H. & NORMAN, D. A. (1972). A process model for long-term memory. In TULVING, E. and DONALDSON, W. (eds.), *Organisation and Memory*. New York: Academic Press.

RYLE, G. (1949). *The Concept of Mind*. London: Hutchinson.

SAKOMOTO, T. & MAKITA, K. (1973) Japan. In DOWNING, J. (ed.) *Comparative Reading*. New York: Macmillan.

SANDERS, A. F. & SCHROOTS, J. J. (1969). Cognitive categories and memory span. III. Effects of similarity on recall. *Quarterly Journal of Experimental Psychology*, **21**, 21–28.

SANFORD, A. J., GARROD, S. & BOYLE, J. M. (1977). An independence of mechanism in the origins of reading and classification-related semantic distance effects. *Memory & Cognition*, **5**, 214–220.

SANFORD, A. J. & SEYMOUR, P. H. K. (1974a). Semantic distance effects in naming superordinates. *Memory & Cognition*, **2**, 714–720.

SANFORD, A. J. & SEYMOUR, P. H. K. (1974b). The influence of response compatibility on a semantic classification task. *Acta Psychologica*, **38**, 405–412.

SAPIR, E. (1944). Grading: a study in semantics. *Philosophy of Science*, **2**, 93–116.

SARAGA, E. & SHALLICE, T. (1973). Parallel processing of the attributes of single stimuli. *Perception & Psychophysics*, **13**, 261–270.

SCARBOROUGH, D. L. (1972). Memory for brief visual displays of symbols. *Cognitive Psychology*, **3**, 408–429.

SCARBOROUGH, D. L., CORTESE, C. & SCARBOROUGH, H. S. (1977). Frequency and repetition effects in lexical memory. *Journal of Experimental Psychology: Human Perception and Performance*, **3**, 1–17.

SCARBOROUGH, D. L. & SPRINGER, L. (1973). Noun–verb differences in word recognition. Paper presented to the Psychonomic Society in St. Louis, November 1973.

SCHAEFFER, B. & WALLACE, R. (1969). Semantic similarity and the comparison of word meanings. *Journal of Experimental Psychology*, **82**, 343–346.

SCHAEFFER, B. & WALLACE, R. (1970). The comparison of word meanings. *Journal of Experimental Psychology*, **86**, 144–152.

SCHEERER, E. (1972). Order of report and order of scanning in tachistoscopic recognition. *Canadian Journal of Psychology*, **26**, 382–390.

SCHEERER, E. (1973). A further test of the scanning hypothesis in tachistoscopic recognition. *Canadian Journal of Psychology*, **27**, 95–102.

SCHEERER-NEUMANN, G. (1974). Formation and utilization of the visual and verbal codes of pictures and words. *Psychological Research*, **37**, 81–106.

SCHILLER, P. H. (1966). Developmental study of color–word interference. *Journal of Experimental Psychology*, **72**, 105–108.

SCHINDLER, R. M., WELL, A. D. & POLLATSEK, A. (1974). Effects of segmentation and expectancy on matching time for words and nonwords. *Journal of Experimental Psychology*, **103**, 107–111.

SCHUBERTH, R. E. & EIMAS, P. D. (1977). Effects of context on the classification of words and nonwords. *Journal of Experimental Psychology: Human Perception and Performance*, **3**, 27–36.

SCHVANEVELDT, R. W. & MEYER, D. E. (1973). Retrieval and comparison processes in semantic memory. In KORNBLUM, S. (ed.), *Attention and Performance IV*. London: Academic Press.

SCHVANEVELDT, R. W., MEYER, D. E. & BECKER, C. A. (1976). Lexical ambiguity, semantic context, and visual word recognition. *Journal of Experimental Psychology: Human Perception and Performance*, **2**, 243–256.

SEGUI, J. & FRAISSE, P. (1968). Le temps de réaction verbale, III: Réponses specifiques et réponses categorielles à des stimulus-objets. *L'Annie Psychologique*, **68**, 69–82.

SEKULER, R. & NASH, D. (1972). Speed of size scaling in human vision. *Psychonomic Science*, **27**, 93–94.

SEYMOUR, P. H. K. (1969a). Response Latencies in judgements of spatial location. *British Journal of Psychology*, **60**, 31–39.

SEYMOUR, P. H. K. (1969b). Response latencies in classification of word–shape pairs. *British Journal of Psychology*, **60**, 312–321.

SEYMOUR, P. H. K. (1970a). Representational processes in comprehension of printed words. *British Journal of Psychology*, **61**, 222–233.

SEYMOUR, P. H. K. (1970b). Conceptual uncertainty and the latency of judgements of the congruence of word–shape pairs. *Acta Psychologica*, **34**, 451–461.

SEYMOUR, P. H. K. (1971). Perceptual and judgemental bias in classification of word–shape displays. *Acta Psychologica*, **35**, 461–477.

SEYMOUR, P. H. K. (1973a). A model for reading, naming and comparison. *British Journal of Psychology*, **64**, 35–49.

SEYMOUR, P. H. K. (1973b). Semantic representation of shape names. *Quarterly Journal of Experimental Psychology*, **25**, 265–277.

SEYMOUR, P. H. K. (1973c). Stroop interference in naming and verifying spatial locations. *Perception & Psychophysics*, **14**, 95–100.

SEYMOUR, P. H. K. (1973d). Judgements of verticality and response availability. *Bulletin of the Psychonomic Society*, **1**, 196–198.

SEYMOUR, P. H. K. (1974a). Stroop interference with response, comparison and encoding stages in a sentence–picture comparison task. *Memory & Cognition*, **2**, 19–26.

SEYMOUR, P. H. K. (1974b). Asymmetries in judgments of verticality. *Journal of Experimental Psychology*, **102**, 447–455.

SEYMOUR, P. H. K. (1974c). Generation of a pictorial code. *Memory & Cognition*, **2**, 224–232.

SEYMOUR, P. H. K. (1974d). Pictorial coding of verbal descriptions. *Quarterly Journal of Experimental Psychology*, **26**, 39–51.

SEYMOUR, P. H. K. (1975). Semantic equivalence of verbal and pictorial displays. In KENNEDY, R. A. and WILKES, A. L. (eds.), *Studies in Long Term Memory*. London: Wiley.

SEYMOUR, P. H. K. (1976a). Knowledge of structured categories. Volume II of Final Report on Project HR 1833/1 submitted to the Social Science Research Council, London.

SEYMOUR, P. H. K. (1976b). Retrieval and comparison operations in permanent memory. In HAMILTON, V. and VERNON, M. D. (eds.), *The Development of Cognitive Processes*. London: Academic Press.

SEYMOUR, P. H. K. (1977). Conceptual encoding and locus of the Stroop effect. *Quarterly Journal of Experimental Psychology*, **29**, 245–265.

SEYMOUR, P. H. K. & JACK, M. V. (1978). Effects of visual familiarity on 'same' and 'different' decision processes. *Quarterly Journal of Experimental Psychology*, **30**, 455–469.

SEYMOUR, P. H. K. & PORPODAS, C. D. (1978). Coding of spelling by normal and dyslexic readers. In Gruneberg, M. M., Morris, P. E. and Sykes, R. N. (eds.), *Practical Aspects of Memory*. London: Academic Press.

SEYMOUR, P. H. K. & SANFORD, A. J. (1975). Interaction of concurrent generative and expressive activity in production of typewritten lists. *Acta Psychologica*, **39**, 141–152.

SHALLICE, T. & WARRINGTON. E. K. (1975). Word recognition in a phonemic dyslexic patient. *Quarterly Journal of Experimental Psychology*, **27**, 187–199.

SHALLICE, T. & WARRINGTON, E. K. (1977). The possible role of selective attention in acquired dyslexia. *Neuropsychologia*, **15**, 31–41.

SHAW, P. (1969). Processing of tachistoscopic displays with controlled order of characters and spaces. *Perception & Psychophysics*, **6**, 257–266.

SHEPARD, R. N. (1964). Attention and the metric structure of the stimulus space. *Journal of Mathematical Psychology*, **1**, 54–87.

SHEPARD, R. N. & PODGORNY, P. (1977). Cognitive processes that resemble perceptual processes. In ESTES, W. K. (ed.), *Handbook of Learning and Cognitive Processes*. Hillsdale: Erlbaum.

SHOBEN, E. J. (1976). The verification of semantic relations in a same–different paradigm: an asymmetry in semantic memory. *Journal of Verbal Learning and Verbal Behavior*, **15**, 365–379.

SHOR, R. E., HATCH, R. P., HUDSON, L. J., LANDRIGAN, D. T. & SHAFFER, H. J. (1972). Effect of practice on a Stroop-like spatial directions task. *Journal of Experimental Psychology*, **94**, 168–172.

SHULMAN, H. G. & DAVISON, T. C. B. (1977). Control properties of semantic coding in a lexical decision task. *Journal of Verbal Learning and Verbal Behavior*, **16**, 91–98.

SIMMEL, M. L. & GOLDSCHMIDT, K. H. (1953). Prolonged posteclamptic aphasia. *Archives of Neurology and Psychiatry*, **69**, 80–83.

SLOBODA, J. A. (1976). Decision times for word and letter search: a holistic word identification model examined. *Journal of Verbal Learning and Verbal Behavior*, **15**, 93–101.

SILVERMAN, W. P. & GOLDBERG, S. L. (1975). Further confirmation of *same* vs. *different* processing differences. *Perception & Psychophysics*, **17**, 189–193.

SMITH, E. E., BALZANO, G. J. & WALKER, J. (1977). Nominal, perceptual and semantic codes in picture categorisation. In COTTON, J. and KLATZKY, R. L. (eds.), *Semantic Factors in Cognition*. Hillsdale: Erlbaum.

SMITH, E. E., SHOBEN, E. J. & RIPS, L. J. (1974). Structure and process in semantic memory: a featural model for semantic decisions. *Psychological Review*, **81**, 214–241.

SMITH, F. (1971). *Understanding Reading: A Psycholinguistic Analysis of Reading and Learning to Read*. New York: Holt, Rinehart and Winston.

SMITH, F. & CAREY, P. (1966). Temporal factors in visual information processing. *Canadian Journal of Psychology*, **20**, 337–342.

SMITH, P. T. & BAKER, R. G. (1976). The influence of English spelling patterns on pronunciation. *Journal of Verbal Learning and Verbal Behavior*, **16**, 267–285.

SNODGRASS, J. G. & JARVELLA, R. J. (1972). Some linguistic determinants of word classification times. *Psychonomic Science*, **27**, 220–222.

SOLOMON, R. L. & POSTMAN, L. (1952). Frequency of usage as a determinant of recognition thresholds for words. *Journal of Experimental Psychology*, **43**, 195–201.

SPENCER, T. J. (1969). Some effects of different masking stimuli on iconic storage. *Journal of Experimental Psychology*, **81**, 132–140.

SPERLING, G. (1960). The information available in brief visual presentations. *Psychological Monographs*, **74**, 11.

SPERLING, G. (1963). A model for visual memory tasks. *Human Factors*, **5**, 19–31.

SPERLING, G. (1967). Successive approximations to a model for short-term memory. *Acta Psychologica*, **27**, 285–292.

SPERLING, G., BUDIANSKI, J., SPIVAK, J. G. & JOHNSON, M. C. (1971). Extremely rapid visual search: the maximum rate of scanning letters for the presence of a numeral. *Science*, **174**, 307–311.

SPOEHR, K. T. & SMITH, E. E. (1973). The role of syllables in perceptual processing. *Cognitive Psychology*, **5**, 71–89.

SPOEHR, K. T. & SMITH, E. E. (1975). The role of orthographic and phonotactic rules in perceiving letter patterns. *Journal of Experimental Psychology: Human Perception and Performance*, **1**, 21–34.

STANNERS, R. F. & FORBACH, G. B. (1973). Analysis of letter strings in word recognition. *Journal of Experimental Psychology*, **98**, 31–35.

STANNERS, R. F., JASTRZEMBSKI, J. E. & WESTBROOK, A. (1975). Frequency and visual quality in a word–nonword classification task. *Journal of Verbal Learning and Verbal Behavior*, **14**, 259–264.

STERNBERG, S. (1966). High speed scanning in human memory. *Science*, **153**, 652–654.

STERNBERG, S. (1967). Two operations in character recognition: some evidence from reaction time measurements. *Perception & Psychophysics*, **2**, 45–53.

STERNBERG, S. (1969a). The discovery of processing stages; extensions of Donders' method. *Acta Psychologica*, **30**, 276–315.

STERNBERG, S. (1969b). Memory-scanning: mental processes revealed by reaction-time experiments. *American Scientist*, **57**, 421–457.

STERNBERG, S. (1971). Decomposing mental processes with reaction-time data. Paper presented at meeting of the Midwestern Psychological Association, Detroit, 1971.

STERNBERG, S. (1975). Memory scanning: new findings and current controversies. *Quarterly Journal of Experimental Psychology*, **27**, 1–32.

STEVENS, S. S. (1951). Mathematics, measurement and psychophysics. In STEVENS, S. S. (ed.), *Handbook of Experimental Psychology*. New York: Wiley.

STROOP, J. R. (1935). Studies of interference in serial verbal reactions. *Journal of Experimental Psychology*, **18**, 643–662.

SUTHERLAND, N. S. (1968). Outlines of a theory of visual pattern recognition in animals and man. *Proceedings of the Royal Society, Series B*, **171**, 297–317.

SUTHERLAND, N. S. (1973). Object recognition. In CARTERETTE, E. and FRIEDMAN, M. (eds.), *Handbook of Perception*. New York: Academic Press.

TAFT, M. & FORSTER, K. I. (1975). Lexical storage and retrieval of polymorphemic and *of Verbal Learning and Verbal Behavior*, **14**, 638–647.

TAFT, M. & FORSTER, K. I. (1976). Lexical storage and retrieval of polymorphemic and polysyllabic words. *Journal of Verbal Learning and Verbal Behaviour*, **15**, 607–620.

TANENHAUS, M. K., CARROLL, J. M. & BEVER, T. G. (1976). Sentence–picture verification models as theories of sentence comprehension: a critique of Carpenter and Just. *Psychological Review*, **83**, 310–317.

TAYLOR, A. & WARRINGTON, E. K. (1971). Visual agnosia: a single case report. *Cortex*, **7**, 152–161.

TAYLOR, D. A. (1976a). Effect of identity in the multiletter matching task. *Journal of Experimental Psychology: Human Perception and Performance*, **2**, 417–428.

TAYLOR, D. A. (1976b). Stage analysis of reaction time. *Psychological Bulletin*, **83**, 161–191.

TAYLOR, D. A. (1976c). Holistic and analytic processes in the comparison of letters. *Perception & Psychophysics*, **20**, 187–190.

TELLER, P. (1969). Some discussion and extension of Manfred Bierwisch's work on German adjectivals. *Foundations of Language*, **5**, 185–217.

THEIOS, J. (1972). Reaction time arrangements in the study of memory processes: theory and data. University of Wisconsin, Report 72–2.

THOMPSON, M. C. & MASSARO, D. W. (1973). Visual information and redundancy in reading. *Journal of Experimental Psychology*, **98**, 49–54.

THOMSEN, I. V. & HARMSEN, P. (1968). Retraining in a case of agnosic alexia. *Folia Phoniatica*, **20**, 342–347.

THORNDIKE, E. L. & LORGE, I. (1944). *The Teacher's Word Book of 30,000 Words*. New York: Columbia University Press.

TINKER, M. A. (1958). Recent studies of eye movements in reading. *Psychological Bulletin*, **55**, 215–231.

TOWNSEND, J. T. (1971). A note on the identifiability of parallel and serial processes. *Perception & Psychophysics*, **10**, 161–163.

TOWNSEND, J. T. (1972). Some results concerning the identifiability of parallel and serial processes. *British Journal of Mathematical and Statistical Psychology*, **25**, 168–199.

TRABASSO, T., ROLLINS, H., & SHAUGHNESSY, E. (1971). Storage and verification stages in processing concepts. *Cognitive Psychology*, **2**, 239–289.

TREISMAN, A. M. & FEARNLEY, S. (1969). The Stroop test: selective attention to colours and words. *Nature*, **222**, 437–439.

TSVETKOVA, L. S. (1965). The naming process and its impairment. In LENNEBERG, E. M. & LENNEBERG, E. (eds.), *Foundations of Language Development: A Multidisciplinary Approach, Volume 2.* Academic Press: London.

TULVING, E. (1972). Episodic and semantic memory. In TULVING, E. and DONALDSON, W. (eds.), *Organization of Memory*. New York: Academic Press.

TULVING, E. & GOLD, G. (1963). Stimulus information and contextual information as determinants of tachistoscopic recognition of words. *Journal of Experimental Psychology*, **66**, 319–327.

TULVING, E., MANDLER, G. & BAUMAL, R. (1964). Interaction of two sources of information in tachistoscopic word recognition. *Canadian Journal of Psychology*, **18**, 62–71.

TVERSKY, B. (1969). Pictorial and verbal encoding in a short-term memory task. *Perception & Psychophysics*, **6**, 225–233.

TVERSKY, B. (1975. Pictorial encoding of sentences in sentence-picture comparison. *Quarterly Journal of Experimental Psychology*, **27**, 405–410.

ULEMAN, J. S. & REEVES, J. (1971). A reversal of the Stroop interference effect through scanning. *Perception & Psychophysics*, **9**, 293–295.

VENEZKY, R. L. (1962). A computer programme for deriving spelling-to-sound correlations. Unpublished MA thesis, Cornell University.

VERNON, P. E. (1951). *The Stucture of Human Abilities*. London: Methuen.

VON WRIGHT, J. M. (1968). Selection in visual immediate memory. *Quarterly Journal of Experimental Psychology*, **20**, 62–68.

WARREN, R. E. (1972). Stimulus encoding and memory. *Journal of Experimental Psychology*, **94**, 90–100.

WARRINGTON, E. K. (1973). Object recognition in patients with left and right hemisphere lesions. Paper presented at Queen's Square Hospital, London, 1973.

WARRINGTON, E. K. (1975). The selective impairment of semantic memory. *Quarterly Journal of Experimental Psychology*, **27**, 635–657.

WARRINGTON, E. K. & TAYLOR, A. M. (1973). The contribution of the right parietal lobe to object recognition. *Cortex*, **7**, 152–164.

WARRINGTON, E. K. & ZANGWILL, O. L. (1957). A study of dyslexia. *Journal of Neurology, Neurosurgery and Psychiatry*, **20**, 208–215.

WASON, P. C. (1961). Response to affirmative and negative binary statements. *British Journal of Psychology*, **52**, 133–142.

WASON, P. C. & JOHNSON-LAIRD, P. N. (1972). *Psychology of Reasoning: Structure and Content.* London: Batsford.

WAUGH, N. C. & ANDERS, T. (1973). Searching through long-term verbal memory. In KORNBLUM, S. (ed.), *Attention & Performance IV.* London: Academic Press.

WEBER, R. J. & CASTLEMAN, J. (1970). The time it takes to imagine. *Perception & Psychophysics*, **8**, 165–168.

WEBER, R. J., KELLEY, J. & LITTLE, S. (1972). Is visual image sequencing under verbal control? *Journal of Experimental Psychology*, **96**, 354–362.

WELFORD, A. T. (1968). *Fundamentals of Skill.* London: Methuen.

WELL, A. S., POLLATSEK, A. & SCHINLDER, R. M. (1975). Facilitation of both 'same' and 'different' judgments of letter strings by familiarity of letter sequence. *Perception &Psychophysics*, **17**, 511–520.

WELL, A. E. & GREEN, J. (1972). Effects of color differences in a letter matching task. *Psychonomic Science*, **29**, 109–110.

WHEELER, D. D. (1970). Processes in word recognition. *Cognitive Psychology*, **1**, 59–85.

WILKINS, A. J. (1971). Conjoint frequency, category size, and categorization time. *Journal of Verbal Learning and Verbal Behavior*, **10**, 382–385.

WINER, B. J. (1962). *Statistical Principles in Experimental Design.* New York: McGraw Hill.

WINGFIELD, A. (1967). Perceptual and response hierarchies in object identification. *Acta Psychologica*, **26**, 216–226.

WINGFIELD, A. (1968). Effects of frequency on identification and naming of objects. *American Journal of Psychology*, **81**, 226–234.

WINGFIELD, A. (1973). Effects of serial position and set size in auditory recognition memory. *Memory & Cognition*, **1**, 53–55.

WINNICK, W. A. & DANIEL, S. A. (1970). Two kinds of response priming in tachistoscopic recognition. *Journal of Experimental Psychology*, **84**, 74–81.

WINOGRAD, T. (1972). *Understanding Natural Language.* Edinburgh: Edinburgh University Press.

WITTGENSTEIN, L. (1953). *Philosophical Investigations.* Oxford: Blackwell.

Author Index

Subject Index